Radu Gheorghita

The Role of the Septuagint in Hebrews

An Investigation of its Influence with Special Consideration to the Use of Hab 2:3-4 in Heb 10:37-38

Mohr Siebeck

RADU GHEORGHITA, born 1961; 1984 B.S. in Physics at University of Cluj, Romania; 1991 M.Div. at Trinity Evangelical Divinity School, Deerfield, U.S.A.; 2000 Ph.D. Cambridge University, U.K.; currently Scholar in Residence at Midwestern Baptist Theological Seminary, Kansas City, U.S.A., and Lecturer; in Biblical Studies at Universitatea Emanuel, Oradea, Romania.

ISBN 3-16-148014-7
ISSN 0340-9570 (Wissenschaftliche Untersuchungen zum Neuen Testament, 2. Reihe)

Die Deutsche Bibliothek lists this publication in the Deutsche Nationalbibliographie; detailed bibliographic data is available in the Internet at *http://dnb.ddb.de*.

The book was printed by Druckpartner Rübelmann GmbH in Hemsbach on non-aging paper and bound by Buchbinderei Schaumann in Darmstadt.

Printed in Germany.

Preface

Ἔστιν δὲ πίστις ἐλπιζομένων ὑπόστασις,
πραγμάτων ἔλεγχος οὐ βλεπομένων.

Now faith is the assurance of things hoped for,
the conviction of things not seen.

During four immensely enjoyable years, that which lies between these covers was hoped for though not yet seen. Now that the end of these days has come, it behoves me to mention with gratitude those people and institutions who contributed to its completion.

By unsurpassed scholarly example and guidance, Professor William Horbury of Cambridge University has supervised the development of this project from its infancy to maturity, all the while dealing gently with the ignorant and wayward. His expertise, encouragement, and patience created an atmosphere in which the research lost tediousness and became a treasured experience and an unexpected pleasure. It is beyond dispute that the inferior was blessed by the superior.

By valuable encouragement and priceless fellowship, the Tyndale House community under the wardenship of Dr. Bruce Winter, has shown that the stirring up of one another to love and good works is just as valuable today as it was in the days of the Epistle to the Hebrews.

By providing generous financial support and stimulating camaraderie, Corpus Christi College, a truly great college in the University, has clearly not neglected the doing of good and the sharing of what they have, sacrifices that are pleasing to God.

By indispensable prayer, seasoned advice, and substantial financial assistance, both my parents, Nick and Cornelia, and my parents-in-law, John, now a righteous man made perfect, and Betsey, have offered faithful support and joyfully accepted the plundering of their property. They have played a part in that great cloud of witnesses, and without their encouragement along the way this project would have been less enjoyable and meaningful.

By partaking in the same calling, two academic institutions have allowed me the time to complete this project: Universitatea Emanuel Oradea, Romania, during the dissertation phase, and Midwestern Baptist Theological Seminary, Kansas City, during the monograph preparation.

Their worthy presidents, Dr. Paul Negruţ and Dr. Phil Roberts, are to be thanked, as well as my colleagues who stepped in and carried the teaching load in my absence.

Elizabeth, Nicholas, William, Edward, and most recently Margaret, though perhaps not as numerous as the stars of heaven or the sand of the sea, nevertheless have been a priceless help in keeping a healthy perspective on this dissertation and monograph. Hours away from the library, be they spent playing football, going punting, reading stories, or playing recorders, are not regretted.

In many and various ways, Liz, who by her name reminds me of God's oath, has been a sure and steadfast anchor in this earthly and spiritual sojourn. While her hope that I would not dedicate this work to her has been disappointed, her love, patience, and sacrifice are more deeply appreciated than can be expressed.

And what more shall I say? For time would fail me to tell of all those who have advised, encouraged, helped, and challenged me along the way, of Professor Robert Gordon, Rev. Dr. Arnold Browne, Mrs. Margaret Cathie, Dr. Andrew Turkanik, Dr. Emil Bartoş, and Dr. Iosif Ţon, during the completion of the dissertation, and of Professor Dr. Jörg Frey, Dr. Georg Siebeck, Dr. Henning Ziebritzki, and the staff of Mohr Siebeck in Tübingen, during the revision process. To all of them and, supremely, to the One who is ὁ τῆς πίστεως ἀρχηγὸς καὶ τελειωτής, my deepest gratitude.

Kansas City, February 2003   Radu Gheorghiţă

Table of Contents

List of Abbreviations

ANE   Ancient Near East

BAGD   Bauer, Walter. *A Greek – English Lexicon of the New Testament and Other Early Christian Literature*

BDB   Brown, F., S. R. Driver, and C. A. Briggs. *The New Brown – Driver – Briggs – Gesenius Hebrew and English Lexicon*

BDF   Blass, F., and A. Debrunner. *A Greek Grammar of the New Testament and Other Early Christian Literature*

BHK   Kittel, R., and P. Kahle. *Biblia Hebraica*

BHS   Elliger, K., and W. Rudolph. *Biblia Hebraica Stuttgartensia*

DCH   Clines, D. J. A. *The Dictionary of Classical Hebrew*

DT   Jastrow, Marcus. *A Dictionary of the Targumim, the Talmud Babli and Yerushalmi, and the Midrashic Literature*

EDNT   Balz, Horst, and Gerhard Schneider. *Exegetical Dictionary of the New Testament*

GEL   Louw, Johannes P., and Eugene A. Nida. *Greek – English Lexicon of the New Testament. Based on Semantic Domains*

GELSMP Muraoka, Takamitsu. *A Greek – English Lexicon of the Septuagint. Twelve Prophets*

KB   Koehler, Ludwig, and Walter Baumgartner. *The Hebrew and Aramaic Lexicon of the Old Testament*

κτλ   καὶ τὰ λοιπά

LEH   Lust, J., E. Eynikel, and K. Hauspie. *A Greek – English Lexicon of the Septuagint*

LXX   Septuagint

MT   Masoretic Text

NIDOTTE VanGemeren, Willem A. *The New International Dictionary of Old Testament Theology and Exegesis*

NT   New Testament

OT   Old Testament

PLD   Patrologia Latina Database

TDNT   Kittel, G., and G. Friedrich. *Theological Dictionary of the New Testament*

TDOT   Botterweck, G. Johannes, and Helmer Ringgren. *Theological Dictionary of the Old Testament*

Tg   Targum

TLG   Thesaurus Linguae Graecae

Chapter One

Introduction

1. Prolegomena

Πολυμερῶς καὶ πολυτρόπως, "in many and various ways", the alliterative collocation describing God's revelation in times past (1:1) suitably characterises the way the Author of Hebrews (the Author, henceforth) made use of the Scriptures. The Author's scriptural repertoire includes numerous quotations from the Old Testament (OT, henceforth), extensive use of OT language and ideas, references to the OT's important cultic institutions, events and persons, and a variety of OT summaries, parallels, allusions, and echoes of scriptural texts.[1] An assessment such as Paul Ellingworth's, "the language and thought of the epistle are steeped in the OT",[2] is frequently found in current scholarship which has reached an undeniable consensus regarding the importance of the Jewish Scriptures and their contribution to the theology of the Epistle to the Hebrews.

It is widely acknowledged that a common characteristic of New Testament (NT, henceforth) writings is the blending of two important sources that have contributed to the formation of each author's theology, one being the Jewish Scriptures, and the other, the Christ-event, which encompasses the teachings, ministry, life, death and resurrection of Jesus of Nazareth. The part played by the Jewish Scriptures in the formation of the theology of the New Testament writers offers a complex field of inquiry. Although the majority of the authors were Jews, their writings were composed most probably in the Greek language, the indisputable *lingua franca* of the Graeco-Roman world in New Testament times. If Greek was the language of choice for their *theolegomena,* it can safely be

---

[1] The terminology employed here to refer to the Scriptures used by the Author to the Hebrews will be predominantly "the Old Testament", especially from today's reader's point of view. At times, however, an alternative expression such as "the Jewish Scriptures" and its variations will prove to be a better label from the Author's point of view. Similarly, the traditional B.C. and A.D. will be used throughout to reflect the theological standpoint of the present writer.

[2] Paul Ellingworth, "The Old Testament in Hebrews: Exegesis, Method and Hermeneutics" (Ph. D., University of Aberdeen, 1978) 307.

assumed that the most accessible and convenient Scriptures for them was the Greek translation of the Jewish sacred writings, the Septuagint.

While one must agree with Origen's assertion that τίς δὲ ὁ γράψας τὴν Ἐπιστολὴν, τὸ μὲν ἀληθὲς Θεὸς οἶδε,[3] it can be said that the Author fits very well within the above description. First, he possessed a profound knowledge and understanding of the Jewish Scriptures, which even a casual reading of the epistle demonstrates. His knowledge and appropriation of the Scriptures as well as their crucial importance in the development of his theological argument are second to none among the NT writers. Second, when one considers the question of what constituted the Jewish Scriptures for the Author, the evidence points unambiguously toward the Septuagint.[4] It was the Greek text of the Jewish Scriptures that he used for his quotations with much more uniformity and precision than most of the other NT writers. His remarkable command of the Jewish sacred writings was acquired as a result of the study of the Greek Scriptures, and it was from that vantage point that he reflected upon the Christ-event.

The background of the Author's thought has been admirably explored by L. D. Hurst in a new synthesis of alleged influences on the Author.[5] The conveniently arranged and critically assessed proposals have put many of Hebrews' students in his debt. The monograph investigates both the non-Christian backgrounds, including Qumran, Pre-Christian Gnosticism, Samaritan and Merkabah mysticism, as well as the possible Christian influence from contemporary sources such as the Stephen tradition, Pauline theology, and Petrine influence. Hurst records among his presuppositions the role played by the Septuagint as the source of the epistle's quotations, which, for an author so dependent on the Scriptures, were clearly "one of the major influences upon the formation of his argument".[6] While this assumption accompanies Hurst's study throughout, to this writer, the absence of a separate, explicit, and detailed discussion of the Septuagint among the factors that have directly influenced the Epistle to the Hebrews is the only drawback of an otherwise extremely insightful and helpful monograph.

These observations raise a number of pertinent questions that provide the springboard for the present investigation. If the argument of the epistle depends so heavily on the OT and if its author relies solely on the Greek

---

[3] Origen in *Ex Homiliis in epistulam ad Hebraeos*, *Thesaurus Linguae Graecae* (6.01) (Chadwyck-Healey, Silver Mountain Software, 1997) 14.1309.4.

[4] See *infra* (3.1) the discussion on textual issues.

[5] Lincoln D. Hurst, *The Epistle to the Hebrews. Its Background of Thought* (SNTS-MS 65; Cambridge: Cambridge University Press, 1990).

[6] Hurst, *Background* 4.

text of the Jewish Scriptures, is it conceivable that the Greek Jewish Scriptures might have had a distinct and discernible influence on his theology? Has the Author formulated his argument on the basis of the Septuagint translation in a way that he would not have done had he been expounding the Hebrew text? Is it legitimate to affirm that the Septuagint had a determinant role in the shaping of the epistle? To what extent can the Septuagint be considered as having exerted a distinct influence on the Author and on the epistle's argument, and in what ways was that influence exercised? Is the use of the OT in Hebrews determined in any way by the use of the Greek Scriptures as opposed to the Hebrew Scriptures?

Doubtless there are other important factors that contributed to the crystallisation of the Author's theology, and the delimitation of his formative influences to just one factor, the Scriptures, could well be regarded as reductionistic. Yet the question surfaces over and over again especially at those junctures where the Author builds his argument on particular ideas or nuances present in the Greek Old Testament.

As will soon be evident, the scholarship on the use of the OT in the Epistle to the Hebrews is extensive, and this study could not have been undertaken if not for the outstanding work of those who have wrestled with the textual, exegetical, and hermeneutical aspects. The research undertaken in this thesis builds on several monumental studies in the field, primarily K. J. Thomas, F. Schröger, J. J. McCullough, and P. Ellingworth, and proposes an approach that could further the scholarly dialogue in the exploration of factors that contributed to the genesis of this epistle.[7] It seeks to address more explicitly certain aspects pertaining to the relationship between the epistle and the Septuagint, the Bible of the Author. Its special interest is directed toward unfolding some of the major ways in which the Greek OT contributed to the content and the thought of this first century Christian document.

2. The Septuagint – Beyond Textual Criticism

The increasing attention given by NT scholars to the role of the Septuagint in the writing of the NT is a predictable outcome of the renewed interest in Septuagintal studies themselves, best seen in the two volumes of classified bibliography by S. P. Brock and C. Dogniez.[8]

---

[7] Ellingworth, "Old Testament"; J. C. McCullough, "Hebrews and the Old Testament" (Ph. D., Queen's University, 1971); F. Schröger, *Der Verfasser des Hebräerbriefes als Schriftausleger* (Regensburg: Pustet, 1968); Kenneth J. Thomas, "The Use of the Septuagint in the Epistle to the Hebrews" (Ph. D., University of Manchester, 1959).

[8] S. P. Brock, C. T. Fritsch, and S. Jellicoe, eds., *A Classified Bibliography of the*

Prior to the discoveries in the Judaean Desert, the study of the Septuagint was conducted with the primary interest of recovering the original Hebrew text. This emphasis continues unabated to this day, even after the discoveries of other older textual witnesses, as eminent scholars advocate for keeping the focus on textual criticism as the major goal in LXX studies. After acknowledging the proliferation of interest in this field, Emanuel Tov affirms that "one should always try to integrate the results of these studies into the larger area of textual criticism or exegesis ... all other sub-areas of LXX research ... should always have the next stage in mind, that of the reconstruction of the *Vorlage* of the LXX".[9] Albert Pietersma echoes a similar concern when he concludes his survey of Septuagintal research with the emphatic plea to return to "what must always remain the first priority of LXX research, viz. the systematic and methodical uncovering of the Old Greek text".[10]

This perspective on the nature of LXX studies seems to be the dominant approach of the English-speaking schools, although not all Septuagintalists share it. John W. Wevers, through his comparative analyses of the Greek and Hebrew texts of the books of the Pentateuch,[11] or William Horbury, in the study of the theological nuances of several themes in the Septuagint,[12] deserve special mention in this respect. There is indeed, a growing consensus, especially in continental circles, that the Septuagint cannot be looked upon merely as a witness to the original Hebrew text or as an instrument for its reconstruction. No one disputes that the Septuagint is valuable in this respect. However, to limit the scope of Septuagintal

---

Septuagint (ALGHJ 6; Leiden: E. J. Brill, 1973); Cécile Dogniez, *Bibliography of the Septuagint (1970-1993)* (SVT 60; Leiden: E. J. Brill, 1993). See also Robert A. Kraft, and E. Tov, eds., *Computer Tools for Septuagint Studies* (SBL-SCS 20; Atlanta: Scholars Press, 1988).

[9] Emanuel Tov, "Textual Criticism of the Hebrew Bible 1947-1997", in *Perspectives in the Study of the Old Testament and Early Judaism. A Symposium in Honour of Adam S. van der Woude on the Occasion of His 70th Birthday*, eds. Florentino Garcia Martinez and Ed Noort (Leiden / Boston / Köln: E. J. Brill, 1998) 62.

[10] A. Pietersma, "Septuagint Research: A Plea to Return to Basic Issues", *Vetus Testamentum* 35, no. 3 (1985) 311.

[11] John William Wevers, *Notes on the Greek Text of Exodus* (SBL-SCS 30; Atlanta: Scholars Press, 1990), *idem, Notes on the Greek Text of Genesis* (SBL-SCS 35; Atlanta: Scholars Press, 1993), *idem, Notes on the Greek Text of Deuteronomy* (SBL-SCS 39; Atlanta: Scholars Press, 1995), *idem, Notes on the Greek Text of Leviticus* (SBL-SCS 44; Atlanta: Scholars Press, 1997), *idem, Notes on the Greek Text of Numbers* (SBL-SCS 46; Atlanta: Scholars Press, 1998).

[12] William Horbury, "Septuagintal and New Testament Conceptions of the Church", in *A Vision for the Church. Studies in Early Christian Ecclesiology in Honour of J. P. M. Sweet*, eds. Markus Bockmuehl and Michael B. Thompson (Edinburgh: T. & T. Clark, 1997).

studies to matters of textual criticism ignores one of the essential and unique roles that the Septuagint played in the Christian Church from its inception. The extent to which the NT writers and the Church Fathers depended on the Septuagint strongly suggests that the right approach is to consider the Greek Bible not only as a textual witness to the Jewish Scriptures but as a theological text in its own right. To disregard this function of the Septuagint is at best reductionistic and at worst misguided.[13]

J. Trebolle Barrera, while not denying the value of the LXX for textual criticism, emphasises the eclipsed exegetical value of the LXX. "The LXX version," he writes, "had enormous influence on the formulation of the Christian faith and on the language and literature of the Fathers, an aspect generally ignored by biblical scholars".[14] A similar concern is voiced by the French Septuagint scholar Marguerite Harl, the director of the impressive project *La Bible d'Alexandrie*. Since the LXX reflects the maturing process of Jewish thought, she asserts that "la connaissance de la LXX ... est nécessaire pour mieux lire le NT, pour comprendre comment il recueille les croyances et la foi juives, et en donne un interprétation qui en 'renouvelle' le sens".[15] The Scandinavian school, while primarily known for their intense pursuit of the technique exhibited by the translators of the Septuagint, has not neglected to give proper attention to the theological motivation behind the translators' choice of equivalents as well as to their implications.[16] Likewise, Robert Hanhart, Martin Hengel, and Joachim Schaper, three German voices, have contributed immensely to the appreciation of the theological significance of the Septuagint for NT studies.[17] One of the most vocal advocates of this approach is the Danish

---

[13] John W. Wevers, "The Interpretative Character and Significance of the Septuagint Version", in *Hebrew Bible / Old Testament. The History of Its Interpretation. From the Beginnings to the Middle Ages (until 1300)*, eds. Magne Saebo, Chris Brekelmans, and Menahem Haran (Göttingen: Vandenhoeck & Ruprecht, 1996) 87.

[14] Julio Trebolle Barrera, *The Jewish Bible and the Christian Bible. An Introduction to the History of the Bible*, trans. Wilfred G. E. Watson (Leiden / Grand Rapids: E. J. Brill / Eerdmans, 1998) 439.

[15] Marguerite Harl, Gilles Dorival, and Olivier Munnich, *La Bible grecque des Septante: du judaïsme hellénistique au Christianisme ancien* (Paris: Éditions du Cerf, 1988) 218.

[16] S. Olofsson, *God is My Rock. A Study of Translation Technique and Theological Exegesis in the Septuagint* (Stockholm: Almqvist, 1990).

[17] Representative contributions include Robert Hanhart, "Die Bedeutung der Septuaginta in neutestamentlicher Zeit", *Zeitschrift für Theologie und Kirche* 81, no. 4 (1984); M. Hengel and R. Deines, "Die Septuaginta als 'Christliche Schriftensammlung', ihre Vorgeschichte und das Problem ihres Kanons", in *Die Septuaginta: zwischen Judentum und Christentum*, eds. Martin Hengel and Anna Maria Schwemer (WUNT 72; Tübingen: Mohr Siebeck, 1994); Joachim Schaper, *Eschatology in the Greek Psalter*

scholar Mogens Müller, who in a recently published collection of essays entitled *The First Bible of the Church: A Plea for the Septuagint* undertakes to prove that "the Septuagint does in fact convey, more convincingly than Biblia Hebraica what the NT authors understood as their Holy Writ".[18]

The present study seeks to evaluate this particular perspective on the alleged influence exerted by the Greek Scriptures on the writings of the New Testament and their authors by focusing on the Epistle to the Hebrews as one of the most suitable candidates for such an enquiry. As already mentioned, the Author of Hebrews recommends himself not only on account of his knowledge and interest in the Scriptures, which was, judging by his writings, unsurpassed among the other NT authors, but also because of his repeated and consistent use of the Greek textual tradition of the Scriptures, the Septuagint. Can the Septuagint stand on its own either as a distinct influence on the Author or as a discernible component of the Old Testament influence? Is it correct to affirm that the LXX had a determinant or unique role in the shaping of the epistle? Has the Author of Hebrews formulated the argument on the basis of the Septuagint translation in a way that he would not have done had he been expounding the Hebrew text? These questions delineate the parameters of the present study as a quest toward a thorough assessment of the role played by the Greek Scriptures, the Septuagint, in shaping the theological message of the writings of first-century Christianity.

The term "Septuagint" should be clarified at the outset.[19] The term generally is used to designate either the Greek translation of the Hebrew Torah (etymologically, the Septuagint proper), or the translation of the entire Hebrew canon (the Old Greek Version), or, in its broadest sense, the Alexandrian canon, which includes the deutero-canonical writings along side the Greek version of the Hebrew Scriptures.[20] This investigation uses

---

(WUNT II 76; Tübingen: Mohr Siebeck, 1995); Martin Hengel, *The Septuagint as Christian Scripture. Its Prehistory and the Problem of Its Canon* (Edinburgh: T. & T. Clark, 2002).

[18] Mogens Müller, *The First Bible of the Church. A Plea for the Septuagint* (JSOT-SS 206; Sheffield: Sheffield Academic Press, 1996) 121. It is worth mentioning that the Orthodox Church considers the Septuagint as its primary textual witness of the Old Testament. H. Cunliffe-Jones writes, "so far as the text of the Bible is concerned it is natural that the Orthodox Church should hold that the *Greek text* of both the Old as well as the New Testament *is the authoritative one*" (author's emphasis); "Scripture and Tradition in Orthodox Theology", in *Holy Book and Holy Tradition*, eds. F. F. Bruce and E. G. Rupp (Manchester: Manchester University Press, 1968) 191.

[19] Leonard Greenspoon, "The Use and Abuse of the Term 'LXX' and Related Terminology in Recent Scholarship", *Bulletin of the International Organization for Septuagint and Cognate Studies* 20 (1987).

[20] Wevers, "Significance" 86.

the term Septuagint as a common idiom, without any particular associations to either specific manuscript traditions (such as the Codices A or B) or to specific Septuagintal families (such as the ones grouped by the Göttingen Septuagint). Since the data on the history of the Greek translation of the Hebrew Scriptures and its history of transmission is far from being conclusive, the term Septuagint will be used with a less precise meaning denoting nothing more than the Greek version of the Jewish Scriptures used by the Author in composing the epistle. While this usage does not offer any assistance in locating more precisely the Author's text in the transmission history of the LXX, it gives perhaps a more realistic picture of such matters as the Author's access to, use of, and ownership of the Greek Scriptures.[21]

3. Use of the Old Testament in Hebrews: State of Research

Due to the wealth of material it supplies, the Epistle to the Hebrews is among the most well researched NT writings with respect to its use of the OT. Practical considerations require that the focus be limited only to those works that made a significant impact in this field, selected from the contributions of the past five decades, primarily by English-speaking authors. The present survey traces chronologically the developments in three major areas of interest with regard to the use of the OT in Hebrews, which have led to three distinct approaches: textual, exegetical-hermeneutical, and rhetorical.

3.1. Use of the OT in Hebrews: Textual Approach

Studies dealing primarily with textual matters have investigated questions pertaining to the text used by the Author in quotations in an attempt to

---

[21] Many issues deserve to be addressed here. Foremost are the considerations of the status of the Greek Scriptures in the first century A.D., including the debate on the Alexandrian Canon and the status of the non-canonical writings. These matters will receive brief consideration at several junctures throughout this study. For several standard works on these matters, see Roger Beckwith, *The Old Testament Canon of the New Testament Church and Its Background in Early Judaism* (Grand Rapids: Eerdmans, 1985); E. Earle Ellis, "The Old Testament Canon in the Early Church", in *Mikra. Text, Translation, Reading and Interpretation of the Hebrew Bible in Ancient Judaism and Early Christianity*, ed. Martin Jan Mulder (CRINT 2/I ; Minneapolis: Fortress Press, 1990) 653-90; Hengel, *Scripture*; Albert C. Sundberg, *The Old Testament of the Early Church* (New York: Kraus Reprint Co., 1969).

align it to the major textual witnesses. The following selection marks the more significant developments in this very intensely studied area.[22]

3.1.1. K. J. Thomas

Thomas' dissertation, summarised in a subsequent article, was arguably the harbinger of the scholarly interest in the following decades in textual matters regarding the use of the OT in the epistle.[23] The research interest was to compare the text of the Author's quotations against two major textual witnesses, LXX^A and LXX^B. Thomas asserts that where the text of the epistle differs from that of the LXX^A or LXX^B, almost invariably the changes were intentional and interpretative. The major part of the study consists of an analysis of more than fifty variations in the quotations with no parallels in the LXX^A or LXX^B, with only non-uncial parallels, with parallels in uncials other than LXX^A or LXX^B, with parallels in LXX^A or LXX^B, and with parallels in LXX^A and LXX^B but in cases where other significant variants are present. The last chapter analyses the alleged Philonic influence on the Author, by presenting both the similarities and the differences between the two writers in handling certain OT texts. Thomas concludes that it is possible to reconstruct the Greek OT used by the Author, since the intentional variations from LXX^A and LXX^B can be safely determined. Thus where Codex A differed from B, the Author used the text he had, and where LXX^A was identical to LXX^B, but different from other witnesses, the Author used the common text. Taking the lead from Katz,[24] Thomas discusses the issue of primitive vs. edited text, and concludes that the text used by the Author uses almost all primitive readings, both when LXX^A is different from LXX^B, and when they are identical but different from other witnesses.[25] Thomas' analysis has bearing also on the history of the Septuagint. Indeed, Thomas contends that:

---

[22] An important work on this topic often referred to is E. Ahlborn, "Die Septuaginta Vorlage des Hebräerbriefes" (Ph. D., Göttingen, 1966). Unfortunately, the attempts to secure a copy proved fruitless.

[23] Kenneth J. Thomas, "The Old Testament Citations in the Epistle to the Hebrews", *New Testament Studies* 11 (1965); *idem*, "Septuagint".

[24] P. Katz, "The Quotations from Dt. in Heb.", *Zeitschrift für die neutestamentliche Wissenschaft* 49 (1958). Katz discusses the five passages in Hebrews considered by most commentators to be quotations from Deuteronomy, Heb. 1:6, 10:30, 12:15, 21, and 13:5. He concludes that these texts display no common characteristics that can be grouped together and that they supply no evidence for a Greek text different from the LXX. Katz proposes that the old and mistaken quest for the LXX^A or LXX^B as the quotation-supplying texts be replaced by a more appropriate one, i.e., seeking to determine if the text of a given quotation follows a primitive text or an edited one.

[25] Thomas, "Septuagint" 324.

[LXX] A and [LXX] B represent two traditions from a single translation, which may be called the Septuagint. The author of Hebrews had a text of this translation still in its comparatively pure, 'primitive' form. It appears that this text was used by the Author before it had been subjected to any very extensive editing.[26]

3.1.2. G. Howard

Developments in pre-Masoretic textual studies led Howard to defend the theory of the Author's dependence on a Hebrew text.[27] He challenges the popular view of the Author's dependence on the LXX and of his unfamiliarity with the Hebrew text or language. In the first part Howard presents a general inventory of the similarities between the quotations in the epistle and either the Hebrew or the Greek text. Although there is a predominance of LXX text influences as opposed to the Hebrew text, there are six cases in which the quotations in the epistle are identical to the Hebrew text as opposed to the LXX, and only two identical to the LXX as opposed to the Hebrew. The second part deals more closely with the quotations that show dependence on a Hebrew text.[28] In the concluding remarks, Howard suggests "it is incorrect to characterise the quotations in Hebrews as always Septuagintal. A great many of them do not correspond exactly to any Septuagint, and some agree with a known Hebrew text, either whole or in part, against the Septuagint."[29]

Howard's conclusions, not always the result of a fair assessment of all possibilities,[30] have been accepted by several scholars,[31] although subsequent scholarship has shown that the study overlooked the wealth of the Greek textual variants which supply a more reasonable explanation for the textual deviations in the quotations.[32]

3.1.3. J. C. McCullough

McCullough's dissertation and the subsequent article are among the most comprehensive contributions to the discussion, and could easily feature in

---

[26] Thomas, "Septuagint" 337.

[27] George Howard, "Hebrews and the Old Testament Quotations", *Novum Testamentum* 10 (1968).

[28] The quotations listed under this heading are: Dt. 32:35, Is. 35:3, Is. 8:7, 12:2, 2 Sam. 22:3, Pr. 3:11-12, Jos. 1:5, Dt. 32:43, Ps. 47:7, Ex. 24:8, Ps. 22:23, and Ps. 110:4.

[29] Howard, "Quotations" 215.

[30] J. H. Luther deals at length with this criticism, "The Use of the Old Testament by the Author of Hebrews" (Ph. D., Bob Jones University, 1977).

[31] *Inter alios*, J. A. Fitzmyer, "Habakkuk 2:3-4 and the New Testament", in *De la Torah au Messie. Melanges Henri Cazelles*, eds. J. Dore, P. Grelot, and M. Carrez (Paris: Descleé, 1981) 447-57.

[32] See especially McCullough, "Hebrews".

any of the three areas delineated by this survey.[33]   He engages in a
thorough analysis of the epistle's employment of OT quotations and
allusions and conducts a comparative study of the Author's exegetical
approach with those of his contemporaries.

The recent developments in Septuagint studies, especially the massive
collection of variants in the Göttingen Septuagint, have convinced
McCullough that one "can no longer think in terms of great manuscripts A
or B as being LXX, and therefore it is no longer relevant to try to
assimilate the text behind the quotations in Hebrews with these, explaining
all differences by reference to the intentional changes of the Author".[34]
The proposed alternative is the search for the text-types to which the
quotations belong in order to assess whether the differences in the text are
more likely to be due to LXX recensional activity or to the influence of the
author.   McCullough analyses all the quotations in their OT context and
traces the textual variants to a particular family, when available.   Each
variation is labelled according to the degree of intentionality displayed by
the change.

McCullough's main contribution is to focus on readings not reflected in
most LXX manuscripts, but on those that are found in the main
manuscripts representing the recension thought to be used by the Author.
He considers in detail the instances where the text of the epistle differs
from that of the main reading of the recension in order to determine
whether or not the Author deliberately introduced a variant reading.   In the
cases where the textual modifications could be confidently traced to the
Author's activity, a series of reasons, such as the effort to add either a
particular emphasis or to achieve a better fit with the context or to avoid
possible misunderstandings, are held responsible.[35]

McCullough's work also engages in a comparative analysis of the
Author's exegetical approach to the OT against the background of
contemporary exegetical and hermeneutic practices.   *Sensus plenior* and
typology are the most suitable hermeneutic frameworks for understanding
the Author's use of the OT, with due appreciation given to the role of the
One who fulfilled the OT, Jesus Christ, as the hermeneutical key for
opening the OT.   Further consideration given to other types of OT material
present in the epistle, i.e., figures, events, and institutions, conclude
McCullough's assessment of the Author's theological contribution.   His
overall conclusion deserves to be quoted in full:

---

[33] McCullough, "Hebrews"; *idem*, "The Old Testament Quotations in Hebrews", *New
Testament Studies* 26 (1980).

[34] McCullough, "Hebrews" 46.

[35] McCullough, "Quotations" 378.

The author of the Epistle to the Hebrews was a man of his time. He used the text which he found in common use in his day, without being too concerned with LXX textual criticism, he used methods of exegesis common in his day, and was influenced by exegetical traditions familiar to him. He was, however, above all a Christian, and as such, his main concern was to find Christ in the Old Testament. This ability to range over such wide tracks of Old Testament and interpret it in this way is his greatest contribution.[36]

3.1.4. A. H. Cadwallader

Cadwallader undertakes a detailed investigation of many of the cases which attest the epistle's assimilation of the LXX text, a difficult topic given the larger spectrum of the issues involved in a study of this nature, not least "the attitudes of Christian scribes concerning the relationship between (Greek) Old and New Testaments".[37] Cadwallader contends that the Author's assimilation of the LXX displays several characteristics. First, there are the expansions determined either by the need for clarification or by unsuccessful attempts to reflect the original thought or preserve a particular tradition. Second, there is the removal or creation of conflations. A third characteristic is the corrections of syntactical or grammatical form, word addition or omission or the change of word order. In the same category Cadwallader includes word substitutions, corrections which make more explicit perceived allusions or to concord with a previously given quotation. Fourth, there are the common expressions showing a preference for Septuagintal language. The study concludes that the work of the Christian scribes reflects a wide spectrum of practices, ranging from corrections affecting the substance of a text to the simple modification of expressions without a change of meaning.[38] While Cadwallader's contribution has drawn attention to the interdependence between different textual traditions in their transmission, it has dealt with the issues too unevenly, without giving equal consideration to the possibility that the Hebrews' textual transmission itself influenced the textual history of the Septuagint.

3.2. Use of the OT in Hebrews: Exegetical – Hermeneutical Approach

There are too many studies investigating the exegetical aspects of the Author's use of the OT to give them full justice in the space available,

---

[36] McCullough, "Hebrews" 479.

[37] A. H. Cadwallader, "The Correction of the Text of Hebrews towards the LXX", *Novum Testamentum* 34, no. 3 (1992) 275.

[38] Cadwallader, "The Correction" 286.

therefore the selection presented here outlines only some of the major contributions.[39]

3.2.1. G. B. Caird

Caird mounts a rigorous defence against the groundless accusation that the Author mishandled the OT in an Alexandrine or Philonic fashion, in an epistle that is "one of the earliest and most successful attempts to define the relation between the Old and New Testaments".[40]   Caird proposes a fresh look at what the epistle reveals about the Old Testament as revelation, which had been superseded and fulfilled but not abrogated. Caird is mostly known for his insight on the OT's "constant disclaimer of finality".[41]   Although God spoke in times past, the final, full word of salvation was spoken only in Christ. The range of OT quotations proves that the Author regarded the OT as a prophetic work, which pointed to the eschatological future. In the analysis of the self-confessed validity of the old order, Caird draws attention to the four major OT quotations on which the argument of the Author rests (Pss. 8, 95, 110, Jer. 31), arguing that the Author's purpose "is not to prove the superiority of the New over the Old, nor to establish the inadequacy of the Old. His interest is in the confessed inadequacy of the old order."[42]   The need for a new and fully adequate covenant, for a new priesthood, for a proper understanding of God's offer of "rest" and of the glory for which man was destined, have been testified to already by the key OT passages used by the Author. Thus the major contribution of the OT to the faith and worship of the New Testament community is to provide the "aspirations to which only Christ supplies the fulfilment", to supply the "picture language for the preaching of the gospel", to testify to the "partial anticipation of the realities which were fully present in Jesus", and to provide models of faith.[43]

3.2.2. M. Barth

Barth reviews three hermeneutical approaches, the anthropo-centric, the *sensus plenior* and the typological, which try to explain the Author's interpretation of the Old Testament, and finds all three to be

---

[39] It should be noted that several studies grouped under this heading, such as Ellingworth, "Old Testament", or McCullough, "Hebrews", give equally extensive consideration to textual matters. They seem, however, to devote their main attention to exegetical and hermeneutical issues.

[40] George B. Caird, "The Exegetical Method of the Epistle to the Hebrews", *Canadian Journal of Theology* 5 (1959) 45.

[41] Caird, "Method" 46.

[42] Caird, "Method" 47.

[43] Caird, "Method" 51.

unsatisfactory.[44]   The variety of references to the OT, the direct and indirect quotations, the allusions, the summaries or reflections and the names, show the extent of the epistle's use of the OT. Barth contends that the Author works with a "canon within the canon" and that canon is "the Lord who comes in the world".[45]

Based on observations regarding the use of the OT, Barth outlines the qualities of correct exegetical process, a process that must be characterised by a "willingness to listen and the invitation to heed [God's word]"[46] and a participation in the dialogue between God and his people.[47]   Furthermore, the Author understands exegesis to be research done in the history and in the literature of Israel in the pursuit of learning more about the Messiah and his relevance for the life and situation of the recipients,[48] as well as an act of hearing the OT as a call to worship in truth for all true believers. Barth concludes that the Author's exegetical method is "essentially dialogical, Christological, and homiletical, ... , one among many New Testament ways of approaching, respecting, and using the Old Testament for its witness to Jesus Christ".[49]

3.2.3. F. Schröger

Schröger's contribution ranks alongside those of McCullough and Ellingworth as one of the most detailed analyses of the use of the OT in Hebrews.[50] Each quotation and allusion in the epistle is analysed, first, by exploring its meaning in the *Urtext* (MT) and in the LXX rendering, concentrating on the differences between the two traditions. Focus then is shifted to the ways in which these OT texts are used in the epistle, their meaning and the methods of interpretation as appropriated by the Author. One of the most important sections considers the hermeneutic method behind each individual quotation, a large canvas that includes the direct and indirect messianic interpretations according to the pattern "Promise-Fulfilment", the typological interpretation, the allegorical interpretation, the interpretation according to the Midrash-Pesher and Midrash-Haggadah

---

[44]   Markus Barth, "The Old Testament in Hebrews: An Essay in Biblical Hermeneutics", in *Current Issues in New Testament Interpretation*, eds. W. Klassen and G. F. Snyder (New York: Harper & Row, 1962) 53-78.

[45] Barth, "Hermeneutics" 57.

[46] Barth, "Hermeneutics" 61.

[47] Barth, "Hermeneutics" 63.

[48] Barth, "Hermeneutics" 71.

[49] Barth, "Hermeneutics" 77.

[50]   F. Schröger, "Das hermeneutische Instrumentarium des Hebräerbriefverfassers", *Theologie und Glaube* 60 (1970) 344-59; *idem*, *Verfasser*.

methods, and the interpretation according to the literal meaning.[51] The foremost distinctiveness of the Author's hermeneutics, however, is his *heilsgeschichtliche* approach.[52]

The use of this impressive "hermeneutische Instrumentarium" was necessary, Schröger contends, to solve the "Schriftenkreises" [*sic*] in which his readers found themselves when trying to connect the past to the present, or to relate the new community of faith to the nation and synagogue of Israel. The Author's approach has implications for the present-day exegete, who, just like the Author, must be conscious of both his indebtedness to the assumptions of the hermeneutics employed, as well as to the necessity of faith being the prerequisite for dealing with a text that claims to be divine revelation.[53]

3.2.4. P. Ellingworth

It would be difficult to find a more comprehensive treatment of the textual, exegetical and hermeneutical issues involved in the use of the OT in the epistle.[54] The essence of this study is encapsulated in the keen observation that "the phrase 'the understanding of the Old Testament in Hebrews' may be construed in two ways, depending on whether attention is focused on the understanding by the author of Heb. or by ourselves".[55] Questions pertaining to the OT material, form and function, the text-form of the quotation, awareness of the original context and comparison with other contemporary authors are being asked throughout the study of quotations and allusions in the epistle. Ellingworth concludes that the use of the OT is "far more extensive than a mere list of quotations and verbal allusions would suggest".[56]

Many of the generally accepted positions regarding the Scriptures used by the Author, his fidelity to the text or his main theological interests,

---

[51] The first pattern is that of "Prophecy–Fulfilment" which includes the direct messianic promises fulfilled in the "last of days", (Jer. 31, Hab. 2, Hag. 2) and the promises fulfilled in the person of Christ (Ps. 2, 2 Sam. 7, Ps. 45, Ps. 110, Is. 8, Ps. 22). Second, the typological approach is defined as the prefiguration of the work and person of Jesus Christ (the reality) in the persons, historical events and cultic institutions of the OT (Num. 12, Ps. 95, Gen. 22, Gen. 14, Ps. 40, Gen. 4, as well as the texts in which the argument קל וחמר is used). Third, the Midrash–Pesher method is illustrated by the use of Dt. 32, Ps. 102, Ps. 8, and Ps. 40. Fourth, the Rabbinic method of interpretation is evident especially in certain procedures and ways of reasoning. Finally, the interpretation according to the literal meaning underlies the use of Ps. 104, Ex. 24, Dt. 32, Gen. 21, Gen. 47, Pr. 3, and Ex. 19.

[52] Schröger, *Verfasser* 307.

[53] Schröger, "Instrumentarium" 329.

[54] Ellingworth, "Old Testament".

[55] Ellingworth, "Old Testament" v.

[56] Ellingworth, "Old Testament" 466.

receive firmer grounding as a result of Ellingworth's analysis. The most unique contribution of his study is the insightful exploration of the quotations and allusions in their Septuagintal context, which became the direct precursor of the present investigation.

The second part of the study covers questions of method and hermeneutics. As far as exegetical method is concerned, Ellingworth provides a useful theoretical framework against which one can assess the different exegetical methods employed by the Author, such as allegory, the prophecy-fulfilment schema, typology, midrash, Rabbinic rules, the *sensus plenior*, the "real-presence of Christ in the OT" and the "Christ-Witness argument". Ellingworth concludes that whereas in the direct quotations "the prophecy-fulfilment schema was the method most widely used ... the typological approach was the most deeply rooted in the epistle as a whole".[57]

In the section which focuses on issues of hermeneutics, Ellingworth turns to the hermeneutical philosophy of Georg Gadamer, developed primarily in the work *Truth and Method*, as offering the best framework with which to analyse two given perspectives on the OT. On the one hand is the perspective of the first-century Jews and Christians, and on the other, that of the modern reader or exegete, each group having its own set of axiomatic presuppositions. Are there elements of continuity and discontinuity between the ways in which each group approaches and understands the OT? Although both the Author's understanding of the OT and our modern understanding are considered justified and valid, from the point of view of each system of reference, they both are liable to be considered defective when analysed from the other's reference system; "Gadamer's insights made it possible to avert this danger by recognising validity in different interpretations of a text each embodying an authentic response to the substance of the text in different historical situations".[58]

3.2.5. G. Hughes

Hughes devotes his entire study to the hermeneutical issues underlying the epistle of a theologian who "more diligently and successfully than any other of the New Testament writers, has worked at what we now describe as hermeneutics".[59] Hughes discusses the Author's perspective on Scriptures, which, even when subjected to historical processes, remain the

---

[57] Ellingworth, "Old Testament" 468.

[58] Ellingworth, "Old Testament" 469.

[59] Graham Hughes, *Hebrews and Hermeneutics: The Epistle to the Hebrews as a New Testament Example of Biblical Interpretation* (SNTS-MS 36; Cambridge: Cambridge University Press, 1979) 3.

Word of God, unfortunately without giving serious consideration to many exegetical issues that bear directly on these issues.

Hughes argues that the prologue of the epistle focuses on the Son who is the new and superior form of God's address, the perfect and final revelation of God. The revelation in the Son is superior to, although in continuity with the revelation mediated by angels, Moses and Aaron, since Christ is superior to them. The main theological aspects of the epistle have to be understood then in terms of the dialectic nature of continuity and discontinuity, which underlies the revelation process and the required response to this revelation, the covenants, the community of the addressees, and the priesthood.

As far as the use of the OT is concerned, Hughes draws attention to the key hermeneutical dilemma raised by the epistle, i.e., how could the Scriptures of a covenant declared obsolete still function as a valid form of the Word of God.[60] To answer this question, Hughes uses the concept of "promise" to link history and the Word of God. Hughes selects Heb. 5:11-6:20 as the best example of the way in which the OT functions as revelation for Christians.[61] The three indispensable ingredients for such a process are first, "the creative, interpretative, reflective activity of one member of the congregation for the others", second, a "Christian (i.e., faith-) context" and third, an "openness to and receptivity for the Word of God".[62] After describing the main role of the Scriptures as paraenetic, Hughes classifies the OT citations in three categories, the messianic, the ones originally addressed to Yahweh and transferred to Jesus, and finally, the ones attributed to Jesus himself. Important for Hughes' considerations is the eschatological factor that operates in the same dialectical framework of continuity and discontinuity between the covenants. The epistle presents a "realised eschatology" in the doctrinal passages, which emphasises the discontinuity, while the "futurist eschatology" in the paraenetic passages highlights the continuity.[63]

3.2.6. D. F. Leschert

Leschert's main concern is the hermeneutical validity of the Author's use of the Old Testament, especially whether or not he employs the OT in a manner consistent with the intended meaning of the original authors.[64]

---

[60] Hughes, *Hermeneutics* 35.

[61] Hughes, *Hermeneutics* 47.

[62] Hughes, *Hermeneutics* 51 f.

[63] Hughes, *Hermeneutics* 70.

[64] Dale F. Leschert, *Hermeneutical Foundations of Hebrews: A Study in the Validity of the Epistle's Interpretation of Some Core Citations from the Psalms* (Lewiston: Edwin Mellen Press, 1994).

The approach taken in this study is based on a detailed examination of several important citations in order to restore credibility to the Author's use of the OT, and more generally, to the message of the epistle.[65] Leschert justifies his particular approach by the fact that the epistle itself rests "on a limited number of core citations which control the development of the book. All other citations are ancillary to these and explain, illustrate or apply points that they make."[66] The exegetical analysis seeks to prove that "[the Author] interprets [the OT] in a manner consistent with historical-grammatical hermeneutics without distorting the intended meaning of the OT".[67] In the section devoted to hermeneutical considerations, the study examines "the writer's methodology to see if he uses creative methods of interpretation that are capable of distorting the OT's meaning"[68] with the purpose of analysing the Author's use of midrash, typology, and possible allegory.

With regard to the exegetical procedures, Leschert concludes that there is considerable exegetical continuity between the Author's interpretation of the OT and the intended meaning of the original writers. Furthermore, the Author proves his faithfulness to his *Vorlage*, the Septuagint, by treating it as authoritative "even where it departs from the MT".[69] The continuity is manifested also with regard to the traditional interpretations of the OT within the canonical literature, even though one must grant the Author a measure of freedom in the exploration of the OT citations. Furthermore, concerning the methodological issue, the consistency of the Author with historical-grammatical hermeneutics is proven by the avoidance of "creative methodologies" such as midrash and allegory, and the employment of the "standard expository methods: explanation, illustration and application".[70]

While Leschert's work is commendable, the limitation of his study to a sample of quotations, albeit the principle ones in the epistle, does not provide the strongest defence of the Author's historical-grammatical approach to the OT interpretation. The variety of exegetical and

---

[65] Leschert, *Foundations* 16.

[66] Leschert, *Foundations* 16. The OT passages selected are as follows: the catena in ch.1, Ps. 8:4-6, Ps. 95:7-11, Ps. 110:4, and Jer. 31:31-34.

[67] Leschert, *Foundations* 16. In this part attention is given to the messianic interpretation of Ps. 45:6-7 in Heb. 1:8-9, the messianic application of Ps. 8:4-6 to Jesus in Heb. 2:5-9, and the application of the concept of "rest" in Ps. 95 to the generation in Heb. 3:7-4:11.

[68] Leschert, *Foundations* 20. The investigation of the Author's methodology deals with the validity of the midrashic features in Heb. 3:7-4:11 and with the validity of the typological interpretation of Melchizedek in Hebrews 7.

[69] Leschert, *Foundations* 246.

[70] Leschert, *Foundations* 251.

hermeneutical approaches that characterises the epistle, as thoroughly developed by Schröger and Ellingworth, prevents one from extrapolating too hastily from a few quotations to the entire epistle. Even more, the use of the OT in Hebrews cannot be reduced just to the quotations. The entire epistle is impregnated with the thought and the world of the OT, and the conclusions reached by analysing the quotations could not by default be extended to the OT material found outside the quotations.[71]

3.2.7. S. Stanley

Stanley launches his exegetico-hermeneutical investigation from the fundamental theological tension presented to the reader of the epistle.[72] On the one hand, the Author argues that the Old Covenant is obsolete, and about to be replaced (8:13), but on the other hand, he appeals to the Scriptures of the Old Covenant to support his argument. The main part of the thesis consists of a detailed exegetical-theological analysis of Heb. 8-10, "the theological heart and paraenetic core of the book of homily".[73] The investigation confirms several positions defended earlier, such as the resemblance of the Author's text to the codices LXX[A] and LXX[B], and the possibility of influence from other sources, not only other LXX traditions, but also possibly the writings of Philo, since the Author "may have extracted passages for the texts of the LXX that he studied, even texts to which he gained access in a variety of locations, to create his own anthology of Scripture passages".[74]

In considering the function of the OT for the people of the New Covenant, Stanley modifies and improves the solution offered by Hughes. Whereas Hughes charges the Author with inconsistency for using parts of the OT while considering others obsolete, Stanley argues that the Author's choice of certain OT passages, and not their interpretation was determined by his eschatological outlook.[75] He continues, "for the author of Hebrews, Old Covenant Scripture is fulfilled in the New Covenant situation, but not all Scripture is fulfilled in the same way, and it is precisely the differences in the way Scripture is fulfilled in the new situation, in the view of our

---

[71] One could also observe a certain level of circularity in Leschert's thesis. He sets himself up to defend that "[the Author] interprets in a manner consistent with historical-grammatical hermeneutics without distorting the intended meaning of the OT", but if "his interpretations transcend the historical-grammatical meaning of the OT", a rescuing alternative will be advanced to offer "an explanation of how they may be consistent with it without being identical to it", *Foundations* 16.

[72] S. Stanley, "A New Covenant Hermeneutic: The Use of Scripture in Hebrews 8-10" (Ph. D., University of Sheffield, 1994).

[73] Stanley, "Hermeneutic" 11.

[74] Stanley, "Hermeneutic" 214.

[75] Stanley, "Hermeneutic" 244.

author, that determine its application".[76]   These considerations cause
Stanley to distinguish between three types of Old Covenant Scripture
fulfilment, the prophetic, the typological and the universal.[77] Thus the
function of the Old Covenant Scripture in the New Covenant setting and
for the New Covenant people can be properly understood in terms of
"fulfilment".

3.2.8. H. W. Bateman

Bateman's dissertation, while not a study covering the use of the OT
within the entire epistle, is nonetheless an investigation that must be
acknowledged in a survey of current scholarship.[78] The limitation to the
first chapter is legitimate since this chapter contains not only an extensive
number of OT quotations, but also shows the Author engaged in a variety
of interpretative approaches to the OT, thus offering a representative
sample for the rest of the epistle.

Bateman analyses Hillel's rules of exegesis and the Author's awareness
and employment of them, as well as three literary genres (Targum,
Midrash, Pesher) and hermeneutical processes (targumic, midrashic,
pesher), which were current among the Author's contemporaries.   The
overarching goal is an attempt to prove that awareness of first century
Jewish hermeneutics, exegesis and concepts helps in understanding how
and why the OT is used in Heb. 1:5-13. The main part of the dissertation
consists of a comparative examination of the quotations in ch. 1 in light of
the textual forms of both the Septuagint and the Hebrew Bible, as well as
those found in other intertestamental literature.   Bateman concludes by
highlighting the theological program of the Author, who interpreted the OT
passages as testimonies to Jesus' status as Davidic King and eternal Son-
Creator. The Author's interpretative route from the scriptural text to its
implications is a process that is better understood when viewed in light of
the wide range of contemporary approaches to the Scriptures.

---

[76] Stanley, "Hermeneutic" 245.

[77] Stanley, "Hermeneutic" 200 f. The Author builds his application of Scripture to
Christ and the New Covenant situation on the prophetic fulfilment type. This type of
Scripture fulfilment is foundational to the other two, the typological fulfilment, pointing
to the elements of continuity and discontinuity between the Old and New Covenants, and
the universal, the direct application of Old Covenant Scriptures in the New Covenant
context.

[78] Herbert W. Bateman IV, *Early Jewish Hermeneutics and Hebrews 1:5-13. The
Impact of Early Jewish Exegesis on the Interpretation of a Significant New Testament
Passage* (AUS VII.193; New York: Peter Lang, 1997).

3.3. Use of the OT in Hebrews: Rhetorical Approach

The rhetorical analysis of the Scriptures resulting from the recent growing interest in ancient rhetoric[79] has left its imprint on the scholarship on Hebrews, which is, in Lindars' memorable assessment, a "work of persuasion from start to finish".[80] The rhetorical function of the OT in the structure and the argument of the epistle, a spin-off of rhetorical criticism of the epistle, has been the focus of several recent studies, with valuable results in assessing the role of the Scriptures in shaping the epistle.

One should perhaps start by mentioning a long-standing stream of studies on the structure of the epistle,[81] culminating with the most recent contribution of George Guthrie.[82] These precursors to the rhetorical criticism of the epistle have provided the springboard for the subsequent rhetorical analyses. As far as the Epistle to the Hebrews is concerned, pride of place goes to the extensive rhetorical analysis of Überlacker, a

---

[79] George Kennedy, *New Testament Interpretation through Rhetorical Criticism* (Chapel Hill: University of North Carolina Press, 1984); Stanley E. Porter, *Handbook of Classical Rhetoric in the Hellenistic Period (330 B.C. – A.D. 400)* (Leiden / New York / Köln: E. J. Brill, 1997); Stanley E. Porter, ed., *The Rhetorical Interpretation of Scripture. Essays from the 1996 Malibu Conference* (JSNT-SS 180; Sheffield: Sheffield Academic Press, 1999); Stanley E. Porter and Thomas H. Olbricht, eds., *Rhetoric and the New Testament. Essays from the 1992 Heidelberg Conference* (JSNT-SS 90; Sheffield: Sheffield Academic Press, 1993); Stanley E. Porter and Thomas H. Olbricht, eds., *Rhetoric, Scripture and Theology. Essays from the 1994 Pretoria Conference* (JSNT-SS 131; Sheffield: Sheffield Academic Press, 1996); Stanley E. Porter and Thomas H. Olbricht, eds., *The Rhetorical Analysis of Scripture. Essays from the 1995 London Conference* (JSNT-SS 146; Sheffield: Sheffield Academic Press, 1997); Stanley E. Porter and Dennis Stamps, eds., *Rhetorical Criticism and the Bible. Essays from the 1998 Florence Conference* (JSNT-SS 195; Sheffield: Sheffield Academic Press, 2002).

[80] Barnabas Lindars, *The Theology of the Letter to the Hebrews* (Cambridge: Cambridge University Press, 1991) 2. See also his article on the rhetoric structure of Hebrews, Barnabas Lindars, "The Rhetorical Structure of Hebrews", *New Testament Studies* 35 (1989) 382-406.

[81] David J. MacLeod, "The Literary Structure of the Book of Hebrews", *Bibliotheca Sacra* 146 (1989); Linda Lloyd Neeley, "A Discourse Analysis of Hebrews", *OPTAT* 3-4 (1987); James Swetnam, "Form and Content in Heb. 1-6", *Biblica* 53 (1972); *idem*, "Form and Content in Heb. 7-13", *Biblica* 55 (1974); *idem*, "The Structure of Hebrews: A Fresh Look. On the Occasion of a New Commentary", *MelTheol* 41, no. 1 (1990); Albert Vanhoye, *Structure and Message of the Epistle to the Hebrews* (SB 12; Rome: Pontificio Institutio Biblico, 1989).

[82] George H. Guthrie, *The Structure of Hebrews: A Text-Linguistic Analysis* (SNT 73; Leiden: E. J. Brill, 1994). He contends that the linear structure assumption of most of the current scholarship on the issue should be dropped in favour of a more complex and possibly more realistic approach that recognizes two divisions in the discourse of Hebrews, the expository and the hortatory, which run simultaneously.

groundbreaking achievement for the new approach.[83] While Überlacker does not deal primarily with the rhetorical function of the OT in the epistle, the proposed structure and analysis provide a solid base for appreciating the rhetorical elements of the epistle, a document whose entire argument develops from the opening passage.[84] Also noteworthy, albeit not specifically addressing the rhetorical function of the OT in Hebrews, are the contributions of Cosby on the rhetorical criticism of Heb. 11, Olbricht's examination of the Hebrews' rhetoric of amplification on the background of ancient funeral oratory, and deSilva's monograph on the language of "honour and shame", a suitable background for understanding the Author's rhetoric in several central passages, as well as his commentary on Hebrews in a series devoted to the analysis of the socio-rhetoric dimension underlying the NT writings.[85]

3.3.1. R. E. Davis

The purpose of Davis' study was to investigate, by means of rhetorical analysis, the function of the Old Testament citations in the structure of the argument of Hebrews, "to understand the purpose in the author's use of the Old Testament citations within Hebrews".[86] Dissatisfied with the insignificant level of attention given to this particular aspect, Davis

---

[83] Walter G. Überlacker, *Der Hebräierbrief als Appell: Untersuchungen zu Exordium, Narratio, und Postscriptum (Hebr 1-2 und 13, 22-25)* (ConB-NTS 21; Stockholm: Almqvist und Wiksell, 1989). Überlacker's study has given to the scholarship on Hebrews a similar milestone as did Betz' study on Galatians two decades earlier; see Hans Dieter Betz, *Galatians. A Commentary on Paul's Letter to the Churches in Galatia* (Hermeneia; Philadelphia: Fortress Press, 1979).

[84] The resulting structure for the Epistle to the Hebrews is *Exordium* (1:1-4); *Narratio* with *Propositio* (1:5-2:18); *Argumentatio*, with *Probatio* and *Refutatio* (3:1-12:29); *Peroratio* (13:1-21) and *Postscriptum* (13:22-25). For a more extensive evaluation and critique of Überlacker's work see, *inter alios*, Guthrie, *Structure* 31; Ronald E. Davis, "The Function of the Old Testament Texts in the Structure of Hebrews: A Rhetorical Analysis" (Ph. D., Southern Baptist Theological Seminary, 1994) 105; Daniel E. Buck, "The Rhetorical Arrangement and Function of OT Citations in the Book of Hebrews: Uncovering Their Role in the Paraenetic Discourse of Access" (Ph. D., Dallas Theological Seminary, 2002) 91.

[85] Michael R. Cosby, *The Rhetorical Composition and Function of Hebrews 11 in Light of Example Lists in Antiquity* (Macon: Mercer University Press, 1988); David A. deSilva, *Despising Shame. Honor Discourse and Community Maintenance in the Epistle to the Hebrews* (SBL-DS 152; Atlanta: Scholars Press, 1995); David Arthur deSilva, *Perseverance in Gratitude. A Socio-Rhetorical Commentary on the Epistle "to the Hebrews"* (Grand Rapids: Eerdmans, 2000); Thomas H. Olbricht, "Hebrews as Amplification", in *Rhetoric and the New Testament. Essays from the 1992 Heidelberg Conference*, eds. Stanley E. Porter and Thomas H. Olbricht (JSNT-SS 90; Sheffield: Sheffield Academic Press, 1993) 375-87.

[86] Davis, "Function" 108.

bemoans, "it is puzzling that so little has been written with regard to the function of the texts in the development of the argument of Hebrews."[87] This contention probably should have been defended better, especially in light of Ellingworth's, Schröger's, and McCullough's studies, which, while not necessarily dealing with the rhetorical function of the OT texts as such, wrestle extensively with the function of the OT quotations and allusions in the epistle.

Davis uncovers seven rhetorical units in the epistle, which supply the structure of the epistle with the following layout, "the Nature and Work of the Son (1:1-2:4), "Necessity of the Suffering of the Son" (2:5-18), "Contrast of Faith and Non-Faith" (3:1-4:16); "Jesus Established as High Priest" (4:14-7:28), "Work of Jesus as High Priest" (8:1-10:35), "The Righteous Live by Faith" (10:36-12:3), "Necessity of the Suffering of the 'Sons'" (12:1-13:25). As result of his investigation, first emerges, a division of the OT material (primary citations, secondary citations, and scriptural allusions) and second, an understanding of its role within each rhetorical unit. Thus the primary citations function as introduction, transition, development, and support, while the secondary citations are employed as support, development, and introduction, and finally, the allusions serve as support and development. The role of the OT passages, Davis contends, is foundational to the shape of the epistle, since "not only do primary texts provide a structure in establishing rhetorical units, but secondary texts and scriptural allusions provide validation and development throughout the discourse".[88] Davis has rightly delineated the two principles operating at the rhetorical level, the employment of the OT as support for the epistle's developing argument and the structuring of the argument according to the use of key OT citations. Not entirely clear, however, is the methodological basis for distinguishing between the two aspects, and more importantly, the grounds for which one can be considered predominant over the other, i.e., the OT texts determining the argument, or the pre-existing argument selecting the OT texts.

3.3.2. D. E. Buck

Buck's analysis develops from the observation that the presence of the OT citations in the epistle is unmistakable, and they serve both a structural and argumentative role in the theology of the book. The theological theme of access to God's presence is proposed as the primary theological motif of the epistle, a document consisting of a persuasive argument stringed on several primary OT citations, Ps. 110, Ps. 8, Ps. 95, Jer. 31, Ps. 40, and Hab. 2, which calls the recipients to embrace Jesus' provision of a way of

---

[87] Davis, "Function" 45.
[88] Davis, "Function" 299.

access to the very throne of God. The two-pronged analysis, by way of deductive and inductive investigation of the selection and arrangement of key OT citations, is conducted in order to secure a cohesive picture of both the content and the ethos of the Author's persuasive project. The study itself develops, first, by presenting the historical exegetical principles in order to understand the Author's view and approach to the OT Scriptures, then, by considering the hermeneutics operative in the Author's contextualisation of the Scriptures to his audience, and finally, by tracing the Author's thought process from the message to its form of delivery, which essentially is a message of persuasion.

The work indeed offers a cohesive message that brings together the citations as the vehicle which advances and supports the central message of Hebrews, which according to Buck is "a theological-hermeneutical enterprise in the reading of the OT Scriptures for the purpose of addressing the ongoing demands of living life in relationship with God through the provision of the new covenant in Jesus the Son".[89] The study perhaps is less successful first, in defending the theme proposed by means of a comparative analysis of other contenders, and second, in showing how rhetorical criticism can help decide with certainty between competing and equally legitimate overall theological messages.

Καὶ τί ἔτι λέγω; ἐπιλείψει με γὰρ ὁ χρόνος (Heb. 11:32) is a fitting phrase with which to conclude this selective incursion in the field, leaving aside many worthwhile contributions which can only be acknowledged here, such as Ploeg's analysis of *sensus plenior*, Rendall's view of the OT as progressive revelation up to the New, Synge's claim of the independent origins of the doctrinal and exhortative sections, Kistemaker's valuable examination of the Psalms quotations, McGaughey's study of the citation formulae, Reid's exploration of the Author's biblical-eschatological thinking, Sowers' Christ-Witness argument, Longenecker's motif of anticipation-consummation, Hanson's insistence on Christ's real-presence in the OT times, Clements' view on the dialectic relationship between the OT and the Author, Luther's defence of the Author's exploration the literal and historical meaning of the OT, Hofius' analysis of *katapausis*, France's exploration of the Author's homiletical prowess, Gleason's interpretation of the Heb. 6 and Heb. 3 in light of OT themes, Laansma's exploration of the "rest" motif, Blackstone's hermeneutics of recontextualisation, Motyer's typology as a guiding hermeneutic,[90] as well as many valuable insights in several commentaries.[91]

---

[89] Buck, "Function" 297.

[90] J. van der Ploeg, "L'exégèse de l'Ancien Testament dans l'épître aux Hébreux", *Revue Biblique* 54 (1947) 187-228; R. Rendall, "The Method of the Writer to the

There is undoubtedly a solid consensus on many issues pertaining to the use of the OT in the epistle, and the recent trend in narrowing the focus of the study to either a selected theme or a selected passage is a welcome and needed development. Two final considerations that relate directly to the present study are in order. First, as far as textual matters are concerned, Septuagintal studies will continue to be an fruitful area of cross-pollination with scholarship on Hebrews, primarily due to their importance in clarifying text-critical issues of either the Greek OT or of the Epistle to the Hebrews. Any progress in these matters is intrinsically dependent on the progress made in the field of Septuagint studies. In the time frame

---

Hebrews in Using Old Testament Quotations", *Evangelical Quarterly* 27 (1955) 214-220; F. G. Synge, *Hebrews and the Scriptures* (London: SPCK, 1959); Simon Kistemaker, *The Psalm Citations in the Epistle to the Hebrews* (Amsterdam: Van Soest, 1961); D. H. McGaughey, "The Hermeneutic Method of the Epistle to the Hebrews" (Ph. D., Boston University, 1963); R. Reid, "The Use of the Old Testament in the Epistle to the Hebrews" (Th.D., Union Theological Seminary, 1964); S. G. Sowers, *The Hermeneutics of Philo and Hebrews: A Comparison of the Interpretation of the Old Testament in Philo Judaeus and the Epistle to the Hebrews* (Richmond / Zürich: Knox, 1965); Richard N. Longenecker, *Biblical Exegesis in the Apostolic Period* (Grand Rapids: Eerdmans, 1975); Anthony. T. Hanson, "Christ in the Old Testament according to Hebrews", *Studia Evangelica* (1964) 393-407; Ronald E. Clements, "The Use of the Old Testament in Hebrews", *Southwestern Journal of Theology* 28 (1985) 36-45; Luther, "Old Testament"; Otfried Hofius, *Katapausis. Die Vorstellung vom endzeitlichen Ruheort im Hebräerbrief* (WUNT 11; Tübingen: Mohr Siebeck, 1970); Richard France, "The Writer of Hebrews as a Biblical Expositor," *Tyndale Bulletin* 47 (1996) 245-76; Randall C. Gleason, "The Old Testament Background of the Warning in Hebrews 6:4-6", *Bibliotheca Sacra* 155, no. Jan-Mar (1998) 62-91; *idem*, "The Old Testament Background of Rest in Hebrews 3:7-4:11", *Bibliotheca Sacra* 157, no. Jul-Sep (2000) 281-303; Jon Laansma, *'I will give you rest': The Rest Motif in the New Testament with Special Reference to Mt 11 and Heb 3-4* (WUNT II 97; Tübingen: Mohr Siebeck, 1997); Thomas L. Blackstone, "The Hermeneutics of Recontextualization in the Epistle to the Hebrews" (Ph. D., Emory University, 1995); Stephen Motyer, "The Psalm Quotations of Hebrews 1: A Hermeneutical-Free Zone?", *Tyndale Bulletin* 50, no. 1 (1999) 3-22.

[91] Harold W. Attridge, *The Epistle to the Hebrews* (Hermeneia; Philadelphia: Fortress Press, 1989); Herbert Braun, *An die Hebräer* (HNT 14; Tübingen: Mohr Siebeck, 1984); F. F. Bruce, *Commentary on the Epistle to the Hebrews* (NICNT; Grand Rapids: Eerdmans, 1965[1990 ed.]); George W. Buchanan, *To the Hebrews* (AB; Garden City, NY: Doubleday, 1972); Paul Ellingworth, *Commentary on Hebrews* (NIGTC; Grand Rapids: Eerdmans, 1993); Erich Grässer, *An die Hebräer (Hebr 1-6) (Hebr 7,1-10,18) (Hebr 10,19-13,25)*, 3 vols., (EKKNT VII:1,2,3; Zürich / Neukirchen-Vluyn: Benzinger / Neukirchener, 1990, 1993, 1997); William L. Lane, *Hebrews 1-8, 9-13*, 2 vols., (WBC; Dallas: Word, 1991); J. Moffatt, *A Critical and Exegetical Commentary on The Epistle to the Hebrews* (ICC; Edinburgh: T. & T. Clark, 1924 [1979 ed.]); Ceslas Spicq, *L'Épître aux Hébreux*, 2 vols., (Paris: Gabalda, 1952-1953); H.-F. Weiss, *Der Brief an die Hebräer* (KEK; Göttingen: Vandenhoeck & Ruprecht, 1991); deSilva, *Perseverance*; Robert P. Gordon, *Hebrews* (Sheffield: Sheffield Academic Press, 2000); Helmut Koester, *To the Hebrews* (AB; Garden City, NY: Doubleday, 2001).

surveyed there has been a significant shift in the quest for the Author's *Vorlage*. Whereas in the first part of the century scholars were particularly interested in sorting out whether the text of Codex A or B constituted the source of the quotations, the works of Thomas and McCullough have altered the course of this quest. This led in turn to an increased awareness of the extremely complex factors involved in the elucidation of these issues, and any subsequent study will have to reckon with the possibility, indeed, the probability of the changes introduced by the Author in using the text of his *Vorlage* for either grammatical, stylistic, contextual, rhetorical, or theological reasons. To this rather daunting set of variables one must add the complicated process of reciprocal influences of the epistle and the Septuagint in the process of their respective transmissions.

Second, most studies surveyed agree on exegetical and hermeneutical matters, particularly on the variety of exegetical procedures employed by the Author. It has been established that the Author read and interpreted the OT not in isolation from practices commonly found among his contemporaries. In fact, there is extensive continuity between his methods and theirs. Agreement has not been reached with regard to the extent to which he uses these methods. What sets him and the other NT writers apart from their contemporaries is the Christ-event. The interdependence between reading the OT in light of the Christ-event and interpreting the Christ-event in light of the OT is at the heart of understanding the Author's use of the OT.

4. Methodological Considerations and Assumptions

The influence that the Septuagint exerted on the writers and the writings of the New Testament is a complex area of investigation in which there is an ongoing quest for precise methodology and clear parameters. A thorough and conclusive assessment must be built on both qualitative and quantitative investigation of the data, which even for a relatively short piece, such as the Epistle to the Hebrews, is indeed a daunting endeavour.

The main methodological concern of research on the influence of the Septuagint on the Author has to steer the fine line that avoids both the danger of stating a truism on the one hand, and of trying to argue for what is indefensible, on the other. Indeed, since the Septuagint was the Author's Scriptures, it could not have but influenced the Author. The research consequently must focus primarily on questions of degree of influence and nuances on the legitimate assumption that a theological writing of the epistle's magnitude must show various signs of direct dependence on the Septuagint. At the other extreme, an extrapolation from the given data into the speculative area of how the epistle and the Author's argument would have looked had the Author used the Hebrew Scriptures borders on methodological impossibility.

The methodological problems presented by both sides are avoided when the issue is stated in the positive, that is, the quest to discover and evaluate the influences of the LXX on the epistle. Consequently the emphasis is on the various ways in which the LXX has contributed specifically to the argument of the epistle. Ideally, for a definitive assessment of the LXX influence one should engage in a full-scale investigation of the entire epistle, a task that would be required if a thorough quantitative evaluation would be the intended goal. The present study pursues a less ambitious objective characterised by a predominantly qualitative evaluation, on considerations of space and need for further refinement of the investigation methodology.

By necessity, therefore this investigation cannot be exhaustive; it can only hope to address some of the more representative cases chosen from the vast group of candidates. Selection of texts from the epistle enabling the collection of evidence to be assessed was guided by three factors. First, since a distinct Septuagintal influence, as opposed to a more general one, i.e., scriptural, is under scrutiny, the OT texts targeted for this approach are passages that present various degrees of differences between the LXX and the MT. In order to insure that one deals indeed with a particular Septuagintal influence, a second criterion was established by selecting for analysis those passages in which it could be reasonably proven that the argument of the epistle hinges on the very section of the Septuagint in which the Greek text differs from its parallel MT text.[92] Third, in order to minimize the effect of our limited knowledge of the genesis and transmission of both textual traditions, the Hebrew and Greek texts, as well as to limit the number of text-critical variables to be handled, the examples selected are characterised by either the absence or reduced significance of the textual variants attested for the texts involved.

The study of the distinct role played by the Septuagint in the Author's use of the OT focuses on a number of areas, arguably, the most important areas in which the Greek OT left its distinct mark on the use of the OT in the Epistle to the Hebrews. The five areas under scrutiny are the text of

---

[92] By selecting the MT, this study assumes that this Hebrew text tradition resembles closely the Hebrew texts that the Author could have used had he possessed knowledge of the Hebrew language, an issue which itself raises other adjacent questions that cannot be addressed in this study.

the quotations, the context of the quotations, the use of the OT outside the quotations, the Septuagintal language, and the theology of the Septuagint.[93]

To establish a more secure database for the investigation, this study will engage in a two dimensional analysis. Part One of the study examines each of the individual aspects outlined above, concentrating on several examples selected from different sections of the epistle. Chapter Two investigates the text of the quotations in the epistle. Particular attention is given to textual matters, especially to the way in which divergences between the Hebrew and Greek textual traditions affected both the text and the use of the quotation in the epistle. Chapter Three deals with the role and importance of the quotations' original context, particularly the way in which the context was instrumental in the Author's use of that particular text in the epistle. Chapter Four samples the use of the OT material that lies outside of the quotations or their immediate context. Specifically, allusions or echoes from both canonical and extra-canonical books are surveyed to assess the role of the Septuagint in several aspects of the Author's extensive use of OT material. Chapter Five considers the possible influences exerted on the language and thought of the Author by the Septuagintal language, which is the acknowledged linguistic and theological background of the Author. Finally, Chapter Six directs its attention to theological matters. Eschatology and Messianism are selected as two distinct theological emphases within the Septuagint with the view to ascertaining if any specific Septuagintal influence on the epistle can be detected.

Part Two of this study selects one test case, the use of Hab. 2:3-4 in Heb. 10:37-38, for the purpose of a more detailed analysis of the possible Septuagintal influences outlined above. This particular quotation recommends itself on at least two counts. First, the quotation incorporates several significant differences between the Greek and Hebrew texts of the passage on which divergent traditions of interpretation were subsequently developed. Second, the quotation from Habakkuk is arguably one of the very few OT quotations in which there is evidence that the quotation as it stands in the epistle has undergone considerable changes at the hands of the Author, changes that are primarily theological in nature. For the test case, three separate aspects will be given more extensive coverage: Chapter Seven deals with the text critical issues in the three relevant textual traditions, Hab. 2 MT, Hab. 2 LXX, and Heb. 10; Chapter Eight covers issues related to the literary and historical contexts of Hab. 2 and

---

[93] These areas correspond roughly to the ones delineated by I. Howard Marshall, "An Assessment of Recent Developments", in *It Is Written: Scripture Citing Scripture*, eds. D. A. Carson and H. G. M. Williamson (Cambridge, UK: Cambridge University Press, 1988) 1-21.

Heb. 10; Chapter Nine focuses on the theological implications of the use of Hab. 2 LXX for the eschatology and Messianism of the epistle.

As will soon become evident, the division suggested above is somewhat artificial, since many cases in one category could well have fit into another as well. The main reason for dividing the material in such a way was primarily pragmatic, in as much as it ensures a better appreciation of the various ways in which the Septuagint has left its imprint on the epistle. No particular attention is devoted to the question of the Septuagint's influence on the Author as distinct from its influence on the epistle. While the primary interest of this study is clearly set on the latter influence, as the influence that could be more easily be determined when working with the text of the epistle, it is assumed throughout this work that the two are inseparable and the latter is a correct representation of the former.

Each of the cases analysed in this study is essentially a comparative analysis of three textual traditions, the Hebrew text, its Greek translation, and the text as it appears in the epistle. Such a comparative study would proceed without much difficulty if we knew with certainty the precise text in each tradition. The basis for an objective appraisal would be secure only in this ideal situation. Unfortunately, in all of these textual traditions our knowledge of both the original writings as well as of the history of their transmission is restricted to a limited amount of manuscript evidence.

The lack of precise knowledge regarding the nature of the Jewish Scriptures' translation into Greek and the circumstances in which the translation took place are an even greater impediment for a comparative study of this nature. The text of the translators' *Vorlage*, its degree of similarity to the Masoretic text (MT, henceforth), its historical evolution "from pluriformity to uniformity", as argued by Kahle, or "from uniformity to pluriformity", as maintained by de Lagarde, to use van der Woude's matrix,[94] are issues that continue to divide Septuagintalists in their ongoing quest for clarity in the history of the textual witnesses.

This study does not intend to investigate the history of the transmission of the textual witnesses of any of the texts under discussion. Due to the complexity of the issues involved in such an exhaustive study, it is virtually impossible to achieve satisfactory results within the constraints of this study. The textual matters will be addressed on a case-by-case basis without pursuing an over-arching conclusion. Nevertheless, several assumptions that can be legitimately held will serve as starting points.

---

[94] Adam S. van der Woude, "Pluriformity and Uniformity. Reflections on the Transmission of the Text of the Old Testament", in *Sacred History and Sacred Texts in Early Judaism. A Symposium in Honour of A. S. van der Woude*, eds. J. N. Bremmer and F. Garcia Martinez (Kampen: Kok Pharos, 1992) 151-69.

First, as far as the Hebrew text of the Scriptures is concerned, this study assumes that the Masoretic text represents a very important textual tradition, one that "was held in esteem by the temple circles and later, the Pharisees".[95] This assumption does not exclude the possibility of the coexistence of several Hebrew textual traditions during the Second Temple period, traditions that were generated, as in the case of the Septuagint, either in the development from pluriformity to uniformity, or from uniformity to pluriformity.[96] Consequently, the MT could be safely considered to represent a text that would have been very close to the text that the Author might have used in the first century A.D. had he possessed a working knowledge of the Hebrew language.

Second, with regard to the Greek text that the Author had, the Göttingen Septuagint provides the needed textual information to help establish with a reasonable degree of confidence what might have been the Author's *Vorlage*. Attempts to align the Author's text with one of the Septuagintal textual traditions preserved in the major codices seem to have been abandoned, at least for the present time. Therefore, an eclectic approach, based on a careful assessment of the textual variants in each case, is the preferred way forward.

Third, as mentioned before, the Author depended primarily, if not exclusively, on the use of a Greek text of the Jewish Scriptures. While this position still awaits a strong and irrefutable defence, it is concurrent with most of the textual and interpretative data in the Epistle, and it continues, with slight variations, to be the dominant assumption of the students of the Epistle.

It is to the use of the Greek textual tradition of the Scriptures by the Author to the Hebrews that the present investigation now turns.

---

[95] Tov, "Textual Criticism" 65.

[96] For a good overview of the evidence and the issues involved see Emanuel Tov, "The History and Significance of a Standard Text of the Hebrew Bible", in *Hebrew Bible / Old Testament. The History of Its Interpretation. From the Beginnings to the Middle Ages (until 1300)*, eds. Magne Saebo, Chris Brekelmans, and Menahem Haran (Göttingen: Vandenhoeck & Ruprecht, 1996), and Martin Jan Mulder, "The Transmission of the Biblical Text", in *Mikra. Text, Translation, Reading and Interpretation of the Hebrew Bible in Ancient Judaism and Early Christianity*, ed. Martin Jan Mulder (CRINT 2/I; Minneapolis: Fortress Press, 1990).

Part One

The Septuagint in the Epistle to the Hebrews

Chapter Two

Septuagintal Quotations in Hebrews: Text

1. Quotations in Hebrews

The study of the distinct role played by the Septuagint in the Epistle to the Hebrews commences with an analysis of several quotations. Any study of the Author's use of the OT should begin with the scriptural quotations for the following reasons. First, the number of quotations relative to the length of the book is among the highest in the New Testament.[1] Second, the prevalent opinion is that these quotations form, if not the backbone of the argument, at least a significant structure with direct contribution to the overall argument of the epistle. Indeed, some of the particular ways in which the quotations are used, such as the prominence of several OT texts[2] or the recurrences of quotations from and allusions to Ps. 109 [110 MT],[3] seem to indicate the important role played by the quotations in the epistle not only in its argument but also its structure.[4] Lastly, and more importantly for the methodology adopted here, study of the use of the OT in Hebrews must commence with the quotations because of the relatively

---

[1] The number of quotations in the epistle varies considerably depending on the criteria established by each scholar. The following list exemplifies some of the more representative tallies: 36 – Spicq, *Hébreux* 331; 29 – Caird, "Method" 47; 32 – Kistemaker, *Citations* 16; 29 – Thomas, "Citations" 303; 35 – Schröger, *Verfasser*; 35 – Howard, "Quotations" 211; 38 – Longenecker, *Exegesis* 164; 35 – Ellingworth, "Old Testament" 303; 39 – Gleason L. Archer and G. C. Chirichigno, eds., *Old Testament Quotations in the New Testament: A Complete Survey* (Chicago: Moody Press, 1983) xxii; 35 – Lane, *Hebrews* cxvi; 30 – Blackstone, "Recontextualization" 19; 31 – Pamela M. Eisenbaum, "Heroes and History in Hebrews 11", in *Early Christian Interpretation of the Scriptures of Israel*, eds. C. A. Evans and J. A. Sanders, (JSNT-SS 148; Sheffield: Sheffield Academic Press, 1997) 92; 36 – George H. Guthrie, "The Old Testament in Hebrews", in *The Dictionary of the Later New Testament and Its Developments*, eds. Ralph P. Martin and Peter H. Davids, (Downers Grove / Leicester: Inter Varsity Press, 1997) 846 f. Even according to some of the less generous totals, the Epistle to the Hebrews ranks second only to Matthew and Romans among NT writings with the most frequent OT quotations.

[2] Ps. 2, Ps. 8, Ps. 94 [95 MT], Ps. 109 [110 MT], Jer. 38 [31 MT], etc.

[3] Heb. 1:3, 13, 5:6, 10, 6:20, 7:3, 17, 21, 8:1, 10:12, 13, and 12:2.

[4] Guthrie, *Structure* 21 ff.; Steve Stanley, "The Structure of Hebrews from Three Perspectives" *Tyndale Bulletin* 45, no. 2 (1994) 253 f.

high degree of objectivity with which quotations can be investigated, as opposed to other forms of OT usage. Since the emphasis will be placed on the differences between the Hebrew and Greek texts of the OT, the cases of textual divergence are easier to spot in quotations than in any other aspects of OT usage. Furthermore, once particular divergences are identified, it is easier to evaluate their contribution to the flow of the argument.

The intent of this chapter is to assess whether or not the Septuagint, as the supplier of the quotation texts, has played a distinct role in the way in which the quotations are employed in the epistle. By distinct role, the present study understands a role that is intrinsically and directly linked with the linguistic nature of the OT used by the Author, a Greek text as opposed to a Hebrew text. Although there are many examples of quotations that qualify for such an approach, the investigation will concentrate on some of the more representative texts.

1.1. Definition

At the outset, the lack of a precise definition of or the dissipating scholarly consensus on what constitutes an OT quotation ought to be signalled, especially for an epistle with an unsurpassed volume of quotation material among the NT writings. Lack of precision in the definition of a quotation or in the setting out the precise criteria to distinguish between quotations and other types of OT usage has implications in the overall picture of the Author's use of the OT, either restricting too narrowly or expanding too broadly the number of instances to be considered as quotations. Recent studies have drawn attention to this shortcoming,[5] evident even in some of the major studies on the subject.[6]

---

[5] Stanley Porter bemoans the lack of precision and consistency in most studies dealing with the use of the OT in the NT, "The Use of the Old Testament in the New Testament: A Brief Comment on Method and Terminology," in *Early Christian Interpretation of the Scriptures of Israel*, eds. Craig A. Evans and James A. Sanders (JSNT-SS 148; Sheffield: Sheffield Academic Press, 1997) 92. The most affected field of study is the area of OT quotations, an area in which "the vast majority of those discussing the issue don't bother to define their terms"("Use" 81).

[6] The definition of what constitutes a quotation is conspicuously absent from several standard works covering the NT corpus, such as Archer and Chirichigno, eds., *Quotations*; D. A. Carson and H. G. M. Williamson, *It Is Written: Scripture Citing Scripture. Essays in Honor of Barnabas Lindars, S.S.F.* (Cambridge: Cambridge University Press, 1988), Hans Hübner, *Vetus Testamentum in Novo. Corpus Paulinus*, vol. 2, (Göttingen: Vandenhoeck & Ruprecht, 1997); Bradley H. McLean, *Citations and Allusions to Jewish Scripture in Early Christian and Jewish Writings through 180 C.E.* (Lewiston / Queenston / Lampeter: Edwin Mellen Press, 1992). Even studies focusing on the citations either in a NT book or by an NT author often have the same weakness.

Two recent monographs of Koch and Stanley brought a corrective change in this regard to the scholarly dialogue in the Pauline corpus.[7] Both authors propose lists of criteria for identifying OT citations in the NT. As a result their studies proceed with better methodological precision than any of the studies previously undertaken.[8]

The Epistle to the Hebrews has not fared as well as Pauline studies have regarding precision in the definition of OT quotations. In part the reason is somewhat pragmatic, since most studies on the topic actually use an implicit definition of what constitutes a quotation, in order to differentiate them from other forms of OT usage, such as allusions, parallels, summaries or even just plain biblical phraseology.[9] Apparently, the

---

[7] Dietrich-Alex Koch, *Die Schrift als Zeuge des Evangeliums: Untersuchungen zur Verwendung und zum Verständis der Schrift bei Paulus* (BHT 69; Tübingen: Mohr Siebeck, 1986); Christopher D. Stanley, *Paul and the Language of Scripture: Citation Technique in the Pauline Epistles and Contemporary Literature* (SNTS-MS 74; Cambridge: Cambridge University Press, 1992).

[8] Koch proposes a set of seven criteria for labelling a Pauline text as a quotation. According to him, one can legitimately treat a Pauline text as an OT quotation in any of the following seven cases: (1) when a citation formula is used; (2) when the same text is introduced by a citation formula when used in another place; (3) when it is followed by an interpretative gloss; (4) when syntactical tension sets the quotation words aside from the present Pauline context; (5) when there are stylistic differences from the surrounding verse; (6) when different introductory particles signal the insertion of a quotation; or (7) when reproducing a tradition (*Schrift* 11 ff.). Stanley proposes a similar but modified list that attempts to resolve an essential deficiency of Koch's theory, namely, the "level of literary competency required by his [Koch's] definition" (*Language* 35). Consequently, he narrows down the list to just three criteria for identifying quotations, contending that only the texts which are: (1) introduced by an explicit quotation formula; (2) accompanied by a clear interpretative gloss; or (3) stand in demonstrable syntactical tension with their present Pauline surroundings can be considered as citations (*Language* 37). While Stanley's list adds to the precision with which quotations can be determined, it is itself subject to criticism primarily due to its narrow criteria, which seem to eliminate a relatively high number of borderline cases. More importantly still, Stanley's argument displays a certain degree of question-begging, when he writes, "at the same time, restricting the study to this narrower body of texts should make it possible to establish a homogeneous data base from which to derive reliable conclusions about the normal citation technique of the apostle Paul" (*Language* 37). The "normal citation technique" seems to be at the same time a premise and a conclusion of Stanley's study.

[9] Even some of the best studies on the quotations in Hebrews do not wrestle at length with the definition of the quotations. Ellingworth ("Old Testament" 3) briefly describes them as explicit, when accompanied by a quotation formula, and implicit, when there is no quotation formula. Neither McCullough ("Hebrews"), nor Schröger (*Verfasser*) supply any definition.

relative uniformity with which the quotations are inserted into the epistle facilitates an almost intuitive demarcation of the quotations.[10]

The present study follows the criteria established by Koch and Stanley, which are adapted slightly to the characteristics of the Epistle to the Hebrews. Since this study does not undertake an exhaustive treatment of the quotations in the epistle, a less strict set of criteria seems to be sufficient to guide the selection of the cases under scrutiny. The two criteria are: (1) The presence of specific textual markers, such as an introductory formula, particles with the role of introducing a quotation, explanatory glosses, grammatical or syntactical discontinuities introduced by the quotation, and parallel usages; and (2) The substantial qualitative and quantitative textual identity with a Septuagintal passage.[11] The two criteria outlined above give preference to an author-oriented as opposed to reader-oriented approach, which seems to be better suited to an analysis of the possible influences of the Septuagint on the Author. It is important to note, however, that even when these criteria to establish the presence of a quotation are followed, a reasonable degree of flexibility seems to be required since it is unlikely that the author held himself to such strict criteria.

1.2. Sources of Quotations

The particular focus of this sub-section is to trace the role of the Greek OT in the actual process of selection of the quotations, and of its main corollary, the grouping of these texts. As a first century theologian the Author wrote in a literary, cultural, and theological context, in which a multiplicity of factors determined the selection of the biblical texts used for quotations. The developing Christian tradition clearly played an important role, as the Author himself acknowledges in 2:1-4, and as evidenced in the overlap of scriptural texts and themes with other NT writers.[12] As in other NT writings, the specific situation of the epistle's addressees has also played a determinant role in the Author's particular

---

[10] While the uniformity of the quotation forms cannot be denied, it has to be stressed that there is a considerable amount of variety in the actual format in which quotations appear in the epistle. Thus the Author's quotations are sometimes with or without introductory formula, long or short, used once or repeatedly, independent or fused with other texts, text perfect or modified, in their entirety or summarised, expounded or simply quoted, launching or concluding a point, with the biblical author given or without, crucial or secondary for the argument, supplying a needed word or just the gist, and in the doctrinal or in the paraenetic passages.

[11] For a similar approach, see Eisenbaum, "Heroes and History" 90 ff.

[12] Paul quotes from Ps. 8 and Ps. 109 LXX in 1 Cor. 15 and uses Hab. 2:4 in Rom. 1:17 and Gal. 3:11.

theological agenda. Doubtless, these two paramount factors have guided the selection of the OT texts used by the Author.

As important as these factors were, the Author's profound knowledge of the OT, the creative and rich employment of OT texts, concepts and ideas, the originality of thinking and exclusive treatment of several themes clearly indicate that, at least in part, the texts selected to buttress his argument were the direct result of his reading of and reflection on the Jewish Scriptures, in his case, the Septuagint.

The obvious question then is why has Author used these texts? What led him to choose these particular texts? While no one answer can fully explain the data available, the considerations that follow attempt to answer these questions by focusing on the role that the Septuagint played in the selection of texts, a selective process by which certain Scriptures were not only supportive of, but also indispensable for his argument. Prior to exploring that process a brief overview is in order to highlight several major hypotheses that have been advanced in order to explain the reason for which the Author employed these texts.

1.2.1. Testimonia Book

In the first part of this century, Rendall Harris gave attention to the idea that the NT authors extracted their scriptural quotations from the so-called *testimonia*, a compilation of biblical texts allegedly used by early Christians primarily for apologetic and missionary purposes.[13] This hypothesis was advocated in order to explain peculiar facts about the way the NT uses the OT, such as the identical grouping of OT quotations by different Christian writers, the similar misidentifications of certain OT passages, and identical textual variants unsupported by any manuscript evidence, MT, LXX, or other Versions.[14] Other considerations such as the alleged lack of interest in the original context of the texts, as well as the presence of similar lists of texts in the writings of the Church Fathers strengthened the hypothesis.[15]

---

[13] R. Harris, *Testimonies*, 2 vols., (Cambridge: Cambridge University Press, 1920); see also Martin C. Albl, *And Scripture Cannot Be Broken. The Form and Function of the Early Christian Testimonia Collections* (SNT 46; Leiden / Boston / Köln: E. J. Brill, 1999) for an excellent investigation of the issue of *testimonia*, providing also a thorough historical survey of major trends and positions in this century.

[14] Harris, *Testimonies*. i: 18; see also Albert C. Sundberg, "On Testimonies", *Novum Testamentum* 3 (1959) 268; McCullough, "Hebrews" 14; and Robert Hodgson, "The Testimony Hypothesis", *Journal of Biblical Literature* 98, no. 3 (1979) 361 ff.

[15] Hodgson, "Testimony" 371; Albl, *Scripture*; Hugh Montefiore, *A Commentary on the Epistle to the Hebrews*, *Black's New Testament Commentaries* (London: Adam & Charles Black, 1964) 43.

As far as Hebrews is concerned, the most ardent advocates of the Author's dependence on *testimonia* were Synge, Montefiore, and Sowers.[16] The main reasons for the appeal of this hypothesis are three distinctive features of the Author's quotation style, namely, quoting without supplying any reference to the original author, splitting the quotations that come from the same source,[17] and an alleged disregard for the original context of the quotation.[18]

The *testimonia* hypothesis as advocated by Harris has never found extensive support, and although the discovery of the Qumran documents 4QTestimonia and 4QFlorilegium have revived it,[19] the subsequent research into the exegetical methods of the Author has gradually led to the abandonment of the hypothesis. Among the main reasons adduced against the *testimonia* are the growing consensus that the Author used the quotations mindful of the original, i.e., Septuagintal, context and the evidence that indicates a considerable measure of authorial intent in the way the quotations are employed.[20] It became clearer not only that the theory based on the *testimonia* hypothesis outruns the evidence,[21] but also that the problems that the hypothesis was formulated to answer, could be answered more satisfactorily by other theories. Overall, it is more probable that the Author, possessing such a deep knowledge of the Scriptures as well as such a creative mind, would rely on the results of his own investigation of the Scriptures than on another's compilation.[22]

1.2.2. *Jewish Hellenistic Liturgical Cycle*

A second possible factor that might have contributed to the Author's choice of scriptural texts is the dependence on the synagogue lectionary.

---

[16] Synge, *Hebrews* 54; Montefiore, *Hebrews* 46; Sowers, *Hermeneutics* 84 ff. Synge categorically maintains, "the author has not got the Scriptures in front of him at all. What he has in front of him is a catena of passages, a Testimony Book ... Hebrews expounds them as they stand in the Testimony Book, not as they stand in the Bible" (*Hebrews* 34).

[17] The phenomenon takes place in the quotations from Is. 8, Ps. 94 [95 MT], and Dt. 32.

[18] Synge, *Hebrews* 34.

[19] McCullough, "Hebrews" 17; see also Bateman, *Hermeneutics*.

[20] Ellingworth, *Hebrews*; *idem*, "Old Testament".

[21] C. H. Dodd, *According to the Scriptures: The Sub-structure of New Testament Theology* (New York: Charles Scribner's Sons, 1952) 26.

[22] McCullough concludes, "we must still reckon that [the Author] is quoting directly from some version of the OT and find that version, rather than look for a Testimony Book" ("Hebrews" 141). See also Ellingworth, *Hebrews* 109. A similar argument is put forward by Koch (*Schrift* 99) and Stanley (*Language* 73 ff.), who suggest the possibility that Paul used a personal *testimonia* collection. Alternatively, Albl (*Scripture* 160) dismisses this suggestion.

Essentially, it is argued that the Author selected the OT texts as *haphtarot* which build on the *sedarim* of the reading cycle of the Torah. This explanation is advanced by A. Guilding who contends that "the early chapters of the Epistle seem quite clearly to be based on the lectionary readings for Pentecost, Genesis 14:18-15:21, Exodus 19, and Numbers 18, while in chapter 12 the lections of Pentecost and New Year are telescoped to illustrate the contrast between the old and new covenants".[23]   Burch, Spicq, Kistemaker, and Moule are scholars that have been associated with different variations of this position.[24]   Although the epistle has characteristics similar to the Jewish – Hellenistic synagogue homilies, such as the frequent use of Scriptures, the alternation of exposition and paraenesis, the use of rhetorical devices and a distinct type of argumentation,[25] the evidence for a direct link between the portions of Scripture used by the Author and the synagogue lectionary seems to be unconvincing. The freedom that the homilist was able to exercise both in the choice of the *haftarah* and in its length makes a precise association between certain *sedarim* and *haftarot* speculative.[26]

1.2.3. Primitive Christian Kerygma

One of the most remarkable contributions in this area was penned by C. H. Dodd, who proposed that the OT texts used by the NT authors came from a selection of Scriptures that essentially supplied the theological framework for the understanding and portrayal of the life and ministry of Jesus the Messiah. In effect Dodd argues that the first century Christians used a "canon within the canon" approach to the Scriptures, the inner canon consisting of passages that were germane for christological interpretation. Although Dodd's theory might look more like a modified version of Harris' theory,[27] it proposes a fundamental shift: "The quotation of passages for the Old Testament is not to be accounted for by the postulate of a primitive anthology of isolated proof texts. The composition of 'testimony-books' was the result, not the presupposition, of the work of

---

[23] Aileen Guilding, *The Fourth Gospel and Jewish Worship* (Oxford: Clarendon Press, 1960) 72.

[24] Varcher Burch, *The Epistle to the Hebrews. Its Sources and Message* (London: Williams & Norgate, 1936); Spicq, *Hébreux*; Kistemaker, *Citations*; C. F. D. Moule, *The Birth of the New Testament* (San Francisco: Harper & Row, 1984 [1962 ed.]); cf. Schröger, *Verfasser* 30.

[25] Lane, *Hebrews* lxx.

[26] Charles Perrot, "The Reading of the Bible in the Ancient Synagogue", in *Mikra. Text, Translation, Reading and Interpretation of the Hebrew Bible in Ancient Judaism and Early Christianity*, ed. M. J. Mulder (CRINT 2/I; Minneapolis: Fortress Press, 1990) 138.

[27] Sundberg, "Testimonies" 280.

early Christian biblical scholars."[28] The NT writers in their endeavour to present and defend the kerygma appealed to a common tradition of textual "fields", namely, OT texts that provided a relevant scriptural framework within which the Christ event was to be understood.[29]

Dodd's thesis has been developed further by the momentous contribution of Lindars, who sought to establish a causal link between the Scriptures used by early Christians and their apologetic activity.[30] Subsequent studies in this area have sharpened the focus on particular issues related to the use of the OT in the NT, but the overall conclusion seems to remain essentially unaltered.[31]

The research as to why early Christians used the OT is likely to continue. The selection of texts for quotation was most likely a multifaceted process, with several factors involved in the decision, and consequently no single answer can explain entirely the choice. Regardless of the exact source of the texts used, be it a copy of the LXX, or a *testimonia*-like collection of scriptural texts, or perhaps the Author's own memory, it is essential to acknowledge that the text used was the Greek Scriptures, a factor which, as this study seeks to prove, played a distinct role in the selection and the use of these passages.

2. Quotations from Texts with Divergent Hebrew – Greek Textual Traditions

The most problematic issue in assessing Septuagintal influence in the quotations rests with the text critical issues involved, more precisely, with the high number of variables to be considered in evaluating and comparing the three texts involved, the Greek text incorporated by the Author in the epistle's quotations, the Greek OT read by the Author, and the Hebrew text against which one compares the presumed *Vorlage* of the Septuagint

---

[28] Dodd, *Sub-structure* 126.

[29] Continuing on the lines of Dodd's hypothesis, Moule maintains that "the choice of OT passages is determined by the Christian events and their interpretation dictated by Christian tradition ... The Christians thus found themselves pushed by the pressure of events into a new way of selecting, relating, grouping, and interpreting what we call 'Old Testament' passages, and, while the scriptures of the Jews undoubtedly exercised a great influence upon the form in which they presented their material, and ultimately upon the very writing and collecting of the Christian scriptures, this influence was evidently subordinate both to the influence of the apostolic witness to Jesus and to the living inspiration of Christian prophets in the Church." (*Birth* 85).

[30] Barnabas Lindars, *New Testament Apologetic* (Philadelphia: Westminster Press, 1961).

[31] Albl, *Scripture* 3.

translators. Each one of these texts has a complex history of coming into being and of transmission, and to discuss each quotation and textual variant separately would require considerably more space than permitted by this work.[32]

2.1. Text and Function of the Quotations

The cases selected for analysis display at least one major divergence between the Greek and Hebrew OT texts. Selection was based primarily on consideration of the minimal text-critical issues involved in order to acquire a higher degree of certainty concerning the resemblance between the texts as we now posses them and those which the Author handled, namely, the texts of the epistle, the Greek *Vorlage* of the Author, and the Hebrew *Vorlage* behind the OT translation. Once the divergence has been determined, it will be necessary to trace its effect on the argument of the epistle in order to assess whether or not, in expounding that quotation, the Author based his argument in any discernible way on the very point where the Greek text differs from the Hebrew.

2.1.1. Dt. 32: 43 [LXX] in Heb. 1:6

The most likely candidate for the quotation in Heb. 1:6 is Dt. 32:43, a text that has various forms in different textual traditions. The Masoretic tradition and the Septuagint preserved the following texts:

Dt. 32:43b MT	Dt. 32:43a LXX	Heb. 1:6 NTG
wanting	εὐφράνθητε οὐρανοί ἅμα αὐτῷ καὶ προσκυνησάτωσαν αὐτῷ πάντες υἱοὶ θεοῦ	καὶ προσκυνησάτωσαν αὐτῷ
הַרְנִינוּ גוֹיִם עַמּוֹ	εὐφράνθητε ἔθνη μετὰ τοῦ λαοῦ αὐτοῦ καὶ ἐνισχυσάτωσαν αὐτῷ πάντες ἄγγελοι θεοῦ	πάντες ἄγγελοι θεοῦ.

The Hebrew text of Dt. 32:43 was preserved in a slightly different form in the Dead Sea Scrolls than the Masoretic tradition. As the parallel text shows, the Septuagint resembles better the Hebrew text form in 4 Q Deut[q]:

---

[32] This approach is undertaken in a number of studies, such as Ellingworth, "Old Testament"; McCullough, "Hebrews"; Schröger, *Verfasser*; Thomas, "Citations", and by the major commentaries on Hebrews.

Dt. 32:43b 4QDeut^q	Dt. 32:43a LXX	Heb. 1:6 NTG
השתחוו־לו כל־אלהים	καὶ προσκυνησάτωσαν αὐτῷ πάντες ἄγγελοι θεοῦ	καὶ προσκυνησάτωσαν αὐτῷ πάντες ἄγγελοι θεοῦ.

The quotation in Heb. 1:6 raises questions on several fronts, which will be considered briefly here. First, there is the issue of the text source for the quotation. There are three possible sources for this quotation, Dt. 32:43, Ps. 96:7 [97:7 MT], and Odes 2:43, none of which explains completely all the textual evidence. The Septuagint text of Dt. 32:43 has two lines that correspond partially to the quotation in Hebrews. If the book of Deuteronomy was indeed the source of the quotation then the Author has either adjusted the text to better suit his needs or followed a textual tradition no longer extant.[33]

Alternatively, there are two other possible sources for the quotation, which should be considered. First, there is Ps. 96 [97 MT]:

Ps. 97:7b MT	Ps. 96:7b LXX	Heb. 1:6 NTG
השתחוו־לו כל־אלהים:	προσκυνήσατε αὐτῷ πάντες οἱ ἄγγελοι αὐτοῦ	προσκυνησάτωσαν αὐτῷ πάντες ἄγγελοι θεοῦ

If Ps. 96 [97 MT] was used by the Author for the quotation in Heb. 1:6, the parallelism is indeed very close. In this case, the Author either modified his text, by changing the person of the verb from the 2nd to the 3rd,[34] deleting the article, and replacing the pronoun αὐτοῦ with the proper noun θεοῦ, or simply followed his *Vorlage*. These two cases are by no means the only possible explanations for the differences that exist between the two Greek texts; rather they stand at the ends of a large spectrum of possibilities.

If the book of Odes supplied the quotation, the parallel texts of the two textual traditions are as follows:

---

[33] This option is preferred by most commentators, see Ellingworth, *Hebrews ad loc.*

[34] The change in the morphology of the phrase from προσκυνήσατε αὐτῷ πάντες to προσκυνησάτωσαν αὐτῷ πάντες might have been triggered by the similarity of the opening line in the verse, αἰσχυνθήτωσαν πάντες κτλ. Similar morphological changes take place in the quotations from Gen. 22:16 in 6:13 f., and Dt. 31:6, 8 in 13:5.

no MT	Odes 2:43 LXX	Heb. 1:6 NTG
	εὐφράνθητε οὐρανοί ἅμα αὐτῷ καὶ προσκυνησάτωσαν αὐτῷ πάντες ἄγγελοι θεοῦ εὐφράνθητε ἔθνη μετὰ τοῦ λαοῦ αὐτοῦ καὶ ἐνισχυσάτωσαν αὐτῷ πάντες υἱοὶ θεοῦ	καὶ προσκυνησάτωσαν αὐτῷ πάντες ἄγγελοι θεοῦ

The text from Odes, the third possibility, fits the Hebrews text perfectly, but considerations of origin, availability and probable Christian editing of this hymn-compilation make one hesitant to decide in its favour.[35] The decisive factor seems to be the context of the alleged quotation sources. Although there are points of contact between Ps. 96 [97 MT] and Hebrews,[36] the text in Deuteronomy seems to have the edge in this respect, not only because of the numerous allusions to Dt. 31-33,[37] but, as astutely observed by Andriessen and Lane, because the entrance of Israel into the Promised Land supplies a better typological framework for the Author's presentation of Christ.[38]

The second issue is the relationship of the Septuagint text to its Hebrew parent text. The Masoretic tradition has not preserved the portion in Dt. 32:43 quoted in Hebrews, but the Hebrew text of the Qumran 4QDeut^q did. Skehan and Ulrich explain the longer Greek text by suggesting that the Septuagint tradition renders two Hebrew forms of the text known to the translators, "the first agrees with 4QDeut^q and the first line of the second

---

[35] Ellingworth, *Hebrews*; Schröger, *Verfasser*. Moffatt conjectures that since Justin Martyr's quotation of this LXX text uses ἄγγελοι, "this may have been the text current among the primitive Christians" (*Hebrews* 11).

[36] Ellingworth, *Hebrews* 119.

[37] Ellingworth draws attention to the following parallels: ἔσχατον τῶν ἡμερῶν in Dt. 31:29 (cf. Heb. 1:1), σήμερον in Dt. 31:21, 27 (cf. Heb. 3:7, 15), the danger of apostasy in Dt. 32:20 (cf. Heb. 3:12 ff.), ἐκκαθαριεῖ κύριος in Dt. 32:43 (cf. Heb. 1:3) and προσέχετε τῇ καρδίᾳ in Dt. 32:46 (cf. Heb. 2:1); "The Old Testament in Hebrews: Exegesis, Method and Hermeneutics" *ad loc.*

[38] P. Andriessen points to the similarity of language between Dt. 6:10, 11:29 and Heb. 1:6; "La teneur judéo-chrétienne de Hé 1:6 et 2:14b-3:2", *Novum Testamentum* 18 (1976) 293-313.

happens to agree with MT".[39] More important than the length of the text, however, are the divergences between the Hebrew and Greek texts of Dt. 32. First, the Greek verb εὐφραίνειν, "rejoice", translates the hiphil of רָנַן, "praise", the only occurrence of this equivalence in the Pentateuch. Second, resulting from the verb choice, the suffixed noun עַמּוֹ, "his people", is translated as עִמּוֹ, "with him", a possible consequence of the translators' discomfort with attributing praise to anyone except God.[40]

Two implications of Dt. 32:43 LXX for the epistle surface immediately. First, the pronoun αὐτῷ in the Greek phrase καὶ προσκυνησάτωσαν αὐτῷ πάντες υἱοὶ θεοῦ, due to its lack of a clear antecedent, made the reading of Dt. 32 more christologically germane from the standpoint of the Author.[41] Second, the noun ἄγγελοι played a crucial role in the inclusion of this verse in the catena, a matter that will be discussed later in the chapter.[42]

2.1.2. Ps. 101:26-27 [102:25-27 MT] in Heb. 1:10-12

The quotation in Heb. 1:10-12 from Ps. 101 [102 MT] is the longest text in the catena of quotations in Heb. 1.

Ps. 102:25 MT	Ps. 101:26 LXX	Heb. 1:10-12 NTG
לְפָנִים	κατ' ἀρχὰς σύ κύριε	σὺ κατ' ἀρχάς, κύριε,
הָאָרֶץ יָסַדְתָּ	τὴν γῆν ἐθεμελίωσας	τὴν γῆν ἐθεμελίωσας,
וּמַעֲשֵׂה יָדֶיךָ	καὶ ἔργα τῶν χειρῶν σού	καὶ ἔργα τῶν χειρῶν σού
שָׁמָיִם׃	εἰσιν οἱ οὐρανοί	εἰσιν οἱ οὐρανοί

The example will focus on only one item from this Psalm quotation, even though there are other possible points of interest.[43] The appellative σύ κύριε is attested in most manuscripts for both the epistle and the LXX. For the epistle, only Chrysostom and the Latin version omit it.[44] As far as

---

[39] Eugen Ulrich et al., *Qumran Cave 4. Deuteronomy, Joshua, Judges, Kings* (DJD XIV; Oxford: Clarendon Press, 1995) 141.

[40] George W. Buchanan, "The Priestly Teacher of Righteousness", *Revue de Qumran* 6, no. 24 (1969) 17.

[41] T. F. Glasson, "'Plurality of Divine Persons' and the Quotations in Hebrews 1.6 ff.", *New Testament Studies* 12 (1965-1966) 271; see also Ellingworth, *Hebrews* 119.

[42] See *infra* (2.2.1).

[43] Two other translation choices are notable. First, the Greek text translates the plural ἔργα for the Hebrew singular מַעֲשֵׂה, possibly either on stylistic grounds or to agree with the plural οἱ οὐρανοί. Second, the lexical choice describing the future of the created universe, ἀλλαγήσονται, "they will be changed", for the Hebrew וְיַחֲלֹפוּ, "they will pass away", must have shaped the eschatological perspective of the Author.

[44] Cadwallader, "Correction" 262.

Septuagint evidence goes, although the reading does not appear in S (cf. MT) it is attested in the rest of the evidence, albeit in a number of different sequences, such as τὴν γῆν σύ κύριε ἐθεμελίωσας in B, or τὴν γῆν σύ ἐθεμελίωσας κύριε evidenced in La[G] and Augustin. It seems legitimate to assume that the vocative was part of the Author's *Vorlage*.[45] The appellative, however, has no counterpart in the Hebrew text, but was supplied by the translators who correctly read it as the implied subject of the verb יָסַדְתָּ.

The effect of the use of the Septuagintal form of the quotation is twofold. First, the explicit use of σύ κύριε adds an unequivocal note of emphasis on the Creator,[46] the emphasis being heightened by the Author's transferring the pronoun to the very beginning of the sentence.[47] Second, and more important, the Septuagint appellative used in the epistle facilitates the association of the Old Testament κύριος with Jesus, the Lord in the epistle.[48] Reading 1:10 in light of the description of the Son's role in creation (1:3), on the one hand, and of the explicit reference to Jesus as κύριος (2:3), on the other, leads to the conclusion that Jesus' agency in Creation was exercised on account of his Sonship as well as of his Lordship.

2.1.3. *Ps. 8:5-7 [LXX] in Heb. 2:6-8*

The quotation in Heb. 2:7 is from Ps. 8, a psalm whose importance for the Author's argument is recognised unanimously by commentators.

Ps. 8:6 MT	Ps. 8:6 LXX	Heb. 2:7 NTG
וַתְּחַסְּרֵהוּ	ἠλάττωσας αὐτὸν	ἠλάττωσας αὐτὸν
מְעַט	βραχύ τι	βραχύ τι
מֵאֱלֹהִים	παρ' ἀγγέλους	παρ' ἀγγέλους,
וְכָבוֹד וְהָדָר	δόξῃ καὶ τιμῇ	δόξῃ καὶ τιμῇ
תְּעַטְּרֵהוּ:	ἐστεφάνωσας αὐτόν	ἐστεφάνωσας αὐτόν

The quotation from Ps. 8 occupies a strategic place in the Author's argument, as evidenced not only by its centring on the key word ἀγγέλους, which is both the *mot-crochet* in Heb. 1:4-5 and the *terme caractéristique*

---

[45] Ellingworth, "Old Testament"; McCullough, "Quotations"; Thomas, "Septuagint".

[46] Bateman, *Hermeneutics* 137.

[47] Ellingworth, "Old Testament" 56.

[48] In Heb. 2:3, 7:17, 13:20 explicitly, and in Heb. 1:13, 2:6-9 implicitly. See also Attridge, *Hebrews* 60.

of the first two chapters,[49] but also by its being the first quotation in the epistle that is both cited and expounded. The quotation as a whole presents a high degree of conformity to the source text, with one notable exception, the omission of the complete line καὶ κατέστησας αὐτὸν ἐπὶ τὰ ἔργα τῶν χειρῶν σου (v. 7a) from the description of God's mandate given to man (vv. 6-7).[50]

The focus of this example is on the middle part of the quotation, in which the noun אֱלֹהִים is translated as ἀγγέλους, an equivalent usually reserved for מַלְאָךְ, which, although legitimate, it is very rare in the Septuagint.[51] With such extensive usage in the Psalter as well as in the Hebrew Bible, it is not surprising that while the basic meaning of the Hebrew אֱלֹהִים is that of god(s), deity, there is a vast range of referents throughout, which include not only the one true God but also the pagan gods of people or of lands, king(s) and idols. This inevitably has implications for the understanding of each individual passage. Several traditions of Ps. 8:6 reflect the ambiguity of the Hebrew term. The Septuagint translated it as "angels", probably due to either theological concerns,[52] or to the "the apparent interchangeability of the terms 'gods' (אֱלֹהִים), 'sons of God' (בְּנֵי אֱלֹהִים or υἱοὶ τοῦ θεοῦ), and 'angels of God' (ἄγγελοι θεοῦ)".[53] This was the choice of the Syriac, the Targum, and the Vulgate.[54] While אֱלֹהִים can be construed as a generic term referring to "heavenly beings",[55] the sense in 8:6 is most probably that of God.[56] This was also the way Aquila, Symmachus and Theodotion rendered the term.[57] The significance of the Septuagint reading stands in the clarification of the

---

[49] Albert Vanhoye, *La structurelle litéraire de l'épître aux Hébreux*, 2nd ed., (Paris: Desclée de Brouwer, 1976) 38.

[50] The textual evidence is extensive for both variants, with ℵ A C D* P Y 0121b 6 33 81 104 365 629 1739 1881 2464 it vg syr[p.h] cop [sa, bo, fay] arm eth *al* having the line, and alternatively 𝔓[46] B D[2] K L vg[ms] *al* not including it. The internal evidence is just as equivocal since the form and style of the quotations employed by the Author could support either the argument for the presence of the line, since the deletion of an entire line would be unparalleled in the epistle, (Ps. 94 [95 MT], Jer. 38 [31 MT], Hab. 2) or alternatively, the freedom he felt in adjusting the quotation to better suit his particular point, such as the condensation of quotation from Jer. 38 [31 MT] in Heb. 10.

[51] See *infra* (2.2.1).

[52] Peter C. Craigie, *Psalms 1-50* (WBC; Dallas: Word, 1983) 108.

[53] Leschert, *Foundations* 88.

[54] Craigie, *Psalms* 108.

[55] Hans-Joachim Kraus, *Psalms 1-59, 60-150*, trans. Hilton C. Oswald, 2 vols., (Minneapolis: Augsburg, 1989) 183.

[56] Craigie, *Psalms* 105; Robert G. Bratcher and William D. Reyburn, *A Handbook on Psalms* (New York: UBS, 1991) 82.

[57] The text according to Field reads βραχύ τι παρὰ θεόν Fridericus Field, *Origenis Hexaplorum cum supersunt*, 2 vols., (Oxford: Clarendon Press, 1875) ii: 96.

Hebrew term's ambiguity through the translation equivalent chosen, ἄγγελος, a noun which in 8:6a as well as in the other thirteen occurrences in the Psalter, can be construed only as "angels".[58]

The two text traditions differ as to which being man is compared with in the psalm. The Hebrew text is probably best construed as "you made him [man] lower than God", while the Septuagint conveys the meaning "you made him [man] lower than the angels". By using the Greek text of Ps. 8 the Author not only understood the Psalm in the translation tradition of the Septuagint, but also expounded its message by building on the particular meaning of ἀγγέλους in Ps. 8:6 LXX. The gist of the main section of the epistle, 1:5-2:18 is the Son's superiority over the angels, as proven by the name "Son" which he inherited. The noun ἄγγελος is used 11 times in the first section (1:4-2:18), always referring to angelic host which have never been granted either the privilege of being υἱός (1:5), or κύριος over the enemies (1:13), or over the creation (2:5). According to the Author, they are not to be worshipped but they are to worship the Son, not to be ministered to but to minister τοὺς μέλλοντας κληρονομεῖν σωτηρίαν. While it can never be known how the Author would have expounded Ps. 8 had he used a Hebrew text, it is clear that the particular rendering of Ps. 8:6 LXX fitted nicely within his argument, and probably even contributed distinctly to its development.

2.1.4. Ps. 94:7-11 [95:7-11 MT] in Heb. 3:7-11

The use of Ps. 94 [95 MT] in Heb. 3:7-4:10 is one of the most extensive OT quotations in the entire epistle, spanning over 5 verses.

Ps. 95:8 MT	Ps. 94:8-9a LXX	Heb. 3:8-9a NTG
אַל־תַּקְשׁוּ	μὴ σκληρύνητε	μὴ σκληρύνητε
לְבַבְכֶם	τὰς καρδίας ὑμῶν	τὰς καρδίας ὑμῶν
כִּמְרִיבָה	ὡς ἐν τῷ παραπικρασμῷ	ὡς ἐν τῷ παραπικρασμῷ
כְּיוֹם	κατὰ τὴν ἡμέραν	κατὰ τὴν ἡμέραν
מַסָּה	τοῦ πειρασμοῦ	τοῦ πειρασμοῦ
בַּמִּדְבָּר:	ἐν τῇ ἐρήμῳ	ἐν τῇ ἐρήμῳ
אֲשֶׁר נִסּוּנִי	οὗ ἐπείρασαν	οὗ ἐπείρασαν
אֲבוֹתֵיכֶם	οἱ πατέρες ὑμῶν	οἱ πατέρες ὑμῶν

---

[58] As well as in Ps. 8:5, ἄγγελος is used in 33:7 [34 MT], 34:5, 6 [35 MT], 77:25, 49 [78 MT], 90:11 [91 MT] 96:7 [97 MT], 102:20 [103 MT], 103:4 [104 MT], 137:1 [138 MT], 148:2 [149 MT], and 151:4 [150 MT].

From the numerous potential cases of interest, attention will be given to just one instance of a significant divergence between the Greek and Hebrew texts that sheds light on the importance of the Greek text for the Author's argument.[59]

The translator of Ps. 95 [94 LXX] opted for a literal rendering of the proper nouns in the Hebrew text, ἐν τῷ παραπικρασμῷ for כִּמְרִיבָה and κατὰ τὴν ἡμέραν τοῦ πειρασμοῦ for כְּיוֹם מַסָּה.[60] Since there are other clues in the text of the quotation which draw attention to the interpretative nature of the Author's quotation,[61] it is reasonable to argue that these Septuagintal readings determined a significant shift of focus from a precise geographical localisation of the memorable events in the history of Israel (in the Hebrew text) to a more spiritual outlook, the rebellion and the testing which lay at the foundation of the conflict between God and the people of Israel in the desert (in the Greek text).

The Greek text of the Psalm is quoted *ad litteram* by the Author, and the two nouns, παραπικρασμῷ and πειρασμοῦ, play a significant role in the appropriation of this Scripture in the context of the New Covenant. First, the cognate verb παραπικραίνειν is used in 3:16 leading off a string of terms describing the sin of the desert generation. The summary of the forty years in Heb. 3:16-19 is delivered with powerful rhetorical force and is filled with paraenetic injunctions. The New Covenant believers are warned that the sin of rebellion could easily terminate their pilgrimage. In a similar way, the cognate verb πειράζειν is used in 2:18 and 4:15 to remind the New Covenant generation that the life of faith is a life of constant testing as it was for Israel and for Jesus himself.

---

[59] There are at least three other differences, the use of the conditional particle ἐάν for the Hebrew אִם, here expressing a wish; the plural τὰς καρδίας for the generic singular, and the addition of ἀεί in v. 10; Ellingworth, *Hebrews* 218.

[60] Although there are many text critical issues in this passage with a number of significant differences between the Septuagint text and the quotation in Hebrews, there are no textual variants for the words chosen here for discussion, παραπικρασμῷ and πειρασμοῦ in 3:8.

[61] Two such clues particularly stand out. First, the intercalation of the conjunction διό in 3:10 which divides the text in such a way that the period of 40 years depicts not the duration of God's anger, (cf. LXX=MT), but the duration of the people's witnessing of God's work. Several verses later (3:17), however, the Author reverts to the reading and the meaning of the LXX text. Similarly in 3:10, the modification of the phrase τῇ γενεᾷ ἐκείνῃ to read τῇ γενεᾷ ταύτῃ is a clear indication of the Author's desire to contextualise Ps. 94 [95 MT] for his audience, cf. Peter Enns, "The Interpretation of Psalm 95 in Hebrews 3.1-4.13", in *Early Christian Interpretation of the Scriptures of Israel*, eds. C. A. Evans and J. A. Sanders (JSNT-SS 148; Sheffield: Sheffield Academic Press, 1997) 353.

2.1.5. Ps. 39:7-9 [40:6-8 MT] in Heb. 10:5-7

Ps. 39 [40 MT] supplies another example of the way in which a significant textual divergence between the Hebrew text and its Greek translation is imported into the Author's argument via the quotation text from the Septuagint.

Ps. 40:6-8 MT	Ps. 39:7-9 LXX	Heb. 10:5-7 NTG
זֶבַח וּמִנְחָה לֹא־חָפַצְתָּ אָזְנַיִם כָּרִיתָ לִּי	θυσίαν καὶ προσφορὰν οὐκ ἠθέλησας σῶμα δὲ κατηρτίσω μοι	θυσίαν καὶ προσφορὰν οὐκ ἠθέλησας σῶμα δὲ κατηρτίσω μοι

Following the first part of the psalm, a declaration of trust and the subsequent deliverance (Ps. 40:1-4 MT), the psalmist reveals the essence of submission to God, which is found not in the numerous sacrificial regulations, as important as they were, but in the immutable resolve and desire to do his will (Ps. 40:6-8 MT). The Greek translation of the Psalm is quite literal with one significant divergence in the second line of v. 7, in which the Hebrew אָזְנַיִם כָּרִיתָ לִּי is translated as σῶμα δὲ κατηρτίσω μοι. Commentators have not reached consensus over the provenance of this particular Septuagintal reading. The reading σῶμα δέ could be either a case of an interpretative translation of the Hebrew idiom, which was subsequently corrected in the revisions of Aquila, Theodotion, and Symmachus to read ὠτία, in conformity with the Hebrew text.[62] Alternatively, the original ὠτία, chosen by the Göttingen Septuagint as the *lectio difficilior*, might have evolved to read σῶμα as result of corruption in the transmission of the Greek text.[63]

Textual evidence suggests that the reading σῶμα and not ὠτία was more likely to have been the text in the Author's *Vorlage*. This variant also provides a more plausible explanation of the development of the other variants. The Septuagintal reading obviously is more conducive to a christological interpretation than the Hebrew parallel text.[64] In the subsequent exposition of the quotation (Heb. 10:9-18), the Author substantiates the way in which this Scripture found its fulfilment in Christ. Attention is drawn to the superior value of Jesus' one-time sacrifice that

---

[62] Attridge, *Hebrews*; Bruce, *Hebrews*; Lane, *Hebrews*.

[63] Ellingworth suggests ΗΘΕΛΗΣΑΣΘΤΙΑ read as ΗΘΕΛΗΣΑΣ(Σ)ΩΜΑ (*Hebrews ad loc*).

[64] Karen H. Jobes argues unconvincingly that the reading ὠτία in the Author's *Vorlage* was modified to read σῶμα on rhetorical considerations, "Rhetorical Achievement in the Hebrews 10 'Misquote' of Ps 40," *Biblica* 72 (1991) 388.

replaced the sacrificial system of the Old Covenant and to the Saviour's perfectly submissive will as epitomised in his "coming in the world ... to do [God's] will". While both these aspects hang on the Author's understanding of Ps. 39 LXX [40 MT], the application of this Scripture to the Incarnation of Christ is directly provided by the Septuagint of Ps. 39 LXX [40 MT].

2.1.6. Gen. 47:31 in Heb. 11:21

The quotation from Gen. 47:31 is one of only two OT quotations included in the Author's retrospective on the heroes of faith in Heb. 11:

Gen. 47:31 MT	Gen. 47:31 LXX	Heb. 11:21 NTG
וַיִּשְׁתַּחוּ יִשְׂרָאֵל עַל־רֹאשׁ הַמִּטָּה:	καὶ προσεκύνησεν Ἰσραηλ ἐπὶ τὸ ἄκρον τῆς ῥάβδου αὐτοῦ	καὶ προσεκύνησεν ἐπὶ τὸ ἄκρον τῆς ῥάβδου αὐτοῦ

There are no textual variants for this verse in the text of Hebrews. The variants in the Septuagint, as well as the possible stylistic omission of Ἰσραηλ by the Author, do not relate to the problem addressed here. The LXX translators have probably read the word המטה as הַמַּטֶּה, "staff" not as הַמִּטָּה, "bed" (cf. MT), and the Greek text was employed as such by the Author. Although the Greek and the Hebrew texts differ significantly in this respect, it seems that the Author does not exploit the difference in any way, even though the Greek equivalent of "staff", ἡ ῥάβδος, forms a part of a quotation used earlier (the catena of the first chapter) and appears in Ps. 109:2 [110:3 MT], one of the more prominent OT texts used in the epistle. There are no particular inferences drawn from this verbal link.[65]

2.1.7. Pr. 3:11-12 in Heb. 12:5-6

The Author of Hebrews quotes only once from the book of Proverbs:

Pr. 3:11-12 MT	Pr 3:11-12 LXX	Heb. 12:5-6 NTG
מוּסַר יְהוָה בְּנִי אַל־תִּמְאָס	υἱέ μὴ ὀλιγώρει παιδείας κυρίου	υἱέ μου μὴ ὀλιγώρει παιδείας κυρίου

---

[65] Attridge, *Hebrews* 336; Ellingworth, *Hebrews* 243.

וְאַל־תָּקֹץ	μηδὲ ἐκλύου	μηδὲ ἐκλύου
בְּתוֹכַחְתּוֹ:	ὑπ' αὐτοῦ ἐλεγχόμενος	ὑπ' αὐτοῦ ἐλεγχόμενος
כִּי אֶת אֲשֶׁר יֶאֱהַב	ὃν γὰρ ἀγαπᾳ	ὃν γὰρ ἀγαπᾳ
יְהוָה יוֹכִיחַ	κύριος παιδεύει	κύριος παιδεύει
וּכְאָב אֶת־בֵּן	μαστιγοῖ δὲ πάντα υἱὸν	μαστιγοῖ δὲ πάντα υἱὸν
יִרְצֶה:	ὃν παραδέχεται	ὃν παραδέχεται

There are a number of textual variants for the texts of the epistle and the Septuagint. The readings υἱέ μου / υἱέ are attested by manuscripts of both the epistle and of the book of Proverbs,[66] one possible case of cross-influence in the transmission history of the texts.[67] The only other notable variant in the text of the epistle is the omission in 𝔓46 of 12:6b-7a, due to the homoioteleuton involved. These text-critical issues do not affect the one important divergence between the Greek and Hebrew texts. The Septuagintal μαστιγοῖ and πάντα both contribute to the overall meaning of the Pr. 3:11-12 with nuances that are not explicit in the Hebrew text.

The fairly common Septuagint addition of the adjective πᾶς[68] introduces an emphasis on the individual character of the Lord's discipline. A more significant difference is introduced by the words μαστιγοῖ δέ translating וּכְאָב, a translation choice difficult to explain.[69] Whatever the reason for this translation equivalence, the Greek text incorporates a more overt reference to physical punishment, which is absent from the Hebrew text of Pr. 3. By means of the Septuagintal quotation this nuance of the text is imported not only as the text of the epistle but, more importantly, as reinforcement of the Author's thought in this section. Although the idea of the unpleasantness of any disciplinary measure is communicated by such terms as παιδεύει / παιδειά or ἐλεγχόμενος, the term μαστιγοῖ brings to the fore the idea of physical suffering so dominant in this section. Since both the people of the Old Covenant (Heb. 11:36-38) and Christ himself (Heb. 12:2-3) underwent physical suffering, the New Covenant community should likewise anticipate its presence in their lives (Heb. 12:4). As their forerunner (Heb. 6:20), Christ must be followed not only on the "new and

---

[66] The preponderance of the textual variants favour the reading υἱέ for the Greek text with the exception of 23, Clement of Alexandria, Chrysostom and Theodoret, and υἱέ μου for the Hebrews text, with the exception of D* 81 614 630 1241ˢ pc b. See Thomas, "Septuagint" ad loc.; McCullough, "Hebrews" 138; and Ellingworth, "Old Testament" 257.

[67] Ellingworth, Hebrews 648.

[68] In Pr. 3 seven out of ten occurrences of the adjective πᾶς have no correspondent in the Hebrew text.

[69] William Mc Kane suggests that the translators might have read וַיַּכְאֵב the hiphil of כאב, Proverbs. A New Approach, Old Testament Library (London: SCM Press, 1970) 294. Buchanan advocates a similar solution (Hebrews 212).

better way" (Heb. 10:20) leading to the holy place, but also on his way to the cross with its shame and humiliation (cf. Heb. 13:13).[70]

2.1.8. Ps. 117:6 [118:7 MT] in Heb. 13:6

For the last quotation in the epistle, the Author returns to the book of Psalms:

Ps. 118:7 MT	Ps. 117:6 LXX	Heb. 13:6 NTG
יְהוָה לִי לֹא אִירָא מַה־יַּעֲשֶׂה לִי אָדָם:	κύριος ἐμοὶ βοηθός οὐ φοβηθήσομαι τί ποιήσει μοι ἄνθρωπος;	κύριος ἐμοὶ βοηθός [καὶ] οὐ φοβηθήσομαι τί ποιήσει μοι ἄνθρωπος;

The Greek translation supplies βοηθός either as an attempt to clarify the Hebrew idiom יְהוָה לִי, or as a result of dittography caused by the homoioarcton of vv. 6 and 7 [117:7 and 8 LXX].[71] Regardless of the reason behind the Greek translation, the Author uses it in this form as a fresh reminder of God's help in adversities of all sorts (cf. Heb. 2:18, 4:16). It must also be mentioned that both the noun βοηθός and the verb βοηθεῖν are used repeatedly in Dt. 32-33,[72] which follow immediately after the passage from which the quotation in Heb. 13:5 was taken. The quotation is a suitable scriptural injunction intended to calm the legitimate fears of a community that had already suffered from persecution and the seizure of their property.[73]

2.2. Selection and Grouping of the Quotations

Besides the role played by the Septuagint text of the quotations in developing certain points of the argument, the process of selection and the grouping of the scriptural texts are two further aspects often considered as indicative of Septuagintal influence on the epistle. The issue of text selection has already been addressed by this study, for now it will suffice to consider three such instances in which a certain word(s) in the

---

[70] The LXX rendering of Pr. 3:12 facilitates a thematic link with 2 Sam. 7:14, an important text in the beginning section of the epistle.

[71] The text-critical variants for this quotation include the articular reading ὁ κύριος of 𝔓*vid and the omission καί in A* C* P 0285 33 1739 1175 and three Versions, for the epistle text. The addition of the copula is evidenced in the groups L'' and A' for the Septuagint text. The major divergence between the Greek and Hebrew text, the addition of βοηθός, is not affected by these textual variants and therefore they will not be discussed further.

[72] Dt. 32:32, 33:7, 26, and 29.

[73] Cf. Heb. 10:32 ff.

Septuagint-based quotation was, if not solely responsible, at least instrumental in the selection of those texts.[74]

The contribution of these parallels is better perceived in view of the Jewish hermeneutical practice, especially the Hillel's *middoth*, a set of seven "general hermeneutical principles of inference, analogy and context",[75] ascribed to the famous rabbi Hillel by rabbinical tradition. It has often been recognised that the NT writers, both in their argumentation as well as in their use of Scriptures often used arguments that resemble the aforementioned *middoth*.[76] Among them, the Author and the apostle Paul made use of similar hermeneutical principles with greater frequency and diversity than any other NT writer.[77] Several of these principles, which in time became known as the seven rules of Hillel, could be responsible for the selection of the OT texts employed.[78]

The epistle abounds in textual markers that offer clues for unpacking its literary structure. Two such structural markers, the announcement of the subject and the catchword, are the most evident, especially in the use of the quotations. Prominent among many examples in the epistle are ἄγγελοι for the catena in Heb. 1:5-13 and its link with the quotation from Ps. 8 in Heb. 2:6 ff., κατάπαυσις for the exposition of Ps. 94 [95 MT] in chs. 3, 4, ἀρχιερεύς for the main theological exposition in chs. 7-10, πίστις for the encomium in ch. 11, and παιδεία in ch. 12. Whether the catchword technique has as its procedural guide the hermeneutical principles of Hillel or the pattern of the Hellenistic Jewish homily, it is important to draw attention to the fact that the words in the quotations, and hence the Septuagint text, were instrumental for these developments.

---

[74] The similarities extend well beyond the simple technical details of the selection and grouping of scriptural texts. For an in-depth analysis of these similarities, see Bateman, *Hermeneutics*; Ellingworth, "Old Testament"; Kistemaker, *Citations*; McCullough, "Hebrews", Schröger, *Verfasser*.

[75] E. Earle Ellis, "Biblical Interpretation in the New Testament Church," in *Mikra. Text, Translation, Reading and Interpretation of the Hebrew Bible in Ancient Judaism and Early Christianity*, ed. M. J. Mulder (CRINT 2/I; Minneapolis: Fortress Press, 1990) 699.

[76] Ellis, "Biblical Interpretation" 700-02, *inter alios*.

[77] Treatment of this particular aspect can be found in most studies of the use of the OT in Hebrews, especially in Bateman, *Hermeneutics*; Ellingworth, "Old Testament"; Kistemaker, *Citations*; Schröger, *Verfasser*. The debate over the provenance of these rules, as well as the correctness of referring to Hillel's rules when analysing the Author's use of the Scriptures, has not achieved definitive results. The present study uses the traditional nomenclature primarily for practical purposes.

[78] The Author's procedure is similar to the rule nr. 3, בנין אב מכתוב אחד, to rule nr. 4, בנין אב משני כתובים, which state the procedure for building of a family of texts based on one or two verses, and to rule nr. 6, כיוצא בו במקום אחר, which draws inferences from an analogous passage.

2.2.1. Heb. 1:6 πάντες ἄγγελοι θεοῦ

An argument for a specific Septuagintal influence in this area can be substantiated only by a very limited number of examples where the choice of the texts or their grouping can be traced directly to the Septuagint texts, which differ from their Hebrew counterparts. The following cases exemplify the point.

Dt. 32:43b MT	Dt. 32:43a LXX	Heb. 1:6 NTG
wanting	καὶ προσκυνησάτωσαν αὐτῷ πάντες υἱοὶ θεοῦ	καὶ προσκυνησάτωσαν αὐτῷ
הַרְנִינוּ גוֹיִם עַמּוֹ	εὐφράνθητε ἔθνη μετὰ τοῦ λαοῦ αὐτοῦ καὶ ἐνισχυσάτωσαν αὐτῷ πάντες ἄγγελοι θεοῦ	πάντες ἄγγελοι θεοῦ.

The quotation from Dt. 32:43 has already been discussed at some length. It is important to observe that the Septuagintal ἄγγελοι is precisely the catchword needed to construct the catena that gives Scriptural support for the Son's superiority over the angels. The Hebrew counterpart for ἄγγελοι is either missing, as in Dt. 32:43 MT or is a phrase for which ἄγγελοι only rarely was used as a translation equivalent, as in 4QDeut.[79] It seems reasonable to conclude that the Greek text of Dt. 32:43 is the most suitable text tradition to justify the inclusion of this passage in the catena of quotations in Heb. 1:5-13.

2.2.2. Heb. 3:7-4:11 εἰς τὴν κατάπαυσίν μου

A direct corollary of the mechanism behind the selection of the OT texts for quotations is the process of concatenating OT texts in several stages of the epistle's argument. The rules of Hillel or the Jewish Hellenistic homily are again the most obvious background for understanding this procedure. The clearest example of verbal association as the basis for the quotations' concatenation is Heb. 5:5-6. The two verses contain quotations from two OT passages, Ps. 2:7 and Ps. 109:4 [110 MT], brought together on the basis of the verbal parallel explored by the Author.

---

[79] The equivalence ἄγγελοι for אֱלֹהִים is attested only three times in over 250 occurrences, in Ps. 8:5, Ps. 96: 7 [97 MT], and Ps. 137:1 [138 MT]. It should also be mentioned that there are five cases in which ἄγγελοι translates the collocation בֶּן-אֱלֹהִים, Gen. 6:2, Dt. 32:8, Job 1:6, 2:1, and 38:7.

Ps. 2:7 MT	Ps. 2:7 LXX	Heb. 5:5 NTG
בְּנִי אַתָּה	υἱός μου εἶ σύ	υἱός μου εἶ σύ

Ps. 110:4 MT	Ps. 109:4 LXX	Heb. 5:6 NTG
אַתָּה־כֹהֵן לְעוֹלָם	σὺ εἶ ἱερεὺς εἰς τὸν αἰῶνα	σὺ ἱερεὺς εἰς τὸν αἰῶνα

By stating ἀλλ' ὁ λαλήσας πρὸς αὐτόν· υἱός μου εἶ σύ, ... καθὼς καὶ ἐν ἑτέρῳ λέγει· σὺ ἱερεὺς εἰς τὸν αἰῶνα, the Author explicitly indicates that the verbal similarity between the two passages stands as the main reason for their fusion.[80]

It is important to note that the association of these two texts although facilitated by the Septuagintal reading, is not intrinsically dependent on it. A Hebrew text could just as easily have supported this as well as other associations in the book, since similarity of words was not the exclusive reason behind the concatenation of texts. Thematic and contextual considerations seem to have played an important role as well.

There are however other instances, albeit very limited, in which the reason for fusing the texts was supplied primarily by the Greek OT text, in a way in which the corresponding Hebrew texts would have been less suitable. One of the clearest examples is the association of Ps. 94:11 [95 MT] and Gen. 2:3 [2:4 MT] in Heb. 4:3:

Ps. 95:11 MT	Ps. 94:11 LXX	Heb. 4:3 NTG
אֲשֶׁר־נִשְׁבַּעְתִּי בְאַפִּי אִם־יְבֹאוּן אֶל־מְנוּחָתִי:	ὡς ὤμοσα ἐν τῇ ὀργῇ μου εἰ εἰσελεύσονται εἰς τὴν κατάπαυσίν μου	ὡς ὤμοσα ἐν τῇ ὀργῇ μου εἰ εἰσελεύσονται εἰς τὴν κατάπαυσίν μου

---

[80] The dialogue between divine persons plays as well a significant role among the thematic links between verses. This aspect will be considered in more detail in a later section; see *infra* (ch. 6, 3.3).

| Gen. 2:4b | Gen. 2:3 | Heb. 4:4 |
MT	LXX	NTG
וַיְבָרֶךְ אֱלֹהִים	καὶ ηὐλόγησεν ὁ θεὸς	
אֶת־יוֹם הַשְּׁבִיעִי	τὴν ἡμέραν τὴν ἑβδόμην	
וַיְקַדֵּשׁ אֹתוֹ	καὶ ἡγίασεν αὐτήν	
כִּי בוֹ שָׁבַת	ὅτι ἐν αὐτῇ κατέπαυσεν	καὶ κατέπαυσεν ὁ θεὸς
		ἐν τῇ ἡμέρᾳ τῇ ἑβδόμῃ
מִכָּל־מְלַאכְתּוֹ	ἀπὸ πάντων τῶν	ἀπὸ πάντων τῶν
	ἔργων αὐτοῦ	ἔργων αὐτοῦ

The stringing together of these two verses was probably enhanced by the cognates κατάπαυσιν in Ps. 94:11 LXX and κατέπαυσεν in Gen. 2:3 LXX. The key in the exposition of the Scriptures in paragraph 3:7-4:11 is the term "rest". The association of Gen. 2:4 MT and Ps. 95:11 MT, although possible when working with a Hebrew text, is more likely to have arisen as a consequence of the Author's using a Greek text.[81] The two verses could still have been grouped even when working with a Hebrew text, based on thematic considerations, since the two verbs, שָׁבַת and נוּחַ (cognate of מְנוּחָתִי), are synonymous. The associations, however, were more effective when built on cognate catchwords rather then on thematic parallelism.

3. Conclusion

Several passages were analysed for an assessment of the specific role played by the Septuagint quotation texts in the Author's use of Scriptures. In each example the focus was directed to the part in the quotation where the Hebrew and Greek texts diverge due to translation. Furthermore, it can be argued that in several cases the divergence was to some degree exploited in the epistle's argument and consequently it left discernible Septuagintal traces on the epistle's use of quotations.[82] These marks

---

[81] See also Schröger, *Verfasser* 109 f.

[82] Space allows only for a brief mention of another important phenomenon in the Author's use of quotations, namely, the cases in which the Author, who normally seeks to abide by the text of the quotations, modifies the Septuagint text itself. The more noteworthy examples include Pss. 8, 39 LXX, and 94 LXX. In Ps. 94 [95 MT], the insertion of the conjunction διό changes the description of the desert wanderings, so that the 40 years of God's provocation in Ps. 94 [95 MT] is construed as 40 years of Israel's witnessing God's work. In Ps. 39 [40 MT] the end of the quotation as given by the Author renders a different meaning to the quotation. In Ps. 8 there is the already mentioned omission of an entire stich. Lastly, the complete rearrangement of the

cannot be reduced simply to the quotation text *per se*. In several cases the analysis of the quotations reveals that the Septuagintal influences go beyond the mere insertion of an LXX text in the epistle. Often the particular form and content of the Greek text finds reverberations in the argument of the epistle.

It is important to acknowledge that not all the divergences between the Hebrew and Greek texts have equally marked the epistle. A significant number of them are immaterial to the use of that particular quotation, and in such cases the Septuagintal influence is strictly limited to the form and content of the citation text, without flowing into the function of the quotation. In other cases, however, particular nuances of the Septuagintal text, distinct from those of the Hebrew text, are exploited by the Author in the exposition of that quotation. A similar statement can be made regarding the distinct role of the Septuagint text in the selection and combination of several passages. For all these cases the Septuagintal influence has to be acknowledged as a significant part of the complex system of factors that contributed to the shaping of the Author's thought as reflected in the epistle.

---

quotation from the book of Habakkuk will be analysed in more detailed as a test case. There is considerable debate over the reasons behind these particular modifications; some certainly were intended to heighten the rhetorical force of the text, others betray stylistic concerns, while others still might be theologically motivated changes.

Chapter Three

Septuagintal Quotations in Hebrews: Original Context

1. Original Context of the Quotations in Hebrews

The importance of both the immediate and larger contexts for a correct understanding of biblical passages is one of the axioms of modern exegesis, yet it would be an anachronism to expect the ancient interpreters to display the same interest in context. Their exegetical and hermeneutical principles generally differ from those developed in the modern period, and often mirror the practices of their contemporaries. This particularly seems to be true in the Author's case. Although it would be wrong to expect his method to correspond to post-Enlightenment approaches to the Scriptures, it would be equally wrong to assume that he is completely uninterested in the original context of the quotations.

Scholarship on Hebrews is divided on this issue. For a considerable period in the history of the research the dominating view was that the Scripture quotations were used by the Author as proof-texts, an atomistic approach to reading the Scriptures without any consideration for the context of the quotation employed. Synge, a representative of this position, describes the Author as one who "ignores the human element, the original context, the original meaning, the original purpose [of the Old Testament]".[1] Recent studies, however, have challenged this position on different counts, not least because of the growing evidence that the Author emulated many Jewish exegetical procedures and hermeneutical principles of contemporaries who did not disregard the context.[2] Current opinion now swings more towards admitting that the Author quotes from the OT with full awareness of the texts' original contexts, evidenced in the way the quotations frequently align themselves with ideas from the passage in which they originate. Ellingworth concludes a thorough investigation of this aspect by affirming that the Author's approach to the OT "is the opposite of atomistic exposition".[3]

---

[1] Synge, *Hebrews* 61. Caird ("Method" 44) and, more recently, Leschert (*Foundations* 2) list further examples of exponents of this view.

[2] David I. Brewer, *Techniques and Assumptions in Jewish Exegesis before 70 CE* (TSAJ 30; Tübingen: Mohr Siebeck, 1992).

[3] Ellingworth, *Hebrews* 41.

This growing consensus forms the departure point for the following section of the present study. On the legitimate assumption that the original context from which the quotations were extracted was important to the Author, the study intends to investigate whether or not the original Septuagintal context has played any discernible and distinct role in the way in which the Author employed the quotations. As in the previous chapter, the search for distinctiveness will concentrate on the quotations originating from contexts that display discernible differences between the Hebrew and Greek texts.

2. Quotations from Texts with Divergent Hebrew – Greek Contexts

One can expect translation differences between the Greek and Hebrew texts to appear not only in the texts, which constitute the quotations *per se*, but also in the contexts from which the quotations were extracted, in large part due to their relatively uniform distribution throughout the Septuagint. While some of these contextual differences are inconsequential, others arguably affect the meaning of the entire passage, often influencing the very text selected for quotation. Differences of this nature are the focus of the present section. Once the dissimilarities are identified for a given passage, the next step is to assess whether or not these divergences have played a role in the way in which the Author read and understood the context, and inevitably, the quotation he used. According to Dodd, when NT authors quote a passage they usually limited the size of the quotation to the most representative part of the text, even though they, as well as their readers, knew that attention was drawn not simply to the part quoted but to its entire context.[4] Dodd's position has more recently been confirmed by Hays in his analysis of the linguistic phenomenon of metalepsis as a key to a more correct understanding of the use of the OT in the NT.[5] Consequently, the context of the quotations becomes an important informative element, both for the Author's interpretative horizon and for our own. The more significant differences between the Greek and Hebrew contexts deserves special attention as they might shed light on a specific Septuagintal contribution to the way the Author read and understood the passage. Four such passages are selected for closer scrutiny.

---

[4] Dodd, *Sub-structure* 57.
[5] Richard B. Hays, *Echoes of Scripture in the Letters of Paul* (New Haven: Yale University Press, 1989).

2.1. Ps. 44:7-8 [45:6-7 MT] in Heb. 1:8-9

The discussion of the quotation from Ps. 44:7-8 [45:6-7 MT] in Heb. 1:8-9 usually centres on the *cruces interpretum* in vv. 8, 9; the meaning of the pivotal phrases ὁ θρόνος σου ὁ θεός εἰς τὸν αἰῶνα and ἔχρισέν σε ὁ θεὸς ὁ θεός σου, the proper way of construing the syntax of the phrase ἡ ῥάβδος εὐθύτητος ἡ ῥάβδος τῆς βασιλείας σου[6] and the text critical issue in v. 8, that is, the choice between the 2nd or 3rd person of the pronoun σου / αὐτοῦ. The clues in the Septuagint of Ps. 44 [45 MT] generally receive less attention than they deserve, yet they shed light on the legitimacy of reading vv. 7-8 as a reference to Christ, and implicitly on the justification for the Author's quoting from this psalm. Although the translation of the psalm is quite literal,[7] there are various differences between the Hebrew and Greek texts that must be singled out for consideration. The most notable divergence is the title of the Greek psalm:

Ps. 45:1 MT	Ps. 44:1 LXX
לַמְנַצֵּחַ	εἰς τὸ τέλος
עַל־שֹׁשַׁנִּים	ὑπὲρ τῶν ἀλλοιωθησομένων
לִבְנֵי־קֹרַח מַשְׂכִּיל	τοῖς υἱοῖς Κορε εἰς σύνεσιν
שִׁיר יְדִידֹת:	ᾠδὴ ὑπὲρ τοῦ ἀγαπητοῦ

Here, as well as in over fifty other instances, the psalm's superscription לַמְנַצֵּחַ is rendered εἰς τὸ τέλος, possibly on account of the equivalence נצח, "end", for מנצח, "choir conductor" (LEH). The phrase ὑπὲρ τῶν ἀλλοιωθησομένων, "for the ones who will be changed", translating עַל־שֹׁשַׁנִּים, "for the lilies", suggests a possible confusion of roots, שׁנה taken as שׁושׁן (LEH). The third equivalence ᾠδὴ ὑπὲρ τοῦ ἀγαπητοῦ is an appropriate rendering of the consonantal שִׁיר יְדִידֹת, with the difference that the adjectival rendering ἀγαπητός, "beloved", was preferred over the substantival one, יְדִידֹת, "love" (BDB). In the target Greek text, the phrases εἰς τὸ τέλος and ὑπὲρ τοῦ ἀγαπητοῦ have potential Christian resonance that probably attracted the attention of the Author.

A second set of differences, such as the insertion of δυνατέ in Ps. 44:6a LXX without a Hebrew correspondent[8] and the rendering of the genitive suffix in בָּנֶיךָ as a dative construction ἐγενήθησάν σοι υἱοί in 44:17 LXX,

---

[6] Notably the text in Hebrews differs from the majority of Septuagintal readings with regard to the articular state of the nouns.

[7] Murray J. Harris, *Jesus as God. The New Testament Use of Theos in Reference to Jesus* (Grand Rapids: Baker, 1992) 203.

[8] Harris detects the influence of v. 4a (*Jesus* 203).

supply additional points of contact between the psalm and the first chapters of the epistle.[9] The former alludes to Christ's role in the creation and sustenance of the universe (Heb. 1:3), and the latter anticipates the development of the theme of Christ's and the believers' sonship in Heb. 2:10 ff. These differences coupled with the correct as well as convenient rendering of מְשָׁחֲךָ as the aorist ἔχρισέν σε, a cognate of Χριστός,[10] and with the pregnant expression ὅτι αὐτός ἐστιν ὁ κύριός σου in Ps. 44:12b LXX probably strengthened the Author's perception regarding the appropriateness of including the psalm in the collection of Scriptures that refer to Christ.

Even though the precise original setting for the psalm continues to be debated, it would be safe to assume that the language and the imagery of this royal psalm have contributed to the development of its Messianic interpretation. The development of the Messianic reading of the psalm was primarily determined by the psalm itself, and not by a particular text form, be it Greek or Hebrew. Yet, the Greek text has several nuances that plausibly have contributed, in the case of the Author, toward the Messianic application of this psalm to Christ.

2.2. Ps.101:26-28 [102:26-28 MT] in Heb. 1:10-12

In the catena of Heb. 1:5-13, the quotation from Ps. 101:26-28 [102 MT] follows immediately after the quotation from Ps. 44 [45 MT] discussed above, and continues the address to the Son in which the Author's main concern is to support the claim that, unlike the angels (1:7), or the created world (1:10, 11), the Son's existence extends from everlasting to everlasting. The eternal existence of the Son, expressed by phrases such as εἰς τὸν αἰῶνα τοῦ αἰῶνος in 1:8, σὺ δὲ διαμένεις, σὺ δὲ ὁ αὐτὸς εἶ, and τὰ ἔτη σου οὐκ ἐκλείψουσιν in 1:10-12, forms the main thematic link between the two psalms.

According to the title, the psalm is a prayer of an afflicted person who cries out to God, pleading for help and salvation. The psalm does not follow the general pattern of the lament psalms, i.e., an opening lament followed by an affirmation of praise and trust, but has a more convoluted structure in which the themes of lament and trust repeatedly alternate with one another. The main image in the psalm is that of contrast between the ephemeral life of the afflicted psalmist (Ps. 101:3, 4, 11 [102 MT]) and the everlasting life of God (vv. 12, 25 ff.), an idea that stands at the heart of the psalmist's plea for mercy and life (v. 24). Undoubtedly the recurrent theme of God's eternal existence found resonance with the Author. The

---

[9] Ellingworth, *Hebrews* 125.
[10] Attridge, *Hebrews* 60.

justification for extending this description of God to the Son, however, is found exclusively in the LXX context.

The Greek translation of the Psalm is fairly literal throughout with only a few exceptions in the verses quoted in Hebrews, such as the addition of σὺ κύριε, the plural noun ἔργα and the lexical choice ἀλλαγήσονται, which already have been noted.[11] Verse 24, in the immediate context of the passage quoted in Hebrews, contains several differences that are significant for the overall message of the psalm.

Ps. 102:24-25 MT	Ps. 101:24-25 LXX
עִנָּה בַדֶּרֶךְ (כֹּחוֹ) [כֹּחִי]	ἀπεκρίθη αὐτῷ ἐν ὁδῷ ἰσχύος αὐτοῦ
קִצַּר יָמָי:	τὴν ὀλιγότητα τῶν ἡμερῶν μου
אֹמַר אֵלִי	ἀνάγγειλόν μοι
אַל־תַּעֲלֵנִי בַּחֲצִי יָמָי	μὴ ἀναγάγῃς με ἐν ἡμίσει ἡμερῶν μου
בְּדוֹר דּוֹרִים שְׁנוֹתֶיךָ:	ἐν γενεᾷ γενεῶν τὰ ἔτη σου

First, the verb עָנָה is translated as ἀπεκρίθη, the probable result of reading the consonantal text as עָנָה instead of with the vocalisation preserved by the Masoretic tradition עִנָּה. Second, the translation inserts a dative pronoun αὐτῷ as indirect complement for the previous verb. Third, the translation ἰσχύος αὐτοῦ reflects the Ketiv כֹּחוֹ and not the Qere כֹּחִי. Fourth, the translation of the phrase אֹמַר אֵלִי, "I say, 'my God'", as ἀνάγγειλόν μοι, "proclaim to me", perfectly legitimate in light of the consonantal text, supplies the verb for the preceding direct complement τὴν ὀλιγότητα κτλ and was probably required by the logic of the text as the translator read it.

The result of the translation is significant on several counts. The meaning and the verse division of the Greek text are different from that of the Hebrew text. The desolate cry of the person afflicted in the Hebrew text, "he has broken my strength on the way, my days he has shortened", is translated as a testimony of answered prayer in the Greek text, "he answered him in the way of his strength". Furthermore the dialogue in the Hebrew text between the one afflicted and God is altered by the insertion of the pronoun αὐτῷ, which can be neither the psalmist, nor God. The referent of this inserted pronoun can be, however, the κύριος of vv. 13-22, the Davidic king who shall build up Zion and appear in his glory, as Motyer, exploring the suggestions of Bacon and Moule, contends in a recent study.[12] Several elements in the LXX context of Ps. 101:25, 27

---

[11] See *supra* (ch. 2, 2.1.2).

[12] Motyer, "Quotations" 20.

[102 MT], such as the ambiguity of the antecedent for the pronouns αὐτῷ and αὐτοῦ in v. 24a, the alternating referent for κύριος as either the Lord or the Davidic king, as well as the LXX text's addition of κύριος in v. 25 supply reasonable grounds to justify the Author's incorporation of this psalm in the Scripture catena of Heb.1:5-13.

2.3. Ps. 21:23 [22:23 MT] in Heb. 2:12

Ps. 21 [22 MT] is one of the most frequently quoted from or alluded to psalms in the NT[13] and one of the paramount texts in Dodd's list of Scriptures that shaped the substructure of NT theology. Two particular episodes in Christ's passion, the cry of dereliction and the fate of Jesus' garments are portrayed in the Gospels as direct fulfilment of this psalm. The psalm itself consists mainly of two parts, the lament in vv. 1-22, and the praise of the one whose prayer was heard and answered.[14] Commentators often note that while other NT writers use the first part of the psalm, the Author is unique in quoting from the second part of the Psalm.[15]

Ps. 22:22 MT	Ps. 21:23 LXX	Heb. 2:12 NTG
אֲסַפְּרָה שִׁמְךָ לְאֶחָי בְּתוֹךְ קָהָל אֲהַלְלֶךָּ׃	διηγήσομαι τὸ ὄνομά σου τοῖς ἀδελφοῖς μου ἐν μέσῳ ἐκκλησίας ὑμνήσω σε	ἀπαγγελῶ τὸ ὄνομά σου τοῖς ἀδελφοῖς μου ἐν μέσῳ ἐκκλησίας ὑμνήσω σε

The translation of the verse quoted is straightforward and the only noteworthy departure of the Author from the Septuagint rendering is the use of ἀπαγγελῶ for διηγήσομαι, a change that most probably originated with the Author.[16] More fruitful for this analysis are the multiple points of

---

[13] For an extensive list, see Schröger, *Verfasser* 89.

[14] Craigie, *Psalms* 197.

[15] The treatment of this quotation follows, in part, Ellingworth's thorough analysis, "Old Testament" 81 ff.

[16] McCullough ("Hebrews" 77) explains the use of the verb ἀπαγγελῶ as a more suitable parallel to εὐαγγελίζομαι in 4:2, while Thomas ("Use" 40) suggests that its provenance is due to the special Christian meaning of this verb. Kistemaker is uncertain (*Citations* 32), while Ellingworth ("Old Testament" 81) interprets it as a more common term and cognate with the important words in ch. 1 (ἄγγελος) and ch. 4 (ἐπαγγελία), and Howard ("Quotations" 211) explains it as Hebrew influence divergent from the LXX. Attridge (*Hebrews* 90) sees it as more suitable description of Christ's mission, while Jobes ("Achievement" 392) invokes rhetoric.

contact between the psalm and the new context of the quotation in the epistle.

Even though the Author does not quote from the first part of the psalm as do the Evangelists, it is indisputable that the writer associates this psalm with the Passion of Christ. Immediately preceding the quotation from Ps. 21:23 LXX, the Author brings into focus the suffering and death of the Son as part of God's overall plan for humankind (Heb. 2:9-11). In quoting from the second part of the psalm, the Author reveals his primary interest in the themes of the psalm's latter part. The Greek translation of this psalm has several nuances that might have been important for the way in which this quotation was employed. The first one is in v. 21:

Ps. 22:21 MT	Ps. 21:21 LXX
הַצִּילָה מֵחֶרֶב נַפְשִׁי מִיַּד־כֶּלֶב יְחִידָתִי:	ῥῦσαι ἀπὸ ῥομφαίας τὴν ψυχήν μου καὶ ἐκ χειρὸς κυνὸς τὴν μονογενῆ μου

The variety of ways in which the verse is translated by the English versions suggests that the meaning of the Hebrew text is not straightforward and presents difficulties that were also encountered by the Greek translators.[17] The verse contains an important christological clue in the rendering of יְחִידָתִי by τὴν μονογενῆ μου, an adjective used only three other times in the Psalter. Although the equivalence is legitimate, it is the specific usage of μονογενής in the Christian tradition that makes the verse pertinent for a christological interpretation.

Second, it is also important to note that the extensive use of the future tense[18] gives a more pronounced future dimension to the Greek text than that of the Hebrew text - especially in reference to the future people of God in vv. 31, 32.[19] Third, the emphasis on the brotherhood of Jesus and the believers, so important in the immediate context of Heb. 2:10-18, is well served by the equivalents ἀδελφοῖς μου / ἐκκλησίας, set in

---

[17] *RSV*: "Deliver my soul from the sword; my darling / my life from the power of the dog",

NEB: "Deliver my very self from the sword, my precious life from the axe",

NASB: "Deliver my soul from the sword, my only life from the power of the dog",

NIV: "Deliver my life from the sword, my precious life from the power of the dogs",

TNK: "Save my life from the sword, my precious life [n. only one] from the clutches of a dog."

[18] The future tense is used at least fifteen times in the second part of the psalm. See also John Sailhamer, *The Translation Technique of the Greek Septuagint for the Hebrew Verbs and Participles in Psalms 3-41* (New York: Peter Lang, 1991).

[19] Ellingworth, "Old Testament" 85 and Schaper, *Eschatology* 50.

synonymous parallelism. Commenting on this passage Ellingworth concludes, "LXX was open to an application to Christ and his people which has its roots in Jesus' own understanding of the Psalm".[20]

2.4. Is. 8:17, 18 in Heb. 2:13

The quotation in Heb. 2:13 is a composite quotation:

Is. 8: 17 b-18a MT	Is. 8:17b-18a LXX	Heb. 2:13 NTG
		καὶ πάλιν ἐγὼ
וְקִוֵּיתִי־לֹו׃	πεποιθὼς ἔσομαι ἐπ᾽ αὐτῷ	ἔσομαι πεποιθὼς ἐπ᾽ αὐτῷ καὶ πάλιν
הִנֵּה אָנֹכִי וְהַיְלָדִים אֲשֶׁר נָתַן־לִי יְהוָה	ἰδοὺ ἐγὼ καὶ τὰ παιδία ἅ μοι ἔδωκεν ὁ θεός	ἰδοὺ ἐγὼ καὶ τὰ παιδία ἅ μοι ἔδωκεν ὁ θεός

The provenance of the first part of the quotation is disputed by commentators since there are three possibilities, 2 Km. 22:3, Is. 8:17, and Is. 12:2.[21] Because the second part of Heb. 2:13 consists of a quotation from Is. 8:18, it is reasonable to assume that the quotation in the first part was taken from Is. 8:18 as well.[22]

The Greek translation of this verse mirrors the Hebrew text, and there are no important changes in the Greek text of Is. 8:17 quoted in the epistle, other than the emphatic addition of the personal pronoun and the change of word order. There are, however, significant contextual divergences between the Hebrew and Greek texts,[23] some of which may have contributed to the selection of this text for quotation and to its distinct application in Hebrews 2.

Is. 8:17 MT	Is. 8:17 LXX
וְחִכִּיתִי לַיהוָה הַמַּסְתִּיר	καὶ ἐρεῖ μενῶ τὸν θεὸν τὸν ἀποστρέψαντα

---

[20] Ellingworth, "Old Testament" 86.

[21] Ellingworth, *Hebrews* 169.

[22] The split of the quotation into two parts separated by the connective καὶ πάλιν is not a serious contra-argument for this position. The Author applied the same quotation technique of dividing the quotations text in at least one other instance, the quotation from Dt. 32:35-36 in Heb. 10:30.

[23] According to Seeligmann the "translator not only struggled with the wording, but also with the theological signification of expressions", I. L. Seeligmann, *The Septuagint Version of Isaiah. A Discussion of Its Problems* (Leiden: E. J. Brill, 1948) 106.

פָּנָיו	τὸ πρόσωπον αὐτοῦ
מִבֵּית יַעֲקֹב	ἀπὸ τοῦ οἴκου Ιακωβ
וְקִוֵּיתִי־לֹו׃	καὶ πεποιθὼς ἔσομαι ἐπ' αὐτῷ

First, the Septuagintal phrase καὶ ἐρεῖ has no equivalent in the Hebrew text, a point to which Moule and Ellingworth draw attention.[24] As a result of this insertion there is a shift in the speaker's identity from that of prophet, the unmistakable reading of the Hebrew text, to that of a different person in the Greek text. A series of differences starting with 8:11, such as the insertion of κύριος in the last part of 8:10, the absence of an equivalent for the addressee אֵלַי in 8:11 and the change in the subjects of the verbs in 8:12, all contribute to occasional rifts in meaning between the Greek and Hebrew texts. All these changes obscure the relationship between certain words, their referents and antecedents. The most notable case is the dative pronoun in 8:14a, καὶ ἐὰν ἐπ' αὐτῷ πεποιθὼς ᾖς which, in the intricate picture of the antecedents and the context of the verse, could have generated the reading of the verse as "a dialogue between divine persons, in which the Father speaks to the Son as to a second κύριος".[25] Once such a reading was entertained, the messianic potential of these verses was explored by the authors of three NT writings, Hebrews, Romans, and First Peter.

3. Quotations from Texts with Parallels in their Contexts

3.1. Verbal and Thematic Parallels. Selection of the Quotations

Another aspect of the original context important for tracing Septuagintal influences is the presence of verbal and thematic parallels between the contexts of the quotations. The existence of two separate categories of OT texts from which quotations derive has long been recognised. The first category consists of texts that are of primary importance for the development of the overall argument of the epistle, while the texts of the second category have a more limited scope that does not extend beyond the paragraph in which they are inserted. While most scholars would concur with Caird's assertion that "all other scriptural references are ancillary to these [four scriptural passages], which control the drift of the argument",[26] not all would agree with his selection of main texts. In fact, the proposals

---

[24] C. F. D. Moule, *Birth* 80; Ellingworth, "Old Testament" 88.

[25] Ellingworth, "Old Testament" 88.

[26] Caird, "Method" 47.

for the number of primary texts vary considerably, with advocates for one,[27] four,[28] five,[29] and seven[30] main texts.

As important as this division of primary and secondary texts is, it has often obstructed the perception of the extensive thematic and verbal parallels between the OT passages quoted in the epistle. Most of these parallels are evident in the themes of the primary OT passages, but are certainly not restricted to them. Verbal and thematic links surface also in the contexts of primary and secondary texts, and even between secondary texts. The following considerations maintain that the overlap, far from being merely coincidental, was instead an important element in the selection process of the OT texts. A reading of these passages in both the Hebrew and Greek traditions reveals that while many of the thematic links between passages are supported by either text, several links are observable only in the Greek text. In each of the above cases, the role of the Septuagint, when it has either a reading similar to the Hebrew text or a distinct one, must be acknowledged as directly influencing the form and content of the OT use in the epistle.

Doubtless, there are other factors that contributed to the selection of the texts. As well as the early Christian tradition and the particular needs of the community addressed, a wide range of common denominators have been proposed in recent scholarship, such as the "confessed inadequacy of the old order",[31] or the "plurality of divine persons",[32] which generally opened the OT texts to Christian interpretation. Sometimes the association of texts is more subtle than it appears, as Flusser has astutely observed regarding the use of Ps. 94 [95 MT] to support the paraenesis in Heb. 3.[33]

Stanley, continuing the quest for the common denominator of OT texts quoted in the epistle, has correctly identified the parallels that exist between the texts employed as a possible solution.[34] But while he primarily addressed the overlap of Ps. 109 [110 MT] with other OT texts,

---

[27] Ps. 109 [110 MT], cf. Buchanan, *Hebrews* xxvii.

[28] Pss. 8, 95, 110 and Jer. 31, cf. Caird, "Method" 47.

[29] The catena in Heb. 1:5-13 (Ps. 2 and Dt. 32), Pss. 8, 95, 110 and Jer. 31; cf. Longenecker, *Exegesis* 175 ff.

[30] Pss. 8, 95, 110, Jer. 31, Hab. 2, Pr. 3, and Ex. 19-20; cf. France, "Writer" 259.

[31] Astutely proposed by Caird ("Method" 47) and developed recently by Motyer ("Quotation" 3 ff.).

[32] Glasson ("Plurality" 270) and Ellingworth (*Hebrews* 41).

[33] The association of Ps. 94 LXX and Lev. 19:17 is made on the basis of the adverb σήμερον and the injunction to watch over the errant brother; cf. David Flusser, "'Today if you will listen to His voice': Creative Jewish Exegesis in Hebrews 3-4", in *Creative Biblical Exegesis. Christian and Jewish Hermeneutics Through the Centuries*, eds. B. Uffenheimer and H. G. Reventlow (JSOT-SS 59; Sheffield: Sheffield Academic Press, 1988) 56.

[34] Stanley, "Hermeneutic" 41 ff.

it is just as important to realise that his suggestion can be extended on a larger scale to include an extensive network of parallels. It is this particular aspect of the importance of the quotation's context that this subsection intends to develop more fully, drawing attention to the specific, albeit not exclusive, role that the Greek text played in supporting these links.

3.1.1. Pre-eminence of Ps. 109 [110 MT]

The centrality of Ps. 109 [110 MT] to the epistle is admitted by most scholars. Buchanan even goes so far as to propose that the main part of the epistle, chs. 1-12, was originally a midrash on Ps. 109 [110 MT].[35] On the basis of the frequent quotations from and allusions to Ps. 109 [110 MT] throughout all major sections of the epistle, Stanley also argues for the pre-eminence of this psalm, but does not venture as far as Buchanan.[36] An aspect that has received less attention is the amount of parallels of language and thought between Ps. 109 [110 MT] and the contexts of the other quotations, both primary and secondary texts, as highlighted in the tables below.

Between Ps. 109 [110 MT] and Ps. 2, there are the following verbal and thematic parallels:

Ps. 109 LXX	Ps. 2 LXX
v.2 ἐξαποστελεῖ κύριος ἐκ Σιων	v.6 ἐπὶ Σιων ὄρος τὸ ἅγιον αὐτοῦ
v.5 συνέθλασεν ... βασιλεῖς	v.10 καὶ νῦν βασιλεῖς σύνετε
v.6 κρινεῖ ἐν τοῖς ἔθνεσιν	v.1 ἵνα τί ἐφρύαξαν ἔθνη
v.6 κρινεῖ ἐν τοῖς ἔθνεσιν	v.8 δώσω σοι ἔθνη τὴν κληρονομίαν
v.2 ῥάβδον δυνάμεώς σου	v.9 ποιμανεῖς ... ἐν ῥάβδῳ σιδηρᾷ
v.3 ἐκ γαστρὸς ... ἐξεγέννησά σε	v.7 ἐγὼ σήμερον γεγέννηκά σε
v.1 εἶπεν ὁ κύριος τῷ κυρίῳ μου	v.1 κύριος εἶπεν πρός με
v.4 σὺ εἶ ἱερεὺς εἰς τὸν αἰῶνα	v.7 υἱός μου εἶ σύ
v.5 κύριος ἐκ δεξιῶν σου	v.2 συνήχθησαν ... κατὰ τοῦ κυρίου
v.5 κύριος ἐκ δεξιῶν σου	v. 4 ὁ κύριος ἐκμυκτηριεῖ αὐτούς
v.5 ἐν ἡμέρᾳ ὀργῆς αὐτοῦ	v.12 μήποτε ὀργισθῇ κύριος
v.7 ἐκ χειμάρρου ἐν ὁδῷ πίεται	v.12 καὶ ἀπολεῖσθε ἐξ ὁδοῦ δικαίας
v.3 ἐν ἡμέρᾳ τῆς δυνάμεώς σου	v.7 ἐγὼ σήμερον γεγέννηκά σε
v.5 ἐν ἡμέρᾳ ὀργῆς αὐτοῦ	v. 5 ἐν τῷ θυμῷ αὐτοῦ

---

[35] Buchanan, *Hebrews* xxvii.
[36] Stanley, "Hermeneutic" 7 f.

A comparable list of parallels is discernible between Ps. 109 [110 MT] and Ps. 94 [95 MT]:

Ps. 109 LXX	Ps. 94 LXX
v.1 εἶπεν ὁ κύριος τῷ κυρίῳ μου	v.1 ἀγαλλιασώμεθα τῷ κυρίῳ
v.5 κύριος ἐκ δεξιῶν σου	v.3 ὅτι θεὸς μέγας κύριος
v.4 ὤμοσεν κύριος	v.11 ὡς ὤμοσα ἐν τῇ ὀργῇ μου
v.5 ἐν ἡμέρᾳ ὀργῆς αὐτοῦ	v.11 ἐν τῇ ὀργῇ μου
v.6 ἐπὶ γῆς πολλῶν	v.4 τὰ πέρατα τῆς γῆς
v.7 ἐκ χειμάρρου ἐν ὁδῷ πίεται	v.10 οὐκ ἔγνωσαν τὰς ὁδούς μου
v.5 ἐν ἡμέρᾳ ὀργῆς αὐτοῦ	v.7 σήμερον ἐὰν ... ἀκούσητε

There are several parallels between Ps. 109 [110 MT] and Ps. 8:

Ps. 109 LXX	Ps. 8 LXX
v.1 ἕως ἂν θῶ τοὺς ἐχθρούς σου	v.3 τοῦ καταλῦσαι ἐχθρόν
v.3 ἐν μέσῳ τῶν ἐχθρῶν σου	v.3 ἕνεκα τῶν ἐχθρῶν σου
v.1 εἶπεν ὁ κύριος τῷ κυρίῳ μου	v.2,10 κύριε ὁ κύριος ἡμῶν
v.1 ὑποπόδιον τῶν ποδῶν σου	v.7 ὑποκάτω τῶν ποδῶν αὐτοῦ
v.6 ἐπὶ γῆς πολλῶν	v.2,10 ἐν πάσῃ τῇ γῇ

A similar, although not as extensive picture emerges when Ps. 109 [110 MT] is compared with the secondary OT texts from which the Author quotes, such as Ps. 39 [40 MT], Ps. 44 [45 MT], and Ps. 101 [102 MT].

3.1.2. Parallels between the Contexts of Other Quotations in Hebrews

A comparable phenomenon of language and theme overlap is observable when the contexts of other quotations are examined. The following table highlights the most representative cases.

Between Ps. 94 [95 MT] and Ps. 8:

Ps. 94 LXX	Ps. 8 LXX
v.3 ὅτι θεὸς μέγας κύριος	v.2 κύριε ὁ κύριος ἡμῶν
v.9 εἴδοσαν τὰ ἔργα μου	v.7 τὰ ἔργα τῶν χειρῶν σου
v.5 αἱ χεῖρες αὐτοῦ ἔπλασαν	v.7 τὰ ἔργα τῶν χειρῶν σου
v.5 ὅτι αὐτοῦ ἐστιν ἡ θάλασσα	v.9 τοὺς ἰχθύας τῆς θαλάσσης

Finally, between Ps. 94 [95 MT] and Ps. 2:

Ps. 94 LXX	Ps. 2 LXX
v.3 καὶ βασιλεὺς μέγας	v.6 ἐγὼ δὲ κατεστάθην βασιλεύς
v.1 ἀγαλλιασώμεθα τῷ κυρίῳ	v.11 καὶ ἀγαλλιᾶσθε αὐτῷ ἐν τρόμῳ
v.7 σήμερον ἐὰν ... ἀκούσητε	v.7 ἐγὼ σήμερον γεγέννηκά σε
v.10 οὐκ ἔγνωσαν τὰς ὁδούς μου	v.12 καὶ ἀπολεῖσθε ἐξ ὁδοῦ δικαίας
v.11 ὡς ὤμοσα ἐν τῇ ὀργῇ μου	v.5 ἐν τῷ θυμῷ αὐτοῦ
	v.12 ὅταν ἐκκαυθῇ ... ὁ θυμὸς αὐτοῦ

The list could continue with other examples that display similar parallels, Ps. 2 and Ps. 8, Ps. 39 [40 MT] and Jer. 38 [31 MT], and Ps. 39 [40 MT] and Hab. 1-3. The picture that emerges from these comparisons is one of a network of OT texts which where selected by the Author on considerations of their verbal and thematic affinities. Undoubtedly the Author was extremely familiar with these Scriptures, and probably had even committed them to memory.[37] In this scenario, it seems extremely likely that the Author was indeed aware of the context of his quotations, and that the context itself played a significant role in shaping the use of the quotations.

3.2. *Verbal and Thematic Parallels. Grouping of the Quotations*

As noted earlier, the practice of building a family of quotations, so prevalent among the Author's contemporaries, intimately linked the text selection process to that of the grouping of the texts. Stanley correctly contends that the frequency with which the conceptual and verbal links recur establishes the "pattern of the author's *modus operandi*".[38] This phenomenon extends beyond the level of the quotations' texts to include their contexts as well, where in fact, it is even more noticeable. Since the Author seldom uses an OT text disconnected from others, most of the examples that were presented above could serve equally as evidence for

---

[37] Unfortunately because of methodological indeterminacy, a case for quoting from memory cannot be either demonstrated or refuted, cf. Ellingworth, "Old Testament". Consequently, scholarship has given only secondary attention to this possibility. It is, however, the explanation that seems most plausible to this writer. Memorizing large portions of the Scriptures, as was customary in Early Judaism, significantly increased the ability to make multiple and various connections between scriptural passages. For a comprehensive treatment of the role of Scripture memorization in Early Judaism, see the standard work of Birger Gerhardsson, *Memory and Manuscript. Oral Tradition and Written Transmission in Rabbinic Judaism and Early Christianity* (Uppsala: Almqvist and Wiksells, 1961).

[38] Stanley, "Hermeneutic" 43.

the mechanism behind the grouping of the texts. The example selected here intends to show that in several cases, the concatenation of two passages was the result not of the texts in the quotations but of their contexts.

Dt. 31:6 LXX	Heb. 13:5-6 NTG
ἀνδρίζου καὶ ἴσχυε μὴ φοβοῦ μηδὲ δειλία μηδὲ πτοηθῇς ἀπὸ προσώπου αὐτῶν ὅτι κύριος ὁ θεός σου ὁ προπορευόμενος μεθ' ὑμῶν ἐν ὑμῖν οὐ μή σε ἀνῇ οὔτε μή σε ἐγκαταλίπῃ	 αὐτὸς γὰρ εἴρηκεν οὐ μή σε ἀνῶ οὐδ' οὐ μή σε ἐγκαταλίπω ὥστε θαρροῦντας ἡμᾶς λέγειν κύριος ἐμοὶ βοηθός [καὶ] οὐ φοβηθήσομαι τί ποιήσει μοι ἄνθρωπος;

The short catena of Dt. 31:6 and Ps. 117:6 [118 MT] in Heb. 13:5-6 seems to have no obvious common denominator, only a loose thematic overlap between the promise of permanent divine presence in Deuteronomy, and the resolve of the psalmist as he reflects on God's being his helper in Ps. 117 [118 MT]. The link between the two texts becomes clearer when Dt. 31:6 is read in its context. Previous to the divine promise iterated in Dt. 31:6, there is a string of five imperatives and the third one, μὴ φοβοῦ, provides the verbal element that links with the other quotation. In this case the immediate context of Dt. 31:6, and not the quotation text itself, facilitated the catena link.

4. Conclusion

The investigation of the context of several quotations in the epistle has traced discernible links between the Septuagintal context, on the one hand, and either the use of the quotation or the reason behind its selection, on the other. If these links are found in some of the more obscure quotations in the epistle, such as the ones selected above, one could reasonably expect that they are even more evident in the case of the epistle's important quotations. While this study is not exhaustive, its conclusions on the issue of the quotations' context are clearly in line with the more recent school of thought that seeks to vindicate the Author of the long-standing charge of an atomistic and proof-text type approach to the Scriptures.

Once the importance of the context is established, it becomes clear that certain features of the Greek text used by the Author were potentially more suitable for application to Christ than their corresponding Hebrew source texts. The divergences between the Greek and Hebrew texts in the literary contexts of the four quotations selected have shown that the Greek translation is characterised by linguistic or theological nuances that were germane for christological interpretations. The distinct role of the Septuagint was just as much that of a supplier of texts for the Author's word of exhortation as a theological guide for understanding and portraying the life and ministry of Christ. Furthermore, the Septuagintal contexts, through an extensive network of verbal and conceptual parallels, have supplied the needed ingredient for the selection and the grouping of most of these particular texts; however, one must concede that the Hebrew text also supports most of these associations.

While not as unambiguous as the case for the quotations' text, the analysis of the quotations' context offers support for a distinct contribution of the Septuagint to the epistle. The Septuagint contexts, both in their content and extensive overlap have exemplified the Septuagint's role in the epistle's selection and use of quotations. One can sustain that the Greek OT passages were more resonant with the Christian message than their parallel Hebrew text on the basis of particular lexical or grammatical renderings of a word, additions or deletions of a word, or specific nuances which coincided with the developing Christian tradition.

What shape the epistle might have taken if the Author had read the Hebrew Scriptures is impossible to know. Yet, if the conclusion of this selective study can be extrapolated, it can be maintained that the Septuagint context supplies good evidence that the quotations were not randomly or thoughtlessly chosen. Their context often supplied a more favourable reading, at times absent from the corresponding Hebrew text, which justified the application of that Scripture to Christ.

Chapter Four

Septuagintal Allusions in Hebrews

1. Intertextuality and Scriptural Allusions in Hebrews

The use of the Old Testament in the Epistle to the Hebrews extends beyond that of quotations. A wide selection of biblical names and events, cultic motifs and institutions, and other themes and ideas are frequently alluded to and, consequently, form a substantial part of the epistle's overall argument, bearing witness to the extensive range of the Author's engagement with the Jewish Scriptures.

This chapter focuses on the OT material outside of the quotations in an attempt to trace cases of specific Septuagintal influence. The scope of the investigation will be broadened to include allusions not only from the canonical books of the Jewish Scriptures but also from the Apocrypha and Pseudepigrapha.[1] A principle justification for this expansion is the renewed interest in these two corpora of writings from the Second Temple period. Their contribution to the writing and the understanding of the NT is currently undergoing a reassessment, as such issues as authorship, location, original language, date, transmission and Christian influence continue to generate scholarly dialogue.[2]

A second, and more important reason for including these writings in the present investigation is the consideration that books belonging to these corpora most probably were a part of the literary context of the Author. The books of the Apocrypha, although not included in the Jewish canon, have been preserved, transmitted and used by the Christian church since its inception. Evidence shows that at least some of them were valued by Christians even as early as the second century, and as a group of "non-canonical, but acceptable" books,[3] they were included in the Septuagint alongside the Greek translation of the canonical books.[4]

---

[1] For a recent pertinent discussion of the canonicity issues, see Siegfried Meurer, ed., *The Apocrypha in Ecumenical Perspective* (UBS-MS 6; Reading / New York: UBS, 1991), and the earlier works of Sundberg, *Old Testament of the Early Church*, and Beckwith, *Canon*.

[2] J. H. Charlesworth, *The Old Testament Pseudepigrapha and the New Testament* (Cambridge: Cambridge University Press, 1985).

[3] William Horbury, "The Christian Use and the Jewish Origins of the Wisdom of

It is true that while quotations from the canonical writings abound in the epistle, there is no direct or indirect quotation from the Apocrypha or from any other extra-canonical sources. On this ground alone, it is reasonable to contend that the Author maintained a distinction between canonical and extra-canonical sources both in his reading and employment of written sources. Based on the Author's quotation formulas, it would be fair to conclude that the canonical books held a privileged place over other sources, yet, the frequent parallels between the epistle and the extra-canonical writings suggest that the Author was acquainted with this corpus of writings. If indeed this was the case, the extracanonical writings can be counted among the factors that contributed to the form and content of several passages in the epistle.

As with previous areas of investigation, only representative cases from both canonical and extra-canonical books will be scrutinised. The selection of these examples is not random; they are part of a larger group of texts that exhibit dependence on Greek textual traditions divergent from the parallel Hebrew texts. In each case the analysis will focus exclusively on the elements of textual difference between the two traditions and on their usage in the epistle.

Recent interest in interdisciplinary studies has given rise to several new approaches in biblical criticism, especially in the area of confluence between biblical studies and that of literary and linguistic studies. One such approach is the area of intertextuality. In essence, intertextuality refers to the relationship that exists between different texts, particularly in instances when authors of literary texts make use of pre-existing texts.[5] In the area of biblical studies the study of the use of the Old Testament in the New has proven to be fertile ground for this approach, which has rapidly generated new presuppositions, methodologies and terminology.

In biblical approaches to intertextuality, failure to specify the distinct ways in which the term is construed leads to unnecessary confusion. Foremost in the list of needed clarifications is the differentiation between the traditional understanding of and approach to intertextuality, and the more recent developments that are associated with post-structuralism and deconstructionist theories.[6]

Solomon", in *Wisdom in Ancient Israel. Essays in Honour of J. A. Emerton*, eds. John Day, R. P. Gordon, and H. G. M. Williamson, (Cambridge: Cambridge University Press, 1995).

[4] Wevers, "Significance" 86.

[5] Thomas R. Hatina, "Intertextuality and Historical Criticism in New Testament Studies: Is There a Relationship?", *Biblical Interpretation* 7, no. 1 (1999) 28.

[6] In the first case, intertextuality is seen more as a static and diachronic concept, which depicts various ways in which authors make use of previously written texts. Whether by direct quotations, allusions, or other means, authors allow, either consciously

The two ways of understanding the phenomenon of "intertextuality" are mutually exclusive.[7] This friction has been particularly felt in the area of biblical studies, where the poststructuralist framework is rarely taken into consideration, in spite of the use of terminology and methodology associated with those schools of thought.[8] In fact, as Hatina argues, "intertextuality, as it is commonly understood in the poststructuralist contexts, is inimical to current historical-critical inquiry".[9]

One of the most influential approaches to intertextuality in the NT was pioneered by Richard Hays, who applied the concept of "echo" or "metalepsis", derived from literary criticism, to the study of St. Paul's use of Scripture. The approach marked an important development in the area of the use of the OT in the NT by emphasising, among other things, the importance of a reader-oriented analysis of the quotations and allusions. Hays directs the attention of the readers of the Pauline epistles to the need "to interpret a citation or allusion by recalling aspects of the original

---

or not, a text to bear the influence of an earlier text or texts. Intertextuality construed in this way is essentially a study of the formative and informative influences exerted by precursor texts on successor texts, bearing witness to an interconnectedness between texts, which as Tallis observes, has been "the very stuff of literature since ancient times", (quoted in Hans-Peter Mai, "Bypassing Intertextuality. Hermeneutics, Textual Practice, Hypertext", in *Intertextuality*, ed. Heinrich F. Plett [Berlin / New York: Walter de Gruyter, 1991] 31). A different use of intertextuality originated in the new trends in literary theory, especially those related to poststructuralist and deconstructionist theory. There is a considerable range of nuances within this framework, at times conflicting with each other and incoherent, cf. Mai, "Intertextuality" 31; Stanley E. Porter, "Use" 84; Heinrich F. Plett, "Intertextualities", in *Intertextuality*, ed. *idem* (Berlin / New York: Walter de Gruyter, 1991) 3. The term "intertextuality" is employed to refer to a dynamic and synchronic relationship between texts, a relationship more complex than the earlier theory of literary influence suggests. Developed primarily by Julia Kristeva, Roland Barthes, and Jacques Derrida, intertextuality is understood "as a concept that discloses every text's dependence on and infiltration by prior codes and concepts – thus being closely aligned with deconstruction in which language serves as the ground of existence and the world emerges as infinite text" (Hatina, "Intertextuality" 31). Intertextuality construed in this way was the product of a radical analysis of the acts of writing, reading and interpretation. A precursor text can never be just a simple presence in the successor text. According to Miscall, the tension generated by the interference of the two texts proves that the relationship between the two texts is equivocal, including simultaneously "both acceptance and rejection, recognition and denial, understanding and misunderstanding, and supporting and undermining. To recognise that a text is related to another text is both to affirm and to deny the earlier texts." Peter D. Miscall, "Isaiah: New Heavens, New Earth, New Book", in *Reading Between Texts. Intertextuality and the Hebrew Bible*, ed. Danna Nolan Fewell (Louisville: John Knox Press, 1992) 44.

[7] Mai, "Intertextuality" 51.

[8] Porter, "Use" 84.

[9] Hatina, "Intertextuality?" 29.

context that are not explicitly quoted".[10] One of the results of Hays'
analysis was the drafting of a more precise methodology for identifying
and interpreting scriptural echoes or allusions. The seven criteria proposed
by him, availability, volume, recurrence, thematic coherence, historical
plausibility, history of interpretation, and satisfaction,[11] have become the
guidelines by which later studies have been conducted.[12]

The present study does not attempt to follow Hays' approach, but opts
for a primarily author-centred perspective in place of a reader-centred one.
Although the importance of the reader's perspective cannot be denied,
especially in an exhaustive study of the allusions, an author-centred
approach provides a more suitable framework within which one can assess
the particular Septuagintal influence in the use of scriptural allusions.

Consequently, Hays' criteria for locating scriptural allusions need to be
narrowed down to just two, those of availability and volume.[13] With this
approach, scriptural allusions will be identified in passages of the epistle
which display a reasonable amount of linguistic or conceptual overlap with
an OT text that the Author "could reasonably have been expected to
know".[14] Needless to say a more nuanced definition is required for a
comprehensive analysis of the OT allusions in the epistle. For the specific
purpose of identifying samples of Septuagintal influence in allusions the
parameters set above are sufficient.

2. Septuagintal Allusions in Hebrews

2.1 Septuagintal Allusions from Canonical Books

The canonical books, besides being the exclusive source for the quotations
in the epistle, are responsible for the majority of the allusions in the epistle

---

[10] Richard B. Hays, "Echoes of Scripture in the Letter of Paul: Abstract", in *Paul and
the Scriptures of Israel*, eds. Craig A. Evans and James A. Sanders (JSNT-SS 83;
Sheffield: Sheffield Academic Press, 1993) 43.

[11] Hays, "Echoes" 29 ff.

[12] See, *inter alios*, Robert L. Brawley, *Text to Text Pours Forth Speech. Voices of
Scripture in Luke-Acts* (Bloomington: Indiana University Press, 1995); Steve Moyise,
The Old Testament in the Book of Revelation (JSNT-SS 115; Sheffield: Sheffield
Academic Press, 1995); Brian S. Rosner, *Paul, Scripture and Ethics. A Study of 1
Corinthians 5-7* (AGAJU 22; Leiden: E. J. Brill, 1994); Michael Thompson, *Clothed
with Christ. The Example and Teaching of Jesus in Romans 12:1-15:13* (JSNT-SS 59;
Sheffield: Sheffield Academic Press, 1991).

[13] A similar approach is proposed by Brawley, *Text* 13.

[14] Porter, "Use" 95. Ellingworth ("Old Testament" 3) proposes a grid that
distinguishes between allusions to a particular text, either verbal or non-verbal, and the
use of OT vocabulary.

as well. Clearly the number of allusions to canonical books varies according to each author's criteria for identifying them.[15] Several comprehensive studies of allusions that have been conducted in the past guided the selection of cases for this study.[16]

2.1.1. Dt. 33 in Heb. 2:1-5

The first paraenetic section of the epistle contains two unusual allusions to the ministry of the angels. The first one in 2:2 pertains to the Author's understanding of the role of the angels in the Sinaitic revelatory act and the second one in 2:5 refers to angelic dominion over the world.

2.1.1.1. Heb. 2:2 εἰ γὰρ ὁ δι' ἀγγέλων λαληθεὶς λόγος ἐγένετο βέβαιος

In the first case, allusion is made to the giving of the law, and the Author's words ὁ δι' ἀγγέλων λαληθεὶς λόγος could be no more than a reference to a tradition attested elsewhere in contemporary literature. The importance of angelic mediation for the argument in Heb. 2:1-4 needs no defence, as the very essence of the Author's injunction depends on it. With the aid of a common Jewish form of argumentation, *a minori ad maius*, the Author draws attention to the overwhelming responsibility of the New Covenant believers to abide by the message proclaimed. Their responsibility surpasses even that of the Israelites after receiving the law at Sinai because it is determined by the special quality of God's speech in the last days. Unlike at Sinai, when angels mediated the giving of the law, this time the message was not only attested in the midst of unquestionable evidence of the Spirit's activity and power (Heb. 2:3-4), but it was delivered by the Lord himself, the messenger and apostle of God *par excellence* (cf. vv. 1:1-2, 3:1). Essentially, the Author argues that different degrees of responsibility correspond with different degrees of privilege. Therefore it is to be expected that the punishment for not considering the final Word from God will be more severe than that which befell the desert generation.

While the Author's allusion to the mediation of the angels could rest on the Jewish tradition, an alternative explanation is also plausible, especially for an author who consistently tries to substantiate his ideas by appealing to the Scriptures. The text of Dt. 33:2, particularly due to its divergence from the Hebrew text, could prove such a scriptural passage, which supports the Author's idea. Dt. 33:2 is part of the Song of Moses, and the distinct way in which the verse in the Greek translation speaks of the giving of the law might have caught the attention of the Author.

---

[15] Longenecker identifies fifty-five "clear Old Testament allusions" (*Exegesis* 166), while Spicq lists sixty-five "citations virtuelles" (*Hébreux* i: 332 f.).

[16] *Inter alios*, Ellingworth, "Old Testament".

Dt. 33:2 MT	Dt. 33:2 LXX	Heb. 2:2 NTG
יְהוָה מִסִּינַי בָּא	κύριος ἐκ Σινα ἥκει	
וְזָרַח מִשֵּׂעִיר	καὶ ἐπέφανεν ἐκ Σηιρ	
לָמוֹ הוֹפִיעַ	ἡμῖν καὶ κατέσπευσεν	
מֵהַר פָּארָן	ἐξ ὄρους Φαραν	
וְאָתָה מֵרִבְבֹת קֹדֶשׁ	σὺν μυριάσιν Καδης	
מִימִינוֹ (אֵשְׁדָּת)	ἐκ δεξιῶν αὐτοῦ	εἰ γὰρ
[אֵשׁ] [דָּת] לָמוֹ׃	ἄγγελοι μετ' αὐτοῦ	ὁ δι' ἀγγέλων λαληθεὶς λόγος ἐγένετο βέβαιος

The Greek text of Dt. 33:2 differs from the Hebrew text in three places. First, the 3rd pl. לָמוֹ is rendered as a 1st pl. ἡμῖν, which aided by the equivalence ἐπέφανεν for וְזָרַח, makes the text more adaptable to a Christian reading.[17] Second, the phrase וְאָתָה מֵרִבְבֹת קֹדֶשׁ is translated as σὺν μυριάσιν Καδης, with the meaning not of God descending "from his holy assembly", as the Masoretic text reads, but of his descending together "with his holy ones", a possible reading of an otherwise unintelligible Greek syntagm.[18] The Greek translation of the next stich upholds this meaning by supplying the parallel line ἐκ δεξιῶν αὐτοῦ ἄγγελοι μετ' αὐτοῦ, which renders מִימִינוֹ אֵשְׁדָּת לָמוֹ, a "completely opaque" Hebrew text.[19]

The idea of angelic mediation in the giving of the law is present in other Jewish streams such as *Jubilees* (1:27, 29, 2:1 etc.) and Josephus (*Ant.* 15.5.3), as well as in some rabbinical traditions.[20] Closer yet to the background of the Author, two other NT authors mention it in no ambiguous terms, Stephen's speech in Acts 7:38, 53 and Paul in Gal. 3:19. With such wide contemporary attestation, this tradition and not the Greek text of Dt. 33:2 could well have served as the source for the Author's remark, although probably an either-or explanation is unnecessary. It is more reasonable to contend that someone keen to uphold his argument with Scriptures would seek support from those same Scriptures for contemporary traditions as well. The Greek text of Dt. 33:2, an oblique depiction of the angelic mediation in the law giving fits well in the

---

[17] C. Dogniez and M. Harl, *Le Deutéronome*, ed. M. Harl, vol. 5, *La Bible d'Alexandrie. Traduction et annotation de la Septante* (Paris: Éditions du Cerf, 1992) 343.

[18] Wevers, *Deuteronomy* 539.

[19] Wevers, *Deuteronomy* 540.

[20] Attridge, *Hebrews* 65; Lane, *Hebrews* 38.

category of texts that either directly or indirectly contributed to the Author's argument for the responsibility of obedience to the divine Word.

2.1.1.2. *Heb. 2:5* οὐ γὰρ ἀγγέλοις ὑπέταξεν τὴν οἰκουμένην τὴν μέλλουσαν

The second allusion involving the angelic beings is similarly traceable to an OT text where the Greek textual tradition differs from its parent Hebrew text. The Author's treatment of the allusion fits more comfortably with the Greek textual tradition, contributing to the case for a specific Septuagintal influence.

The opening statement in Heb. 2:5, οὐ γὰρ ἀγγέλοις ὑπέταξεν τὴν οἰκουμένην τὴν μέλλουσαν, similar in form and function to the one in 2:16, οὐ γὰρ δήπου ἀγγέλων ἐπιλαμβάνεται, sets the stage for the quotation from Ps. 8. It affirms that the world to come was not placed under subjection to the angels, with two obvious implications. First, if not the angels, then whom? The identity of that being is revealed with rhetorical skill in an exploration of Ps. 8, from which the Author quotes at this junction. It is only in 2:9 that the Author reveals that the world to come is subjected to humankind, through the mediation of their arch-representative Jesus. The second implication, just as important as the first, is that the dominion under subjection is not the world to come but the present world. The concept of angelic dominion over people, nations, and historical events was an idea that acquired wide attestation in Jewish literature (Dan. 10:13, Sir. 17:17, *Jub.* 15:31). A major scriptural support for this idea is offered by the peculiar translation in Dt. 32:8 LXX, a verse that belongs to the Song of Moses (Dt. 32), a text that has already supplied one quotation in the catena in Heb. 1:5-13. Textually, Dt. 32:8 and Heb. 2:5 share only the noun ἀγγέλος (ἀγγέλων / ἀγγέλοις), which is, however, the announced subject in Heb. 1:4 and one of the key catchwords in this section.

Dt. 32:8 MT	Dt. 32:8 LXX	Heb. 2:5 NTG
בְּהַנְחֵל	ὅτε διεμέριζεν	
עֶלְיוֹן גּוֹיִם	ὁ ὕψιστος ἔθνη	
בְּהַפְרִידוֹ בְּנֵי אָדָם	ὡς διέσπειρεν υἱοὺς Αδαμ	
יַצֵּב גְּבֻלֹת עַמִּים	ἔστησεν ὅρια ἐθνῶν	οὐ γὰρ ἀγγέλοις ὑπέταξεν
לְמִסְפַּר	κατὰ ἀριθμὸν	τὴν οἰκουμένην
בְּנֵי יִשְׂרָאֵל:	ἀγγέλων θεοῦ	τὴν μέλλουσαν

The Hebrew text describes the time when God set the boundaries for the nations, עַמִּים גְּבֻלֹת יַצֵּב, specifying that it was done "according to the number of the sons of Israel", יִשְׂרָאֵל בְּנֵי לְמִסְפַּר. While the Greek text translates appropriately the first phrase as ἔστησεν ὅρια ἐθνῶν, it construes the Hebrew phrase יִשְׂרָאֵל בְּנֵי as ἀγγέλων θεοῦ. The meaning of the Greek text is that "the Most High divided up the nations in such a way that each one had a divine protector".[21] While the textual history of this verse is rather complex,[22] it is reasonable to assume that the Author's *Vorlage* had the above reading, which supports better than its Hebrew counterpart the Author's inference on the present world's subjection to the angels.

2.1.2. Num. 14 in Heb. 3: 11-17

One of the longest treatments of a quotation in the epistle, the exposition of Ps. 94 [95 MT] in Heb. 3:12-19, offers a further example of the Author's use of scriptural allusions, in particular, allusions to events from the history of Israel.[23] The quotation from Ps. 94, its exposition and application to the readers' situation constitute the second warning passage in the epistle. The threefold use of the inclusio following the text of the quotation, ἀπιστία in vv. 3:12 and 19, εἰσελθεῖν εἰς τὴν κατάπαυσιν in vv. 4:1 and 5, and ἀπείθεια in vv. 4:6 and 11, provides a convenient way to divide the passage into three paragraphs.

The main thrust of this second warning passage is the call to faithfulness as inspired by the faithfulness of Moses and Christ. If heeded, the warning would prevent the readers from repeating the disastrous experience of the desert generation that failed to enter into God's rest (4:11); if not heeded, the only prospect is a life of faithlessness (3:12, 4:2) and apostasy (3:12). The frequent use of words from the semantic domains of faith (3:12, 19, 4:2, 3) and obedience (3:18, 4:6, 11) leads one to believe that the Author considers the desert generation essentially guilty of two sins, i.e., disobedience and lack of faith, the cardinal sins which were the very root of Israel's rebellion, παραπικραίνειν (3:16).[24]

---

[21] Wevers, *Deuteronomy* 513.

[22] Notable among the Greek manuscript variants is 848 which reads υἱῶν instead of ἀγγέλων, and the Hebrew text attested at Qumran reads אל בני; cf. Wevers, *Deuteronomy* 513. *La Bible d'Alexandrie* suggests a slightly different interpretation of the evidence and retains the reading of Dt. 32:8d "selon le nombre des fils de Dieu", Dogniez and Harl, *Le Deutéronome* 326.

[23] France, "Writer"; Judith H. Wray, *Rest as a Theological Metaphor in the Epistle to the Hebrews and the Gospel of Truth. Early Christian Homiletics of Rest* (SBL-DS 166; Atlanta: Scholars Press, 1997).

[24] Scot McKnight, "The Warning Passages of Hebrews: A Formal Analysis and Theological Considerations", *Trinity Journal* 13, no. 1 (1992) 25 ff.

Although all three paragraphs are infused with OT allusions from the Pentateuch, the first one, 3:12-19, a summary of a particular event recorded in Numbers 14, is the most fruitful for tracing scriptural allusions and possible Septuagintal influences. Most studies acknowledge the extensive parallels between the two passages.[25] The warning against καρδία πονηρά (3:12), characterised by ἀπιστία, echoes the description of the desert generation, ἡ συναγωγὴ ἡ πονηρά (Num. 14:27), and its characteristic unbelief, οὐ πιστεύουσίν μοι (Num. 14:11). Furthermore, the sin of apostasy from the living God, ἐν τῷ ἀποστῆναι ἀπὸ θεοῦ ζῶντος (3:12), echoes the Israelites' apostasy from God, ἀπὸ τοῦ κυρίου μὴ ἀποστάται γίνεσθε (Num. 14:9), the God who describes himself as ζῶ ἐγὼ καὶ ζῶν τὸ ὄνομά μου (Num. 14:21). Similarly key points in the Num. 14 episode, the forty years, the sin of the people, God's anger and subsequent oath, and dying in the wilderness as punishment are included in the Author's summary in 3:12-19.

The parallels between Heb. 3 and Num. 14 extend to the wider context of the two passages as well, supplying further evidence that the Author alludes to passages of Scripture with full knowledge of their original context. The episode of the spying expedition into Canaan and its consequences is preceded by Num. 12, from which the quotations in Heb. 3:2 and 3:5 derive. It is also followed by a discussion of the wilful sin in Num. 15:22 ff. and the Korait revolt in Num. 16, both themes being frequently alluded to in Hebrews, especially in ch. 10.[26] Moreover, as Gleason points out, the Author's depiction of the Christian experience of the readers in 6:4 ff. is more properly understood when read in light of the history of the desert generation.[27]

The particular ways in which the reading of Num. 14, based on a Greek and not a Hebrew text, might have coloured the Author's reading of the events can be traced by comparing the Hebrew text with its translation and exploring the differences. The LXX translation of Num. 14 is quite literal, with notable divergences in vv. 9, 23, 43, and 45. Verse 43 provides the most relevant example for locating the distinctive contribution of the LXX to the Author's allusions from this portion of Scripture.

---

[25] For a complete list of textual parallels, see Hofius, *Katapausis* 117-37 and Ellingworth, "Old Testament" 110.

[26] Ellingworth, "Old Testament" 111.

[27] Gleason writes, "the four characteristics described in 6:4-5 unite the spiritual condition of the readers with that of the Exodus generation" ("Warning" 57 ff.). Each of the four participles is a direct parallel for the LXX description of the desert generation.

Num. 14:43 MT	Num. 14:43 LXX	Heb. 3:18, 4:6, 11 NTG
כִּי הָעֲמָלֵקִי	ὅτι ὁ Αμαληκ	
וְהַכְּנַעֲנִי	καὶ ὁ Χαναναῖος	
שָׁם לִפְנֵיכֶם	ἐκεῖ ἔμπροσθεν ὑμῶν	
וּנְפַלְתֶּם בֶּחָרֶב	καὶ πεσεῖσθε μαχαίρᾳ	
כִּי־עַל־כֵּן שַׁבְתֶּם	οὗ εἵνεκεν ἀπεστράφητε	
מֵאַחֲרֵי יְהוָה	ἀπειθοῦντες κυρίῳ	3:18 τοῖς ἀπειθήσασιν
וְלֹא־יִהְיֶה יְהוָה	καὶ οὐκ ἔσται κύριος	4:6 δι' ἀπείθειαν
עִמָּכֶם:	ἐν ὑμῖν	4:11 τῆς ἀπειθείας

The most notable factor is the presence of the participle ἀπειθοῦντες supplied in the Greek text without a direct correspondent in the Hebrew text. One of three explanations is possible, either the translators had a different *Vorlage*, or they decided to paraphrase and not translate the text,[28] or the prepositional noun מֵאַחֲרֵי was read as a derivative of the Hebrew root מרה, usually translated by the verb ἀπειθεῖν.[29] The Greek translation of this verse, especially its use of the verb ἀπειθεῖν, is significant for understanding the way in which the Author read Num. 14. As suggested by both the frequency with which the verb is used (Heb. 3:18, 4:6, 11) and the concluding remark in 4:11, ἀπειθεῖν was chosen by the Author to describe most accurately the desert generation from a theological perspective.[30]

The allusions in Heb. 3, 4 are restricted neither to Num. 14 nor to the use of the verb ἀπειθεῖν. Other OT passages that recount this event (Dt. chs. 1, 16, Ps. 105 [106 MT]) as well as other terms from Num. 14, such as εἰσακούειν, informed the Author's reading of the event.[31] But while it is reasonable to contend that the overall understanding of this event is independent of the language of the Author's Scripture, some of the specific nuances, especially the Author's selection of ἀπείθεια and ἀπειθεῖν as a prominent theme in Num. 14, can be traced directly to the textual tradition of the Septuagint.

---

[28] Wevers, *Numbers* 234.

[29] Dt. 1:26, 9:7, 23, and 24.

[30] A similar phenomenon can be noted in the translation of Dt. 1:26; see also *infra* (ch. 5, 3).

[31] See Hofius, *Katapausis* 117 ff.

2.1.3. Num. 24:6 in Heb. 8:1-5

In the margin of Heb. 8:2, Nestle-Aland (27th ed.) directs the reader to Num. 24:6 as a possible source for the allusion to the heavenly tabernacle, ἣν ἔπηξεν ὁ κύριος οὐκ ἄνθρωπος. With this statement the Author makes the first explicit reference to a different tabernacle, the true tabernacle where the λειτουργός is Christ. The relation between this tabernacle and the earthly one, described throughout the epistle in terms such as ὑπόδειγμα, σκιά, or ἀντίτυπος (8:5, 9:23, 24), receives a fuller development in the central part of the epistle, in which the Author explores the High Priestly ministry of Christ. If Heb. 8:2 is a case of a biblical allusion from Num. 24:6 due to similarity of language, this could have happened only as a result of the Author's reading the Greek text and not the Hebrew.

Num. 24:6 MT	Num. 24:6 LXX	Heb. 8:2 NTG
כִּנְחָלִים נִטָּיוּ	ὡσεὶ νάπαι σκιάζουσαι	
כְּגַנֹּת	καὶ ὡσεὶ παράδεισοι	
עֲלֵי נָהָר	ἐπὶ ποταμῶν	λειτουργὸς ...
כַּאֲהָלִים	καὶ ὡσεὶ σκηναί	τῆς σκηνῆς τῆς ἀληθινῆς
נָטַע יְהוָה	ἃς ἔπηξεν κύριος	ἣν ἔπηξεν ὁ κύριος
כַּאֲרָזִים עֲלֵי־מָיִם:	ὡσεὶ κέδροι παρ' ὕδατα	οὐκ ἄνθρωπος

Num. 24:6 is part of Balaam's prophetic oracle uttered from the summit of Peor (Num. 23:28) in full view of Israel's camp (Num. 24:2). In this oracle "Israel's tents are compared among other things for their beauty with σκηναί ἃς ἔπηξεν κύριος".[32] The Greek translation of Num. 24:6 follows literally the Hebrew text except for the third comparison; the "tents pitched by the Lord" translates the Hebrew כַּאֲהָלִים נָטַע יְהוָה as "aloes planted by the Lord". The two different meanings are a result of the two readings of the consonantal text, כַּאֲהָלִים read by the *BHS* and the Targum, and כַּאֲהָלִים as read by the translators of the LXX, Syriac, and Vulgate.[33] It is generally agreed that the translation of the passage also displays elements of exegesis and not merely translation.[34] With this particular

---

[32] Ellingworth, *Hebrews* 402.

[33] Geza Vermes, *Scripture and Tradition in Judaism. Haggadic Studies* (Leiden: E. J. Brill, 1961) 158.

[34] Vermes, *Scripture* 157; cf. also Wevers, *Deuteronomy* 404.

rendering, the Septuagint text stands as the most plausible source for the language and thought behind the Author's allusion in Heb. 8:2.[35]

It must be noted that the Heb. 8:2 allusion to the heavenly tent, though plausibly based on Num. 24:6, is supported by other OT texts as well. Ellingworth draws attention to two passages in Isaiah, 42:5 κύριος ὁ θεὸς ὁ ποιήσας τὸν οὐρανὸν καὶ πήξας αὐτόν and 40:22 ὁ στήσας ὡς καμάραν τὸν οὐρανὸν καὶ διατείνας ὡς σκηνὴν κατοικεῖν as being instrumental in the way in which "the wider reference in Hebrews to the creation of a heavenly σκηνή is anticipated in the LXX".[36] Similarly, the motif of God's pitching a tent in the heavens is used in other psalms, such as Ps. 18:5 [19:5 MT], where the unusual translation of the preposition and the pronominal suffix, ἐν τῷ ἡλίῳ ἔθετο τὸ σκήνωμα αὐτοῦ for לַשֶּׁמֶשׁ שָׂם־אֹהֶל בָּהֶם, results in associating God, and not the sun, with the tent. The Targumic tradition elaborates on the themes of scribes, schools of law, and Israel's privileges, but only Targum Neofiti 1 possibly comes close to the imagery in the LXX, in interpreting the Hebrew text as indicative of the "heavens which God has spread out as the house of the Shekinah".[37]

The larger context in which this allusion must be read is the prominent tradition in early Judaism which refers to the heavenly City and Temple as the patterns in whose image the correspondent realities on Earth were modelled. This tradition is supported by many ancient texts such as Ex. 25:9, 40 (v. 40 quoted in Heb. 8:5), and 1 Ch. 28:11 f., possibly even more suggestive in their Greek forms, and is reiterated in the corpus of extra-canonical writings (Wis. 9:8, *inter alia*). Doubtless, a measure of Platonic influence cannot be denied,[38] even though its extent has been vigorously

---

[35] Given the poetic and metaphorical language of the oracle, the shift from a plural form in Numbers to a singular in Hebrews is unimportant, since, according to Ellingworth (*Hebrews* 402), the emphasis is on God's act of setting up the tent / tents.

[36] Ellingworth, *Hebrews* 402.

[37] The Targum Pseudo-Jonathan reads "as gardens planted by the river torrents", M. McNamara and E. G. Clarke, *The Targum Neofiti 1: Numbers; and Pseudo-Jonathan: Numbers*, vol. 4, *The Aramaic Bible. The Targums* (Edinburgh: T. & T. Clark, 1995) 259.

The Targum Neofiti 1 reads "like gardens planted beside sources of water", McNamara and Clarke, *The Targum Neofiti 1: Numbers; and Pseudo-Jonathan: Numbers* 137.

The Targum Onqelos has a different reading "like aromatics which the Lord has planted, like cedars that were planted by the waters", B. Grossfeld, *The Targum Onqelos to Leviticus and The Targum Onqelos to Numbers*, vol. 8, *The Aramaic Bible. The Targums* (Edinburgh: T. & T. Clark, 1988) 136.

[38] Robert P. Gordon, "Better Promises: Two Passages in Hebrews against the Background of the Old Testament Cultus", in *Templum Amicitiae. Essays on the Second Temple Presented to Ernst Bammel*, ed. William Horbury (JSNT-SS 48; Sheffield: Sheffield Academic Press, 1991) 448.

challenged by Williamson and Hurst.[39] The key factor in the debate, i.e., the correct way to construe the epistle's use of the terms ὑπόδειγμα, σκιά, and ἀντίτυπος, will continue to preoccupy scholarship. While the Philonic background was for a while the undisputed framework for understanding the Author's terminology, the Jewish apocalyptic background seems to offer a better perspective on the Author's thought, as Barrett concludes "the heavenly Tabernacle in Hebrews is not the product of Platonic idealism, but the eschatological temple of apocalyptic Judaism, the temple which is in heaven primarily in order that it may be manifested on earth".[40]

It is difficult to establish with certainty whether the ideas in Heb. 8:2-5 about the heavenly tabernacle and its relation to the earthly one are the result of the Author's dependency on contemporary traditions or of his direct engagement with the Greek Scriptures, which themselves may have either mirrored or generated those traditions. The fact that Heb. 8:2 is imbedded in a paragraph that opens with a clear allusion to Ps. 109 [110 MT], and ends with a quotation from Ex. 25:40, increases the probability that 8:2 was also intended as a scriptural allusion. In this case, the Author's allusive language and thought is supported by the particular form of the Num. 24:6 LXX and not its Hebrew equivalent.

2.1.4. Ex. 25-30 in Heb. 9:1-5

The description of the tabernacle and its contents in Heb. 9:1-5 poses some of the more difficult exegetical issues in the epistle as far as scriptural allusions are concerned, since there are several instances in which the Author diverges from the Hebrew OT account. Attention will be directed to four examples, selected primarily for their importance in evaluating whether or not the Author's dependence on the LXX account of the tabernacle can explain the epistle's peculiar depiction of several cultic elements.[41]

---

[39] Hurst, *Background*; R. Williamson, *Philo and the Epistle to the Hebrews* (Leiden: E. J. Brill, 1970).

[40] C. K. Barrett, "The Eschatology of the Epistle to the Hebrews", in *The Background of the New Testament and Its Eschatology. In Honour of Charles Harold Dodd*, eds. W. D. Davies and D. Daube (Cambridge: Cambridge University Press, 1956) 389.

[41] The following textual variants are directly relevant for the present argument. In 9:2, following the listing of the lamp, the table and the showbread, B sa^mss insert και το χρυσον θυμιατηριον a reading that, consequently, is absent from 9:4. As the less difficult reading, it is almost certain that this insertion was intended to align the text of the epistle with the Exodus account by locating the incense altar in the Holy Place and not in the Holy of Holies (Ex. 30:6 f.); cf. Bruce M. Metzger, *Textual Commentary on the Greek New Testament* (London: UBS, 1971) 667. A more complex text critical issue revolves around the name given to the parts of the tabernacle mentioned in vv. 2 and 3. In v. 2 the variants include the feminine singular ἀγία in 365 629 *al* b, the neutral plural τα αγια in B, the collocation αγια αγιων in 𝔓^46 A D* vg^ms, and the reading

2.1.4.1. The Tabernacle Accounts in LXX and Hebrews

The epistle's divergence from the tabernacle account based on the Masoretic text involves the tabernacle's cultic items and their position. The more notable are the specific mention of a "second" curtain, τὸ δεύτερον καταπέτασμα (9:3), the designation and the position of the incense altar, χρυσοῦν θυμιατήριον (9:4), the placing of the manna pot and Aaron's rod in the ark of the covenant, ἐν ᾗ στάμνος χρυσῆ ἔχουσα τὸ μάννα καὶ ἡ ῥάβδος 'Ααρὼν ἡ βλαστήσασα (9:4), and the golden manna pot, στάμνος χρυσῆ (9:4). Each case will be considered separately.

At the outset it is appropriate to acknowledge that the tabernacle account in Exodus in the Hebrew tradition represented by the MT differs considerably from the one in the Greek tradition. The ongoing discussion seems to oscillate between two representative positions formulated by Gooding and Aejmelaeus. Gooding regards the two accounts of the tabernacle in the LXX Exodus as the work of one translator, and contends that the considerable differences between the accounts, i.e., omissions, mistranslation and additions, especially in the second section, are the result of liberties taken in the process of translation.[42] At the other end of the spectrum, Aejmelaeus charges Gooding with assuming too much regarding the large scale editorial activity in the Greek text and suggests that more serious attention needs to be paid to the "possibility of a different Hebrew *Vorlage*".[43]

The tabernacle account consists of two major sections, the first one covering Ex. 25-31, the giving of the instructions ending with the call of Bezalel and Oholiab, and the second, Ex. 36-40, repeating much of the material in the first section, narrates the accomplishment of the project.

---

adopted by the Nestle-Aland text, αγια in 𝔐 ℵ D² P I. Conversely, the attested readings in v. 3 are αγια αγιων in ℵ* A D* I^vid 𝔐, with the two further variations τα αγια των αγιων in ℵ² B D¹ K L 1241 *al* and αγια των αγιων in P 1739 *pc*, and ανα (*sic*) in 𝔓⁴⁶. Although Attridge (*Hebrews* 65) defends the reading of 𝔓⁴⁶ on grounds of *lectio difficilior*, the present analysis follows the decision of most commentators who opt for the reading of the Majority text, cf. *inter alios*, Bruce, *Hebrews*; Buchanan, *Hebrews*; Grässer, *An die Hebräer*; Lane, *Hebrews*; Spicq, *Hébreux*; Weiss, *An die Hebräer*.

[42] David W. Gooding, *The Account of the Tabernacle. Translation and Textual Problems of the Greek Exodus* (Cambridge: Cambridge University Press, 1959) 99 f.

[43] Anneli Aejmalaeus, "Septuagintal Translation Techniques – A Solution to the Problem of the Tabernacle Account", in *Septuagint, Scrolls and Cognate Writings*, eds. George J. Brooke and Barnabas Lindars (SBL-SCS 33; Atlanta: Scholars Press, 1992) 387.

Whereas in the first part the LXX follows closely the Hebrew text,[44] in the second section one finds numerous divergences not only from the sequence of the items in the first section,[45] but also between the two textual traditions.[46] For this study attention is given to the LXX account itself in order to assess the above-mentioned discrepancies within the context of this textual tradition.

2.1.4.2. The Golden Pot of Manna

On the list of the cultic items pertaining to the ἅγιον κοσμικόν the Author explicitly mentions a golden pot of manna, a reference that cannot be traced to any Hebrew text.

Ex. 16:33 MT	Ex. 16:33 LXX	Heb. 9:4 NTG
וַיֹּאמֶר מֹשֶׁה	καὶ εἶπεν Μωυσῆς	
אֶל־אַהֲרֹן	πρὸς Ααρων	
קַח	λαβὲ	ἐν ᾗ
צִנְצֶנֶת אַחַת	στάμνον χρυσοῦν ἕνα	στάμνος χρυσῆ
וְתֶן־שָׁמָּה	καὶ ἔμβαλε εἰς αὐτὸν	
מְלֹא־הָעֹמֶר מָן	πλῆρες τὸ γομορ τοῦ μαν	ἔχουσα τὸ μάννα
וְהַנַּח אֹתוֹ	καὶ ἀποθήσεις αὐτὸ	
לִפְנֵי יְהוָה	ἐναντίον τοῦ θεοῦ	
לְמִשְׁמָרֶת	εἰς διατήρησιν	
לְדֹרֹתֵיכֶם:	εἰς τὰς γενεὰς ὑμῶν	

The Hebrew hapax-logomenon צִנְצֶנֶת is translated as στάμνον to which the adjective χρυσοῦν is appended. Although the adjective has generated different textual traditions because of the ambiguity of its gender,[47] it is nevertheless attested in all Greek manuscripts. Yet, the Hebrew text

---

[44] The furniture in ch. 25; curtains, frames and pillars in ch. 26; altar of burnt offering, court in ch. 27; vestments of priest in ch. 28 and their ordination in ch. 29; altar of incense, laver and the anointing oil in ch. 30.

[45] The change of order is in both accounts; for the MT: tabernacle, furniture, court, and vestments, for the LXX: vestment, tabernacle, court, and furniture.

[46] The LXX notably has a much briefer account of the making of the tabernacle in ch. 36, neglects the altar of incense in ch. 37 (mentioned though in ch. 40) and omits several other details. Moreover, the Septuagint supplies unsuitable equivalents for different structural items, makes occasional contradictory statements, and expands the text with midrash-type additions in the section describing the metal work. For a thorough presentation of the details, both Gooding (*Tabernacle*, especially 99 f.) and Aejmalaeus ("Tabernacle", especially 387) are indispensable.

[47] Göttingen Septuagint lists four such traditions, cf. Wevers, *Exodus* 260.

makes no explicit mention about the material from which the pot was to be manufactured. Wevers contends that it "seems to be a free invention of [the LXX] Exod, possibly in view of the gold of so many of the tabernacle utensils, and cf. also the use of gold for the ark itself 38:1-8".[48] Josephus makes no explicit mention as to where the manna pot was to be preserved, but Philo refers to it in similar terms, τὸ μνημεῖον ἐν στάμνῳ χρυσῷ (*Congr.* 100). The epistle's depiction of the manna pot as στάμνος χρυσῆ is most probably a consequence of following the Septuagintal tradition, whose addition is not supported in any Hebrew textual traditions.

2.1.4.3. *The Second Curtain*

Most commentators remark that the OT account does not explicitly refer to a "second" curtain, hence the epistle's language seems novel. The account of the curtains is given in Ex. 26:31-37, where reference is made to the κατάπέτασμα (v. 31), corresponding to the Hebrew פָּרֹכֶת which was to separate the Holy and the Holy of Holies (v. 33), and to the ἐπίσπαστρον (v. 36), corresponding to the Hebrew מָסָךְ, the screen used as the door of the tent. The Author's explicit mention of the second curtain, implying the presence of a first curtain, is interpreted in a number of ways by commentators. Bruce, for example, observes that the Author's specific terminology is reflected also in the Rabbinic literature,[49] whereas Buchanan correlates it with archaeological data.[50] Ellingworth draws attention to the idiom ἀνὰ μέσον τοῦ ἁγίου καὶ ἀνὰ μέσον τοῦ ἁγίου τῶν ἁγίων in v. 33, which might have been read as a reference to a double curtain.[51] Philo refers to the tabernacle's veils, reserving the κατάπέτασμα for the inner veil dividing the Holy and the Most Holy place, and κάλυμμα for the outer covering (*Vit. Mos.* 2. 101). Likewise, Josephus mentions that the tabernacle was veiled, κατεπετάνυσαν δὲ τήν σκηνήν, and describes the two veils as τό πρῶτον, and τό ἕτερον (*Ant.* 3. 125-127).

The explanation for these diverse traditions has to do just as much with the flexibility of language as with the inconsistency with which the Exodus translator refers to the two distinct curtains. He uses κατάπέτασμα to refer both to the curtain separating the Holy of Holies in Ex. 26:31 LXX, and to what should have more properly been ἐπίσπαστρον in v. 37 if he had been consistent with the terminology in v. 36. The degree of synonymity between the two dividers in the tabernacle, not supported by the Hebrew

---

[48] Wevers, *Exodus* 260.
[49] Bruce, *Hebrews* 184, n.14.
[50] Buchanan, *Hebrews* 140 f.
[51] Ellingworth, *Hebrews* 424.

text, but perceptible in the Greek translation, might have led the Author to use this term.[52]

2.1.4.4. The Placement of the Incense Altar

The position of this altar is generally considered to be the most striking anomaly in the epistle's portrayal of the tabernacle, since the Author locates the incense altar in the Holy of Holies, χρυσοῦν ἔχουσα θυμιατήριον καὶ τὴν κιβωτὸν τῆς διαθήκης περικεκαλυμμένην πάντοθεν χρυσίῳ, whereas the Exodus account, as well as other writings contemporary to the Author, such as Philo (*Vit. Mos.* 2, 94-95) and Josephus (*Ant.* 3.139-147, *J. W.* 5. 216-219) place the altar in the Holy place. The departure point in the following discussion is the commentators' general consensus that although the θυμιατήριον usually designates the incense burner, the Author really has in mind the θυσιαστήριον, the incense altar, designated in Ex. 30:1 as θυσιαστήριον θυμιάματος.[53]

The relevant passages are as follows:

Ex. 30:6-7 MT	Ex. 30:6-7 LXX	Heb. 9:4 NTG
וְנָתַתָּה אֹתוֹ לִפְנֵי	καὶ θήσεις αὐτὸ ἀπέναντι	μετὰ δὲ τὸ δεύτερον
הַפָּרֹכֶת	τοῦ καταπετάσματος	καταπέτασμα σκηνὴ ἡ
אֲשֶׁר עַל־אֲרֹן	τοῦ ὄντος ἐπὶ τῆς	λεγομένη "Αγια Ἁγίων
הָעֵדֻת	κιβωτοῦ τῶν μαρτυρίων	χρυσοῦν ἔχουσα
לִפְנֵי הַכַּפֹּרֶת		θυμιατήριον
אֲשֶׁר עַל־הָעֵדֻת		καὶ
אֲשֶׁר אִוָּעֵד לְךָ	ἐν οἷς γνωσθήσομαί σοι	τὴν κιβωτὸν
שָׁמָּה:	ἐκεῖθεν	τῆς διαθήκης
וְהִקְטִיר עָלָיו	καὶ θυμιάσει ἐπ' αὐτοῦ	
אַהֲרֹן	Ααρων	
קְטֹרֶת סַמִּים	θυμίαμα σύνθετον λεπτόν	
בַּבֹּקֶר בַּבֹּקֶר	τὸ πρωὶ πρωί	
בְּהֵיטִיבוֹ	ὅταν ἐπισκευάζῃ	
אֶת־הַנֵּרֹת	τοὺς λύχνους	
יַקְטִירֶנָּה:	θυμιάσει ἐπ' αὐτοῦ	

---

[52] Attridge's different explanation rests on his solution for the text critical issues in vv. 2 and 3 (*Hebrews* 236).

[53] Variant readings for θυσιαστήριον in Ex. 30:1 are τω θυσιαστηριω θυμιατηριον 509, θυμιατηριον αφιον 72, θυμιατηριον 75, and others, which add θυμιατηριον M^mg 376 131^c 127 85-343'. Also significantly, Symmachus and Theodotion translate θυμιατήριον; cf. Wevers, *Exodus* 338.

Ellingworth provides a thorough summary of the proposed solutions, the more probable being, first, a wilful or involuntary lack of precision in the Author's description of the tabernacle, since the primary interest is in the broad picture and not in the details. Second, there is the possibility that the participle ἔχουσα should be construed as an indicator of the altar's function, i.e., "associated with" and not of its location, as in the case of the same verb when used in Heb. 9:2. The third explanation suggests that the placement of the altar is at least a partial result of reading the LXX passage regarding the incense altar.[54]

Three aspects in particular seem to favour this latter explanation. First the preposition ἀπέναντι, "over against", might have been read by the Author to refer not to the outside part of the veil but to the inner part, a reading equally supported by the Greek preposition, but excluded by the more specific Hebrew preposition לִפְנֵי.[55] Second, the translation of the idiomatic Hebrew phrase in Ex. 30:7 MT, בַּבֹּקֶר בַּבֹּקֶר, "daily" or "morning by morning", deserves attention. If the Hebrew text were construed to read "daily", the association of the incense alter with the Most Holy place would be automatically excluded, since the entrance to the Holy of Holies was restricted to one day each year. In the Greek translation, however, the equivalent phrase τὸ πρωὶ πρωί, although literally correct, is ambiguous and can mean either "early" or, in an intensified sense, "very early". The result of this translation choice could have been read then as a temporal reference to the morning of the Day of Atonement, and not to a daily event.[56] Finally, Ellingworth draws attention to the collocation in Ex. 30:10 LXX ἅγιον τῶν ἁγίων ἐστὶν κυρίῳ as another possible reason for the association of the θυμιατήριον with the Most Holy place.[57]

The cumulative effect of these translation equivalents provides a reasonable explanation for the association of the incense altar with the most Holy place as originating from the Author's reading of the Greek account of the tabernacle. The probability of this solution increases even more when one considers that the LXX recounts the instructions regarding the incense altar only once in ch. 30, unlike the text represented by the Masoretic tradition text which reiterates this section in ch. 37:25-29.[58]

---

[54] Ellingworth, *Hebrews* 426 f.

[55] Attridge, *Hebrews* 234.

[56] Attridge, *Hebrews* 235.

[57] Ellingworth, *Hebrews* 426.

[58] Attridge (*Hebrews* 236 ff.) proposes a different explanation, by suggesting that the anomalies in Heb. 9 find a reasonable explanation when read against the background of Numbers, especially the distinction between the Aaronites and Levites maintained throughout the book.

2.1.4.5. The Position of the Manna Pot and Aaron's Rod

The related passages recording the place of the pot and the rod are in Exodus and Numbers. For the manna pot:

Ex. 16:33 MT	Ex. 16:33 LXX	Heb. 9:4 NTG
וַיֹּאמֶר מֹשֶׁה	καὶ εἶπεν Μωυσῆς	
אֶל־אַהֲרֹן קַח	πρὸς Ααρωνλαβὲ	ἐν ᾗ
צִנְצֶנֶת אַחַת	στάμνον χρυσοῦν ἕνα	στάμνος χρυσῆ
וְתֶן־שָׁמָּה	καὶ ἔμβαλε εἰς αὐτὸν	ἔχουσα
מְלֹא־הָעֹמֶר מָן	πλῆρες τὸ γομορ τοῦ μαν	τὸ μάννα
וְהַנַּח אֹתוֹ	καὶ ἀποθήσεις αὐτὸ	
לִפְנֵי יְהוָה	ἐναντίον τοῦ θεοῦ	
לְמִשְׁמָרֶת	εἰς δεατήρησιν	
לְדֹרֹתֵיכֶם:	εἰς τὰς γενεὰς ὑμῶν	

For Aaron's rod there are two relevant passages in the book of Numbers:

Num. 17:25 MT	Num. 17:25 LXX	Heb. 9:4 NTG
וַיֹּאמֶר יְהוָה	καὶ εἶπεν κύριος	
אֶל־מֹשֶׁה הָשֵׁב	πρὸς Μωυσῆν ἀπόθες	
אֶת־מַטֵּה אַהֲרֹן	τὴν ῥάβδον Ααρων	καὶ
לִפְנֵי הָעֵדוּת	ἐνώπιον τῶν μαρτυρίων	ἡ ῥάβδος Ἀαρὼν
לְמִשְׁמֶרֶת לְאוֹת	εἰς διατήρησιν σημεῖον	ἡ βλαστήσασα καὶ
לִבְנֵי־מֶרִי	τοῖς υἱοῖς τῶν ἀνηκόων	αἱ πλάκες τῆς διαθήκης
וּתְכַל	καὶ παυσάσθω	
תְּלוּנֹתָם	ὁ γογγυσμὸς αὐτῶν	
מֵעָלַי	ἀπ' ἐμοῦ	
וְלֹא יָמֻתוּ:	καὶ οὐ μὴ ἀποθάνωσιν	

Num. 17:19 MT	Num. 17:19 LXX	Heb. 9:4 NTG
וְהִנַּחְתָּם	καὶ θήσεις αὐτὰς	καὶ
בְּאֹהֶל	ἐν τῇ σκηνῇ	ἡ ῥάβδος Ἀαρὼν
מוֹעֵד	τοῦ μαρτυρίου	ἡ βλαστήσασα καὶ
לִפְנֵי הָעֵדוּת	κατέναντι τοῦ μαρτυρίου	αἱ πλάκες τῆς διαθήκης
אֲשֶׁר אִוָּעֵד	ἐν οἷς γνωσθήσομαί	
לָכֶם שָׁמָּה:	σοι ἐκεῖ	

The problem of the pot placement is generated by the preposition used in Ex. 16:33, the verse in which Moses instructs Aaron to place the pot לִפְנֵי יְהוָה, having been translated into Greek as ἐναντίον τοῦ θεοῦ. A similar preposition is used in the instructions regarding Aaron's rod and its position relative to "the testimony" in Num. 17:19 MT/LXX, where κατέναντι τοῦ μαρτυρίου translates לִפְנֵי הָעֵדוּת. Likewise in Num. 17:25 MT/LXX, the prepositional phrase ἐνώπιον τῶν μαρτυρίων is rendered as לִפְנֵי הָעֵדוּת. If the preposition is construed in its normal sense, the Hebrews account indeed goes beyond the Exodus and Numbers accounts by placing the pot and the rod into the Ark of the Covenant, ἡ κιβωτὸς τῆς διαθήκης, contrary to what the Hebrew and the Greek texts suggest. The particular placement of the rod and pot can be explained, however, by observing the inconsistency of the Greek translation of the singular הָעֵדוּת, translated as a singular τοῦ μαρτυρίου in v. 19 and as a plural τῶν μαρτυρίων in v. 25. While the noun in its singular form unambiguously refers to the Ark of the Covenant, the plural usually refers to the tablets of the law, τὰ μαρτύρια.[59] This meaning is found in Ex. 25:16, where τὰ μαρτύρια, although translating the singular הָעֵדוּת, clearly refers to the tables of the law. Neither Philo nor Josephus refers explicitly to the position of the manna and Aaron's rod.

The final solution to the alleged discrepancies in Heb. 9 is still to be found. The evidence suggests that the main sources of information were the text of the Greek Bible and the tradition that was common knowledge among Jewish circles, [60] although it is difficult to know the degree to which one source was preferred over the other. The above analysis is an example of how the Author's dependence on the Greek Bible can explain some of the particularities of the epistle.

Doubtless, not all disagreements between the Author and the Hebrew OT account can be resolved by appealing to the Greek Scriptures.[61] The Greek Scriptures, however, must take precedence in resolving such disagreements since the epistle's OT allusions often reflect specific translation equivalencies.

2.2. *Septuagintal Allusions from Extra-Canonical Books*

The inclusion of a number of selected allusions from the extra-canonical books is intended as an adjacent argument for the role that the Septuagint

---

[59] Ellingworth, *Hebrews* 428.

[60] The former position is advocated by Ellingworth (*Hebrews ad loc.*), while the latter by Attridge (*Hebrews ad loc*).

[61] For example, later in the same chapter (9:19 ff.) the Author refers to the inauguration of the Mosaic covenant by introducing elements that are not attested in either Hebrew or Greek texts.

had in the composition of the epistle. The higher esteem that the Author
may have had for the canonical writings should not overshadow the
importance of the extra-canonical writings especially as a source for
different aspects of the epistle, primarily as sources of allusions.

The volume of possible allusions to material from extra-canonical books
is indeed large. In a recent survey, Evans includes more than thirty
allusions and parallels from this corpus, with the books of Ben Sirach,
Wisdom of Solomon and the Maccabees heading the list.[62] An exhaustive
treatment of these allusions, which assesses their role in the epistle, is yet
to be undertaken. The cases selected for analysis in this section, chosen
primarily from the books of Wisdom, Ben Sirach and Maccabees, are
intended to aid the investigation of a possible dependence on the extra-
canonical writings.

It should be mentioned at the outset that the pronounced lexical affinity
between the epistle and the Apocryphal and extra-canonical books
recommends lexicography as a primary area of investigation for such
influences. Williamson draws attention to the extensive lexical overlap
between Hebrews and 1-4 Maccabees,[63] overlap that Ellingworth, in
charting the allusions to these four writings, expanded beyond mere lexical
elements.[64]

2.2.1. Heb. 1:1-4

Since the Apocryphal books of Wisdom of Solomon and Wisdom of Ben
Sirach are both representative of sapiential literature, it is to be expected
that allusions from these writings are most likely to be found in the
sections of the epistle in which language and ideas are similar to the
wisdom literature. The epistle's prologue is one of the clearest examples.

The question of the availability of the Wisdom of Solomon for the
Author can only be briefly addressed here. The date and origin of this
book, most "manifestly Alexandrian in tone and style",[65] can be located in
the first century B.C., and the book's "early and widespread Christian
use",[66] supports an earlier rather than later date, making it quite plausible
that the Author had knowledge of it.

---

[62] Craig A. Evans, *Non Canonical Writings and New Testament Interpretation*
(Peabody: Hendrikson, 1992) 210 ff.

[63] Williamson, *Philo* 15.

[64] Ellingworth, "Old Testament" 332 f.

[65] Henry B. Swete, *Introduction to the Old Testament in Greek*, 2nd ed. (Cambridge:
Cambridge University Press, 1914) 268.

[66] Horbury, "Christian Use" 184.

Heb. 1:1-4 NTG	Wis. LXX
1:2 δι' οὗ καὶ ἐποίησεν τοὺς αἰῶνας 1:3 ὃς ὢν ἀπαύγασμα τῆς δόξης 1:3 ὃς ὢν ἀπαύγασμα τῆς δόξης 1:3 χαρακτὴρ τῆς ὑποστάσεως αὐτοῦ 1:3 τῷ ῥήματι τῆς δυνάμεως αὐτοῦ 1:3 καθαρισμὸν τῶν ἁμαρτιῶν 1:1 ἐκάθισεν ἐν δεξιᾷ τῆς μεγαλωσύνης ἐν ὑψηλοῖς 1:4 τοσούτῳ κρείττων γενόμενος τῶν ἀγγέλων ὅσῳ διαφορώτερον παρ' αὐτοὺς κεκληρονόμηκεν ὄνομα	7:21 ἡ γὰρ πάντων τεχνῖτις 7:26 ἀπαύγασμα ... φωτὸς ἀϊδίου 7:25 ἀπόρροια τῆς ... δόξης 7:26 εἰκὼν τῆς ἀγαθότητος αὐτοῦ 7:26 τῆς τοῦ παντοκράτορος δόξης 7:27 τὰ πάντα καινίζει 9:4 δός μοι τὴν τῶν σῶν θρόνων πάρεδρον σοφίαν 7:29 ἔστιν γὰρ αὕτη εὐπρεπεστέρα ἡλίου καὶ ὑπὲρ πᾶσαν ἄστρων θέσιν φωτὶ συγκρινομένη εὑρίσκεται προτέρα

The parallels between the portrait of wisdom in Wis. 7 and that of the Son in Heb. 1:1-4 are probably the best evidence not only of the Author's familiarity with this apocryphal book, but also of his conscious dependence while sketching the Son's portrait, on its lexical elements and ideas. The distinctive terminology referring to the Son as the Father's ἀπαύγασμα, whether in an active or reflective sense, and as the χαρακτήρ of his nature, as well as his special role in the creation and the redemption of the world, culminating in his privileged and exalted position, are clear echoes of the language and ideas of Wis. 7.[67] Wisdom personified is likewise described in terms of ἀπαύγασμα and εἰκών (Wis. 7:26), and she also participated in the creation of the world ἡ πάντων τεχνῖτις (Wis. 7:21). She contributes to its renewal τὰ πάντα καινίζει (Wis. 7:27), and her elevated position is acknowledged δός μοι τὴν τῶν σῶν θρόνων πάρεδρον σοφίαν (Wis. 9:4).

The portrait of the personified wisdom in Wisdom of Solomon has its antecedents both in the canonical books of Pr. chs. 1, 8, 9 and Job 28, as well as in other extra-canonical writings such as Sir. 24. One Targumic tradition even renders Gen. 1:1, "from the Beginning with wisdom the Memra of the Lord created and perfected the heavens and the earth", associating the time and the manner of Creation.[68] All these writings could potentially have exerted influence on the Author's language and thought in Heb. 1. Some particular nuances in the Wisdom of Solomon more prominent than in any of the other sources listed, favour Wisdom as the

---

[67] Spicq, *Hébreux* i: 49; Williamson, *Philo* 40.

[68] Martin McNamara, *Targum Neofiti 1: Genesis*, vol. 1a, *The Aramaic Bible. The Targums* (Edinburgh: T. & T. Clark, 1992) 52.

prime candidate for the source of the allusions. The most distinctive aspect for Heb. 1:1-4 is the image of wisdom as the primary participant in creation.

While Pr. 8:30 suggests the direct participation of wisdom in creation by the rather difficult word אָמוֹן, "artisan", the Greek translation ἀρμόζουσα, "the one being in harmony with" (LEH), a LXX hapax equivalency, makes that inference less certain. It is quite possible that the Wisdom of Solomon built on Pr. 8:30, and opted for τεχνῖτις as a more proper equivalent for the Hebrew אָמוֹן than ἀρμόζουσα. Notably, the masculine form τεχνῖτις is used for God in Heb. 11:10. The idea of wisdom as an agent in creation reaches its most shaped and unambiguous form in the Wisdom of Solomon. Less prominent, but still worth noting is the possible allusion from Sir. 24:8, 9 where the language of inheritance applied to wisdom might be echoed by the motif of Christ's inheritance in Heb. 1:2, and 4.

The closeness of the language and of these wisdom passages and the Hebrews and other similar NT depictions of Christ,[69] point to the wisdom tradition in Jewish thought as one of the most suitable *loci* to provide the necessary concepts for NT Christology.[70]

The extensive parallels between Heb. 1 and Wis. 7 cannot unequivocally stand as proof of the epistle's literary dependence on either the book of Wisdom or Ben Sirach, yet the extensive vocabulary and conceptual overlap is such that the burden of proof lies on those who exclude the apocryphal books as a source of allusions.

2.2.2. Encomium on Faith

The encomium on faith in Heb. 11 is the section of the epistle that assembles the largest collection of scriptural allusions to both persons and events in the Jewish Scriptures and history. Irrespective of the way this chapter fits within its context, it is sufficiently clear that the Author intended for it to be a self-contained unit, "a well-defined and carefully constructed unit".[71] The repetition of the motif of "faith", first signalled as a catchword in Heb. 10:37-39, as well as the multiple usage of inclusio, ὑπομονῆς γὰρ ἔχετε χρείαν (10:36) and δι᾽ ὑπομονῆς τρέχωμεν τὸν ἀγῶνα (12:1), κομίσησθε τὴν ἐπαγγελίαν (10:36) and οὐκ ἐκομίσαντο τὴν ἐπαγγελίαν (11:39), ἐν ταύτῃ γὰρ ἐμαρτυρήθησαν οἱ πρεσβύτεροι (11:2)

---

[69] John 1, 2 Cor. 4, and Col. 1.

[70] Roland E. Murphy, "The Personification of Wisdom", in *Wisdom in Ancient Israel. Essays in Honour of J. A. Emerton*, eds. John Day, R. P. Gordon, and H. G. M. Williamson (Cambridge: Cambridge University Press, 1995) 232.

[71] Attridge, *Hebrews* 305.

and οὗτοι πάντες μαρτυρηθέντες διὰ τῆς πίστεως (11:39),[72] indicate that the Author intended this section to be either an excursus or a rhetorical device to support the appeal to steadfast faith.

The material selected by the Author consists of a combination of paraphrases, summaries and quotations, derived both from canonical and extra-canonical sources, stringed together on the motif of faith. The debate about the Author's dependence on previously existent lists continues today, but the final answer is immaterial for the argument pursued here, since the primary interest is not in who made it into the list but rather on the Author's distinctive presentation of the heroes of the faith and the way in which the Septuagint has informed his perspective. Since the allusions from the canonical books were discussed earlier, no further mention of them will be made here except the reminder that in some cases the reading of the LXX offers a better explanation of some particularities in the list.[73] The attention will be concentrated on the influence of apocryphal and pseudepigraphic material on the genre and on the content.

2.2.2.1. Literary Genre

As far as the literary genre goes, Heb. 11 resembles the hagiographic writings of antiquity, primarily the *exempla* lists frequently employed by writers contemporary with the Author. Within the Jewish literary milieu, the Apocrypha, more so than any other corpus of writings, including the canonical books, provides the closest literary antecedent for the list of heroes of faith in Hebrews. It is true that the canonical writings are not devoid of summaries of the history of God's covenantal people. On the contrary, the accounts of their salvation history frequently employ such retrospectives.[74] These summaries, however, display a predominant interest in the events and their significance, but not as much in the main characters. Von Rad, commenting on the distinctiveness of Sirach on this matter, contends:

> anyone familiar with the older presentations of history in Israel cannot be sufficiently amazed at the difference in the way in which Sirach looks back into history. The

---

[72] Vanhoye, *Structure* 30.

[73] The Septuagintal text supports better the Author's reference to Enoch (Attridge, *Hebrews* 317). Likewise, the allusion to the involvement of both parents in hiding Moses mirrors the Septuagint text (Ex. 2:2 LXX), since the MT mentions his mother's exclusive involvement; cf. Bruce (*Hebrews* 317) and Marie E. Isaacs, *Sacred Space. An Approach to the Theology of the Epistle to the Hebrews* (JSNT-SS 73; Sheffield: Sheffield Academic Press, 1992) 139. Also noteworthy is the chronologically mixed sequence of the characters listed in Heb. 11:32-34 (Bruce, *Hebrews* 331).

[74] Dt. 1-3, 9, 32, Jos. 24, Ez. 20, Neh. 9, Pss. 78, 89, 105, 106, 135, and 136; Eisenbaum, "Heroes" 21.

concern here is not with the obvious or the hidden examples of God's guidance, nor with his judgements of his decrees of salvation, nor with the relationship of tension between promise and fulfilment, but with great men. ... They ... are the objects of the presentation, even of the praise.[75]

A similar assessment can be made with regard to the lists of *exempla* outside the corpus of Jewish literature. In a recent comparative study of such lists, Eisenbaum argues that the Jewish lists differ significantly from their counterparts in the Greco-Roman literature in almost every aspect from their form, length and structure to their overall philosophy and principles behind the selection of their heroes.[76] When compared with the Apocryphal lists found in Wis. 10, 1 Macc. 2, 4 Macc. 16, 18, and most significantly with Sir. 44-50, the similarities between Heb. 11 and these lists tilt the scales in favour of accepting the Author's dependency on the literary models offered by these apocryphal books. First, as in the apocryphal *exempla*, the heroes are selected from the men and women of the biblical record. Secondly, although Hebrews' selection covers the longest time-span, from creation to the Maccabees, the Apocryphal lists in Wisdom of Solomon, Ben Sirach and 2 Maccabees have compatible time-spans. Finally, the use of "wisdom" as the leit-motif in Wis. 10 might have served the Author by offering a model for a theologically unified perspective on the history of God's people, and thus supplied a literary - theological antecedent for the "faith" anaphora in Hebrews.

2.2.2.2. Content

Since the time line covered by the Author extends beyond the recorded history in the canonical books, the Author inevitably had to make use of information supplied by the extra-canonical books, primarily the books of the Maccabees. Whether the information is derived directly from the written sources or more from the knowledge of heroic traditions in Judaism is difficult to prove. Extensive verbal parallels in the martyrdom of Eleazar and the seven brothers, based on the Maccabees corpus, and the martyrdom of the major Jewish prophets Jeremiah, Isaiah and Ezekiel, based on Pseudepigrapha, favour the former alternative.

2.2.2.3. Maccabeean Martyrdom

The story of the martyrdom of Eleazar, the seven brothers and their mother is recorded in parallels texts in 2 Macc. and 4 Macc. The allusion to this episode in Heb. 11:35b is part of the concluding section in ch. 11 which consists of a series of brief and generic statements (vv. 32-38). With this

---

[75] Gerhard von Rad, *Wisdom in Israel* (London: SCM Press, 1972) 257 f.

[76] Eisenbaum, "Heroes" 74 ff. See also the earlier study by Cosby, *Composition*.

particular allusion the Author departs from history recorded in the canonical books and relies on extra-canonical sources.

The main reason for considering v. 35b as an allusion to the Books of the Maccabees, and not merely an allusion to tradition, is the extensive verbal overlap between the words of the Author and the text that records the story of the Maccabees' martyrs.[77] The three details in Heb. 11:35b about ἄλλοι, the specific form of torture, the martyrs' resolve to refuse any compromises that could have spared their lives and the belief in the resurrection as a reward for the martyrdom, are recorded in the martyrdom of Eleazar, the seven brothers and their mother, who were put to death during the reign of Antiochus Epiphanes on account of their firm opposition to the Hellenization campaign.

Heb. 11:35 NTG	2 Macc. LXX
ἄλλοι δὲ ἐτυμπανίσθησαν	6:19 ἐπὶ τὸ τύμπανον προσῆγεν
	6:28 ἐπὶ τὸ τύμπανον εὐθέως ἦλθεν
οὐ προσδεξάμενοι τὴν ἀπολύτρωσιν	6:22 ἵνα τοῦτο πράξας ἀπολυθῇ τοῦ θανάτου
	6:30 ὅτι δυνάμενος ἀπολυθῆναι τοῦ θανάτου
ἵνα κρείττονος ἀναστάσεως τύχωσιν·	7:9 ὁ δὲ τοῦ κόσμου βασιλεὺς ... εἰς αἰώνιον ἀναβίωσιν ζωῆς ἡμᾶς ἀναστήσει
	7:14 αἱρετὸν μεταλλάσσοντας ὑπ' ἀνθρώπων τὰς ὑπὸ τοῦ θεοῦ προσδοκᾶν ἐλπίδας πάλιν ἀναστήσεσθαι ὑπ' αὐτοῦ σοὶ μὲν γὰρ ἀνάστασις εἰς ζωὴν οὐκ ἔσται

As the description continues in Heb. 11:36, there are further echoes of the martyrdom of the seven brothers and their mother, as described in 2 Maccabees and in 4 Maccabees:

---

[77] The suggestion that 2Macc. 6:18-7:42 is a relatively late interpolation is not sustainable; see William Horbury, "The Cult of Christ and the Cult of the Saints", *New Testament Studies* 44 (1998) 451.

Heb. 11:36 NTG	2 Macc. 7 LXX
ἕτεροι δὲ ἐμπαιγμῶν	v.7 τὸν δεύτερον ἦγον ἐπὶ τὸν ἐμπαιγμόν v.10 ὁ τρίτος ἐνεπαίζετο
μαστίγων πεῖραν ἔλαβον	v.1 μάστιξιν καὶ νευραῖς αἰκιζομένους

Heb. 11:36 NTG	4 Macc. 12:2 LXX
ἔτι δὲ δεσμῶν καὶ φυλακῆς	ὁρῶν ἤδη τὰ δεσμὰ περικείμενα

After the allusion to the martyrdom of Eleazar in 11:35b-36a, it is difficult to trace with any degree of confidence the referents for the terms listed in vv. 37-38, with the possible exception of v. 37, in which most commentators discern allusions to the fate of the three major prophets Jeremiah, Isaiah, and Ezekiel. The tradition according to which the prophet Jeremiah was stoned to death, the prophet Isaiah was sawed in two, and the prophet Ezekiel was put to death by sword can be traced to the Pseudepigrapha. Although literary dependence on pseudepigraphic material for these three cases cannot be proven, it can neither be denied when one evaluates the similarity of vocabulary and content between the epistle and these possible sources.

The stoning ἐλιθάσθησαν in v. 37 parallels the two pseudepigraphic descriptions of the prophet Jeremiah's death in *Vitae Prophetarum* 2:1 Ἰερεμίας ἦν ... λίθοις βληθεὶς ὑπὸ τοῦ λαοῦ ἀποθνήσκει and in *Paralipomena Jeremiae* 9:20 δεῦτε οὖν καὶ ... λίθοις λιθοβολήσωμεν αὐτόν. Similarly, the sawing in two, ἐπρίσθησαν, is paralleled in the recounting of the death of Isaiah both in *Vitae Prophetarum* 1:1, Ἡσαΐας ἀπὸ Ἰερουσαλὴμ θνήσκει ὑπὸ Μανασσῆ πρισθεὶς εἰς δύο, and in the *Ascension of Isaiah* 5:1, 12. An allusion to the death of the prophet Ezekiel in ἐν φόνῳ μαχαίρης ἀπέθανον is more difficult to document, although Wright, following Goodenough, advances a good case in its defence.[78]

---

[78] J. Edward Wright, "Hebrews 11:37 and the Death of the Prophet Ezekiel", in *The Echoes of Many Texts. Reflections on Jewish and Christian Traditions. Essays in Honor of Lou H. Silberman*, eds. William G. Dever and J. Edward Wright (Atlanta: Scholars Press, 1997) 150.

3. Conclusion

The many allusions in Hebrews to OT material are the result of the Author's vast knowledge of the Jewish Scriptures. They are evidence not only of his knowledge of the OT, but also of the versatility with which he draws upon the OT to support the argument at different stages in the epistle. These allusions come from the Scriptures used by the Author, the Septuagint, the canonical and apocryphal books and include numerous references to the history and the religion of the Jewish people.

Since one can only identify allusions, determine their source and assess their function with a lesser degree of certainty than when working with quotations, accordingly it is necessary to draw conclusions with more caution. More needs to be done to develop a methodology with which to distinguish more precisely between cases of parallel language and literary dependence, as well as between dependency on a literary source and on contemporary oral traditions.

The narrow focus of this analysis was to assess the extent to which the Author's use of the Septuagint, as opposed to a Hebrew text, was determinant in the selection and the use of the allusions. It is reasonable to assume that a large number of the allusions are drawn from texts in which the Hebrew and the Greek translations are equivalent and no significant divergence can be discerned. In such a case the Author could have made the same inference if the allusion were drawn from a Hebrew text as if it were based on the Greek text. In other cases, however, there are perceptible differences between the Hebrew text and its translation. An allusion drawn from such a text raises the possibility that the point or points of difference between the Hebrew text and the Greek text determined the selection and use of that allusion. In this case the allusion bears an unequivocal Septuagintal mark, and consequently an identical inference could not have been drawn by the Author had he used a Hebrew text.

A theological perspective on an important passage, a succinct presentation of the cultic instrumentarium, references to some of the heroes in Jewish history, an allusion to an important event that is attested widely in other writings and traditions are all examples which display signs of the Author's engagement with the Septuagint. In each case the Greek text better supports the inferences drawn by the Author than any existent Hebrew text could have done, clearly indicating the Septuagint's role as a formative influence on the epistle's use of allusions.

Chapter Five

Septuagintal Lexical Units and Hebrews

1. Introduction

The Author's rich and eloquent use of the Greek language has long been recognised as unparalleled among NT authors. As Simcox remarked, "[the Author of Hebrews] deals with the biblical language ... as a preacher, whose first duty is to be faithful, but his second to be eloquent".[1] The Author surpasses the literary aptitude of the other NT writers, his language and style being the closest to literary Greek among NT writings. His vocabulary and style, the capacity to elicit a strong rhetorical effect by use of rhythm, rhetorical questions, oratorical imperatives and other literary devices suggest that he was the beneficiary of sound training, which certainly included familiarity with the Classic and Hellenistic writers.[2] Nevertheless, in order to correctly understand the Author's contribution to the NT, one must take into account the fact that the LXX was his primary theological source. Moffatt draws attention to this aspect with the statement, "the whole language of the author is formed on the LXX, not merely his actual quotations from it",[3] an evaluation unchallenged in subsequent scholarship. In view of the Author's dependence on the Septuagint, the area of lexical semantics recommends itself as one area in which distinct LXX influence can be detected. This chapter focuses on the Author's lexicography by analysing selected lexical units with the aim of assessing the relationship between their meaning in the three textual traditions, the Hebrew text, the Septuagint translation and the Epistle to the Hebrews. The difficulties involved in discussing these issues are considerable, not merely because of the intricate and controversial nature of the field of lexical semantics itself, but also because of its

---

[1] Quoted by Moffatt, *Hebrews* lxiv.

[2] Nigel Turner, *Style*, vol. 4, *A Grammar of New Testament Greek* (Edinburgh: T. & T. Clark, 1976) 107.

[3] Moffatt, *Hebrews*.

interconnectedness with other areas of investigation, two of which have direct bearing on the subject.[4]

First, is the fundamental question of the nature of Biblical Greek, whether it is to be considered as Semitic, translation Greek, or Koine. Each position is likely to influence the assessment of the linguistic influence of the Septuagint on the epistle,[5] and while the dispute between opposing positions is far from over,[6] it is possible that they have more in common than it is usually admitted. Silva, who holds this position, took into account several developments in linguistics, especially Saussure's important distinction between *langue* and *parole*. Silva's analysis brings into clearer focus the main deficiencies of previous studies and explains the disagreements between Deissmann and Turner as the result of confounding two distinct levels of linguistic description. Silva concludes, "Deissmann, concerned with grammatical rules (*langue*) insisted rightly that NT Greek cannot be isolated from the Hellenistic form. Turner, who has devoted his efforts to syntactical phenomena – an area of grammar that constantly 'infringes' on stylistics (*parole*) – sees an undeniable distinctiveness in the Biblical language."[7] This observation is important for specifying the influence of the linguistic aspects of the Greek OT on the NT writers. To the often-asked question of where exactly the influence of the Greek OT on the NT writers manifests itself, Silva categorically

---

[4] Silva lists twelve major aspects that have direct implications on the discussion regarding Koine in general, Koine in Alexandria and Koine in Palestine; Moisés Silva, "Semantic Borrowing in the New Testament", *New Testament Studies* 22 (1976) 206 f.

[5] If, on the one hand, with scholars such as Turner and Gehman one considers Biblical Greek to be a special language, in which words, collocations and syntactical structures are distinct from those of non-biblical, contemporary usage, the influence of such a language on the NT will undoubtedly be strong; Nigel Turner, *Christian Words* (Edinburgh: T & T Clark, 1980) and Henry S. Gehman, "The Hebraic Character of Septuagint Greek", in *The Language of the Greek New Testament. Classic Essays*, ed. Stanley E. Porter (JSNT-SS 60; Sheffield: Sheffield Academic Press, 1991). On the other hand, if the Greek biblical language bears an essential continuity with the extra-biblical language, as Deissmann and Moulton maintain, the specific linguistic influence on the NT must be limited and consequently less determinant for the linguistic distinctiveness of the NT; Adolf Deissmann, *Philology of the Greek Bible: Its Present and Future* (London: Hodder and Stoughton, 1908) and J. H. Moulton, *Prolegomena*, vol. 1, *A Grammar of New Testament Greek* (Edinburgh: T. & T. Clark, 1908).

[6] For a helpful historical anthology of several seminal articles on this topic, see Stanley E. Porter, ed., *The Language of the Greek New Testament. Classic Essays* (JSNT-SS 60; Sheffield: Sheffield Academic Press, 1991).

[7] Moisés Silva, "Bilingualism and the Character of Palestinian Greek", in *The Language of the Greek New Testament. Classic Essays*, ed. Stanley E. Porter (JSNT-SS 60; Sheffield: Sheffield Academic Press, 1991) 224.

argues for the *parole*, and not the *langue*, "in idioms, phrases and allusions, not in *linguistic structure* (whether grammatical or lexical)".[8]

The second area with important bearing on the present discussion is that of Greek, especially Septuagintal, lexicography. The area of lexical semantics is almost invariably included among the distinct contributions that the Septuagint has made in NT usage, and it is evident that the fundamental position regarding the nature of Greek lexical stock employed by the LXX and the NT will affect the appraisal of the Septuagint's distinct influence on the NT.[9]

The present study undertakes a more limited approach to determine whether the epistle's use of selected lexical units betrays any distinct Septuagintal influence. In each case analysed there is arguably some measure of semantic divergence between the Hebrew lexeme and its Septuagint equivalent with consequences for the overall meaning of the target text. Furthermore, the semantic divergence is traced in the epistle to determine its possible impact on the Author's usage. The particular

---

[8] Silva, "Bilingualism" 223 f.

[9] Silva, "Borrowing" 109. At the risk of oversimplification, two positions seem to be representative. On the one hand, it is claimed that as the result of the Greek translation of the Hebrew Scriptures, the Hebrew words marked the semantic contours of the Greek equivalent words, which subsequently affected the lexical stock of the NT. Hill, for example, concludes his study on the semantics of soteriological terms by maintaining that many of the theologically loaded words in the NT are used with the sense that reflects not their Greek heritage but rather their Hebraic background. In summing up Paul's understanding of δικαιοσύνη he contends that "Paul so relates its meaning and significance to the work of Christ that, in his hands, δικαιοσύνη has a Christianised content radically different from anything it possessed in Hellenistic thought and usage and linked only with one strand of the Hebraic tradition" (David Hill, *Greek Words and Hebrew Meanings: Studies in the Semantics of Soteriological Terms* [Cambridge: Cambridge University Press, 1967] 300). Hill's conclusion is by no means novel; it agrees with the tradition established by Hermann Cremer, *Biblico-Theological Lexicon of New Testament Greek*, 3rd English ed. (Edinburgh: T. & T. Clark, 1883). It is also similar to the fundamental approach underlying the work of G. Kittel and G. Friedrich, *Theological Dictionary of the New Testament*, 10 vols., (Grand Rapids: Eerdmans, 1964-1976), which, according to Cotterell assumes that the Septuagint and the advent of Christianity "renewed, transformed or even created words" (Peter Cotterell and Max Turner, *Linguistics and Biblical Interpretation* [London: SPCK, 1989] 107). On the other hand is the call for a clearer demarcation between the linguistic study of the biblical languages and the theological implications that can be drawn as result of such an approach. Spear-headed by Barr, who mounted a vigorous attack on the methodology behind the Kittel project and its conclusions, this school of thought is less inclined to accept theological conclusions based solely on the lexical data; James Barr, *The Semantics of Biblical Language* (Oxford: Oxford University Press, 1961). For a helpful dialogue between Barr and his reviewers, see Richard J. Erickson, *James Barr and the Beginnings of Biblical Semantics* (Notre Dame: Foundations Press, 1984) and Francis Watson, *Text and Truth. Redefining Biblical Theology* (Grand Rapids: Eerdmans, 1997).

interest of this present investigation is the meaning shift resulting from the translation process. It is legitimate to expect that the level of synonymity between words in the source language and their equivalents in the receptor language would be affected by translation. It is well known that even within the boundaries of one language perfect synonymity is almost non-existent.[10] Often the connotative spectrum of a word in the source language undergoes a semantic shift in the process of translation, and the connotations of the receptor word, albeit chosen as the most suitable equivalent in the receptor language, matches that spectrum only partially.[11] The shift in meaning is often encountered in instances where the semantic domains of a Hebrew word match only partly those of its Greek equivalent. In such cases the (contextual) meaning of a Greek word, and consequently the inferences drawn from it, are naturally different from that of the Hebrew word. This theoretical possibility deserves to be explored in an epistle such as Hebrews, which relies heavily on the Septuagint for its religious terminology.[12]

The examples selected reflect a variety of statistical characteristics which include the verb ἀφίστημι, used once in the epistle, and the noun διαθήκη which the Author uses more than any other NT author, the seemingly unimportant adverb βραχύ and the theologically charged adjective πιστός. This selection seeks to ensure a typology broad enough to obtain a qualitative appraisal of the phenomenon.

2. Heb. 2:6-8: ἡλάττωσας αὐτὸν βραχύ τι παρ' ἀγγέλους

The adverb βραχύ qualifies man's position in reference to the ἀγγέλους in the quotation from Ps. 8 in Heb. 2:6-8, the first quotation in the epistle to

---

[10] Cotterell and Turner, *Linguistics* 159.

[11] This phenomenon is most evident in the translation of difficult or ambiguous Hebrew words when the Greek translators had either used a loan-word or supplied the word as the result of informed guessing guided either by context, parallelism, etymological considerations or general words Emanuel Tov, "Did the Septuagint Translators always Understand Their Hebrew Text?", in *De Septuaginta*, eds. A. Pietersma and C. Cox (Missiossauga, Ontario: Benben, 1984). Cf. also Barr, *Semantics*.

[12] The Septuagintal linguistic influence on the epistle cannot be limited only to the aspects outlined above, extensive as that influence might be, cf. Moffatt (*Hebrews*), and Williamson (*Philo*). Equally significant are the rare, but not absent Septuagintalisms. Several consecrated syntagmas - ἐπ' ἐσχάτου τῶν ἡμερῶν τούτων, λέγων – or the use of the Semitic genitive, the omission of the article, and other features, must be included in the range of factors that contribute in their own way to the shape of the epistle. For a fuller treatment of the Septuagintalisms in Hebrews see Turner, *Style* 109 f.

be accompanied by a substantial interpretative comment by the Author. The Hebrew text of the Ps. 8:6-7 and its translation are as follows:

Ps. 8:6-7 MT	Ps. 8:6-7 LXX	Heb. 2:7-8 NTG
וַתְּחַסְּרֵהוּ	ἠλάττωσας αὐτὸν	ἠλάττωσας αὐτὸν
מְּעַט	βραχύ τι	βραχύ τι
מֵאֱלֹהִים	παρ' ἀγγέλους	παρ' ἀγγέλους
וְכָבוֹד וְהָדָר	δόξῃ καὶ τιμῇ	δόξῃ καὶ τιμῇ
תְּעַטְּרֵהוּ׃	ἐστεφάνωσας αὐτόν	ἐστεφάνωσας αὐτόν
תַּמְשִׁילֵהוּ	καὶ κατέστησας αὐτὸν	
בְּמַעֲשֵׂי	ἐπὶ τὰ ἔργα	
יָדֶיךָ	τῶν χειρῶν σου	
כֹּל שַׁתָּה	πάντα ὑπέταξας	πάντα ὑπέταξας
תַּחַת־רַגְלָיו׃	ὑποκάτω τῶν ποδῶν αὐτοῦ	ὑποκάτω τῶν ποδῶν αὐτοῦ

Ps. 8 is a unique hymn of praise in the Psalter, which depicts man's place in God's creation in original and distinctive language.[13] The Greek translation of Ps. 8 is literal, and none of the psalm's or its translation's text critical issues pertain to the present discussion. In vv. 6, 7 the psalmist responds to the rhetorical questions of v. 5 with a beautiful presentation of man's dominion over creation as mandated by God.

Some of the equivalents chosen by the translators deserve to be highlighted. First, the syntagm in v. 5b υἱὸς ἀνθρώπου, the legitimate translation of בֶּן־אָדָם, reflects messianic overtones,[14] even though the original psalm has not been considered a messianic psalm.[15] Second, the Greek text follows the Hebrew text's emphasis on man's status and function in the economy of creation. The four finite verbs, three imperfects (חָסֵר, עָטַר, מָשַׁל) and one perfect (שִׁית), are given suitable equivalents,[16] all 2nd singular aorists, ἐλαττόω, στεφανόω, καθίστημι, and ὑπόστασσω. Third, the translation equivalent ἀγγέλους for אֱלֹהִים discussed in an earlier section,[17] has two possible meanings, dependent upon whether the noun ἀγγέλους is construed either as "God" or "angels".

---

[13] Craigie, *Psalms* 106.

[14] Schaper, *Eschatology* 77.

[15] Leschert, *Foundations* 92.

[16] Noteworthy, however, is the unique LXX equivalence מָשַׁל for καθίστημι; see Schaper, *Eschatology* 77.

[17] See *supra* (ch. 2, 2.1.3).

The adverbial expression מְעַט מֵאֱלֹהִים, translated βραχύ τι παρ' ἀγγέλους, requires special attention because of its key contribution to the overall meaning of the psalm. While the phrase's adverbial function was preserved in the target text, the translation caused a shift in its meaning. The Hebrew word מְעַט, "little, few", has a variety of senses determined by the particular collocation in which it is employed. It generally signifies a small, diminished number or quantity (cf. KB). In Ps. 8:6, the phrase מְעַט מֵאֱלֹהִים has several possible meanings. It can be construed qualitatively, as a reference to an inferior status assigned to humankind in comparison with that of אֱלֹהִים, "lower than ...". The causative hiphil תְּחַסְּרֵהוּ, "to diminish, become less" used with the postpositional מֵאֱלֹהִים seems to favour this rendering, generally preferred by commentators, "made him little less than",[18] or "made him inferior only to yourself".[19] Alternatively, מְעַט can be rendered as a reference to a temporal interval, "for a little while", if its other meaning attested in Is. 10:25, Hos. 1:4, or Job 24:24 is considered. For the expression to be construed temporally, however, other contextual clues such as the temporal adverb עַד are needed. In Ps. 8, as in other texts where these indicators are absent, the qualitative sense is to be favoured.

The adverb βραχύ, the main Septuagintal equivalent for מְעַט, can also be understood in various ways, either qualifying a "small" number (Dt. 26:5, 28:62) or quantity, 1Km. 14:29, 43. The collocation βραχύ τι for which the translator opted in Ps. 8:6 is used three other times in the Septuagint. In Is. 57:17 it translates a text without parallel in the Masoretic text, and it unambiguously refers to a short time interval. In its second occurrence in 2Km. 16:1, the phrase βραχύ τι can be construed either spatially, "going a little distance beyond" or temporally, "going for a while". The Septuagintal use of the phrase is not extensive enough to determine with certainty its meaning in Ps. 8:6, even though contextually the temporal meaning seems to have the edge.

The meaning of βραχύ τι in the epistle's use of Ps. 8 is marked by a similar semantic uncertainty. Heb. 2:6 f. quotes Ps. 8:6 f. LXX with only one significant alteration from its alleged *Vorlage*, the exclusion of line three καὶ κατέστησας αὐτὸν ἐπὶ τὰ ἔργα τῶν χειρῶν σου.[20] One option would be to read the adverb as a difference of degree, "a little lower", in

---

[18] Craigie, *Psalms* 105.

[19] Bratcher and Reyburn, *Psalms* 81.

[20] The relevant text critical issues have been overviewed earlier, *supra* (ch. 2, 2.1.3). Certain hermeneutical aspects of the Author's quotation and the legitimacy of the christological reading of the psalm are very intricate and have been amply analysed in other studies such as James D. G. Dunn, *Christology in the Making* (Philadelphia: Westminster Press, 1980); Kistemaker, *Citations*; Leschert, *Foundations*; Schröger, *Verfasser*.

which case the Greek text would mirror perfectly the Hebrew syntagm.[21] Alternatively, the option of most commentators is the temporal sense, "for a little while".[22] The strongest argument for the latter option is supported by the Author's exposition of the psalm, in which the use of the adverbial particle νῦν requires a temporal meaning. The shift in the Author's exposition from the aorist verbs, ἠλάττωσας and ἐστεφάνωσας, to two perfect participles, ἠλαττωμένον and ἐστεφανωμένον, concur with this interpretation.[23] Moreover, a predominant temporal perspective underlies the exposition of other quotations throughout the epistle.[24]

The Hebraic and Greek forms of Ps. 8 have generated several traditions of interpretation in early Judaism and early Christianity. Quotations from Ps. 8 recur frequently in early Rabbinic texts dealing with God's reason for creating humankind. "What is man that Thou are mindful of him?" is the recurrent question that the angelic host pose to God, usually in a remonstrative tone when they contemplate his extraordinary effort in creating man.[25] It is also a reproach against the Holy One at the giving of the Torah, when the angels complain that they, the heavenly host, are better suited to receive the Torah than Israel.[26] Many references that discuss the problem of "What is man?" do not directly elaborate on מְעַט מֵאֱלֹהִים, and the few that do clearly understand the quotation qualitatively and not temporally.[27]

Although the NT frequently quotes from or alludes to Ps. 8, especially in association with Ps. 109 LXX [110 MT],[28] only the Author explicitly

---

[21] Bruce, *Hebrews* 34.

[22] Attridge, *Hebrews* 69 f.; Buchanan, *Hebrews* 57; Lane, *Hebrews* 43; Montefiore, *Hebrews* 54; Moffatt, *Hebrews* 22.

[23] Kistemaker, *Citations* 105 ff.

[24] The ἕως ἄν in Ps. 109:2 LXX, the most dominant OT quotation in the epistle, or ἰδοὺ ἡμέραι ἔρχονται and μετὰ τὰς ἡμέρας ἐκείνας from Jer. 38 LXX, the longest OT quotation in the epistle.

[25] *Gen. Rab.* 8:6 "Said the ministering angels to the Lord: 'Sovereign of the Universe! What is man, that Thou art mindful of him, and the son of man, that Thou thinkest of him? (Ps. 8:5). This trouble, for what has it been created?"

Tosefta (Nashim Sotah 6:5) "At that hour the ministering angels who had come together to cavil [against Israel] before the Holy One blessed be He looked down. When the Holy One blessed be He had created the first man, they had said before him, "Lord of the World, What is man that thou art mindful of him, and the son of man that thou dost care for him? Yet thou hast made him little less than God, and dost crown him with glory and honor. Thou hast given him dominion over the works of thy hands."

[26] *Midr. Teh.* Ps. 8:5.

[27] Usually this understanding is reflected in the Lord's answer to the angelic admonition by situating man, especially his wisdom, above theirs, cf. *Ecc. Rab.* 6:10.

[28] Mk. 12:36, Mt. 22:44, 1 Cor. 15:25, 27, Eph. 1:20, 22, and 1 Pet. 3:22; cf. Dodd, *Sub-structure*. See also Leschert, *Foundations* 95 f.

expounds on the phrase βραχύ τι. In several instances in the epistles, however, there is a clear temporal framework that supports a particular eschatological perspective on the psalm, which can be traced to the Greek textual tradition of Ps. 8.

The Author's interpretation of Ps. 8 clearly builds on the LXX translation βραχύ τι, which has been skilfully employed by him either as the exclusive meaning of Ps. 8 LXX or as a convenient double-entendre. If the former is true, the LXX was determinant in the way in which the Author developed and applied the Scripture christologically. If the latter, the Septuagint played more the role of a catalyst which facilitated the Author's use of an important temporal dimension. In either case, the shift from the qualitative understanding of Ps. 8:6 MT to that of a temporal understanding in Heb. 2:6 ff., was primarily determined by the Ps. 8:6 LXX, a Septuagintal rendering which provided the temporal dimension exploited by the Author.

3. Heb. 3:12: ἐν τῷ ἀποστῆναι ἀπὸ θεοῦ ζῶντος

The negligible frequency with which the epistle uses the verb ἀφίστημι is inversely proportional to its significance in the overall message of the epistle. The verb ἀφίστημι is used for one of the most serious sins in the epistle's rather extensive list of transgressions. Although it appears only once in the epistle, the gravity of the warning passage, as well as its contextual synonyms, suggest that "apostasy" ranks as one of the most serious sins. In fact, a case can be made that the very genesis of the epistle can be traced to the Author's urge to warn the community against apostasy.[29]

In Heb. 3:12, the sin of apostasy is described in terms of separation or departure from God, ἀποστῆναι ἀπὸ θεοῦ ζῶντος, the verb and the preposition usually accompanying each other. Apostasy is the ultimate consequence of having a καρδία πονηρὰ ἀπιστίας, it is failing to keep to the end the confidence and hope, [κατέχειν] τὴν παρρησίαν καὶ τὸ καύχημα τῆς ἐλπίδος (Heb. 3:6), it is forfeiting the status of being a partaker of Christ, μέτοχος τοῦ Χριστοῦ, by losing the firm confidence that characterised the early stages of the Christian life, τὴν ἀρχὴν τῆς ὑποστάσεως (Heb. 3:14). The stern language and imagery employed in ch. 3 are paralleled in the other warning passages of the epistle, most notably,

---

[29] McKnight, "Passages". The debate whether the sin of apostasy was a real or only a virtual possibility is beyond the interest of the discussion here. For a succinct presentation of the arguments, see McKnight, "Passages".

"to drift away" παραρυῶμεν (Heb. 2:1), "to fall away" παραπεσόντας (Heb. 6:6), and "to turn away" ἀποστρεφόμενοι (Heb. 12:23).

In the NT the primary meanings of the verb ἀφίστημι are "to (physically) depart, to be separated from" (Lk. 2:37, 4:13, Acts 12:10, 15:38, 19:10) and "to (be) release(d)", or "to send away" (Lk. 13:27, Acts 3:38, 22:29, 2 Cor. 12:8). In addition to these frequent connotations, the verb ἀφίστημι and its cognate noun ἀποστασία are occasionally employed by other NT writers with the same meaning as in Hebrews. Especially in the latter writings of the NT the verb is used with the specific meaning of "falling away from the faith / Lord"(Lk. 8:13) and it probably acquired the status of *terminus technicus* to describe the falling away from the faith (1 Tim. 4:1, 2 Tim. 2:3).

The range of connotations in the NT is less extensive than in the LXX.[30] The Septuagint employs the verb ἀφίστημι to translate no less than 40 different Hebrew verbs, proof that at least for the Pentateuch, the translators were familiar with the highly idiomatic use of the verb.[31] The versatility of this verb may be responsible for the slightly distinct understanding of its usage in Num. 14, the primary OT text alluded to in Heb. 3:12-19.[32]

Num. 14 recounts the report of the twelve spies returning from Canaan. As on previous occasions, the people showed their disinclination to trust God to take them safely to the Promised Land, thus forfeiting the fulfilment of the promise given to the Patriarchs. The gravity of the sin committed on that occasion is demonstrated by the severity of the punishment of forty years in the wilderness and the interdiction to enter the Land. Num. 14:9 is the most relevant verse for this investigation.

Num. 14:9 MT	Num. 14:9 LXX	Heb. 3:12 NTG
אַ֣ךְ בַּֽיהוָה֮ אַל־תִּמְרֹ֒דוּ֒	ἀλλὰ ἀπὸ τοῦ κυρίου μὴ ἀποστάται γίνεσθε	ἐν τῷ ἀποστῆναι

---

[30] Commenting on the use of the verb in the Pentateuch, Lee contends that the verb is "used in the Pentateuch in a variety of sense, all of which are established in Classical Greek". He then lists the different meanings: 1) "to cause to revolt", 2) "stand back, aloof", 3) "withdraw, depart" (either from an activity or place), 4) "rebel, revolt", 5) "shrink, abstain", J. A. L. Lee, *A Lexical Study of the Septuagint Version of the Pentateuch* (SBL-SCS 14; Chico: Scholars Press, 1983) 35f.

[31] Lee, *Pentateuch* 36.

[32] Besides ἀφίστημι, the LXX uses a closely related verb and its cognate with the more nuanced meaning of "apostate, apostasy". This verb is used in Joshua 22, in the recounting of the building of an altar to the Lord by two of the 12 tribes of Jacob, which remained on the eastern side of Jordan.

וְאַתֶּם אַל־תִּירְאוּ	ὑμεῖς δὲ μὴ φοβηθῆτε	ἀπὸ θεοῦ ζῶντος
אֶת־עַם הָאָרֶץ	τὸν λαὸν τῆς γῆς	
כִּי לַחְמֵנוּ הֵם	ὅτι κατάβρωμα ἡμῖν	
סָר צִלָּם	ἐστιν ἀφέστηκεν γὰρ	
מֵעֲלֵיהֶם	ὁ καιρὸς ἀπ' αὐτῶν	
וַיהוָה אִתָּנוּ	ὁ δὲ κύριος ἐν ἡμῖν	
אַל־תִּירָאֻם:	μὴ φοβηθῆτε αὐτούς	

The phrase μὴ ἀποστάται γίνεσθε translates the Hebrew אַל־תִּמְרֹדוּ and although it uses a different part of speech, it supplies an appropriate semantic equivalent to the Hebrew text. The verb מָרַד and its cognate noun מֶרֶד are translated by the verb ἀφίστημι or its cognates in more than a dozen occurrences throughout the Septuagint.[33] The basic meaning of מָרַד is "to rise in revolt, to rebel" (cf. KB), a meaning that suits well the context of Num. 14:9. The Greek translation uses the noun ἀποστάτης, which has two possible contextual meanings, either "rebel" or "apostate", and only the context can determine which is more suitable.

It should be mentioned that the cognate verb ἀφίστημι used in the same verse offers no help in deciding the meaning of ἀποστάτης.[34] More important is the observation that the prepositions employed by the Hebrew and Greek texts are different. While the Hebrew verb is used in collocation with the preposition בְּ, confirming the meaning "to rebel against",[35] the Greek text employs the preposition ἀπό, which suggests that the Greek phrase should probably be construed as "apostates from, depart from" and not "rebels against" the Lord. This meaning is also recommended by Lust (LEH), although Dorival contends that the meaning "apostate" is not attested before the Christian era, and consequently translates "ne devenez pas des rebelles!"[36] While both meanings seem equally legitimate, contextually the reading "do not become apostates" appears to have a slight advantage.[37] Similarly, Wevers, while suggesting

---

[33] The texts are as follows: Gen. 14:4, Job 22:16, 18, 19(2x), 22, Neh. 2:19, 6:6, 9:26, Ez. 17:15, and Dan. 9:5, 9.

[34] In this instance, the basic meaning of the verb ἀφίστημι, "to depart, to go away", matches closely the meaning of סוּר, the Hebrew verb it translates.

[35] The verb is used with the preposition בְּ referring to the people's revolt against Yahweh, in Num. 14:9, Job 22:16, 18, 19, 29, Ez. 2:3, 20:38, Dan. 9:9, and Neh. 9:26. (cf. KB).

[36] G. Dorival, *Les Nombres*, ed. M. Harl, vol. 4, *La Bible d'Alexandrie. Traduction et annotation de la Septante* (Paris: Éditions du Cerf, 1995) 318.

[37] Although the verb ἀφίστημι is most frequently used in collocation with the preposition ἀπό, this is not an exclusive pattern. The preposition-less use of the verb, as well as its use in conjunction with other prepositions are well attested in the LXX. This

the translation "do not rebel against YHWH", explains the Greek rendering as a fine interpretation of the Hebrew verb "to rebel against", "it is an active turning away from, the antonym of 'following after'".[38]

The case for the meaning of ἀποστάτης in Num. 14:9 understood as "to turn away from the Lord", i.e., "to apostatise, to commit apostasy", as opposed to "to rebel against the Lord", is strengthened by the Greek translation of Num. 32:9 and Dt. 1:28, two subsequent passages relating the particular event that took place during the encampment in Hazeroth (Num. 12:16). The two texts and their translations read as follows:

Num. 32:9 MT	Num. 32:9 LXX
וַיַּעֲלוּ עַד־נַחַל אֶשְׁכּוֹל	καὶ ἀνέβησαν Φάραγγα βότρυος
וַיִּרְאוּ אֶת־הָאָרֶץ	καὶ κατενόησαν τὴν γῆν
וַיָּנִיאוּ אֶת־לֵב	καὶ ἀπέστησαν τὴν καρδίαν
בְּנֵי יִשְׂרָאֵל	τῶν υἱῶν Ισραηλ
לְבִלְתִּי־בֹא אֶל־הָאָרֶץ	ὅπως μὴ εἰσέλθωσιν εἰς τὴν γῆν
אֲשֶׁר־נָתַן לָהֶם יְהוָה:	ἣν ἔδωκεν κύριος αὐτοῖς

Dt. 1:28 MT	Dt. 1:28 LXX
אָנָה אֲנַחְנוּ עֹלִים אַחֵינוּ	ποῦ ἡμεῖς ἀναβαίνομεν οἱ ἀδελφοὶ ὑμῶν
הֵמַסּוּ אֶת־לְבָבֵנוּ לֵאמֹר	ἀπέστησαν ὑμῶν τὴν καρδίαν λέγοντες
עַם גָּדוֹל	ἔθνος μέγα
וָרָם מִמֶּנּוּ	καὶ πολὺ καὶ δυνατώτερον ἡμῶν
עָרִים גְּדֹלֹת	καὶ πόλεις μεγάλαι
וּבְצוּרֹת בַּשָּׁמָיִם	καὶ τετειχισμέναι ἕως τοῦ οὐρανοῦ
וְגַם־בְּנֵי עֲנָקִים רָאִינוּ שָׁם:	ἀλλὰ καὶ υἱοὺς γιγάντων ἑωράκαμεν ἐκεῖ

The two texts relate the effect of the spies' report on the people and both use the verb ἀφίστημι. In Num. 32:9 ἀφίστημι translates the hiphil of the Hebrew verb נוא, "to hinder, to prevent", and in Dt. 1:28 translates the hiphil of the verb מָסַס, "to faint, to grow fearful". In both instances the translation equivalents given are unique in the LXX, even though the corresponding Hebrew verbs are quite extensively used. One reasonable explanation for this peculiar translation is that in rendering Num. 32:9 and the awkward Hebrew expression in Dt. 1:28b, the translator was guided by

---

diverse usage of the verb suggests that the presence of the preposition ἀπό in Num. 14:9 cannot be simply regarded as a default formula for ἀφίστημι.

[38] Wevers, *Numbers* 214.

the lexical choice already made in the translation of Num. 13-14, where the noun ἀποστάτης epitomises the people's sin.

The case for reading the meaning "apostate" in Num. 14:9 remains open to debate, and it is possible that too fine a semantic delimitation among different Hebrew synonyms (סור, שׁוּב, מָאַס, מָרַד), or among their Greek equivalents (ἀφίστημι, ἐπιστρέφω, ἀπειθέω), might reflect an unrealistic understanding of language usage. However, it is important to emphasise the connection between the text in Num. 14 and the epistle, a connection that is primarily mediated by the Septuagint. Whether Num. 14:9 LXX μὴ ἀποστάται γίνεσθε ὑμεῖς should be read "do not become rebels", identical with the Hebrew text, or "do not become apostates", thus departing from the meaning of the Hebrew text, it is almost certain that the Author read it with the latter and not the former meaning. If the former rendering is correct, the meaning shift took place in the process of translation, if the latter, the meaning shift occurred as a result of translation. The Septuagint consequently supplied not only the lexical unit underlying the Author's allusion to Num. 14, but also a particular theological perspective on that event in Israel's history.

4. Heb. 3:2, 5: Μωϋσῆς μὲν πιστὸς ἐν ὅλῳ τῷ οἴκῳ αὐτοῦ

Πιστός is the pivotal lexical unit in Heb. 3:1-6, the passage which portrays Jesus as superior to Moses, the most central figure in Judaism. The word πιστός, used either explicitly or implicitly four times in these verses, lies at the heart of the Author's argument. The present study sides with the majority of commentators who favour the text in Num. 12 as the source for the quotations in Heb 3:2 and 5.[39]

---

[39] Although there is no introductory formula in either of these verses, most commentators consider that at least Heb. 3:5 is an implicit quotation from Num. 12:7. The amount of textual overlap justifies its inclusion among the quotations in the epistle and not just as an allusion. There is no agreement, however, with regard to the quotation in 3:5. An alternative text, 1Par. 17:14 LXX, has been suggested as preferable to Num. 12:7, which many consider to be the more obvious choice in view of the quotation in Heb. 3:5. D'Angelo advocates for 1Par. 17:14 LXX, contending that it better fits the intricacies of the Author's argument, in which "the verbal similarity between the rather unusual πιστώσω of 1Chr. 17:14 and the phrase πιστὸν ὄντα of Heb. 3:2 makes the dependence more clear, clear enough to suggest that the passage cited in 3:2 is not Num. 12:7 but 1Chr. 17:14", Mary R D'Angelo, *Moses in the Letter to the Hebrews* (SBL-DS 42; Missoula: Scholars Press, 1979) 73. D'Angelo has been followed by other commentators, most notably by Lane (*Hebrews* 72), for whom the thematic overlap is decisive. While her assertion that Heb. 3:1-6 is "a very complex midrashic treatment of a number of texts" (D'Angelo, *Moses* 69) seems to be generally accepted, the arguments

Num. 12:7 MT	Num. 12:7 LXX	Heb. 3:5 NTG
לֹא־כֵן עַבְדִּי מֹשֶׁה בְּכָל־בֵּיתִי נֶאֱמָן הוּא:	οὐχ οὕτως ὁ θεράπων μου Μωυσῆς ἐν ὅλῳ τῷ οἴκῳ μου πιστός ἐστιν	Μωϋσῆς μὲν πιστὸς ἐν ὅλῳ τῷ οἴκῳ αὐτοῦ

The larger context of Num. 12:7 is the complaint of Miriam and Aaron against Moses' authority. The two siblings were not primarily set against Moses' role of intermediary between God and the people. Rather, they challenged his unique, unrivalled status in an attempt to become partakers of the same honour.

Num. 12:7, the central verse in the carefully constructed chiastic structure of 12:1-9, is part of God's answer to Miriam and Aaron, which confirms Moses' unique status.[40]   Essentially, God states that while revelation is imparted to other prophets by means of visions and dreams, Moses has been granted the special privilege of direct, unmediated communication; God allows his servant to have a unique kind of access, "he will behold my face".   God's reason for bestowing on Moses this unparalleled stewardship is Moses' quality of נֶאֱמָן in all God's house.

The precise meaning of the participle niphal in Num. 12:7 has generated lengthy discussions.   The niphal participle of אמן is attested with the following meanings.   First, it has the sense of "permanence", "endurance" and "firmness", meanings ruled out for Num. 12:7 by its context.   Second, it can have one of two complementary meanings, "be, prove to be faithful, loyal", or alternatively, "be trustworthy, reliable" (cf. KB, DCH).   Since the quality of being "faithful" is that which engenders trust, "faithful" and "trustworthy" are closely interrelated and in most cases it is difficult to ascertain which meaning better fits a given context.   Thirdly, and with direct significance for Num. 12, the meaning of נֶאֱמָן in several collocations, such as in conjunction with the preposition בְּ, is closer to that of a genuine passive voice "to be trusted, entrusted with", as opposed to its adjectival participial force.[41]

---

promoting 1Chronicles as the text source of the quotation are not, primarily because of extensive verbal similarities between Num. 12 and Heb. 3 (Ellingworth, *Hebrews* 201).

[40] Jacob Milgrom, *Numbers Commentary* (JPSTC; Philadelphia: Jewish Publication Society, 1989).

[41] A similar semantic behaviour is attested for the collocation אָמַן לְ, "to be appointed" cf. 1 Sam. 3:20 (*DCH*).

The difficulty in distinguishing between these meanings in Num. 12:7 is seen also in the major lexica. While most consider that נֶאֱמָן in Num. 12:7 means "to be entrusted with", the alternative meaning "to be faithful, trustworthy, reliable" (cf. KB, *DCH*), is also suggested as a possibility. A similar preference for the passive meaning, "to be entrusted with", or for the participial meaning "trusted, trustworthy" is adopted by most commentaries. Milgrom opts for the participial rendering, "he is trusted", seeing similarities in the position of Abraham's servant and that of Joseph under Pharaoh.[42] The same option is favoured by Gray, "in all My house he showeth himself trustworthy" and Levine, "of all my household he is most trusted".[43] Alternatively Budd and Ashley construe it passively, "he is entrusted with".[44] Since the context focuses on Moses' responsibility, Coats argues that Moses' image should be understood as a "leader whose work can be trusted".[45]

The Greek translation closely follows the Hebrew text throughout this paragraph. Several equivalents in the translation deserve mention since they reveal that in the very act of translation the Septuagint becomes a tradition of interpretation in the making.[46] First, the translation of the preposition בְּ throughout this chapter is idiomatic, the translator being sensitive to the contextual meaning of the collocation דִּבֶּר בְּ, translated either λαλέω κατά in Num. 12:1, 8, or λαλέω plus dative in Num 12:2. The double meaning of the Hebrew expression in v. 2 "speaking through" or "speaking to" is reduced to that of "speaking to" in the Greek text, which would be the more natural way to construe the λαλέω plus the dative.[47] More significantly is Wevers' remark that the choice of tenses in the Greek text, the perfect λελάληκεν and the aorist ἐλάλησεν both translating the same Hebrew form דִּבֶּר, give a more nuanced reading of the complaint, "what Num says is: 'has the Lord spoken only to Moses? Did not he speak to us also?'"[48]

---

[42] Milgrom, *Numbers* 95.

[43] George B. Gray, *Numbers* (ICC; Edinburgh: T. & T. Clark, 1903) 214; Baruch A. Levine, *Numbers 1-20* (AB; New York: Doubleday, 1993) 315.

[44] Timothy R. Ashley, *The Book of Numbers* (NICOT; Grand Rapids: Eerdmans, 1993) 132; Philip J. Budd, *Numbers* (WBC; Waco: Word, 1984) 221.

[45] George W. Coats, *Moses: Heroic Man, Man of God* (JSOT-SS 57; Sheffield: Sheffield Academic Press, 1988) 128.

[46] D'Angelo, *Moses* 100.

[47] The precise meaning of דִּבֶּר בְּ is uncertain, cf. Gray, *Numbers ad loc.* Both meanings "to speak to" and "to speak through" are equally possible; he opts for the former, suggesting that it implies a more intimate communication than the syntagm דִּבֶּר לְ.

[48] Wevers, *Numbers* 184.

A second noteworthy choice is the translation of the difficult Hebrew phrase in v. 6a אִם־יִהְיֶה נְבִיאֲכֶם יְהוָה, which the translator disambiguates by the use of a dative construction, ἐὰν γένηται προφήτης ὑμῶν κυρίῳ, to be construed either as a dative of possession, "should a prophet of yours belong to the Lord",[49] or a dative of association, "pour Seigneur".[50]

Thirdly, in 12:8, the Hebrew imperfect יַבִּיט is surprisingly translated as an aorist, εἶδεν, whereas the other imperfect verbs in the passage, אֶתְוַדָּע and אֲדַבֶּר in 12:6 and אֲדַבֶּר in 12:7, are all translated by future verbs (γνωσθήσομαι, λαλήσω), implying that the translators understood Num. 12:8 as a reference to the earlier event recorded in Ex. 33:18-23.[51]

The meaning of πιστός must be assessed within the framework of these translation choices that qualify the LXX's perspective on Moses' unique role in receiving and imparting divine revelation. The niphal participle נֶאֱמָן in 12:7 is translated by the adjective πιστός, as in more than 90% of its occurrences in the Hebrew Bible. Since this equivalent is clearly the typical rendition of the niphal נאמן (cf. LEH), one can expect to encounter the same difficulty in distinguishing the precise meaning of πιστός. The alternatives for understanding the phrase πιστός ἐστιν are either, "he is faithful, loyal", or "he is trustworthy, reliable" (cf. LEH). Wevers retains the two meanings presumably to indicate that the two concepts are virtually inseparable. He comments, "concerning 'my servant Moses,' the Lord said: 'he is faithful ἐν ὅλῳ τῷ οἴκῳ μου'...the figure is that of one who is πιστός in God's household; he is a trustworthy servant".[52] D'Angelo reaches a similar conclusion and does not commit to either one of the meanings, "not so my servant Moses: in all my house he is faithful/trusted".[53] Noticeably, the passive meaning of the niphal Hebrew verb, "to be entrusted with", one of the primary choices for the meaning of the Hebrew text, is not reflected by either one of these renderings of the Greek text.

Although D'Angelo's large scale investigation of different traditions of interpretation need not be repeated here, a few points worth noting indicate the diversity of thought regarding Moses' portrait in Num. 12. Main traditions based on the Hebrew text seem to have developed along the lines of understanding נֶאֱמָן as "entrusted, trustworthy". The Targumim traditions preserved in the Targum Neofiti, Pseudo-Jonathan, and Onqelos differ with regard to what constitutes God's house in Num. 12:7, but they consistently depict Moses as the one who "is trusted by" (Tg. Onq.), "he is

---

[49] Wevers, *Numbers* 186.

[50] Dorival, *Les Nombres* 302.

[51] D'Angelo, *Moses* 100; Wevers, *Numbers* 187.

[52] Wevers, *Numbers* 187.

[53] D'Angelo, *Moses* 100.

most trusted" (Tg. Neof., note r.) and "he is most reliable" (Tg. Ps.-J.).[54] Similarly, the Rabbinic writings frequently qualify the reference to Moses in Num. 12:7 as "trusted" or "entrusted". God honours Moses with unlimited trust (Sifre Zuta 12:6-8), whether it is with the responsibility of writing the Torah (Ex. Rab. 47:9) or administrating the tabernacle (Mid. Ex. 51:6). This honour is even greater than that bestowed on the ministering angels (Sifre Bemidbar 103).

Some traditions based on the Greek text are more multifaceted. Philo quotes Num. 12:7 four times in *Legum Allegoria*, and each time he highlights a different meaning of πιστός. In ii.67, Moses is πιστός as the result of God's uniting him in marriage to the Ethiopian woman, "who stands for resolve unalterable, intense, and fixed". In the second instance (iii.103) the meaning of πιστός is not expounded, but is set within the context of Moses' special role in the building of the tabernacle, in contrast to that of Bezalel. Moses, with God as his instructor, is the "artificer of the archetypes", whereas Bezalel, with Moses as his instructor, is the artificer of "the copies of these". The third occurrence (iii. 203-4) appears in Philo's response to those who accuse God of impropriety when taking an oath. Philo comments that God, who alone with his friend Moses, is πιστός, is the one who accomplishes his plans on the basis of his strength; "whatever he saith cometh to pass". In this context, the most likely connotation of πιστός is that of "trustworthiness". Finally, in iii.228, collating Gen. 15:6 and Num. 12:7, Philo exploits the active sense of the cognate verb "to believe" and draws a parallel between Moses and Abraham as men who believed God and stand as the perfect model of faith in God.

The Author uses the quotation from Num. 12:7 to support the argument for Jesus' superiority over Moses in a more illustrative than polemic fashion.[55] The attempt to compare someone with Moses was a daunting task in first-century Jewish thought; to have him surpassed was virtually unheard of. The Moses figure was so dominant even in relation to the angels that "contrasting Jesus to Moses is a step beyond Heb. 1:5-13, not a step backward".[56] Essentially the contrast is not one of the degree of πιστός,[57] but rather one of the status of the one displaying the quality.[58] Scott correctly points out that it would have been easy to make a case for

---

[54] For the Targum Onqelos and Targum Pseudo-Jonathan, the house represents the people of Israel, while in Targum Neofiti, it stands for the entire created world.

[55] Erich Grässer, "Mose und Jesus. Zur Auslegung von Hebr 3 1-6", *Zeitschrift für die neutestamentliche Wissenschaft* 75 (1984) 15.

[56] Brett R. Scott, "Jesus' Superiority over Moses in Hebrews 3:1-6", *Bibliotheca Sacra* 155, no. 2 (1998) 203; D'Angelo, *Moses in the Letter to the Hebrews* 125.

[57] Contra Moffatt, *Hebrews*.

[58] Attridge, *Hebrews* 108 f.; Schröger, *Verfasser* 97.

Jesus' superior faithfulness given the ignominious event in Moses' life at the rock of Meribah (cf. Num. 20:10-12).[59]

The correct way to construe the adjective πιστός in the epistle's quotation is a matter of debate, as it is for the LXX's version of Num. 12:7. Several factors have to be considered in order to establish its meaning. First, the adjective is used three times outside the text of Heb. 3:1-6, twice in relation to God (10:23, 11:11) and once to describe Christ as the High Priest ἐλεήμων καὶ πιστός (2:17). When referring to God and his reliability in fulfilling promises, πιστός is best construed as "trustworthiness". In the third instance πιστός is attributed to Christ in his High Priestly role, and the meaning "trustworthy" fits well within this context, reassuring the believer that he can have confidence in Jesus' ministry. Alternatively, the complementary meaning "faithful" is also appropriate, if the Author conveyed the idea that Jesus fulfilled the role and the office to which he was appointed.[60] In a recent investigation of the theme of "faith" in the Epistle, Rhee, while retaining the meaning "faithful" throughout the paragraph, acknowledges the two meanings of πιστός but does not argue strongly for the one he chose since "either one of the translations makes good sense in the context and does not affect the author's inteded purpose for this section".[61]

It is not surprising that the way in which 2:17 is construed affects the reading of πιστός in 3:2 and 3:5 since the verses have roughly the same context. Commentators who opt for the meaning "trustworthy" in Heb. 2:17 read πιστός in 3:2, 5 with the same meaning, i.e., Moses was worthy of God's trust.[62] Alternatively, the meaning "faithful" seems to be better supported by the context. First, as D'Angelo persuasively argues, the LXX texts, which provide the background for the Author's exposition, revolve around the use of πιστεύω in its double meaning of "to appoint" and "to be faithful".[63] Secondly, this sense is confirmed by the following section in Heb. 3:7 ff. with its emphasis on the faithfulness of the believers. Their responsibility in the New Covenant is to display faithfulness to the end, just as Christ and Moses did in their offices. Third, in the list of exempla in ch. 11, the Author returns to the motif of Moses' faithfulness, v. 25, which highlights Moses' faith in no ambiguous terms.[64]

---

[59] Scott, "Superiority" 209.

[60] Attridge, *Hebrews* 109 f.

[61] Victor (Sung-Yul) Rhee, *Faith In Hebrews: Analysis within the Context of Christology, Eschatology, and Ethics* (New York: Peter Lang, 2001) 95.

[62] Ellingworth, *Hebrews* 202.

[63] D'Angelo, *Moses* 76 ff.

[64] Grässer, "Mose" 15.

The case for a particular Septuagintal meaning of the word πιστός in Heb. 3:1-6 is not as unequivocal as some commentators suggest.[65] The richness of the concept, the extensive overlap of the semantic domains of the Hebrew נֶאֱמָן and the Greek πιστός, and the multiple nuances inseparably carried by both lexemes call for caution in assessing whether or not the Septuagintal reading of Num. 12 has set the Author on a different semantic track than the one he would have taken had he worked with the Hebrew text. Complete certainty on this matter is not possible primarily because the evidence indicates that both נֶאֱמָן and πιστός have a wider range of meaning than "entrusted" for the former and "faithful" for the latter. Nevertheless, different traditions of interpretation suggest the possibility of certain preferences or emphases on particular meanings within the spectrum of semantic possibilities. All things considered, the most probable interpretation of the Hebrew and Greek texts of Num. 12:7 and the Author's reading of it seem to indicate the presence of a meaning shift from the meaning of the original Hebrew text either in the Septuagint or in the way in which he construes it. The particular LXX rendering of נֶאֱמָן as πιστός has facilitated, if not determined the Author's perspective on the faithfulness of Moses, of Christ, and that of the New Covenant believer.

5. Heb. 9:16: ὅπου γὰρ διαθήκη

The Epistle to the Hebrews employs the word διαθήκη more often than any other NT writing and also engages in the most extensive and detailed discussion of "covenant". Thus the epistle is at once the legitimate and the ideal place to assess if the Author uses διαθήκη more with the meaning of the Hebrew word-concept בְּרִית, "covenant", or with its Greek counterpart διαθήκη, "testament". The scope of this investigation is limited to one of the more disputed passages, Heb. 9:15-19, in order to determine if an alleged semantic difference between בְּרִית and διαθήκη can be defended, and to evaluate the influence which the Septuagint might have had in this meaning shift.

The word בְּרִית is the primary linguistic expression for the important OT concept of "covenant". Its prominence in the Hebrew Bible is matched in the Greek Bible by διαθήκη, its almost exclusive equivalent. The scholarly dialogue over the last century, while adding to existing proposals, has not succeeded in reaching consensus with regard to the

---

[65] Isaacs comments, "in Heb. 3:2, 5, Num. 12:7 is cited from the LXX, where instead of the MT 'who is entrusted with all my house', the Greek translators have 'who is faithful in all my house" (*Space* 135). Similarly, Schröger, *Verfasser* 97.

word's etymology, its grammatical and linguistic particularities, the range
of similarities and dissimilarities with contemporary practices in the ANE
or the semantic evolution of the word.[66] A similarly unresolved situation is
encountered in the NT, one of the earliest interpretative perspectives on the
OT use of διαθήκη.[67]

Basic linguistic data has been well analysed in a number of studies and
need not be repeated here.[68] The meaning of the Hebrew בְּרִית ranges
from the semantic domains of "oath and commitment" and "love and
friendship",[69] and while precise nuances must be determined by its use and
not by the largely unknown and highly speculative alleged etymologies,[70]
its meaning of "covenant" must be considered as pre-eminent.

The discussion of "covenant" is further complicated by the Septuagint
which translates בְּרִית as διαθήκη in over 250 occurrences, without
significant exception.[71] The reasons behind this translation choice

---

[66] In spite of considerable research, Hahn contends that "a decline of clarity, balance
and consensus" is still prevalent; Scott W. Hahn, "Kinship By Covenant: A Biblical
Theological Study of Covenant Types and Texts in the Old and New Testaments" (Ph.
D., Marquette University, 1995) 1. Barr attributes the state of affairs to the often hasty
endeavour to assemble "covenant" theologies which "too easily and incorrectly build an
entire theological edifice on a word that remains obscure at best", James Barr, "Some
Semantic Notes on the Covenant", in *Beiträge zur Alttestamentlichen Theologie:
Festschrift für Walther Zimmerli zum 70. Geburtstag*, eds. H. Donner, R. Hanhart, and R.
Smend (Göttingen: Vandenhoeck & Ruprecht, 1977) 24.

[67] See the recent study by Susanne Lehne, *The New Covenant in Hebrews* (JSNTS-SS
44; Sheffield: Sheffield Academic Press, 1990) 31. In Hebrews, the variety of
interpretations is best illustrated by two studies that, although they proceeded from the
same data and were guided by virtually identical methodologies and arguments, reach
opposite conclusions. Swetnam undertakes to prove that "the use of διαθήκη in the sense
of testament is not ... ill-advised but is essential for the proper understanding of what the
author [of Hebrews] considered to be the nature of the new διαθήκη"; James Swetnam,
"A Suggested Interpretation of Hebrews 9,15-18", *The Catholic Biblical Quarterly* 27,
no. 4 (1965) 374. Approximately one decade later, Hughes' rejoinder sets out to
demonstrate "not merely the possibility of interpreting διαθήκη as 'covenant' in the OT
sense of בְּרִית in these two pericopae [Heb. 9:15 ff. and Gal. 3:15 ff.], nor even the
probability of such an interpretation, but rather the necessity for so understanding this
word"; John J. Hughes, "Hebrews IX 15 ff. and Galatians III 15 ff. A Study in Covenant
Practice and Procedure", *Novum Testamentum* 21, no. 1 (1979) 28.

[68] Primarily the articles of Weinfeld, "בְּרִית" 2: 253-78; Quell, "διαθήκη" 2: 106-24;
Behm, "διαθήκη" 2: 125-34; McConville, "בְּרִית" 1: 747-55; Hegerman, "διαθήκη" 1:299-
301; see also Knut Backhaus, *Der neue Bund und das Werden der Kirche. Die Diatheke-
Deutung des Hebräerbriefs im Rahmen der frühchristlichen Theologiegeschichte*
(Münster: Aschendorff, 1996); Hahn, "Kinship" and Hughes, "Covenant".

[69] Weinfeld, "בְּרִית" 2: 256.

[70] Cf. McConville, "בְּרִית" 1: 747-755.

[71] The exceptions are of two types, and they are both numerically insignificant. First,
there are the cases in which διαθήκη translates other words than בְּרִית, as in Ex. 31:7, Dt.

continue to elude scholars,[72] especially since the usual Greek meaning of διαθήκη is that of "testament", and a semantically closer word, συνθήκη was available to the translator. Indeed, later revisions of Aquila, Symmachus and Theodotion preferred to render בְּרִית as συνθήκη.[73] Two contrasting positions characterise the ongoing dialogue. On the one hand, it has been proposed that in the search for the closest possible equivalent, translators chose διαθήκη over συνθήκη because the former consistently bore the legal nuance needed for a correct rendering of בְּרִית.[74] Alternatively it is argued that the translator's preference for διαθήκη exhibits a diachronic change in the very meaning of בְּרִית. Commenting on this point, Barr notes that "the semantics of בְּרִית were changing in late biblical and early post-biblical times ... and it may well be that the Greek translation has to be related to specific conditions of Hellenistic Judaism".[75] Proponents of this position understand the use of διαθήκη in light of its semantic evolution. It is argued that the choice, determined by theological motives,[76] reflects the meaning of the Hebrew term בְּרִית at the time of the translation of the Pentateuch into Greek, "will, testament, disposition, gift" as opposed to that of biblical times, "covenant". This position is sustained also by the way Philo uses the word.[77]

Essentially, then the contribution of the LXX has to be assessed against the background of these two possibilities, either διαθήκη has undergone a meaning shift due to its use as the equivalent for the Hebrew בְּרִית, or, alternatively, the term בְּרִית has undergone such a semantic shift that the natural sense of διαθήκη came to capture best its meaning. These two positions are reflected also in the field of the NT. In his endeavour to resist granting the NT language special linguistic status, Deissmann opts for the meaning "will", "testament", in agreement with Greek contemporary usage. Westcott, however, has consistently translated διαθήκη as "covenant" throughout the NT.[78]

This dispute is best illustrated in the interpretation of Heb. 9:15-18, the culmination of the Author's discussion about the covenant, which employs

---

9:5, and Jer. 41:18, and secondly, there are the instances in which other Greek words are supplied as equivalents for בְּרִית, as in Dt. 9:15, 1Ki. 11:11, and Zech. 11:14.

[72] Dennis J. McCarthy, "Covenant in the Old Testament: The Present State of Inquiry", *The Catholic Biblical Quarterly* 27, no. 3 (1965) 217.

[73] Turner, *Christian Words* 92. See also Weinfeld, "בְּרִית" 2: 256.

[74] Hughes, "Covenant" 31.

[75] Barr, "Covenant" 35.

[76] Weinfeld, "בְּרִית" 2: 256.

[77] William Horbury, "Ezekiel Tragicus 106", *Vetus Testamentum* 36, no. 1 (1986) 43 f. See also Behm's study on the reconstruction of the history of the Greek word, which emphasises the semantic shift in the translation; Behm, "διαθήκη" 2: 125-34.

[78] Turner, *Christian Words* 92.

διαθήκη five times explicitly and twice implicitly in the span of four verses.[79] The main difficulty of this passage is that the meaning of διαθήκη, judged by its different collocations, seems to require a sudden and repeated change in connotation. The first collocation, ἡ πρώτη διαθήκη vv. 15, 18 is a clear reference to the Mosaic διαθήκη, "covenant" which is the meaning in the preceding section, most importantly in ch. 8, in which the relationship between the two covenants reaches its clearest expression. Moreover, the Author's mention of the presence of a μεσίτης, "mediator", confirms the meaning "covenant", because the evidence excludes such a role in legal procedures associated with the "will" or "testament". It can be safely concluded that in the opening of the paragraph, the Author uses διαθήκη in the sense of "covenant", and at the end, vv. 18-19, the same connotation of "covenant" for διαθήκη is confirmed by both the explicit reference to Moses and the quotation from Exodus which follows it.

A second set of collocations in the middle section of the paragraph, Heb. 9:16-17, associates διαθήκη with θάνατος, διαθέμενος, κληρονομία and βέβαιος, implying that its proper meaning in these verses should be that of "will, testament", in accordance with the meaning of the widest and almost exclusive attestation in contemporary Greek literature outside the Septuagint. The main idea of these verses is that διαθήκη, as a "will" is operative only when ὁ διαθέμενος, "the testor", has died. Alternatively, to read the meaning "covenant" in this context would imply that death is required in order to enter into a covenant, an idea that "simply is not true".[80]

There are essentially three interpretations for the meaning of διαθήκη in the present passage. The first position advocates reading διαθήκη consistently as "covenant". In the defence already mentioned, Hughes adduces internal textual evidence to argue that the lexic, syntax and semantics of διαθήκη in Heb. 9:15-18 cannot support any other meaning than "covenant". Furthermore he contends that external evidence points to a similar conclusion. At the end of his brief survey of the Hellenistic, Egyptian and Roman legal procedures, he concludes that in none of these legal systems "a will or testament was legally valid only when the testator died".[81] Hughes' overall argument and evidence deserve a detailed answer that is not possible here. While many of his points are correct, especially regarding the overall tenor of Heb. 9 and the particular semantic nuances of the cultic terms, e.g., φέρω,[82] others are less convincing and at times

---

[79] Hahn, "Kinship"; Vanhoye, *Structure*.
[80] Bruce, *Hebrews* 211.
[81] Hughes, "Covenant" 61.
[82] Hughes, "Covenant" 65.

circular.[83] In a recent contribution Hahn develops Hughes' position even further by clarifying some deficiencies in previous studies, including those of Campbell and Hughes.[84] He investigates data provided by the OT and parallel Ancient Near East covenant practices and argues for the existence of three types of covenants: the kinship-type, the treaty-type and the grant-type. Furthermore he probes into the main covenant texts in the NT (Galatians and Hebrews) to show how their authors maintained the distinction between different covenant types in theological discussion. According to Hahn, Hughes fails to observe the distinction between the former covenant, a treaty-type covenant which Israel ratifies by swearing an oath as a (rebellious) vassal, and the new covenant, a grant-type covenant which God ratifies by swearing the oath, the interpretative clue that unlocks Heb. 9:15-18.[85]

The second approach also advocates the consistent use of διαθήκη but argues for retaining the meaning "testament, will" throughout the entire passage. As with the previous position, the argument rejects as highly improbable on stylistic grounds, that an astute writer such as the Author would have changed the meaning of the paragraph's key word in the middle of the argument and without any notice, only to revert to the former meaning once again at the paragraph's end. Since vv. 16, 17 unequivocally require the reading "testament", the same meaning is to be attributed throughout the passage, and in fact throughout the book.[86]

Most commentators opt for a third position, one that essentially credits the Author's literary artistry with the ingenuity of exploiting the double meaning of the word διαθήκη "covenant" and "testament" in order to link the New Covenant with the death of Christ.[87] Moffatt understands the argument of these verses to be the crucial link between διαθήκη and the necessity of death. Starting with v. 16, he argues that the Author "uses διαθήκη as equivalent to 'will' or testamentary disposition, playing effectively upon the double sense of the term ... No natural interpretation of vv. 15-20 is possible, when διαθήκη is understood rigidly either as 'covenant' or as 'will'."[88] A similar position is held by most other major commentators.[89]

---

[83] One could list the meaning of ὁ διαθέμενος as "ratifier" not "testator", or θάνατος as signifying the death of the representative animals.

[84] Hahn, "Kinship".

[85] Hahn, "Kinship". 618.

[86] cf. Swetnam, "Interpretation".

[87] Attridge, *Hebrews* 153.

[88] Moffatt, *Hebrews* 128.

[89] Attridge, *Hebrews* 254 f.; Buchanan, *Hebrews*, Ellingworth, *Hebrews* 462 f., and Spicq, *Hébreux* ii: 285 ff.

The main objection raised against this interpretation is the change of meaning in the middle of the argument, vv. 16-17, and the subsequent return to the initial meaning in the closing verses. Hughes contends that this would amount to a virtually impossible scenario, especially when there are no textual markers to indicate the change.[90] Although the charge cannot be dismissed easily, the following three observations seem to provide reasonable grounds for adopting this position. First, if in Heb. 9:15-18 the Author uses the word διαθήκη with different connotations it would not be unprecedented in the epistle. A similar phenomenon can be found in other sections, albeit not with the same intensity. In the span of four verses in ch. 1 πνεῦμα is used once with the connotation of "wind" (1:7) and then with that of "spirit" (1:14). In 4:12-13 the noun λόγος is used with the different meanings of "word" (4:12) and "account" (4:13). The adjective πρώτη in Heb. 9:1 ff. begins by referring to the covenant and then changes to mean the first room of the tabernacle, while σκηνή in the same context refers first to the tabernacle, and then just to the Holy area of the tabernacle.

Second, Ellingworth makes the pertinent observation that the unarthrous use of διαθήκη in vv. 16, 17 can be considered as the necessary and sufficient marker that indicates a shift in meaning.[91] Third and most important, it must be acknowledged that even advocates for the consistent meaning see the necessity of a shift in the passage, if not in the connotation of διαθήκη, certainly in its referent. For Hahn that shift is the change between the two types of covenant.[92] For Swetnam, the distinction is between a perfect covenant, the New Covenant, a διαθήκη which the Lord διαθήσεται, and an imperfect covenant, the first covenant which although called a covenant by the Author, was never a διαθήκη which the Lord διήθετο.[93] This collocation is exclusively reserved by the Author to refer to the New Covenant. The first covenant is described in conjunction with the verbs συντελέω, or ποιέω, or ἐντέλλω. In support of his argument, Swetnam makes the astute observation that in the quotations the Author replaces the verb διατίθημι with a different verb every time it refers to another entity than the New Covenant.

> The net effect of these changes and retentions is to imply that God did not 'dispose' the διαθήκη at Sinai but that he, as 'the Lord,' will 'dispose' the new διαθήκη. If 'dispose' has for the author the connotation of the one who dies when a διαθήκη (testament) is made (as per 9,17), this usage suggests that at Sinai the animals would have been the ones show death put the διαθήκη into effect, had the Sinai διαθήκη been

---

[90] Hughes, "Covenant" 33 f.
[91] Ellingworth, *Hebrews* 463.
[92] Hahn, "Kinship".
[93] Swetnam, "Interpretation" 376.

a διαθήκη (testament) in the full sense of the word. In the new διαθήκη their place is taken by Christ, who is the one 'disposing'.[94]

This brief discussion of the use of διαθήκη in Heb. 9 has sought to determine what influence, if any, the LXX's διαθήκη may have had on the Author's use of the word. The definitive answer to this question depends not so much on the exegesis of the passage as on the larger semantic and theological issues for both the epistle and its canonical and literary contexts. In view of the enormous complexities involved in this semantic assessment, conclusions regarding the influence of the LXX on the use of διαθήκη must be drawn with caution.

First, it should be acknowledged that while the primary meaning of בְּרִית throughout the OT is "covenant" and that of διαθήκη outside the Greek OT is "will, testament", there is evidence of other meanings. Although the LXX's use of διαθήκη plays a key role in clarifying the NT's use of the term, the reasons behind its choice are unlikely to be settled with any significant degree of consensus. Second, some of the distinct linguistic characteristics of διαθήκη as used in Greek literature are different from those of the Hebrew בְּרִית. The plural of διαθήκη is already employed in 2Macc. and Sirach, and thus provides a direct antecedent for the explicit use of the plural by Paul in Rom. 9:4, and the implicit use by the Author in Heb. 8:8-13. Third, whatever the interpretation of διαθήκη in Heb. 9 might be, either "covenant", "testament" or a semantic compound integrating the two,[95] the Septuagint's contribution should be given due credit. If the meaning is "covenant", the distinct Septuagintal contribution is minimal, since the LXX's role would be reduced to that of supplying a linguistic unit without any distinct contribution to an already established meaning. If, however, either of the other two alternatives is true, the Septuagint has contributed to the enrichment of the biblical notion of "covenant" by providing a semantic nuance that became instrumental in the Christian authors' depiction of the theological link between the Mosaic and the New Covenants.

---

[94] Swetnam, "Interpretation" 377.

[95] Turner comments "the new sense of διαθήκη expresses not a 'will' as in secular Greek, nor strictly a 'covenant', but a one-sided *depositio* which insists on the inevitability of a death before it is put into effect ... we have in mind a one-sided deposition of grace"; Turner, *Words* 93.   Likewise, for Swetnam, "Christ's blood, inaugurating a new arrangement between God and His people, links both ideas, covenant and testament.   The link is something altogether essential and central"; "Interpretation" 389.

6. Conclusion

The aim of this chapter was to assess the contribution made by lexical semantics to the epistle's argument. The primary concern was to locate several lexical units, which arguably cause a certain level of semantic shift due to their translation and to investigate the extent to which the Author's use of these units was affected by the semantic shift. The causes for any shift in meaning are diverse and range from misunderstanding the Hebrew word or phrase to changes prompted by theological motives. Four lexical units were selected and analysed, and doubtless other examples might have been just as suitable.[96] The results can be summarised as follows.

First, the complexity involved in any lexical analysis requires firmer conclusions in adjacent fields of investigation, such as the nature of Biblical Greek and the study of bilingualism. Just as important, as Rabin pointed out, the attention given to the influence of the Hebraic-flavoured Greek of the Septuagint on the NT and on the Greek language in general, has to be balanced by the study of a probable reverse influence of the Greek language on the Hebrew and Aramaic languages.[97] These results would secure a better framework within which to study of the linguistic influence of the LXX on the epistle.

Second, the present study has highlighted a distinct aspect of the Septuagintal influence on the Author by focusing on several Greek words which present a certain degree of semantic divergence from the meaning of the Hebrew source word. Two primary aspects can be identified separately. In several of the investigated cases there is evidence that, either due to a peculiar translation equivalency or to a diachronic semantic shift, the meaning of the Septuagint word in a particular context relevant for the epistle was different from its counterpart in the corresponding Hebrew text. Other words, while not necessarily undergoing a lexical shift, nevertheless diversified their connotative spectrum, often through acquiring new referents. In both such cases, the study was able to identify a certain degree of dependency of the epistle on that particular Septuagintal meaning. While due to the limitation of this study, a definitive assessment of the linguistic influence of the Septuagint on the epistle cannot be formulated, on the basis of the cases analysed it is

---

[96] One can think of theologically loaded words such as ἐλπίς / ἐλπίζω, "hope / to hope for", translating בָּטַח / בֶּטַח, "trust / to trust", and πίστις / πιστεύω for אָמַן / אֱמוּנָה. A comprehensive analysis, necessary for a complete quantitative assessment, still needs to be undertaken.

[97] Chaim Rabin, "Hebrew and Aramaic in the First Century," in *The Jewish People in the First Century. Historical Geography, Political History, Social, Cultural and Religious Life and Institutions*, eds. S. Safrai and M. Stern (CRINT 1/I; Assen: Van Gorcum, 1976).

justifiable to conclude that the Author's engagement with the Greek Bible left unambiguous traces indicating the presence of a distinct Septuagintal influence, which might have been different had the Author based his "word of exhortation" on a Hebrew text of the OT.

Chapter Six

Septuagintal Theology in Hebrews:
Eschatology and Messianism

1. Introduction

The influences of the Septuagint on the epistle's theology can be seen as a logical development of the investigation undertaken in the first four chapters of this work. The goal for this stage is similar to that of previous chapters, namely, an inquiry into the effect that the study and the use of the Septuagint had on the theology of the epistle. The issues involved at this stage are, however, more complex and laborious than at any earlier stage.

One must note at the outset that the way in which this work has been organised may seem to be at times artificial or arbitrary, yet these divisions enable the reader of the Epistle to the Hebrews to appreciate the multifaceted nature of the Author's engagement with the Scriptures, particularly, the Septuagint. The study of the Septuagint's influence on the theology of the epistle can be approached from several different angles. One possible approach would take its lead from the acknowledgement that all the separate aspects studied thus far, the influence on the quotation's text, the quotation's context, the allusions and the Septuagintal lexicography have implications for the theology of the epistle. In the cases previously examined, the differences between the Greek and Hebrew texts affected to some degree the function of that particular text in the epistle. Therefore an exhaustive assessment of the theological impact of the Author's use of the Septuagint would require an integration of all the distinct contributions of this sort, a task that would prove to be very complex and difficult to manage.

A different and more feasible approach would concentrate on a theme in the epistle with the goal of examining aspects pertaining to that particular theme, which were developed as a direct consequence of Author's dependence on the Septuagint. The present study takes this approach and focuses on two of the themes in the epistle, eschatology and Messianism.[1]

---

[1] See Schaper (*Eschatology* 26 ff.) for a lucid presentation of the relationship between the two concepts, the former being the expression of the individual hope whereas the latter expresses of the nationalistic hopes of monarchic restoration.

2. Eschatology

2.1. *Eschatology in the Epistle to the Hebrews*

The epistle addresses a wide range of topics that are generally considered to be the subject matter of eschatology, understood in its wider sense as that branch of theology specifically dealing with the teaching of the Bible regarding the future and the end times.[2]   The extent of the epistle's eschatological interest has never been seriously disputed. Barrett, in his valuable contribution on the topic asserts that in the epistle "the eschatological is the determinant element. Features which do not upon the surface appear to be eschatological show ... traces of eschatological, even apocalyptic, origin, and the thought of the epistle arises out of the eschatological faith of the primitive Church."[3]   Barrett's position, issued almost five decades ago, has continued to be validated by subsequent research.   In particular, attention has been given to the centrality of eschatology in the epistle and its role in clarifying various theological themes or aspects, e.g., the idea of perfection,[4] the structure of the epistle,[5] the profile of the readership,[6] the literary genius of the Author,[7] and the hermeneutical perspective with which he read the OT Scriptures.[8]

Even a cursory reading of the epistle will reveal that no major topic within the field of eschatology was overlooked by the Author of Hebrews. Either explicitly or implicitly, the he refers to a vast spectrum of events that are associated with the end-times: the death and the resurrection of believers (11:35), the eschatological judgement (9:27) with its reward of life for the righteous and destruction for the apostates (10:37-38), the Parousia (9:28, 10:25, 37, 38), the heavenly gathering of the ones made righteous (12:22-23), the severe language of punishment reserved for the immature (10:26 ff.), repeated challenges to persevere until the end (3:14,

---

[2] It should be mentioned that, although distinct, there is considerable continuity between Jewish and Early Christian eschatology; see Andrew Chester, "The Parting of the Ways: Eschatology and Messianic Hope," in *Jews and Christians. The Parting of the Ways A.D. 70 to 135*, ed. James D. G. Dunn (WUNT 66; Tübingen: Mohr Siebeck, 1992). Moreover, while the use of dogmatic categories in analysing NT eschatology is strictly speaking an anachronism, they still serve well the brief analysis undertaken here.

[3] Barrett, "Eschatology" 366.

[4] Moisés Silva, "Perfection and Eschatology in Hebrews", *Westminster Theological Journal* 39 (1976).

[5] Vanhoye, *Structure*.

[6] Stanley D. Toussaint, "The Eschatology of the Warning Passages in the Book of Hebrews", *Grace Theological Journal* 3, no. 1 (1982).

[7] George W. MacRae, "Heavenly Temple and Eschatology in the Letter to the Hebrews", *Semeia* 12 (1978).

[8] Hughes, "Covenant".

6:11), and the final cataclysmic intervention of God (12:25 ff.) are all found within the theological texture of the epistle.

To reduce the eschatological interest of the epistle, however, to just these matters would be short-sighted, since the Author's eschatological perspective clearly extends beyond dealing with these distinct topics. Foremost in the opinion of many commentators is the contention that whichever topic the Author discusses, it is presented within an eschatological framework. The Christ event and its implications are to be understood within a certain understanding of creation, time, history, salvation, and existence, all of which seem to be essentially eschatological issues for him.[9]

Ἐπ' ἐσχάτου τῶν ἡμερῶν τούτων, one of the Septuagintalisms in the epistle (1:2), clearly sets the Author's discourse within a Jewish dualistic perspective on history marked by the two distinct epochs, the age of "these days" and that of "the days to come" (6:5). The frequent temporal references in the epistle confirm this fundamental aspect of understanding history. The Christ-event, seen as a whole, from the incarnation through his earthly life and culminating in his suffering, death, resurrection and exaltation, has both proclaimed and inaugurated the transition from the first age to the last. "These days", just as the covenant established in it, are gradually receding from the scene of human history as they usher in the eschatological age, which has been marked by the establishment of the New Covenant (8:8-13).

The Author's approach to the Scriptures is likewise framed by this eschatological mind-set. The dualistic perspective mentioned above is clearly evident in the epistle's treatment of, among other texts, Ps. 109 [110 MT] and Ps. 8, and Jer. 38 [31 MT], three passages that form the backbone of the epistle. Ps. 109 LXX clearly distinguishes between the moment of the Christ's session and that of the final victory over his enemies. Likewise, Ps. 8 emphasises that the glory and honour intended for mankind is at present experienced only by Christ, and while his brothers can rejoice in this initial fulfilment, the day when they too will share completely in his glory is yet to come. The passage from Jer. 38 LXX, which sets in contrast the two covenants and the ages they represent, is likewise read in light of the New Covenant established by Jesus and its implications. The Author's perspective on the history of salvation undoubtedly affects his reading of the Scriptures. Lane correctly underlines that "the writer of Hebrews ... chose to develop them [certain OT themes] eschatologically".[10]

---

[9] Hughes, "Covenant"; see also Williamson, *Philo*.
[10] Lane, *Hebrews* i: cviii.

The debate over which background best suits the eschatology of the epistle is likely to continue as scholars from three distinct camps dispute which particular type of eschatology underlies the epistle, Hellenistic,[11] Gnostic,[12] or Jewish.[13] Regardless of the outcome, it will probably confirm

---

[11] The extensive verbal similarities between the Author and Philo have naturally led scholars to consider Alexandrian Hellenistic eschatology as the suitable framework for understanding the eschatological language of the epistle. The platonic dualism between the spiritual and the material world as well as the distinction between the world of reality and the world of the senses, essentially a world of copies and shadows of reality, could be considered as the most suitable background for reading several important passages in the epistle. Training in Alexandrian philosophy, it is argued by the proponents of this view, generated a paradigm shift in the eschatological perspective of the Author, for whom "les formules escahtologiques traditionelles sont réinterprétées par Hébr. dans une mentalité alexandrine"; J. Cambier, *Eschatologie ou Hellénisme dans l'épître aux Hébreux*, (ALBO 2; Bruges / Paris: Descles de Brouwer, 1949) 91. Thus the Jewish temporal dualism was replaced by a Hellenistic, spatial dualism; cf. Bertold Klappert, *Die Eschatologie des Hebräerbriefs* (München: Kaiser Verlag, 1969). While, as Moffatt correctly argued, the Author "unlike Philo, ... does not allow his religious idealism to evaporate his eschatology" (*Hebrews* xxxiv), even so the key to understanding the eschatological language of the Author is platonic philosophy; cf. Cambier, *Eschatologie*; Sowers, *Hermeneutics*; James W. Thompson, *The Beginning of Christian Philosophy: The Epistle to the Hebrews* (CBQ-MS 13; Washington, D.C.: The Catholic Biblical Associations of America, 1981). For a convincing critique of this position, see Barrett, "Eschatology"; Williamson, *Philo*; and Lincoln D. Hurst, "Eschatology and 'Platonism' in the Epistle to the Hebrews", *SBL Seminar Papers* 23 (1984) 41-74.

[12] Pre-Christian Gnosticism as the background for the Author's eschatology was developed primarily in the influential work of Käsemann based on the strong thematic and verbal connections between Hebrews and Gnosticism, Ernst Käsemann, *The Wandering People of God: An Investigation of the Letter to the Hebrews*, trans. R. A. Harrisville and I. L. Sandberg (Minneapolis: Augsburg, 1984). This first thorough interpretation of the epistle based on Gnostic motifs seems to explain both several obscure references in the epistle and its dominant themes. The motif of the wandering people of God, the Gnostic myth of the redeemed redeemer and the distinct High priestly theology of the Author are, according to Käsemann, areas of influence of Gnostic ideas on the epistle. Käsemann's approach has been furthered by two German scholars, Grässer and Theissen. As far as eschatology is concerned, the Gnostic influence triggered a shift similar to the one advocated by the proponents of Alexandrian eschatology; "das futurisch-apokalyptische Zeitschema in Hebräerbrief unter dem Einfluss des gnostischen Erlösermythos hinter die Diastase Irdisch / Himmlisch zurückzutreten beginnt" (Klappert, *Eschatologie* 17). The main criticism against this view is the insufficiency of data regarding Pre-Christian Gnosticism, since the primary Gnostic sources are late relative to the NT writings; see especially Hurst, *Background*.

[13] Barrett's proposal for a Judaic-apocalyptic background for understanding the Author's eschatology constitutes a vigorous rebuttal against the alleged influence of Alexandrian philosophy on the eschatology of Hebrews. In analysing three of the main aspects in which the epistle was previously read against a Platonic background, Barrett finds evidence which supports a Jewish complex apocalyptic dualism rather than a Platonic dualism, "God has begun to fulfil his ancient promises; the dawn of the new age has

the present perspective on the epistle as a whole, best summarised by Williamson, "from start to finish, Hebrews is an *eschatological* 'exhortation'".[14]

2.2. *Septuagintal Eschatology*

Debate on the background of the Author's eschatology must be supplemented by considerations of the role played by the Septuagint in shaping and supporting the epistle's argument. This section undertakes to find any nuances of the eschatological language and ideas of the Author that can be traced directly to the Greek Scriptures, especially to texts in which there are notable differences between the Greek and Hebrew texts. These links do not imply that the Author's eschatology was formed exclusively by the Septuagint. As with other theological themes in the epistle, one must assume a variety of formative influences on the Author's eschatology and not limit them to his engagement with the Scriptures. Yet, for an author so preoccupied with the Scriptures one can legitimately expect to find nuances or particular aspects of his eschatological thought which can be directly traced to his use of the Septuagint. In the event that such evidence is found in the epistle, the case for a distinct influence of the Septuagint on the Author will be better supported.

At the outset several preliminary issues must be addressed. First and foremost is the question of the eschatology of the LXX itself, that is, whether or not there is evidence to support the claim that the Septuagint is characterised by an eschatology of its own. One must consider here not only the distinct eschatological nuances of the Greek translation, which are less obvious in their Hebrew text counterparts, but also the substantial contribution to Septuagintal eschatology from the extra-canonical writings, especially the Apocrypha. The key question is to determine whether or not there are portions of the Scriptures whose LXX text tradition have an eschatological overtone different from that of their Hebrew text counterparts.

Second, even in the eventuality of a positive answer to the above question, one must address the methodological difficulty in assessing the existence of a direct causal link between Septuagintal and Hebrews eschatology. As mentioned above, the Greek Scripture was but one of the

---

broken, though the full day has not yet come" ("Eschatology" 391). This position has been developed further by Williamson (*Philo*) and Hurst ("Eschatology"). Both have convincingly argued that while there is indeed linguistic similarity between the Author and Philo, as the major representative of the Hellenistic-Jewish philosophical symbiosis, their perspectives are quite different. Williamson concludes that "on such fundamental subjects as time, history, eschatology, the nature of the physical world, etc., the thoughts of Philo and the Writer of Hebrews are poles apart" (*Philo* 577).

[14] Williamson, *Philo* 145, (italics mine).

formative influences on the Author, which implies that a direct causal link between specific Septuagintal nuances and the Epistle to the Hebrews cannot be assumed. In the case of eschatology, as with any other theological theme, it will be more challenging to trace the LXX influence on the Author because of the intrinsic difficulty in assessing if the epistle's theological distinctiveness results from the Author's engagement with the Greek Jewish Scriptures, or is the product of extra-biblical factors such as Jewish contemporary traditions.

A third aspect concerns the appropriateness of the phrase "LXX eschatology" which might imply that the LXX as a whole is characterised by a uniform and consistent eschatology reflecting the theological intention of the translators. This clearly is not the case, principally because the LXX is not a uniform translation and its renderings reflect varied degrees of literalness determined by the translation technique employed by each individual translator. Yet, it is correct to speak of LXX eschatology if the phrase is limited to individual passages, especially those that display divergences between the Hebrew and the Greek textual traditions. These divergences affect the meaning of the respective texts with implications for the eschatological nuances of each passage. Several studies have conclusively shown that there is indeed strong evidence that the LXX is characterised by eschatological nuances distinct from those transmitted by the Hebrew text, at least the one preserved in the Masoretic tradition. While few would contend that the LXX is an eschatologically oriented translation, or that the eschatological distinctiveness is uniform across individual books, there is agreement that there are numerous LXX passages which, when taken both individually and collectively confer discernible eschatological nuances distinct from the parallel Hebrew texts.

For the book of Isaiah, Seeligmann provided evidence to demonstrate the dual influence on the translators of LXX Isaiah, that of the Bible text and the popular Jewish traditions outside the Bible. According to him, the Jewish-Alexandrian theology, "although its content is for the most part derived from the Bible, it also contains later elements which have their origin partly in popular Jewish traditions that grew outside, and simultaneously with, the Bible and gradually became authoritative, and partly in conscious or unconscious borrowing from the Hellenistic thought-world".[15] When one traces either the translation of different passages, lexical equivalents supplied or different themes it can be concluded that "the translator's interest ... cannot have been just incidental, but that it

---

[15] I. L. Seeligmann, *The Septuagint Version of Isaiah. A Discussion of Its Problems* (Leiden: E. J. Brill, 1948) 95.

originated in the way in which he combined Isaiah's expectation's regarding the future with his own".[16]

A similar conclusion was reached by Gard who undertook an analysis of parallel Greek and Hebrew passages in the book of Job pertaining to the eschatological concept of future life. He concludes that while there is close similarity between the translator's *Vorlage* and the Masoretic tradition, "in regard to the concept of the future life in the book of Job M [MT] and G [LXX] differ significantly".[17] The differences are to be traced not to different *Vorlage* but to "the tendency on the part of the Greek translator to introduce a theological point of view".[18]

Given the prominence of the LXX Psalter numerous studies have analysed the theological distinctiveness of its translation.[19] In a recent study of the eschatological nature of the Greek Psalter as a document reflecting the eschatological milieu in which the translators undertook their task, Schaper sets out to prove that the LXX develops eschatological themes beyond the boundaries set by the Hebrew Psalter. The linguistic and thematic translation choices in the Psalter, and especially their resemblance to other extra-canonical contemporary writings prove that "the whole of the second century is witness to a continual development of the formulation of eschatological and messianic hopes, with the Greek Psalter as one of its main monuments".[20] Starting from contrasting presuppositions and employing radically different methodology than Schaper, Sailhamer reached a similar conclusion in an investigation of the translation techniques used in the First Book of the Psalter. He observes that " the [verb] tense is ... at the heart of one of the central social and religious issues of early Judaism, eschatology. Doubtless, there were other important issues that made their way into the LXX Psalms translation, but this study has been most successful in describing the influence of eschatology on the choice of equivalencies, by considering the feature of past and future tense."[21] He concludes:

> two dominant religious outlooks, thus appear to have influenced the LXX Psalms translator, the centrality of the law for religious life and the hope of a future judgement for the wicked and reward for the righteous ... as far as the present study is

---

[16] Seeligmann, *Isaiah* 116. See also the more recent study of David A. Baer, *When We All Go Home: Translation and Theology in LXX Isaiah 56-66* (JSOT-SS 318; Sheffield: Sheffield Academic Press, 2001).

[17] Donald H. Gard, "The Concept of the Future Life According to the Greek Translator of the Book of Job", *Journal of Biblical Literature* 73 (1954) 143.

[18] Gard, "Concept" 143.

[19] See, *inter alios*, Olofsson, *Theological Exegesis*.

[20] Schaper, *Eschatology* 160.

[21] Sailhamer, *Technique* 214

concerned, it is the eschatology of early Judaism that made itself felt most prominently in the choice of verbal equivalencies in translation.[22]

While it is impossible to talk of an overall eschatology of the LXX as distinct from a Hebrew based eschatology, the works cited above supply sufficient evidence to conclude that, taken case by case, different books of the Jewish Scriptures convey an eschatological dimension distinct and different from that of the Hebrew Scriptures. Furthermore, while the translation choices reflect ideas and nuances that permeated Early Jewish eschatology and were the shaping force behind the translation, it is important to remark that once the Septuagint was completed, these eschatological perspectives became the scriptural *substratum* for continuous theological reflection on eschatology, especially for those readers who relied on the Septuagint as their Scripture.

2.3. *Septuagintal Eschatology in the Epistle to the Hebrews*

If indeed the Septuagint is characterised by a distinct eschatology in the parameters set above, it is legitimate to investigate the extent to which LXX eschatology has influenced the eschatology of the primitive Church, and especially of the canonical authors. As one who based his word of exhortation solely on the Greek Scriptures without recourse to a Hebrew text, the Author stands as a suitable candidate for an inquiry on the influence exerted by the distinct LXX eschatology. With the in-depth knowledge of the Greek Scripture that he possessed, the Author must have been influenced by the textual tradition he appealed to and was most familiar with, and his epistle should inevitably bear the imprint of this influence.

Before looking at the distinct elements of LXX eschatology, it is important to note that the majority of the eschatological aspects mentioned in the epistle can be traced to the Biblical text, preserved just as prominently in the Hebrew textual tradition as in the Greek. Space permits just a sampling from the Author's use of Scripture. The future orientation of Ps. 95 MT is just as clear as in its translation, Ps. 94 LXX. The Author could have argued based on either textual tradition that the invitation to enter eschatological rest is beneficial only for those whose hearts are not hardened by disbelief. Similarly, both Jer. 31 MT and its parallel text Jer. 38 LXX could have been read by the Author as a promise of a new covenant yet to be inaugurated, at least from the prophet's perspective.

---

[22] Sailhamer, *Technique* 214.

Furthermore, the cataclysmic events of the book of Haggai are equally prominent in the Hebrew text as in its Greek translation.[23]

In other instances, however, the Author seems to develop ideas from passages in the Scriptures in which eschatological features preserved in the LXX tradition differ from those of the Masoretic tradition. A first case consists of the titles of several Greek Psalms. Bruce has drawn attention to the value of the Greek Psalter titles for their aid in the interpretation of the psalms, especially the historical psalms.[24] One example of divergent equivalencies in the psalm titles, namely the phrase εἰς τὸ τέλος used to translate the musical title לַמְנַצֵּחַ, is particularly important for the eschatology of Hebrews. The enigmatic εἰς τὸ τέλος title is found in four of the ten Psalms quoted in the epistle[25] and was probably considered by the Author as an eschatological clue, a reference to the message and the acts of God regarding the end of time ἐπ' ἐσχάτου τῶν ἡμερῶν τούτων. It is also notable that the same phrase is used twice in the introductory verses of the Song of Moses, Dt. 31:24, 30, another pivotal scriptural passage for the Author. The noun τέλος is employed with clear eschatological nuances throughout the epistle. It describes in 3:14, μέτοχοι γὰρ τοῦ Χριστοῦ γεγόναμεν, ἐάνπερ τὴν ἀρχὴν τῆς ὑποστάσεως μέχρι τέλους βεβαίαν κατάσχωμεν, and 6:11, ἐπιθυμοῦμεν δὲ ἕκαστον ὑμῶν τὴν αὐτὴν ἐνδείκνυσθαι σπουδὴν πρὸς τὴν πληροφορίαν τῆς ἐλπίδος ἄχρι τέλους, the extent to which Christians are called to demonstrate perseverance and contributes to the metaphorical description of the final judgement in 6:8, ἧς τὸ τέλος εἰς καῦσιν. Neither the Author's selection of psalms nor the eschatological interpretation he gave to them depended exclusively on the εἰς τὸ τέλος phrase, yet it is reasonable to contend that while the Author was drawn to these psalms because of their content, the title supplied a convenient eschatological flavour which contributed to the interpretation and application of the message of the psalm in a new context.

A second type of eschatological link between the Author and the Septuagint consists of passages where the extensive use of the future tense differentiates between the meaning of the Greek text and that of the Hebrew. The differences between the Hebrew and the Greek verbal systems, as well as the lack of uniformity with which the Septuagint translators have rendered the Hebrew modes, gave rise to a semantic divergence between the source and target texts. Since the verb tenses

---

[23] Lane, *Hebrews*; Andrew T. Lincoln, "Sabbath, Rest, and Eschatology in the New Testament (Heb 3:7-4:13)", in *From Sabbath to Lord's Day*, ed. D. Carson (Grand Rapids: Zondervan, 1982).

[24] F. F. Bruce, "The Earliest Old Testament Interpretation", in *The Witness of Tradition*, ed. M. A. Beek, *Oudtestamentische Studiën 17* (Leiden: E. J. Brill, 1972).

[25] Ps. 8, 21 [22 MT], 39 [40 MT], and 44 [45 MT].

provide a straightforward textual basis for developing eschatological themes, these differences will inevitably affect the way in which readers of the two textual traditions understand a passage. Several examples of the Septuagintal usage of the future tense suggest that the Greek text was instrumental in providing those temporal clues, though absent from the Hebrew text, which were read by the Author as indicative of the subsequent work of God in the life and ministry of Christ. Particular renderings of verb tenses by the Septuagint in the context of several quotations such as Ps. 21 [22 MT], Ps. 39 [40 MT], and Is. 8, made the LXX text more suitable for subsequent interpretation of prophecies, which became "a present reality in Christ".[26]

The impact of the LXX on the eschatology of the epistle can be traced also in the area of lexical semantics, in which either distinct renderings of Hebrew words, such as βραχύ τι in Ps. 8:6 LXX, or ἀλλαγήσονται in Ps. 101:27 LXX, or the use of consecrated Septuagintal language, ἐπ᾽ ἐσχάτου τῶν ἡμερῶν, give evidence of the extent to which the Author appropriated LXX eschatology to inform and support his understanding of Christ, the eschatological event *par excellence*.

The eschatology of the epistle incorporates certain aspects that can be best explained by the Author's use of scriptural texts in which variations between the Greek and Hebrew textual traditions were instrumental for his argument. Even so, the entire eschatological interest of the epistle cannot be reduced to these cases in which the Author displays direct dependence on the Septuagint. A complete understanding of the formative influences on the epistle's eschatology must include other factors, not least primitive Christian eschatology. Nevertheless, the Epistle to the Hebrews stands as an example of the way in which distinctive eschatological nuances of the Septuagint exerted influence on the theological reflection of the LXX readers.

3. Messianism

3.1. Messianism in Early Judaism

The dual interest of this study in eschatology and Messianism in the Epistle to the Hebrews is not random; it rather reflects an interrelation between the two topics, which is assumed in the present study. In view of an overwhelming volume of secondary literature devoted to the study of Messianism in Early Judaism, the present study can only adopt a limited perspective that will inevitably leave a number of the main issues

---

[26] Ellingworth, *Hebrews* 41.

unaddressed. This section will focus on selected aspects of the relationship between the messianic ideas present in the Septuagint and their link with the Author's use of Scripture in shaping the Christology of the epistle.[27]

---

[27] Some of the recent representative studies include Martin G. Abegg and Craig A. Evans, "Messianic Passages in the Dead Sea Scrolls," in *Qumran-Messianism. Studies on the Messianic Expectations in the Dead Sea Scrolls*, eds. J. H. Charlesworth, H. Lichtenberger, and G. S. Oegema (Tübingen: Mohr - Siebeck, 1998); H. Anderson, "The Jewish Antecedents of the Christology in Hebrews", in *The Messiah. Developments in Earliest Judaism and Christianity*, ed. J. H. Charlesworth (Minneapolis: Fortress Press, 1992); J. H. Charlesworth, H. Lichtenberger, and G. S. Oegema, eds., *Qumran-Messianism. Studies on the Messianic Expectations in the Dead Sea Scrolls* (Tübingen: Mohr - Siebeck, 1998); James H. Charlesworth, "From Messianology to Christology: Problems and Prospects", in *The Messiah. Developments in Earliest Judaism and Christianity*, ed. J. H. Charlesworth (Minneapolis: Fortress Press, 1992); *idem*, "Introduction: Messianic Ideas in Early Judaism", in *Qumran-Messianism. Studies on the Messianic Expectations in the Dead Sea Scrolls*, eds. J. H. Charlesworth, H. Lichtenberger, and G. S. Oegema (Tübingen: Mohr Siebeck, 1998); *idem*, "Messianology in the Biblical Pseudepigrapha", in *Qumran-Messianism. Studies on the Messianic Expectations in the Dead Sea Scrolls*, eds. J. H. Charlesworth, H. Lichtenberger, and G. S. Oegema (Tübingen: Mohr Siebeck, 1998); *idem*, ed., *The Messiah. Developments in Earliest Judaism and Christianity* (Minneapolis: Fortress Press, 1992); John J. Collins, *The Sceptre and the Star. The Messiahs of the Dead Sea Scrolls and Other Ancient Literature* (New York: Doubleday, 1995); John Day, ed., *King and Messiah in Israel and the Ancient Near East* (JSOT-SS 270; Sheffield: Sheffield Academic Press, 1998); Craig A. Evans and Peter W. Flint, eds., *Eschatology, Messianism and the Dead Seas Scrolls* (Grand Rapids: Eerdmans, 1997); Peter W. Flint and James C. Vanderkam, eds., *The Dead Sea Scrolls after Fifty Years. A Comprehensive Assessment*, 2 vols., (Leiden: E. J. Brill, 1998-1999); I. Gruenwald, S. Shaked, and G. G. Stroumsa, eds., *Messiah and Christos. Studies in the Jewish Origins of Christianity. Presented to David Flusser on the Occasion of His Seventy-Fifth Birthday* (Tübingen: Mohr Siebeck, 1992); Martin Hengel, *Studies in Early Christology* (Edinburgh: T. & T. Clark, 1995); William Horbury, *Jewish Messianism and the Cult of Christ* (London: SCM Press, 1998); *idem*, "Messianism in the Old Testament Apocrypha and Pseudepigrapha", in *King and Messiah in Israel and the Ancient Near East. Proceedings of the Oxford Old Testament Seminar*, ed. John Day, (JSOT-SS 270; Sheffield: Sheffield Academic Press, 1998); Donald H. Juel, *Messianic Exegesis* (Philadelphia: Fortress Press, 1988); Michael A. Knibb, "Eschatology and Messianism in the Dead Sea Scrolls", in *The Dead Sea Scrolls after Fifty Years. A Comprehensive Assessment*, eds. Peter W. Flint and James C. Vanderkam (Leiden: E. J. Brill, 1998 - 1999); H. Lichtenberger, "Messianic Expectations and Messianic Figures During the Second Temple Period", in *Qumran-Messianism. Studies on the Messianic Expectations in the Dead Sea Scrolls*, eds. J. H. Charlesworth, H. Lichtenberger, and G. S. Oegema (Tübingen: Mohr Siebeck, 1998); Jean Lust, "Septuagint and Messianism, with a Special Emphasis on the Pentateuch", in *Theologische Probleme der Septuaginta und der hellenistischen Hermeneutik*, ed. H. G. Reventlow, (Gütersloh: Chr. Kaiser, 1997); Johan Lust, "The Greek Version of Balaam's Third and Fourth Oracles. The ανθρωπος in Num 24:7 and 17. Messianism and Lexicography", in *VIII Congress of the IOSCS*, eds. L. Greenspoon and O. Munnich,

While there seems to be no overarching consensus on a wide range of issues, not least the definition of the concept of the Messiah, for the purposes of this study it will suffice to adopt a working definition that includes several cardinal characteristics of the Messiah, a title given to an eschatological figure, a "divinely appointed and anointed supernatural man",[28] whose task is to see the establishment of God's kingdom on earth.[29]

The scholarly debate over Messianism is far from settled. Its place and importance in the Old Testament and in Early Judaism, as reflected not only in the Greek translation of the Jewish Scriptures, but also in an extensive corpus of apocryphal and pseudepigraphic writings, as well as its connections with developments in the New Testament, are hotly disputed areas of research. The dialogue continues into the present with renewed zeal, especially as a result of both the important textual discoveries from the Judean Desert, as well as of a more focused attention on the corpus of pseudepigraphic writings.

(SCS 41; Atlanta: Scholars Press, 1995); *idem*, "Messianism and Septuagint," in *Congress Volume Salamanca 1983*, ed. J. Emerton (STV 36; Leiden: E. J. Brill, 1985); S. Mowinckel, *He That Cometh* (Oxford: Blackwell, 1956); Bilhah Nitzan, "Eschatological Motives in Qumran Literature: The Messianic Concept", in *Eschatology in the Bible and in Jewish and Christian Tradition*, ed. H. G. Reventlow (JSOT-SS 243; Sheffield: Sheffield Academic Press, 1997); Gerbern S. Oegema, *The Anointed and His People. Messianic Expectations from the Maccabees to Bar Kochba* (JSP-SS 27; Sheffield: Sheffield Academic Press, 1998); *idem*, "Messianic Expectations in the Qumran Writings: Theses on Their Development", in *Qumran-Messianism. Studies on the Messianic Expectations in the Dead Sea Scrolls*, eds. J. H. Charlesworth, H. Lichtenberger, and G. S. Oegema (Tübingen: Mohr Siebeck, 1998); Émile Puech, "Messianism, Resurrection, and Eschatology at Qumran and in the New Testament", in *The Community of the Renewed Covenant. The Notre Dame Symposium on the Dead Sea Scrolls*, eds. E. Ulrich and J. C. VanderKam (Notre Dame: University of Notre Dame Press, 1994); J. J. M. Roberts, "The Old Testament's Contribution to Messianic Expectations", in *The Messiah. Developments in Earliest Judaism and Christianity*, ed. J. H. Charlesworth (Minneapolis: Fortress Press, 1992); P. E. Satterthwaite, R. S. Hess, and G. J. Wenham, eds., *The Lord's Anointed. Interpretation of Old Testament Messianic Texts* (Grand Rapids: Baker, 1995); L. H. Schiffman, "Messianic Figures and Ideas in the Qumran Scrolls", in *The Messiah. Developments in Earliest Judaism and Christianity*, ed. J. H. Charlesworth (Minneapolis: Fortress Press, 1992); S. Talmon, "The Concepts of *Masiah* and Messianism in Early Judaism", in *The Messiah. Developments in Earliest Judaism and Christianity*, ed. J. H. Charlesworth (Minneapolis: Fortress Press, 1992). and James C. VanderKam, "Messianism in the Scrolls," in *The Community of the Renewed Covenant. The Notre Dame Symposium on the Dead Sea Scrolls*, eds. E. Ulrich and J. C. VanderKam (Notre Dame: University of Notre Dame Press, 1994).

[28] Charlesworth, "Christology".

[29] Lust, "Septuagint and Messianism" 73.

At the risk of oversimplification, the following two schools of thought are selected as representative. Charlesworth summarises the basic tenants of the minimalist position by stressing the following aspects that scholarship must answer. First, the textual evidence for the origins and developments of Messianology in Jewish Scriptures is very limited, indicating that Messianism developed much later than previously thought. Second, Messianism was neither a coherent nor a normative doctrine. Third, most Jews in the Second Temple period were not expecting the coming of the Messiah.[30] Obviously the implications of these positions for NT Christology are enormous. Many aspects which were once thought to be irrefutable, such as the smooth transition from Jewish Messianology to Christology and the belief that Jesus fulfilled in his life and teaching all the Jewish expectations for a Messiah, are no longer as clear as they were thought to be.[31] In a recent and fresh approach, Horbury has challenged this interpretation of the data and outlined what might be termed as a maximalist position, maintaining that a different set of answers fit the data, "Messianism grew up in Old Testament times; the Old Testament books especially in their edited and collected form, offered what were understood in the post-exilic age and later as a series of messianic prophecies; and this series formed the heart of a coherent set of expectations which profoundly influenced ancient Judaism and early Christianity."[32]

3.2. Septuagintal Messianism

A similar divergence of opinions can be found when assessing the role of the Septuagint in the development of Jewish Messianism. The importance of the LXX as a document which not only embodied contemporary theological perspectives, but also became the Scripture for subsequent generations of Greek-speaking Jews, cannot be overemphasised in assessing Messianology in the Second Temple period, the historical context of the Author.

Since the Septuagint is not a uniform translation it would be wrong to assume that distinct messianic readings are evenly spread throughout the entire corpus. Scholars have repeatedly pointed out that the Septuagint translation bears evidence of both texts with accentuated as well as diminished messianic nuances.[33] Therefore, since the concept of a unified messianic perspective of the Septuagint is not tenable, it is correct to

---

[30] Charlesworth, "Christology" 35.

[31] Charlesworth, "Christology" 6; see also David Flusser, "Messianology and Christology in the Epistle to the Hebrews," in *Judaism and the Origins of Christianity*, ed. David Flusser (Jerusalem: Magnes Press, 1988) 246-89.

[32] Horbury, *Jewish Messianism* 6.

[33] Harl, Dorival, and Munnich, *Bible grecque* 219 ff.

address only the contribution of several individual texts to Early Jewish Messianism.[34]

While not doing justice to the complexities involved, the following two positions are representative. Lust contends that the LXX does not present a Messianism distinct from that of the Hebrew Scriptures. In the conclusions of his recent study based on the evaluation of relevant passages in the Pentateuch, he contends that "the Septuagint version of the Pentateuch does not seem to emphasise individual messianism".[35] This statement confirms his position articulated in earlier studies, in which he seeks to prove that the LXX, unlike the Targumim, does not display a messianic exegesis.[36] A similar stand has been taken by Oegema in arguing against the trend of overestimating the "messianic" passages in the Septuagint.[37]

Those who defend the distinct Septuagintal Messianism argue both on a level of the individual books, as well as for the Septuagint as a whole. Seeligmann's conclusion regarding the Messianism of LXX Isaiah is similar to the one he reached on the eschatology of LXX Isaiah. He states, "nowhere else does the rendering of biblical images into Greek terminology transpose the content of the text into the Hellenistic sphere of thought more markedly than in the case of this Messianic figure".[38] Along the same lines but with a wider agenda, Schaper's monograph seeks to establish not only that several renderings in the LXX Psalter indicate a clear messianic bias in the translation, but also that the translators have undertaken their task conscientious of a network of messianic texts. Schaper contends that the messianic idea, under the growing influence of Greek thought, "was re-stated and given an *interpretatio graeca*". He continues, "we sense a general inclination towards a more and more refined elaboration of messianism under the influence of Greek thought which showed a tendency towards a universalization of the said concept, a concept which developed into something like a system of messianic belief on the basis of a textual network established in the Septuagint, not least under the impact of the Greek Pentateuch".[39] Horbury advocates a similar position in the study already mentioned. Commenting on the Pentateuch oracles in the LXX, he establishes that:

> they presuppose, already at that time, a developed messianic interpretation which has given rise to a chain of exegetical interconnections, between these great prophecies

---

[34] Lust, "Septuagint and Messianism"; Lust, "Messianism and Septuagint".

[35] Lust, "Septuagint and Messianism" 45.

[36] Lust, "Messianism and Septuagint" 177.

[37] Oegema, "Expectations" 44.

[38] Seeligmann, *Isaiah* 119.

[39] Schaper, *Eschatology* 144.

> within the Pentateuch and also between the Pentateuch and the books of the Prophets ... these LXX passages point to a consistent set of messianic hopes, constituting an expectation centred on a royal messiah which was sufficiently central and widespread among Jews of the third century.[40]

The purpose of this section is to build on the positions outlined above with a view to extending the inquiry into the influence that the messianic overtones of the LXX might have had on the NT authors, and particularly the Author. The underlying idea for this study is a corollary of the position advocating a distinct messianic outlook of the Septuagint. If the Septuagint indeed presents nuances of Messianism distinct from the Hebrew text, one would legitimately expect to see those nuances appealed to and developed by the arguments of Christian theologians in the first century, theologians who not only were representatives of a community with firm beliefs in Jesus of Nazareth as the Messiah, but who also defended their beliefs on the basis of the Scriptures, which for some were the Septuagint.

To a large extent, the issue of the source of Messianism in the LXX, be it the result of deliberate or involuntary translation choices, is not directly important. What is important, however, is the realisation that certain Greek texts communicated messianic ideas with more vividness and nuance than their parallel Hebrew texts. Methodologically, one is confronted again with a recurring case of indeterminacy, since it is impossible to assess with certitude whether the particular messianic ideas of the Author were influenced by the LXX or whether they were the result of a larger range of factors present in his theological milieu. This study is primarily interested in tracing the direct links between the Author's argument and particular nuances of the LXX text without the intention of being exhaustive in collecting and presenting the evidence, a rather daunting task in an epistle with one of the most developed Christologies in the NT. A sample of the diverse evidence is in order.

3.3. Septuagintal Messianism in the Epistle to the Hebrews

Initially this section will turn to several passages that indicate that certain christological aspects of the epistle were drawn directly and distinctly from the Septuagint text. One important common denominator of these texts is a degree of deviation in the Greek text from the Hebrew.

Mention should be made, however, of a group of passages used by the Author that were understood to be messianic by both Christians and Jews. In such cases it is evident that the Hebrew and Greek texts equally support the messianic tradition. This is certainly true for texts such as Ps. 2 and 2

---

[40] Horbury, *Jewish Messianism* 51.

Sam. 7, two texts in which the messianic son – king motif, can be detected in both textual traditions. Further confirmation of this statement is found in the similarity of interpretations of these passages by both subsequent Greek texts, such as Pss. Sol. 17 and the NT, as well as Hebrew texts, such as the 4QFlor.[41] The fusion of these two texts, not only to each other but also with other thematically similar passages in catenae of scriptural quotations is found both among the Qumran texts, and in the NT. Their messianic message is given renewed, as in 4QFlor, or fulfilled, as in the NT, expression.[42]

One aspect of the Author's christological reading of Ps. 2 depends on the particular translation of v. 10 in the Septuagint, where the phrase הִוָּסְרוּ שֹׁפְטֵי אָרֶץ is translated as παιδεύθητε πάντες οἱ κρίνοντες τὴν γῆν and v. 12, where δράξασθε παιδείας translates נַשְּׁקוּ־בַר. The root παιδ- appears twice in the final admonition of Ps. 2 LXX. The first time, the niphal imperative of יָסַר is translated by the aorist imperative παιδεύθητε, by far the most common Greek equivalence in the LXX for the Hebrew verb. The second time, however, παιδείας translates the direct object of the Hebrew collocation נַשְּׁקוּ־בַר, for which a satisfying explanation has yet to be given.[43] Schaper has demonstrated the messianic overtones of this choice, especially when it is seen in light of later passages, Wis. 6:1-11, *1 En.* 51:3, *Pss. Sol.* 17:21, 32, and 18:7. Since these passages are overtly messianic, the very fact that they allude to Ps. 2 and its motifs is sufficient to prove that later authors perceived Ps. 2 as a text with a messianic agenda.[44]

In using Ps. 2, the Author was probably guided by a similar rationale, and while he builds on a text of the psalm where the Greek and Hebrew texts are semantically identical, in other instances important thematic connections with the epistle are drawn from readings in the psalm where the Greek text differs from the Hebrew. The development of the discipline theme, παιδεία in ch. 12 is a foremost example.

Ps. 109 [110MT] also falls in this category. The importance of Ps. 109 LXX for the Author has been acknowledged throughout this study. The focus here is on a series of translation equivalents which caused noticeable divergences between the two text traditions, which in part are responsible not only for making Ps 109 LXX "one of the most remarkable messianic

---

[41] Bateman, *Hermeneutics*.

[42] Herbert W. Bateman IV, "Two First-Century Messianic Uses of the OT: Heb 1:5-13 and 4QFlor 1.1-19", *Journal of the Evangelical Theological Society* 38, no. 1 (1995).

[43] Schaper, *Eschatology* 74.

[44] Schaper, *Eschatology* 75.

interpretations in the Greek Psalter",[45] but also for determining its use in the epistle.

The consistent literalism of the translation of the first part of Ps. 110 MT breaks down in v. 3, where a difficult Hebrew text is translated into a reading with potential messianic overtones.

Ps. 110:3 MT	Ps. 109:3 LXX
עַמְּךָ נְדָבֹת	μετὰ σοῦ ἡ ἀρχὴ
בְּיוֹם חֵילֶךָ	ἐν ἡμέρᾳ τῆς δυνάμεώς σου
בְּהַדְרֵי־קֹדֶשׁ	ἐν ταῖς λαμπρότησιν τῶν ἁγίων
מֵרֶחֶם מִשְׁחָר	ἐκ γαστρὸς
לְךָ טַל יַלְדֻתֶיךָ:	πρὸ ἑωσφόρου ἐξεγέννησά σε

The are several points where the two textual traditions diverge. First, the phrase μετὰ σοῦ ἡ ἀρχή indicates that the translators read the Hebrew עַמְּךָ נְדָבֹת with a different vocalisation עִמְּךָ נְדִבֹת.[46] There are several possibilities for the Hebrew phrase בְּהַדְרֵי־קֹדֶשׁ. It can be taken either as a reference to the holy adornment of worshipers, or, if emended to read בהררי־קדש, " holy mountains", would continue the theme of Zion in v. 2.[47] The Greek translator read it as a reference to the radiance, ἐν ταῖς λαμπρότησιν, of the holy ones, τῶν ἁγίων, which, according to Schaper, is a reference to the likening of the "saints and wise men to the radiance of heavenly bodies".[48]

The most disputed part of this verse is the equivalence ἐκ γαστρὸς πρὸ ἑωσφόρου for the Hebrew מֵרֶחֶם מִשְׁחָר. Acknowledging the difficulties of the Hebrew expression, Schaper favours the Greek text as reading "before the morning star", which, if correct, would strengthen even more the messianic outlook of the psalm by introducing the important messianic motif of "the morning-star".[49]

Lastly, while omitting the לְךָ טַל possibly on the grounds of an inability to make sense of the text in its context, the LXX translator read יַלְדֻתֶיךָ with a different vocalisation יְלִדְתִּיךָ, supplying the translation ἐξεγέννησά σε, reminiscent of the divine adoption granted to the

---

[45] Schaper, *Eschatology* 101.

[46] Leslie C. Allen, *Psalms 101-150* (WBC; Dallas: Word, 1983) 80.

[47] The former position is advocated by Michael D. Goulder (*The Psalms of the Return. [Book V, Psalms 107-150]. Studies in the Psalter* [JSOT-SS 258; Sheffield: Sheffield Academic Press, 1998] 146), while the latter by most commentators, including Allen, *Psalms* 79; Bratcher and Reyburn, *Handbook* 950; and Kraus, *Psalms* ii: 344.

[48] Schaper, *Eschatology* 103.

[49] Schaper, *Eschatology* 102. See also Horbury, *Jewish Messianism*.

Davidic king in Ps. 2.[50] In this way a Hebrew text that was virtually unintelligible, opened the way for a Greek text that "distinctly describes the birth of a child".[51] The cumulative force of these individual translation peculiarities support Schaper's overall evaluation of Ps. 109 LXX as a "psalm of messianic judgement".[52]

In a previous section attention was drawn to the association of Pss. 2 and 109 LXX, which is at the heart of the Author's christological motif of the Son-King.[53] This association was made not only on the basis of the similar language of υἱός μου εἶ σύ and σὺ εἶ ἱερεύς, as they stand collated in 5:5, 6, but also of many other important contextual links. Thus, the motifs of Zion as the chosen place for rulership, the messianic mandate to rule over the kings of the earth, and the Messiah's appointment by Yahweh's decree all point to a close conceptual unity. The text of Ps. 109 LXX draws attention to the motif of the "birth of a monarch", ἐκ γαστρός ... ἐξεγέννησά σε, as a further thematic element which legitimises the fusion of the two psalms, cf. Ps. 2:7 ἐγὼ σήμερον γεγέννηκά σε.

A second category consists of texts for which the difference between the Greek and Hebrew texts was significant enough to suggest that the christological application of that passage was determined primarily by the form or content of the Greek textual tradition. Frequently, the divergences in the wider literary contexts of the Greek texts both explain and justify the Author's use of that text. Particular LXX renderings in these contexts made them conducive for a messianic reading. This holds true in the quotations from Is. 8, Ps. 44 [45 MT], Ps. 101 [102 MT] and Ps. 39 LXX. The most significant difference in these texts, which made them suitable for a christological application, is the recurring theme of dialogue between divine beings. Just as important, several peculiar renderings in the contexts of these quotations[54] further qualified them to offer scriptural support to the Christology of the epistle.

One final example that deserves attention is the use of Ps. 8 in Heb. 2. It has already been argued that the Greek translation added an eschatological emphasis that guided the interpretation and application of the psalm. The messianic overtones of the key nouns in v. 5, ἄνθρωπος and υἱὸς ἀνθρώπου might have fulfilled a similar role for the Christology of the epistle. The inclusion of Ps. 8 among the messianic texts of the OT

---

[50] Allen, *Psalms* 81.

[51] David M. Hay, *Glory at the Right Hand. Psalm 110 in Early Christianity* (New York: Abingdon Press, 1973) 21. See also Martin Hengel, "'Sit at My Right Hand!'" in *Studies in Early Christology*, ed. Martin Hengel (Edinburgh: T. & T. Clark, 1995).

[52] Schaper, *Eschatology* 107.

[53] The association of the two psalms is explicitly mentioned in Heb. chs. 1, 5, and 12.

[54] See *supra* (ch. 3, 2).

is disputed. While it clearly served this function for the Christian church, especially through its association with Ps. 110,[55] in rabbinical circles it was not regarded as messianic.[56] The messianic reading of Ps. 8, which seems to have influenced the Author, could well have had its source in the Christian tradition. The main interpretative question regarding the Messianism of Ps. 8 is whether the readings ἄνθρωπος and υἱὸς ἀνθρώπου were read by the Author with messianic connotations, and if so, what was the source of this reading.

In order to answer this question one must consider several Septuagintal passages in which these terms are used with stronger messianic force. Two such texts are found in Balaam's oracles in Num. 24. The differences between the Hebrew and Greek texts have been often addressed.[57] Both texts use the noun ἄνθρωπος as the equivalent for מַיִם (24:7) and שֵׁבֶט (24:17). A similarly significant change caused by the translation is that of the king אֲגַג as Γωγ. The inclusion of both texts in Numbers among the passages that display an accentuated Messianism is fairly well established,[58] although not all scholars agree with it. Lust has given careful attention to these passages and concludes that "the Greek translation of the LXX bringing the ἄνθρωπος on the scene, does not accentuate the messianic character of the Balaam oracles".[59] Lust is willing to admit an eschatologically distinct nuance in the LXX's replacement of the historical king Agag by the eschatological king Gog, the dominant figure in the apocalyptic scene in Ez 38-39.[60] While one would certainly concur with Lust that the term ἄνθρωπος in the Greek Bible is generally a "neutral" term without messianic connotations,[61] it is difficult to see why he is so reluctant to grant a more messianic overtone to the term ἄνθρωπος in a text which he himself labels as "a prophecy about the final days". Schaper's explanation of reading these texts as part of the "Septuagintal network of messianic texts" seems to be a more logical

---

[55] *Inter alios*, Leschert, *Foundations* 97.

[56] Lincoln D. Hurst, "The Christology of Hebrews 1 and 2", in *The Glory of Christ in the New Testament. Studies in Christology. In Memory of George Bradford Caird*, eds. L. D. Hurst and N. T. Wright (Oxford: Clarendon Press, 1987) 153; Kistemaker, *Citations* 29.

[57] Arie van der Kooij, "Perspectives on the Study of the Septuagint. Who are the Translators?" in *Perspectives in the Study of the Old Testament and Early Judaism. A Symposium in Honour of Adam S. van der Woude on the Occasion of His 70th Birthday*, eds. Florentino Garcia Martinez and Ed Noort (Leiden: E. J. Brill, 1998); Lust, "Septuagint and Messianism"; *idem*, "Messianism and Lexicography".

[58] Harl, Dorival, and Munnich, *Bible grecque*; Horbury, *Messianism*; Schaper, *Eschatology*.

[59] Lust, "Septuagint and Messianism" 44.

[60] Lust, "Septuagint and Messianism" 43.

[61] Lust, "Messianism and Septuagint"; Johan Lust, "Lexicography".

conclusion, sensitive to the culture of the translators.[62] If Schaper's reconstruction of the textual basis for a messianic Septuagint is correct, it would increase the probability of a messianic reading for ἄνθρωπος in Ps. 8 LXX.

The Messianism of the Epistle to the Hebrews is far too complex for a limited study to do it justice. Additional issues such as the son – high priest theme would deserve attention, especially in light of evidence provided by other traditions of interpretation parallel to that of the Author. The theme of Christ as the High Priest, one of the theological *tours de force* of the epistle, was developed by the Author when he combined into one person the twofold office of the Messiah, the Son who was made the High Priest,[63] a development distinct from that of the Qumran community and their double messiahship of Aaron and David.

4. Conclusion

The present chapter has explored several aspects pertaining to the themes of eschatology and Messianism focusing on passages which, due to their distinct meaning in the Septuagint, proved to be more suitable scriptural support for the Author's argument. Doubtless, it must be said that more detailed analysis is necessary in order to establish with certitude if in any of these examples we encounter not so much a Septuagintal influence on the eschatology and the Christology of the epistle, but rather a series of convenient readings and coincidences which were exploited by the Author. While this is indeed a limitation of the approach undertaken in this study, it cannot be denied that the Septuagint, with its distinct eschatological and messianic perspectives, shaped through these very readings the Author's reflection on the Christ-event. This brief presentation of the implications of Septuagintal readings on the epistle's eschatology and Christology will be continued in the test case analysis of the Author's use of the quotation from Hab. 2:3-4 LXX.

---

[62] Schaper, *Eschatology* 116 ff.
[63] Lindars, *Theology* 65.

Part Two

The Use of Hab. 2:3-4 LXX in Heb. 10:37-38

Chapter Seven

The Use of Hab. 2:3-4 in Heb. 10:37-38:
Textual Considerations

1. Introduction

Part two of the present study consists of a detailed examination of the text, context, and theology of the quotation from Hab. 2:3-4 in Heb. 10:37-38. As previously mentioned, this quotation is arguably the result of the most extensive editorial reshaping by the Author of Hebrews, and thus offers itself as a valuable test-case for investigating the presence or the absence of direct Septuagintal influences on its text, literary context, and theology.

The subject matter of this chapter consists of an examination of the text and related text-critical issues with regard to three textual traditions of Habakkuk, the Masoretic text of Hab. 2:3-4, its translation in the Septuagint, and finally Heb. 10:37-38, the text which contains the quotation from the book of Habakkuk.[1] The main objective is to establish the readings that reflect most accurately the original texts and to point out different textual traditions that resulted from the transmission and the translation of Hab. 2:3-4. Special attention will be given to the textual links between Hab. 2:3-4 LXX and Heb. 10:37-38, in order to strengthen the case for the Septuagint's direct and distinct contribution to the text form of the quotation in Hebrews.

---

[1] A similar investigation, Bae Gil Lee, "A Developing Messianic Understanding of Habakkuk 2:3-5 in the New Testament in the Context of Early Jewish Writings" (Ph. D., Southwestern Baptist Theological Seminary, 1997), was on-going roughly at the same time as the writing of this dissertation and was unavailable before this revision. Lee's work, while overlapping partially with this study, extends the investigation of Hab. 2:3-4 to the entire New Testament and does not place particular emphasis on the Septuagintal tradition and its influence, which are the focus of my study. Lee's work stands out as a thorough analysis of the Habakkuk tradition in Early Christianity, with perhaps the notable omission of the classical study on this topic by A. Strobel, *Untersuchungen zum eschatologischen Verzögerungsproblem auf Grund der spätjüdische-urchristlichen Geschichte von Habakuk 2,2 ff* (SNT 2; Leiden: E. J. Brill, 1961).

2. Habakkuk 2:3-4. The Masoretic Text-Tradition

The primary textual tradition for the purpose of this study is the Hebrew tradition, especially the Masoretic text. A brief presentation of the textual data will seek to trace the successive changes that the Hebrew text of Habakkuk underwent before reaching its particular form in Hebrews.

2.1. *Hab. 2:3-4 MT. Text*

2:3a	כִּי עוֹד חָזוֹן לַמּוֹעֵד
2:3b	וְיָפֵחַ לַקֵּץ
2:3c	וְלֹא יְכַזֵּב
2:3d	אִם־יִתְמַהְמָהּ חַכֵּה־לוֹ
2:3e	כִּי־בֹא יָבֹא
2:3f	לֹא יְאַחֵר:
2:4a	הִנֵּה עֻפְּלָה
2:4b	לֹא־יָשְׁרָה נַפְשׁוֹ בּוֹ
2:4c	וְצַדִּיק בֶּאֱמוּנָתוֹ יִחְיֶה:

2.2. *Hab. 2:3-4 MT. Textual Witnesses and Variants*

The following section examines the most important text-critical issues of these verses, selected from the critical *apparatus* in the *BHS*, *BHK*, Kennicott[2] and the primary ancient textual witnesses of this text.

2.2.1. *Masoretic Text*

Notable in Elliger's lists of text critical remarks[3] is the different spelling יפיח in 1QpHab for וְיָפֵחַ, and the absence of the *waw*-conjunctive, a frequent phenomenon when וֹ precedes יֹ.[4] The Septuagint translation καὶ ἀνατελεῖ indicates a *Vorlage* reading ויפרח or ופרח, whereas the Palestinian recension reads καὶ ἐνφανήσ[εται] similar to the Vulgate *apparebit*. The second negative particle לֹא is preceded by the *waw*-conjunctive in 1QpHab as well as in the Septuagint, the Syriac, the Targum and the Vulgate. Furthermore, in 2:4 Elliger suggests that the 3rd fem. sg. pual form עֻפְּלָה is read as the participial form עָפֵל, and that the Septuagint εὐδοκεῖ reflects a possible רָצְתָה in the *Vorlage*. Finally, in agreement with the Greek text, he prefers the 1st ms. sg. suffix נַפְשִׁי to the

---

[2] B. Kennicott, *Vetus Testamentum hebraicum, cum variis lectionibus*, 2 vols. (Oxford: Clarendon Press, 1776-1780).

[3] ויפח 𝔔 prb l וְיָפִיחַ; prp יִפְרַח(וְ), al וּפָתַח et apertio cf 𝔊 l c 𝔔 mlt Mss 𝔊 𝔖 𝔗 𝔙 וְלֹא l עָפֵל vel עָפָל 𝔊 (𝔖) εὐδοκεῖ prb l רָצְתָה; 𝔔 יושרה l c Ms 𝔊 α' נפשׁי 𝔊* ἐκ πίστεώς μου.

[4] William H. Brownlee, *The Text of Habakkuk in the Ancient Commentary from Qumran* (JBL-MS 11; Philadelphia: Society of Biblical Literature, 1959) 43.

3rd ms. sg. נַפְשׁוֹ in the MT, a preference that does not extend to the other pronominal suffix in בֶּאֱמוּנָתוֹ which reads ἐκ πίστεώς μου. Kittel in the *BHK* opts for the same emendations of v. 2:4a, הִנֵּעֲפָל לֹא רָצְתָה נַפְשִׁי בּוֹ, reading with the Greek translation רָצְתָה for יָשְׁרָה and the niphal participle הִנֵּעֲפָל for the MT text הִנֵּה עֻפְּלָה.

Kennicott's consonantal text is identical to that of the *BHS* and his survey provides evidence that most textual traditions in either the Versions or other parallel Hebrew traditions are represented among the 337 medieval manuscripts investigated. Even though Kennicott's massive collection of variants has a rather disputed value for textual criticism, it is remarkable that even the Septuagint readings distinct from the Masoretic tradition have correspondents in the Hebrew manuscripts such as נפשׁי in 17, באמונתי in 320, and the different root עלף in 461 and 531.[5]

2.2.2. Murabba'ât (Mur 88)

The Murabba'ât text of the Scroll of the Minor Prophets,[6] possibly an early second century manuscript,[7] is mostly vacant for Hab. 1:13 - 2:18, and the only legible word in Hab. 2:3-4 appearing in col. xviii, line 19 is ויפח.[8] This reading confirms the consonantal text of the Masoretic tradition.[9]

2.2.3. Qumran Cave 4 (4QXII^g)

The manuscript of the Minor Prophets 4QXII^g is dated on palaeographical grounds in the last half of the first century B.C. The condition of the manuscript is very poor, creating "uncommonly difficult problems" for the editors.[10] There is only one small fragment that has a reading from Hab. 2:4. Fragment 102, 3rd line reads [. ישרה נפש]ו.[11] If this fragment is indeed from Hab. 2:4, it acknowledges a textual tradition identical to the Masoretic textual tradition.

---

[5] Emanuel Tov, *Textual Criticism of the Hebrew Bible* (Minneapolis: Fortress Press, 1992); Ernst Würthwein, *The Text of the Old Testament* (Grand Rapids: Eerdmans, 1979).

[6] P. Benoit et al., eds., *Les Grottes de Murabba'ât* (DJD II; Oxford: Clarendon Press, 1961).

[7] Würthwein, *Text* 30. See also Eugen Ulrich et al., eds., *Qumran Cave 4. The Prophets* (DJD XV; Oxford: Clarendon Press, 1997).

[8] Benoit, *Murabba'ât* 199.

[9] Emanuel Tov, *The Greek Minor Prophets Scroll from Naḥal Ḥever (8Ḥev XIIgr)* (DJD VIII; Oxford: Clarendon Press, 1990) 149.

[10] Ulrich, *Prophets* 270.

[11] Ulrich, *Prophets* 316.

2.2.4. *Qumran Pesher on Habakkuk (1QpHab)*

The Habakkuk Pesher, dated in the second half of the first century B.C.,[12] is one of the most important witnesses to the Hebrew text given its form of a running commentary superimposed on the Biblical text.[13] The thirteen-column commentary covers the first two chapters of the book of Habakkuk and has been preserved almost in its entirety, with the exception of the last lines in each column. The text and commentary on Hab. 2:3-4 extend from the 5th line on col. vii to the 3rd line of col. viii.[14] Generally, the Biblical text in the Habakkuk commentary - *lemmata* - gives strong support for the MT readings. The evidence, however, is not altogether easy to assess due to several orthographic factors, such the extensive use of *scriptio plena* and the impossibility to distinguish with certainty between homeomorphic consonants.[15] Occasionally the difference between the word form in the *lemma* and in the commentary adds to an already difficult textual assessment.[16]

In Hab. 2:3-4 the only notable departures from the MT are in line 6, יפיח for וְיָפֵחַ, in line 9, ולוא for לֹא, and in line 14, יושרה for יָשְׁרָה. These deviations, however, confirm the root preserved in the MT, calling into question the need for an emendation of the MT text. A similar judgement applies to the form עופלה, which is identical morphologically to the much-debated MT form עֻפְּלָה. Unfortunately, the last lines in col. vii are vacant, and a decision on the word באמונת_ can be made only on the basis of the commentary. The commentary on Hab. 2:4b in lines 1-3, col. viii, reads:

> Its prophetic meaning concerns all the doers of the Law in the house of Judah whom God will deliver from the house of damnation, because of their patient suffering and their steadfast faith in the Teacher of Right.[17]

---

[12] William H. Brownlee, *The Midrash Pesher of Habakkuk* (SBL-MS 24; Missoula: Scholars Press, 1979) 23.

[13] Maurya P. Horgan, *Pesharim: Qumran Interpretations of Biblical Books* (CBQ-MS 8; Washington, D.C.: Catholic Biblical Association of America, 1979); Michael A. Knibb, *The Qumran Community* (CCWJCW 2; Cambridge: Cambridge University Press, 1987).

[14] The standard studies include Brownlee, *Pesher*; Brownlee, *Text*; Millar Burrows, *The Dead Sea Scrolls of St. Mark's Monastery. The Isaiah Manuscript and the Habakkuk Commentary*, 2 vols., vol. 1, (New Haven: American Schools of Oriental Research, 1950); Karl Elliger, *Studien zum Habakuk-kommentar vom Toten Meer* (BHT 15; Tübingen: Mohr Siebeck, 1953); and Horgan, *Pesharim*.

[15] Tov, *Textual Criticism of the Hebrew Bible* 108 ff.

[16] Brownlee, *Text* 118.

[17] Brownlee, *Pesher* 125.

The importance of the commentary cannot be overemphasized. First of all, as far as textual matters are concerned, the commentary is congruent with a 3rd ms. sg. suffix in the *lemmata* which is the MT reading as well.[18] Furthermore it supplies interpretative clues with regard to the identity of "the righteous", as the one engaged in "(1) performance of the Torah; (2) endurance of suffering; and (3) אֱמוּנָה as a human virtue, more like "faith" as belief not trust in God or his word."[19]

2.2.5. Targum Jonathan

Targum Jonathan to the Prophets, a translation whose composition and editing extend beyond 70 A.D.,[20] contains the Targum to the Minor Prophets, to which the book of Habakkuk belongs. Since the Targumim are more theological paraphrases than literal translations, their value for textual criticism of the Hebrew text is often questionable and must to be assessed with caution. The Targum for Hab. 2:3-4 reads:

> For the prophecy is ready for a time and the end is fixed, nor shall it fail; if there is delay in the matter wait for it, for it shall come in its time and shall not be deferred. Behold the wicked think that all these things are not so, but the righteous shall live by the truth of them.[21]

For the translation of the difficult form עֻפְּלָה, the Targum uses the contrast between the "righteous" and the "wicked" and their relation to the truths stated in 2:3. The Targum generates a distinct tradition of interpretation of this text, וצדיקיא על קושטהון יתקיימון, in which the truthfulness of the prophetic words replaces the "faithfulness, steadfastness" of either the righteous (Hebrew text) or God (LXX).[22] As important as this tradition is in depicting the way in which the Targumist understood Hab. 2:3-4,[23] it cannot be a reliable guide in establishing with precision the Hebrew text underlying his interpretation.

---

[18] Horgan, *Pesharim* 40.

[19] Francis I. Andersen, *Habakkuk* (AB; Garden City, NY: Doubleday, 2001) 214. The theological differences between the Masoretic tradition and the Pesher on Habakkuk have been the object of several studies, such as Brownlee, *Pesher*; *idem*, *Text*; and more recently Lee, "Understanding" 59-87.

[20] Robert P. Gordon, "The Targum to the Minor Prophets and the Dead Sea Texts: Textual and Exegetical Notes", *Revue de Qumran* 8, no. 31 (1974) 18.

[21] This analysis is based on the translation supplied by Cathcart and Gordon, *The Targum of the Minor Prophets*, vol. 14, *The Aramaic Bible. The Targums* (Edinburgh: T. & T. Clark, 1989) 150 ff.

[22] The antecedent of the pronominal suffix could be the "righteous ones", cf. T. W. Manson, "The Argument from Prophecy", *Journal of Theological Studies* 46 (1945) 133.

[23] For a comparison of the theologies of underlying the Masoretic text and the Targum, see the earlier work of W. H. Brownlee, "The Habakkuk Midrash and the

2.2.6. Septuagint

According to the Göttingen critical edition of the Septuagint,[24] Hab. 2:3-4 reads:

²:³ διότι ἔτι ὅρασις εἰς καιρὸν καὶ ἀνατελεῖ εἰς πέρας καὶ οὐκ εἰς κενόν ἐὰν ὑστερήσῃ ὑπόμεινον αὐτόν ὅτι ἐρχόμενος ἥξει καὶ οὐ μὴ χρονίσῃ ²:⁴ ἐὰν ὑποστείληται οὐκ εὐδοκεῖ ἡ ψυχή μου ἐν αὐτῷ ὁ δὲ δίκαιος ἐκ πίστεώς μου ζήσεται

A closer examination of the text critical issues in the Greek text will follow in a subsequent section.[25] Attention will be given here only to the most significant differences between Ziegler's proposed text and the MT. Set in parallel columns, the two texts read:

Hab. 2:3-4 MT	Hab. 2:3-4 LXX
כִּי עוֹד חָזוֹן לַמּוֹעֵד	διότι ἔτι ὅρασις εἰς καιρὸν
וְיָפֵחַ לַקֵּץ	καὶ ἀνατελεῖ εἰς πέρας
וְלֹא יְכַזֵּב	καὶ οὐκ εἰς κενόν
אִם־יִתְמַהְמָהּ חַכֵּה־לוֹ	ἐὰν ὑστερήσῃ ὑπόμεινον αὐτόν
כִּי־בֹא יָבֹא	ὅτι ἐρχόμενος ἥξει
לֹא יְאַחֵר:	καὶ οὐ μὴ χρονίσῃ
הִנֵּה עֻפְּלָה	ἐὰν ὑποστείληται
לֹא־יָשְׁרָה נַפְשׁוֹ בּוֹ	οὐκ εὐδοκεῖ ἡ ψυχή μου ἐν αὐτῷ
וְצַדִּיק בֶּאֱמוּנָתוֹ יִחְיֶה:	ὁ δὲ δίκαιος ἐκ πίστεώς μου ζήσεται

וְיָפֵחַ   καὶ ἀνατελεῖ
Although the Hatch-Redpath concordance lists this as the only Septuagintal occurrence of ἀνατέλλειν for יפח, it is preferable to understand the Greek form as indicative of a different *Vorlage* reading יפרח.[26]

Targum of Jonathan", *Journal of Jewish Studies* 7 (1956), and the more recent study of Lee, "Understanding" 50-60.

²⁴ Joseph Ziegler, ed., *Septuaginta. Vetus Testamentum Graecum. Auctoritate Societatis Litterarum Gottingensis editum. Duodecim Prophetae*, vol. XIII (Göttingen: Vandenhoeck & Ruprecht, 1943).

²⁵ Mention should be made here of two important studies of the Septuagint of Habakkuk published after the submitting of this dissertation, M. Harl, *Les Douze Prophètes*, ed. M. Harl, vol. 8a, *La Bible d'Alexandrie. Traduction et annotation de la Septante* (Paris: Éditions du Cerf, 1999) and David Cleaver-Bartholomew, "An Analysis of the Old Greek Version of Habakkuk" (Ph. D., Claremont Graduate University, 1998). See also Lee, "Understanding" 87-97.

²⁶ Dominique Barthélemy, *Critique textuelle de l'Ancien Testament*, 3 vols., (OBO

יְכַזֵּב   εἰς κενόν
This is one of the relatively few instances of morphological inconsistency
in the Greek Habakkuk, if indeed the translator's *Vorlage* was identical to
the MT. Lexically the choice is also infrequent, Barthélemy noting only
one other similar instance in Hos. 12:2 LXX where כָּזָב is translated by
κενά.[27]

חַכֵּה־לוֹ   ὑπόμεινον αὐτόν
The translator supplied the accusative ms. sg. pronoun αὐτόν in keeping
with the ms. pronoun in the Hebrew text. As a result, the Greek antecedent
can no longer be ὅρασις as in the Hebrew text, since this would have
required the feminine pronoun αὐτήν. Whether the translator did this
intentionally or, more probably, unintentionally, this modification
triggered a series of divergences between the two texts.[28]

כִּי־בֹא יָבֹא   ὅτι ἐρχόμενος ἥξει
The 3rd ms. sg. ἐρχόμενος ἥξει correctly translates the equivalent masculine
singular construction בֹא יָבֹא. In keeping with the gender in the Hebrew
text, however, the antecedent of the Greek text is necessarily a masculine
singular entity, and no longer the feminine noun ὅρασις, whose equivalent
חָזוֹן is the antecedent for בֹא יָבֹא in the Hebrew text.

הִנֵּה   ἐάν
The Hebrew demonstrative interjection הִנֵּה is rendered by the conditional
ἐάν, a possible, though very rare connotation (KB, BDB). It is possible
that the translator's uncertainty about the form and flow of the text have
contributed to this translation, although the existence of a different reading
in his *Vorlage* cannot be completely ruled out.

עֻפְּלָה   ὑποστείληται
If this is the textual equivalent used by the translator, then it is employed
only here in the entire Greek OT. It is more probable, however, that the
translator either had a *Vorlage* reading a form derived from the root
עלף or he misread his text as such.[29] Since consonantal metathesis was a
common scribal error it is reasonable to presuppose that עלף was in the
translator's *Vorlage*.

50.3; Fribourg / Göttingen: Editions Universitaires Fribourg Suisse / Vandenhoeck &
Ruprecht, 1992) cxlix; Brownlee, *Text* 41.

[27] Barthélemy, *Critique* cl.

[28] For a detailed discussion see *infra* (ch. 9, 3.3).

[29] Paul Humbert, *Problemes du Livre d'Habacuc* (Neuchatel: Université de Neuchatel,
1944) 148.

לֹא־יָשְׁרָה   οὐκ εὐδοκεῖ

Since the verb εὐδοκεῖν is never employed for the translation of יָשַׁר, most commentators indicate that the *Vorlage* might have contained the reading רָצְתָה. The root ישר, however, is confirmed by the *lemma* of the 1QpHab.

נַפְשׁוֹ   ἡ ψυχή μου; בֶּאֱמוּנָתוֹ   ἐκ πίστεώς μου

In both cases the Greek translation has a 1st sg. possessive pronoun corresponding to 3rd ms. sg. suffix in the Hebrew text. As in other similar cases, it is notoriously difficult to ascertain with confidence what caused the deviation, either the transmission of the Hebrew text or the translation process itself. Suffice it to say that the string of antecedents in the Hebrew text is no longer equivalent to the string in the Greek text, and this divergence has implications for the overall meaning of the passage.

2.2.7. Naḥal Ḥever (8 Ḥev XIIgr)

The Naḥal Ḥever Scroll of the Minor Prophets contains a text that is considered to be a revision of the Old Greek translation of the Hebrew Bible, which displays a notable tendency to bring the Greek text into closer affinity with the Hebrew text.[30] The manuscript is dated on palaeographic grounds in the second part of the first century B.C or first part of the first century A.D.[31] Even though there is no consensus regarding the status of this textual witness, whether it is indeed a revision of the Old Greek or a separate translation,[32] the following analysis assumes the former position. The text of Hab. 2:3-4 is located in col. xvii, lines 25-30. Similar to other existent *lacunae* in the scroll, these verses have been damaged quite extensively. The better-preserved portion of the text allows for a reconstruction with a moderate degree of confidence.[33] The texts from the Naḥal Ḥever Scroll and the Septuagint are shown below in parallel columns to highlight the differences.[34]

Hab. 2:3-4 Naḥal Ḥever	Hab. 2:3-4 LXX
ὅτι ἔτ]ι [ὅρασις εἰς κ]αιρὸν καὶ ἐνφανήσετ[αι εἰς πέρας	διότι ἔτι ὅρασις εἰς καιρὸν καὶ ἀνατελεῖ εἰς πέρας

---

[30] Dominique Barthélemy, *Les Devanciers d'Aquila* (SVT 10; Leiden: E. J. Brill, 1963).

[31] Tov, *Naḥal Ḥever* 26.

[32] See, *inter alios*, Fitzmyer, "Habakkuk" and Sidney Jellicoe, *The Septuagint and Modern Study* (Oxford: Clarendon, 1968).

[33] Barthélemy, *Devanciers*; Tov, *Naḥal Ḥever* 83.

[34] See also Harl, *Les Douze Prophètes*; Cleaver-Bartholomew, "Analysis"; and Lee, "Understanding" 98-103.

καὶ οὐ δ]ιαψεύεται.
ἐὰν στραγ[γεύσηται
προσδέχου αὐ]τόν
ὅτι ἐρχόμενος ἥ[ξει
καὶ οὐ - - - - - -]
ἰδ[οὺ] σκοτία
οὐκ εὐθεῖα ψυχὴ αὐτοῦ [ἐν αὐτῷ
καὶ δί]καιος
ἐκ πίστεώς αὐτοῦ
ζήσετ[αι]

καὶ οὐκ εἰς κενόν
ἐὰν ὑστερήσῃ
ὑπόμεινον αὐτόν
ὅτι ἐρχόμενος ἥξει
καὶ οὐ μὴ χρονίσῃ
ἐὰν ὑποστείληται
οὐκ εὐδοκεῖ ἡ ψυχή μου ἐν αὐτῷ
ὁ δὲ δίκαιος
ἐκ πίστεώς μου
ζήσεται

Two categories of differences are significant in these verses. First, in the area of lexical equivalents, the verbs ἐμφαίνω, διαψεύδομαι and στραγγεύομαι in the Naḥal Ḥever Scroll replace ἀνατέλλω, εἰς κενόν and ὑστερέω as lexical units semantically closer to the Hebrew counterparts. Likewise, the adjective εὐθεῖα replaces the verb εὐδοκέω confirming the Hebrew root ישר in the MT, even though the revision might have vocalised the text differently, probably as יְשָׁרָה.[35]

The second area of change is morphological. Included here is the modification of the pronominal elements, resulting in a Greek text in which the two 3rd ms. sg. pronouns are exact equivalents of the Hebrew suffixes. Also, the change to a more correct rendering of the interjection הִנֵּה by ἰδού as opposed to the conjunction ἐάν. The omission of the definite article in οὐκ εὐθεῖα ψυχὴ αὐτοῦ and possibly in καὶ δί]καιος is the result of a more literal translation of the Hebrew text. The rendering σκοτία in 2:4 suggests the presence of the noun אֲפֵלָה as a possible reading in the Vorlage.[36] If this be the case, then the consonantal sequence _פל_ of the MT is confirmed, as opposed to the _לפ_ reflected in the LXX.

2.2.8. Septuagint Revisions: Aquila, Theodotion, and Symmachus

Fragments of Hab. 2:3-4 from the revisions of Aquila, Symmachus and Theodotion, the third, fourth and sixth columns of Origen's Hexapla, have survived in the works of Eusebius, in Jerome's commentaries on Habakkuk and on Galatians, and in the fragmentary material of the Syro-Hexapla.[37] Aquila and Theodotion:

---

[35] Tov, Naḥal Ḥever 152.
[36] Tov, Naḥal Ḥever 152.
[37] Field, Hexaplorum and Tov, Textual Criticism of the Hebrew Bible 144 ff.

Hab. 2:4 Aquila and Theodotion	Hab. 2:4 LXX
ἰδοὺ νωχελευομένου οὐκ εὐθεῖα ἡ ψυχή μου ἐν αὐτῷ καὶ δίκαιος ἐν πίστει αὐτοῦ ζήσετει	ἐὰν ὑποστείληται οὐκ εὐδοκεῖ ἡ ψυχή μου ἐν αὐτῷ ὁ δὲ δίκαιος ἐκ πίστεώς μου ζήσεται

Symmachus:

Hab. 2:4 Symmachus	Hab. 2:4b LXX
ὁ (δὲ) δίκαιος τῇ ἑαυτοῦ πίστει ζήσει	ὁ δὲ δίκαιος ἐκ πίστεώς μου ζήσεται

There is a noticeable similarity between Aquila and the Greek text from Naḥal Ḥever, albeit with significantly different readings νωχελευομένου for עֻפְּלָה and the 1st sg. possessive pronoun in the phrase ἡ ψυχή μου. The first word is the genitive absolute participle of the deponent νωχελεύομαι, "to be sluggish, lazy, heedless", (LEH), which might indicate a *Vorlage* reading הֶעְפַּל,[38] whereas the second word reflects the reading נַפְשִׁי. As in other cases of ' and ו it is impossible to give a certain explanation for the 1st sg. pronoun reading. Symmachus, in his more literary translation,[39] uses the instrumental dative, τῇ ἑαυτοῦ πίστει, instead of the prepositional phrase, ἐν πίστει αὐτοῦ / ἐκ πίστεώς μου, implying a 3rd ms. sg. suffix in the Hebrew text.

2.2.9. New Testament

The quotation from Hab. 2:4 is used three times in the writings of the New Testament, twice by St. Paul in Rom. 1:17 and Gal. 3:11, and once by the Author in Heb. 10:37-38. Since Heb. 10 will be analysed individually in a following section, only the quotations from Paul's Epistles are addressed here. In the Nestle-Aland edition the two texts read:

---

[38] G. R. Driver, "Linguistic and Textual Problems: Minor Prophets. Part I, II, III", *Journal of Theological Studies* 39 (1938) 395.

[39] Jellicoe, *Septuagint* 94; Tov, *Textual Criticism of the Hebrew Bible* 146.

Rom. 1:17 NTG	Hab. 2:4 LXX
ὁ δὲ δίκαιος ἐκ πίστεως ζήσεται	ὁ δὲ δίκαιος ἐκ πίστεώς μου ζήσεται

Gal. 3:11 NTG	Hab. 2:4 LXX
ὅτι ὁ δίκαιος ἐκ πίστεως ζήσεται	ὁ δὲ δίκαιος ἐκ πίστεώς μου ζήσεται

As expected, the textual form of the quotation reflects the Septuagintal rendering of Hab. 2:4, even though generally the Apostle gives no evidence of being bound to a particular text, Greek or Hebrew, in his quotations.[40] With the exception of the uncial C* reading δίκαιός μου in Rom. 1:17, all textual witnesses for both texts have no pronominal elements accompanying either the adjective δίκαιος or the noun πίστεως.[41] Such uniform representation strongly favours an original text devoid of pronouns, suggesting that Paul consciously adapted the Habakkuk text to give better support for his theological argument. In doing so, however, he generated a distinct tradition of Hab. 2:4, a pronoun-less text, which, given the importance of Paul's writings, was likely to influence other textual traditions.[42]

---

[40] Stanley, *Language* 67.

[41] The same is true for the Versions; note, however, the exception in Jerome's commentary on Rom 1:17.

[42] Mention should be made regarding the frequent appearance of Hab. 2:4 in the writings of the Greek Fathers. In most cases the quotations come from their exposition of either the Pauline epistles or Hebrews and display a high degree of inconsistency in the text of the quotation. Eusebius in *Demonstratio Evangelica* uses all three variants within the span of about 50 lines, ὁ δὲ δίκαιος ἐκ πίστεώς μου ζήσεται, *Thesaurus Linguae Graecae* 6.14.1.6, 6.14.3.8; ὁ δὲ δίκαιος ἐκ πίστεως ζήσεται, *Thesaurus Linguae Graecae* 6.14.6.2; and ὁ δὲ δίκαιός μου ἐκ πίστεως ζήσεται, *Thesaurus Linguae Graecae* 6.14.8.5. Clement of Alexandria in *Stromata* quotes the text three times, once in his comments on Romans, keeping the Pauline form tradition, ὁ δὲ δίκαιος ἐκ πίστεως ζήσεται, *Thesaurus Linguae Graecae* 2.6.29.2.1, and twice in comments on Hebrews, preserving the epistle's text tradition, ὁ δὲ δίκαιός μου ἐκ πίστεώς ζήσεται , *Thesaurus Linguae Graecae* 2.2.8.2.2, 4.16.101.3.4, even though he attributes the quote to the "prophet".

2.2.10. Old Latin

The evidence for the Old Latin of Hab. 2:4 comes from the writings of the early Latin Fathers.[43] The main witnesses in this respect are Cyprian of Carthage, Tertullian and possibly Ambrose and Ambrosiaster. Cyprian quotes Hab. 2:4 three times, twice in the *Testimonia adversus Judaeos*, invariably using the first personal pronoun in conjunction with the noun *fides* and not the adjective *justus*, "justus autem ex fide mea vivi(e)t".[44] Even though the text preserved does not include the entire Hab. 2:3-4 passage, the use of the 1st sg. possessive pronoun is similar to that of the Septuagint.

Tertullian, however, quotes the Hab. text using the 3rd ms. pronoun, "Justus ex fide sua vivet",[45] and twice in his comments on the text in Heb. 10 he uses no pronoun at all, "justus ex fide vivit".[46] Likewise, Ambrosiaster uses the quotation primarily in comments on Romans and Hebrews, always without any pronoun, "justus autem ex fide vivit".[47] Ambrose does not quote the Habakkuk text *per se*, but only refers to the NT quotations of that text.

The value of this data for textual criticism has to be considered with caution since the Church Fathers generally did not preserve the text forms in citing Scriptures with rigorous precision.

2.2.11. Vulgate

The Vulgate Hab. 2:3-4 reads:

> 2:3 Quia adhuc visus procul et apparebit in finem et non mentietur si moram fecerit expecta illum quia veniens veniet et non tardabit. 2:4 ecce qui incredulus est non erit recta anima eius in semet ipso iustus autem in fide sua vivet.

The Vulgate translates עֻפְּלָה by *incredulus*, on account of the verse's implied contrast between the subject of 2:4a and the faithful "*iustus*" in 2:4b. The pronouns are identical to the Hebrew text.[48]

---

[43] Since the critical edition of the Vetus Latina on the Minor Prophets is still in preparation, the following evidence has been collected from Migne's *Patrologia Latina*. W. Oesterly's study ("The Old Latin Texts of the Minor Prophets. Part i-iv", *Journal of Theological Studies* 5 [1904] 76, 242-53, 378-86, 570-79) also supplies valuable information.

[44] *Patrologia Latina Database* (5.0) (Chadwyck-Healey Inc., 1995) 0683a, 0757c.

[45] *Patrologia Latina Database* 0403c.

[46] *Patrologia Latina Database* 0474c, 0475c.

[47] In *Commentaria in Epistolam ad Romanos* and *Commentaria in Epistolam ad Galatas*, *Patrologia Latina Database* 0056c, 0354b, etc.

[48] The only significant variant is the alternative reading "non erit recta anima mea in eum" in the Vulgate's manuscripts A Ω, a reading that reflects the Septuagint and Aquila, *Biblia Sacra iuxta latinam Vulgatam versionem. Liber Duodecim Prophetarum*, (Rome:

2.2.12. Peshitta

The translation of the Syriac Peshitta reads:

> [2:4] For his soul does not delight in iniquity, but the righteous man shall live by faith.[49]

The Syriac Peshitta is one of the few ancient versions that do not supply an explicit pronoun to accompany the noun "faith". As mentioned earlier, in the New Testament the pronoun-less version of the verse is used only by St. Paul in Rom. 1:17 and Gal. 3:11, and this could well be a case of the Pauline tradition's influencing the Syriac translation of Habakkuk.

2.3. Hab. 2:4 MT – To Emend or Not To Emend?

Hab. 2:4 raises some of the most difficult *cruces interpretum* for the OT exegete, and although it has been the object of continual scrutiny, scholarly consensus regarding the main exegetical issues remains elusive. This excursus surveys the main interpretative challenges and some of the more tenable solutions proposed in the debate.[50]

2.3.1. Methodological Aspects

The most fundamental methodological aspect hinges on the status of the Masoretic text, and inevitably the solutions proposed mirror the degree of scholars' willingness to emend the MT. Because of the interdependence of the exegetical *cruces* in this passage, the order in which the scholars grapple with the issues will to a great extent determine their conclusions. Since there are few settled issues regarding the verse, this methodological question is one of priority, whether the lexical elements have priority over the syntactical relationships in the verse and the immediate context, or vice versa.

2.3.2. Form Considerations

Most exegetes agree that Hab. 2:4 essentially consists of a parallelism between 2:4a and 2:4b. The consensus, however, extends no further. The

---

Libreria Editrice Vaticana, 1987) 201. Jerome repeatedly comments on the differences between the Hebrew text and the Septuagint. In *Commentariorum in Abacuc* under the text "Justus autem in fide sua vivet" he discusses the divergent reading in the Septuagint "Justus autem ex fide mea vivet", *Patrologia Latina Database* 1289c; similarly in the *Commentarium in Epistolam ad Galatas*, *Patrologia Latina Database* 359c.

[49] George M. Lamsa, *Holy Bible from the Ancient Eastern Text. George M. Lansa's Translation from the Aramaic of the Peshitta* (San Francisco: Harper Collins, 1985).

[50] See Barthélemy, *Critique*; John A. Emerton, "Textual and Linguistic Problems of Habakkuk 2:4-5", *Journal of Theological Studies* 28, no. Ap (1977) 1-18; and George J. Zemek, "Interpretive Challenges Relating to Habakkuk 2:4b", *Grace Theological Journal* 1, no. 1 (1980) 43-69, for earlier similar surveys.

issues still in dispute include the nature of the parallelism, if it is complete or partial, if it is antithetic or synonymous, and whether or not there is a complete morphological parallelism between the lines. Finally, some scholars support a chiastic structure parallelism, 2:4aα // 2:4bβ and 2:4aβ // 2:4bα, while others prefer a linear parallelism. Clearly these preferences determine the lexical connotations attributed to the disputed lexemes. Other studies discuss the meter of the stichs and the extent to which it should be considered in emending the text.

2.3.3. Morphological Considerations

The morphological question is closely linked with the form of this verse. The most disputed part of speech is עֻפְּלָה, whether it should be construed as a verb or as a noun/adjective or, given the nature of a consonantal text, as the collation of two separate words. In the first case, the verse forms a chiastic antithetic parallelism, the verb עפלה pairs with יִחְיֶה, whereas in the second, the noun/adjective עפלה is the counterpart in a linear parallelism to צַדִּיק.

2.3.4. Lexical Considerations

Inconclusive lexical information surrounds several words in Hab. 2:3-4. There is considerable uncertainty about the roots behind וְיָפֵחַ in 2:3 and עֻפְּלָה in 2:4. Furthermore, even for some well-attested lexical elements in the text, it is difficult to assess precisely the intended connotation. The data gets even more intricate as certain Versions testify to different roots in their respective *Vorlage* than those preserved in the MT tradition. Even though most of the differences between proposed roots can be explained as typical scribal errors, it is very difficult to assess which root was in the original text and which has been corrupted in the transmission of the text.

One other related matter of decisive importance is whether or not certain lexical elements have ethical overtones or not. The meaning of the verb יָשַׁר is disputed because, although its cognate adjective is unambiguously used with an ethical overtone, it is uncertain that the verb, especially when used in conjunction with נֶפֶשׁ and not לֵב, would have had the same nuance. Similarly, the understanding of the key lexeme אֱמוּנָה can be influenced by its association with the Greek equivalent πίστις, "faith", and its connotations in the New Testament.

2.3.5. Contextual Considerations

Many issues regarding the context are disputed, the most crucial for the understanding of this verse being the relationship between Hab. 2:4 and 2:5, and the proper understanding of the conjunction וְאַף כִּי in 2:5a. Some see the two verses as integral parts of the argument, while others hold that a considerable discontinuity exists between the two. Furthermore, questions of the larger context remain, namely the role of Hab. 2:4 in the book of Habakkuk as a whole and the way in which similar ideas and words in other verses could inform the understanding of the oracle.

2.3.6. Syntactic Considerations

Although the overall syntax of Hab. 2:3-4 is not particularly difficult, the uncertainty regarding key lexical items affect the way in which the syntactical relationships are understood. There are indeed deviations from normal syntactical patterns, like the unidiomatic Hebrew construction in 2:4a and the lack of a relative pronoun in 2:4a. The debate is whether or not these deviations warrant a modification of the MT tradition, either by a new partition of the consonantal text or by emendation.

Antecedents for the pronominal suffixes and for the implicit grammatical subjects in Hab. 2:3-4 are notoriously difficult. Even within the boundaries of one textual tradition, the antecedents are difficult to determine clearly, and the translation process added further complications by diverging from the antecedents in the MT. This phenomenon alone can be held responsible for generating divergent interpretations of the passage, due to the fundamental differences between the syntax of the source and the target texts.

2.3.7. Semantic Considerations

The semantic riddles of Hab. 2:4 extend beyond the lexical semantics previously discussed. Even when the difficult questions of the antecedents are solved, there remains the problem of the referent; who is the "righteous one" or the one "whose soul is not upright"? Are the nouns and pronouns used collectively throughout the text? Does the verse portray a contrast between the people of Judah and the Chaldeans, or is there a more subtle contrast, which transcends the ethnic boundaries?

2.3.8. Hebrew Text vs. Versions

A closing consideration is the complex issue of the relationship between the Hebrew Masoretic tradition and the early Versions. At a number of crucial exegetical junctures in Hab. 2:3-4 the Versions point to textual traditions allegedly different from the MT. In these cases the exegete has the difficult task of assessing whether the different traditions reflect scribal errors in the transmission of the *Vorlage* or of the target text, if they are the result of faulty translation caused by the translator's insufficient understanding of the Hebrew text, or if they are the result of theologically motivated choices.

2.3.9. Proposed Solutions

A complete list of all the solutions proposed for Hab. 2:3-4 would be exceedingly long.[51] This section reviews the more significant options with emphasis on studies completed since the investigations of Emerton and Zemek.

2.3.9.1. Anderson

> [2:3] For the vision is still for the appointed time. And he is a witness to the end, and he will not deceive. If he delays, wait for him; for he will certainly come, he won't be late. [2:4] Behold, swollen, not straight, is his throat in him, and the righteous person by its trustworthiness will survive.

The most recent commentary on Habakkuk pays special attention to the poetic nature of the prophetic oracle, and the interpretative decisions are guided by considerations of poetic structure and rhythmic patterns in the unit. The author builds his interpretation on the newly reached consensus on several issues, while on others, i.e., Hab. 2:4a, he admits that "in the face of such chaos, all one can do is resign to the likelihood that the original text is irretrievably lost or else struggle to make the best of the MT as it is".[52]

The key issues for the overall message of these verses are the antecedents for the pronominal elements, which, regardless of the way they are interpreted, leave a text full of inner semantic tensions, such as the contradiction between "hurry" and "delay" in 2:3. Anderson proposes a consistent reading of the verses in which חָזוֹן, the "vision" in v. 3, presupposes someone who will reveal it, וְיָפֵחַ, i.e., "the witness" in 2:3,[53] who in turn becomes the antecedent for all subsequent references to the vision, "he will not deceive. If he should (seem to) delay, wait for him! For he will certainly come; he won't be late".[54] In this scenario, one finds a solution also for the apparent contrast mentioned above, in that there are two stages of development, the vision itself and its fulfilment. The

---

[51] Barthélemy provides one of the most extensive lists of translation options reflected in Bible translations, ancient witnesses, medieval Jewish exegesis and modern studies, Barthélemy, *Critique*. While absolute certainty about the text of Hab. 2:4 is ruled out, the Committee for the Textual Analysis of the Hebrew Old Testament decided to maintain the MT in the absence of any serious counter-argument; Barthélemy, *Critique* 844.

[52] Andersen, *Habakkuk* 209.

[53] Andersen follows D. Pardee's seminal study, "YPH 'Witness' in Hebrew and Ugaritic", *Vetus Testamentum* 28, no. 2 (1978) 204-14.

[54] Andersen, *Habakkuk* 207.

suggestion fits well with what seems to have been the way the text was read by the LXX translators.[55]

Anderson's thorough discussion of the exegetical challenges of 2:4 is difficult to summarize. Suffice it to say that the interpretation builds on the three associations of אֱמוּנָה in the Hebrew Bible, "human dutifulness (πίστις), divine reliability in deeds (πίστις), and divine truthfulness in words (ἀλήθεια)",[56] and on the contention that the theme of vv. 2-4 is the "vision". Any one of the three possibilities involves a contrast between two responses to the vision, the one of the righteous who receives the message favourably, and the one of the wicked who perverts the message.[57]

2.3.9.2. Floyd

> [2:4] Once someone's greed has grown so great, it has led him astray; but a just person, in his faithfulness, will live. And because wine [*or* wealth] is treacherous, a man grows arrogant, and he will not succeed. [2:5] He who has made his greed as wide as Sheol becomes like Death and will never have enough ... [58]

Floyd re-evaluates the understanding of the phenomenon of prophecy and argues that the relationship between the oral and written aspects of prophetic material should not be considered entirely unidirectional, i.e., the written record invariably being the result of the oral manifestation. On the basis of Hab. 2:1-5, he argues that prophetic or mantic writing, "was an integral part of the prophetic phenomenon itself, and not merely a secondary or alternative means of representing prophecies".[59]

Floyd asserts that the "vision" to be written down was the speech of Yahweh beginning with 2:4 (arguably up to 2:20), and that the most appropriate connotation of חָזוֹן in this context is its derivative meaning of "revelation". He addresses the controversial meaning of עֻפְּלָה, the antecedents for the pronominal suffixes and for the verbs, and the parallelism in 2:4a/b. The point of departure in his argument is the relationship between 2:4 and 2:5, since it supplies the clues for the interpretation of the text. He prefers the well-attested meaning "appetite" or "greed" for נֶפֶשׁ which provides the semantic link between the two verses. In light of this choice, he interprets עֻפְּלָה as a derivative form of the root עפל, with the meaning of "distension" taken either literally or figuratively. Floyd contends that the antecedent for עֻפְּלָה and בּוֹ is

[55] Andersen, *Habakkuk* 208.

[56] Andersen, *Habakkuk* 213.

[57] Andersen, *Habakkuk* 214.

[58] Michael H. Floyd, "Prophecy and Writing in Habakkuk 2,1-5", *Zeitschrift für die alttestamentliche Wissenschaft* 105, no. 3 (1993) 475.

[59] Floyd, "Prophecy" 477.

ambiguous, but the text elucidates the referent as it unfolds. In 2:5 the identity becomes clear, the referent in 2:4a is the "arrogant man", the Chaldean, by association with 1:9b, and also 1:15a where the same word describes the Chaldeans. The parallelism of 2:4a and 2:4b contrasts two realities and two tendencies, "the process by which greed has corrupted someone", on the one hand, and "the destiny of the person who remains committed to justice", on the other.[60]

2.3.9.3. Haak

> [2:3] For the vision is a 'testifier' at the appointed time, indeed, a witness at the end and does not lie. He tarries? Wait for him! For surely he comes, he will not delay!
> [2:4] Behold, swollen, not smooth, will be his gullet within him, but the righteous because of its fidelity will live.[61]

Following Pardee's seminal study, Haak emends the text in 2:3 and reads עֵד instead of עוֹד.[62] He acknowledges the ambiguity of the antecedents in 2:3 and proposes that God be taken as the referent. Haak sees the key phrase לֹא יָשַׁר in 2:4a as the clue to elucidating the meaning of עֻפְּלָה and argues against reading in ethical overtones, preferring the amoral meaning of "straight, unbent" or "even, smooth". Consequently, the meaning of עֻפְּלָה is "to swell", the main lexical root offered by the major lexica (KB, BDB). In conjunction with these two meanings, the word נֶפֶשׁ must be interpreted in its literal sense of "gullet, throat", according to its use in 2:5. "Fidelity" and not "faith" is the connotation of אֱמוּנָה, with "vision" as its antecedent, even though Haak prefers to keep a loose distinction between the three possible antecedents, "the vision, the content of the vision (the Chaldeans), and the author of the vision (Yahweh). Their reliability is interdependent."[63]

2.3.9.4. Sweeney

Although the main interest of this article concerns the structure and genre of Habakkuk, it also addresses the key exegetical issues in Hab. 2:4 such as the meaning of עֻפְּלָה, the problems of verbal and pronominal antecedents, the lack of full parallelism correspondence between 2:4a and 2:4b and the meaning of key terms. In the absence of a supplied translation it is difficult to understand how the solution proposed by Sweeney comes together.

---

[60] Floyd, "Prophecy" 475.
[61] Robert D. Haak, *Habakkuk* (SVT 44; Leiden: E. J. Brill, 1992) 25.
[62] Pardee, "Witness".
[63] Haak, *Habakkuk* 59.

Regarding the meaning of עֻפְּלָה, he observes, "the basic concept behind each meaning is that of inflation or swelling, whether it is understood literally or in the abstract sense of arrogance".[64] Furthermore, he sees no inherent problem in the lack of explicit antecedents in this verse, a phenomenon occurring earlier in the book. As to the referents in 2:4, verse 1:13 offers the insight, since in both cases the contrast is between the righteous - the people of Judah, and the arrogant - the Chaldean. Sweeney opts for "life" as the meaning of נֶפֶשׁ and "steadfastness" for אֱמוּנָה. Underlying verse 2:4, he sees a contrast between the righteous one and his stability, and the arrogant, whose life is unstable due to the sin of arrogance. In the context of the book, he contends that 2:4a refers to Judah while 2:4b refers to the Chaldeans.[65]

2.3.9.5. Roberts

[2:3] For the vision is a witness to the appointed time; It is a testifier to the end, and it does not lie. If it seems slow, wait for it. [2:4] For it will surely come; it will not delay. Now the fainthearted, his soul will not walk in it, But the righteous person will live by its faithfulness.[66]

Roberts defends his translation based on the following exegetical decisions. He accepts a different pointing, עוֹד, "yet" instead of עֵד, "witness," correcting the alleged error caused by the wrongly construed יָפֵחַ as a verb and not as the noun "testifier." As far as עֻפְּלָה is concerned, Roberts rejects the reading of the 3rd fem. sg. pual "was puffed up" on the grounds of gender incompatibility within 2:4a, even though he apparently fails to observe that while the logical subject requires a masculine verbal form, the grammatical subject נֶפֶשׁ is feminine and agrees with both feminine verbs. Acknowledging עלף, יעף, or עיף as possible roots for the word עֻפְּלָה, Roberts proposes to leave the consonantal text unchanged but to re-divide it to read as a qal participle form, עֵף לָהּ, "the one who faints before it". Roberts adopts the meaning "firmness, steadfastness, fidelity, reliability, trustworthiness" for אֱמוּנָה instead of "faith". In the present context, אֱמוּנָה refers to the reliability of the vision and, implicitly, of God. The verb יִחְיֶה refers to the life promised to the righteous one in the interval preceding the coming of the vision.

---

[64] Marvin A. Sweeney, "Structure, Genre, and Intent in the Book of Habakkuk", *Vetus Testamentum* 41, no. 1 (1991) 75.

[65] Sweeney, "Structure" 76.

[66] Jimmy Jack McBee Roberts, *Nahum, Habakkuk, and Zephaniah* (OTL; Louisville: Westminster - John Knox Press, 1991) 106.

2.3.9.6. Scott

2:4 If indeed Ophel [will be laid waste], unless its people are upright in it – now the righteous (nation) will live (with divine prosperity in the land) by means of its trustworthiness – how much more will the wine deal treacherously, and will not (the) haughty man be destroyed?[67]

Behind the solution proposed by Scott lies the assumption that 2:4 and 2:5 are linked by הִנֵּה and וְאַף כִּי in a *qal waḥomer* argument. The minor premise comprises three cola. In the first colon, he proposes a new interpretation for the word עֻפְּלָה as an alternative form of the toponym Ophel, the fortified acropolis in Jerusalem.[68] He restores an allegedly missing part of the colon, the verb נֶאֱוָא, to supply the meaning "if indeed Ophel [will be laid waste]". The second colon consists of an asyndetic circumstantial clause in which the pronominal suffixes refer collectively to Ophel, and the verb has an unusual ethical meaning. The second colon specifies the conditions without which Ophel would be laid waste by invasion. The third colon supplies the stipulation for abiding prosperously in the land, in which צַדִּיק represents the whole nation and not a segment of it. The preposition בְּ should be given the sense of "means by which", אֱמוּנָה denotes "trustworthiness" not "faith", and the pronominal suffix should be read as subjective genitive. The result of abiding by these conditions is described by the verb יִחְיֶה, which means living under God's covenant blessings. The major premise in 2:5, indicates that the Chaldeans will be punished for their dealings even more certainly than Judah was.

Although some of Scott's proposed solutions deserve attention when taken individually, collectively they make for a very cumbersome reading of the verse. The simple fact that the translation itself requires such extensive buttressing in order to make sense jeopardises Scott's contribution to the discussion.

2.3.9.7. Smith

2:3 For the vision is yet for an appointed time. It hurries to the end and it will not lie. If it tarries, wait for it, because it will surely come. It will not be late. 2:4 Behold, (the oppressor) is puffed up, his soul is not upright in him, but the righteous shall live by his faithfulness.[69]

---

[67] James M. Scott, "A New Approach to Habakkuk 2:4-5a", *Vetus Testamentum* 35, no. Jl (1985) 340.

[68] Scott, "Approach" 332.

[69] Ralph L. Smith, *Micah - Maleachi* (WBC; Waco: Word, 1984).

Smith contends that the subject of the verb in 2:4a was lost and follows Wellhausen's reading הֶעֻול. He prefers the root "to swell" for the meaning of עֻפְּלָה and suggests that the prophetic message that will be written on the tablets should be limited to 2:4.

2.3.9.8. Janzen

[2:3] For the vision is a witness to a rendezvous, a testifier to the end - it does not lie: "If he tarries, wait for him he will surely come, he will not delay!" [2:4] As for the sluggard, he does not go straight on in it; but the righteous through its reliability shall live.[70]

This article addresses lexical and semantic issues on the basis of a philological analysis of the text and presents a number of solutions that are both new and ingenious. The translation reflects his conclusions based on the following evidence. First, he argues that the meaning of the passage rests on four key terms that belong to the same semantic field אֱמוּנָה, יָפֵחַ, כֻּזָב, and עוֹד. He suggests that some of the most important lexemes in the passage have been either misconstrued (יָפֵחַ taken to be derived from the root פּוּחַ) or wrongly vocalised (עוֹד instead of עַד). On the basis of previous studies, especially that of Pardee, he adopts the root יָפֵחַ and the vocalisation עַד.

Second, Janzen describes the dynamic of the passage in terms of two rhetorical vectors in order to clarify the antecedents for the pronominal element, the initiating vector (the vision) and the responsive vector (the answer to the vision). While they provide thematic movement to the passage, both vectors are supported and characterised by lexical elements in the passage, "run" and "wait" for the former, and "if it tarries" and "it will surely come" for the latter. On the basis of this analysis he adopts another emendation of the text, reading עָצֵל in 2:4a as the counterpart of צַדִּיק in 2:4b. In view of these proposals, the antecedent of the 3rd sg. suffix בֶּאֱמוּנָתוֹ in 2:4b is חָזוֹן in 2:2-3.

The last issue addressed is the clarification of the referent for the expression "one who is to come". Janzen asserts that it is God himself, and rests his case on the parallel passages from Isaiah, an earlier member of the prophetic guild, whose traditions Habakkuk upheld.

---

[70] Gerald J. Janzen, "Habakkuk 2:2-4 in the Light of Recent Philological Advances", *Harvard Theological Review* 73, no. Ja-Ap (1980) 76.

2.3.9.9. Emerton

[2:4] Behold, he whose personality within him is not upright will fly away (i.e., pass away, perish), but the righteous man will live because of his faithfulness. [2:5] Furthermore, wealth is treacherous, and the proud man will not be successful …[71]

The article deals with the exegetical issues of vv. 2:5 and 2:4, in this order, and presents a helpful summary of the difficulties involved and the possible solutions. Verse 2:5 holds no particular interest for this excursus, thus it will suffice to note two key elements in Emerton's solution, the translation "furthermore" for the conjunction וְאַף כִּי in 2:5a, and the reading הוֹן, "wealth", instead of הַיִּין, "wine", based on textual evidence provided by 1QpHab.

The second part of the article addresses the challenges of verse 2:4, primarily of its first stich הִנֵּה עֻפְּלָה לֹא־יָשְׁרָה נַפְשׁוֹ בוֹ. Emerton adopts the ethical sense of the verb יָשְׁרָה on the basis of the usual meaning of its cognate adjective. He raises three major objections to the RSV rendering; the lack of support for עֻפְּלָה to have the meaning attributed by the lexica (cf. BDB), the ambiguity of the pronominal antecedents and the awkward form of the verse, since the "will live" in 2:4b has no counterpart in 2:4a.

He then surveys a number of solutions proposed earlier which emend the MT, either by finding a noun in the place of הִנֵּה, or by reading עֻפְּלָה as a noun describing either a blameworthy person or a verb denoting the downfall of the wicked. Emerton's solution is a ingenious proposal that maintains, in essence, the consonantal text but requires a different division of the words and different pointing.[72] The first word עפלה is repartitioned, resulting in the qal participle of עוּף, "to fly", with the sense of "to pass away, perish", and לה, the preposition with an archaic form of the ethic dative ה instead of ו.

The above list would more accurately summarise the discussion if it considered several other proposed solutions,[73] however it offers a selective

---

[71] Emerton, "Problems" 17.

[72] Emerton, "Problems" 16.

[73] Wilhelm Rudolph, *Micha - Nahum - Habakuk - Zephanja*; (KAT 13; Gütersloh: Gerd Mohn, 1975); Jörg Jeremias, *Kultprophetie und Gerichtsverkündigung in der späten Königszeit Israels* (Neukirchen-Vluyn: Neukirchener Verlag, 1970); Adam S. van der Woude, "Der Gerechte wird dürch seine Treue leben",in *Studia Biblica et Semitica. Festschrift Th. C. Vriezen*, eds. Adam S. van der Woude and W. C. vanUnnik (Wageningen: H. Veenman en Zonen, 1966) 367-75; idem, "Habakuk 2:4 [Ez 33:12]", *Zeitschrift für die Alttestamentliche Wissenschaft* 82, no. 2 (1970) 281-82; P. J. M. Southwell, "Note on Habakkuk 2:4", *Journal of Theological Studies* 19 (1968) 614-17; Karl Elliger, *Das Buch der zwölf kleinen Propheten II: Die Propheten Nahum, Habakuk, Zephanja, Haggai, Sacharia, Maleachi* (ATD 25; Göttingen: Vandenhoeck & Ruprecht, 1982); Humbert, *Problemes*; Driver, "Problems"; Ernst Sellin, *Das Zwölfprophetenbuch*

list of the major proposals for solving the difficulties posed by Hab. 2:4, a text that will continue to puzzle the exegetes.

2.3.10. Conclusion

Taking into consideration the current state of research on this matter, this study will proceed on the assumption that the tradition represented in the MT is the best representation of the original text of Hab. 2:4. The position is justified primarily on corroborative grounds between the MT readings and readings from the Dead Sea Scrolls, especially the Habakkuk Pesher. Furthermore, as far as the form of the verse is concerned, neither the deviations from the usual poetic parallelism, be it antithetic or synthetic, chiastic or linear, nor the meter seem to provide sufficient grounds to justify emendation. The unusual expression in 2:4a is understood as a rhetorical device which, not unlike other prophetic texts, employs several layers of literary ambiguity, both of antecedent and referent, which await clarification as the text of the oracle progresses.

3. Habakkuk 2:3-4. The Septuagint Text-Tradition

3.1. Hab. 2:3-4 LXX. Text

3 a	διότι ἔτι ὅρασις εἰς καιρὸν
3 b	καὶ ἀνατελεῖ εἰς πέρας
3 c	καὶ οὐκ εἰς κενόν
3 d	ἐὰν ὑστερήσῃ
3 e	ὑπόμεινον αὐτόν
3 f	ὅτι ἐρχόμενος ἥξει
3 g	καὶ οὐ μὴ χρονίσῃ
4 a	ἐὰν ὑποστείληται
4 b	οὐκ εὐδοκεῖ ἡ ψυχή μου ἐν αὐτῷ
4 c	ὁ δὲ δίκαιος ἐκ πίστεώς μου ζήσεται

(KAT 12; Leipzig: Werner Scholl, 1922); John M. P. Smith, William H. Ward, and Julius A. Bewer, *A Critical and Exegetical Commentary on Micah, Zephaniah, Nahum, Habakkuk, Obadiah and Joel* (ICC; Edinburgh: T. & T. Clark, 1912); A. Van Hoonacker, *Les douze petits prophètes* (Paris: J. Gabalda, 1908); Karl Marti, *Das Dodekapropheton* (KHCAT 13; Tübingen: J. C. B. Mohr, 1904); W. Nowack, *Die kleinen Propheten* (HAT; Göttingen: Vandenhoeck & Ruprecht, 1903); and C. F. Keil and F. Delitzsch, *Biblical Commentary on the Old Testament. The Twelve Minor Prophets*, vol. 2, (Edinburgh: T. & T. Clark, 1871).

3.2. *Hab. 2:3-4 LXX. Textual Witnesses and Variants*

In the Göttingen edition of the Septuagint of the Minor Prophets,[74] Ziegler divides the manuscript witnesses into four distinct groups, the Alexandrian, the Hexaplaric, the Lucianic and the Catena. Four of the most important manuscripts, the codices ℵ, B, V and W do not fit in any of the four text-types and are considered to stand on their own.[75]

ἐρχόμενος / ὁ ἐρχόμενος 46 130 311 Cyr^p Th Thph =Heb.10:37
The only textual witnesses for the articular reading outside the Church Fathers' quotations are the minuscules 46 of the Lucianic Group and 130, 311 of the Catena Group. The textual witness decisively favours the unarthrous reading. Considerations of translation technique cannot be a guide at this juncture because the number of articular participles is relatively equal to the unarthrous ones throughout Habakkuk.[76] The choice must be made on the basis of textual representation. The considerably inferior representation of the articular form, on the one hand, and the possibility of the Heb. 10:37 reading influencing the transmission of the Greek Habakkuk text, on the other, make the choice of the unarthrous reading more reasonable.

οὐ μή / omit μή V *ll* (62 147) *lll* (46 86 711) 410 87* 534
Since this textual issue is directly related to the next text critical problem, it will be discussed in connection with it.

χρονίσῃ / χρονήσει (vel - νησει) *ll* (62 147) 86 410 26 BasN Thph / χρονιεῖ 46 711 613 534 Cyr Tht Thph cf. Heb.
The above text critical issues are addressed together since the mode of the verb χρονίζω and the presence of the second negative adverb μή are closely related. The variants χρονίσει, χρονήσει and χρονιεῖ are all future forms of the verb χρονίζω (BAGD). Therefore, the real choice is between an aorist subjunctive verb and a future indicative. The other text critical issue regards the number of negative adverbs before the verb, whether the text reads οὐ μή or simply οὐ. Generally, the double negative is used with the subjunctive mode to express an emphatic negation, whereas the use of

---

[74] Ziegler, ed., *Duodecim Prophetae.*
[75] 1. The Alexandrian Group: A Q 26 49 106 198 233 393 407 410 449 534 538 544 613 710 764 770 919 La Ach Sa Bo Aeth Arab Cyr BasN 2. The Hexaplaric Recension: Q^mg / Q^c Syh 3. The Lucianic Recension: 22 36 48 51 231 719 763 (*l* = 62 147) (*ll* = 46 86 711) 49 407 410 449 576 613 764 770 96^c 239^c 710^c 764^c 770^c 87^c 91^c S^c Q^c Syh^mg V Arm Constit Chr Th Tht Cyr^p Bas.N Thph 4. The Catena Group: 87 91 490 130 311 538 68 96 239 534 613 Syp Arm Thph Hi.
[76] Hab. 1:2, 4, 6, 9, 13, 14; 2:2, 3, 5, 6, 7, 8, 9, 12, 15, 17, 18, 19; 3:9, 10, 14, and 15. Out of twenty-nine participles, fifteen are unarthrous and fourteen are articular.

only one adverb, οὐ, is in conjunction with a future indicative verb. The mixed combinations οὐ μή plus a future indicative, and conversely, οὐ used with an aorist subjunctive are represented in very few manuscripts, codex V, 87*, 711 for the former, and 26, 613 for the latter, and can be dismissed as scribal errors.

A judgement on style cannot be decisive in this case since both forms are used equally throughout the book; οὐ μή with the aorist subjunctive in 1:2, 5, 12, 2:5 and οὐ with the future indicative in 1:2, 13, 17, 3:17. A further difficulty is posed by the almost complete homophony of the two words. The better attestation favours the aorist subjunctive reading, in which case the other variants are quite possibly the result of a direct influence from the New Testament readings in Heb. 10:37.

ἐάν / καὶ ἐάν 410 Aeth Arm Cyr

The variant reading has a very small attestation and is probably a scribal error due to the extensive use of the conjunction καί in this verse, used three times in addition to the homeomorph noun καιρός.

ὑποστείληται / ὑποστελειται 147

The textual choice is between the aorist subjunctive and the future indicative of the verb ὑποστέλλω. The weak representation of the future indicative form, as well as the frequency of the combination ἐάν with a subjunctive verb, indicate the form ὑποστείληται as the more probable original reading.

εὐδοκεῖ / εὐδοκι[ς] A*

Codex Sinaiticus provides εὐδοκι[ς] as a variant reading for the verb εὐδοκεῖ.[77] Unfortunately the final sigma [ς] is merely reconstructed text, since this letter, the first in the row, has been erased. The most probable reading is εὐδοκεῖ, and the lacuna, whatever the letter might have been, was a scribal error.

δίκαιος ἐκ πίστεώς μου ℵ B Q V W*[vid] 198 233 544 710 764 22 48 51 147 410 613 719 239 534 538 Eus Cyp Spec =Heb. 10:38 (D* pc)

δίκαιος μου ἐκ πίστεως A 26 49 407 36 III (46 86 711) C (87 91 490) 68 Ach Arm[P] Tht Thph =Heb. 10:38 ($\mathfrak{P}^{46}$ al)

δίκαιος ἐκ πίστεώς W[c] [78] 763* 130 311 =Rom. 1:17, Gal. 3:11, Heb. 10:38 ($\mathfrak{P}^{13}$ pl) Bo Aeth Arm Cyr

---

[77] J. de Waard, A Comparative Study of the Old Testament Text in the Dead Sea Scrolls and in the New Testament (STDJ 4; Leiden: E. J. Brill, 1965) 19.

[78] The legitimacy of the W[c] reading in support of this variant is disputed. While some commentators (e.g., Fitzmyer, "Habakkuk") consider it as legitimate support for the

This is the most difficult text critical issue in these verses. Its difficulty rests not only in the diversity of the variants and their relatively equal manuscript support, but also in the complex process of assessing the cross influence in the transmission history of Hab. 2:3-4 and the NT texts quoting it, Rom. 1:17, Gal. 3:11, and Heb. 10:37-38. At the outset the absence of any textual variant representing a precise rendering of the Hebrew text should be noted. The *crux interpretum* is the personal pronoun, its inclusion, its person and its relative position. In the first variant the personal pronoun takes the same position as the Hebrew text, although the person is modified from 3rd ms. sg. to 1st sg., due to either a reading error of the translator or to a different Hebrew *Vorlage* that read באמונתי. Besides Peshitta, no Version tradition of the text of Hab. 2:4 leaves out the pronominal element or attaches it to the noun וצדיק / δίκαιος.

The lack of concordance between pronominal elements of the MT and the Greek translation is not uncommon in Habakkuk, yet the omission of a pronominal element or its attachment to a different lexeme is extremely rare.[79] Internal evidence alone is not sufficient to dismiss either δίκαιος ἐκ πίστεως or δίκαιος μου ἐκ πίστεως as original readings, but it substantially favours the reading δίκαιος ἐκ πίστεώς μου. Consequently, the first two readings must be the result of scribal error, the first, δίκαιος ἐκ πίστεως, either unintentionally by haplography or intentionally from the alignment of the Hab. LXX to the Pauline tradition, and the second, δίκαιος μου ἐκ πίστεως, from the attempt to align the Hab. LXX to the Hebrews' tradition.

External evidence favours a similar conclusion. The possibility of cross-influence in the transmission history of the Septuagint and the NT texts has long been recognised.[80] It is notoriously difficult, however, to attain a reasonable degree of certainty about the direction of influence because the factors involved are so complex. Nevertheless, certain cases can be assessed with more confidence than others, and Hab. 2:4 proves to be one such case.

The manuscript evidence reveals possible connections between certain individual manuscripts of Heb. 10:37-38, and one particular LXX text-group, which in turn helps to evaluate the degree of possibility of the NT

---

reading, others argue against it; see Dietrich-Alex Koch, "Der Text von Hab 2:4b in der Septuaginta und im Neuen Testament", *Zeitschrift für die neutestamentliche Wissenschaft und die Kunde der Älteren Kirche* 76, no. 1-2 (1985) 79 f.

[79] Even though the translation is quite literal, there are numerous cases where pronominal elements, either suffixes or the person of the verb are changed. The following verses are a sample of this phenomenon Hab. 1:11, 2:4, 2:7, 2:11, 2:14, 3:6, 3:8, and 3:10. In 1:13 and 2:6 the pronominal element is not translated.

[80] Cadwallader, "Correction"; Ellingworth, *Hebrews*; *idem*, "Old Testament"; Fitzmyer, "Habakkuk".

manuscripts influencing the LXX manuscripts. Methodologically, one must start with the clearer cases in which the LXX Mss. unequivocally show a NT influence, such as the reading ὁ ἐρχόμενος and οὐ χρονιεῖ discussed above. These LXX Mss. and their families are consequently designated as being more likely to display a NT influence. In the more difficult cases in which there is no certainty about the direction of influence, those LXX Mss. that belong to the designated group are the one more likely to have been influenced by NT readings.

In the case of the clearer variants discussed above,[81] it can be established with a reasonable degree of certainty that the manuscripts of the Lucianic and Catena groups are bearers of NT influence. Most manuscripts that are responsible for the variant readings δίκαιός μου ἐκ πίστεως and δίκαιος ἐκ πίστεως belong also to the same groups, the Lucianic and the Catena.[82] These considerations lead to the conclusion that these two readings have a higher probability of being influenced by the parallel NT traditions.

The case for the originality of the reading δίκαιος ἐκ πίστεώς μου is even stronger when one considers these variants in light of the principle of evaluating which reading could most plausibly explain the development of the other. On this basis, Koch argues for the originality of δίκαιος ἐκ πίστεώς μου in Hab. 2:4 and explains the other two readings as influenced by the NT traditions that originated in St. Paul and the Author.[83] The cumulative force of these arguments strongly favours δίκαιος ἐκ πίστεώς μου as the original reading of Hab 2:4 LXX.

3.3. Conclusion

37 a   ἔτι γὰρ μικρὸν ὅσον ὅσον
37 b   ὁ ἐρχόμενος ἥξει
37 c   καὶ οὐ χρονίσει
38 a   ὁ δὲ δίκαιός μου ἐκ πίστεως ζήσεται
38 b   καὶ ἐὰν ὑποστείληται
38 c   οὐκ εὐδοκεῖ ἡ ψυχή μου ἐν αὐτῷ

---

[81] The readings ὁ ἐρχόμενος and οὐ χρονιεῖ.

[82] For the readings which could confidently be explained as having been influenced by the NT, ὁ ἐρχόμενος is supported by the Lucianic 46 and the Catena 130, 311, the single adverb οὐ by the Lucianic 62, 147, 46, 86, 711, 410 and the Catena 87, 534, and the future indicative χρονίσει / χρονιεῖ by the Lucianic 62, 147, 86, 410, 46, 711, 613 and by the Catena 26, 534. The less clear cases are δίκαιός μου ἐκ πίστεως supported by the Lucianic 36, 46, 86, 711 and Catena 87, 91, 490, 68 and δίκαιος ἐκ πίστεως by the Lucianic 763 and Catena 130, 311.

[83] Koch, "Text" 82 f.

The present study considers Ziegler's assessment to be correct and follows his proposed texts as the basis for the ensuing discussion.

[2:3] For a prophetic vision [is] still for a future time and it shall arise to [the] end and [it shall be] not in vain. If it / he should lag behind, wait for it / him, because coming, he will come and would not be delayed. [2:4] If he draws back, My soul does not find pleasure in him. But, the righteous one will live by my faithfulness.

4. Hebrews 10:37-38

4.1. Heb. 10:37-38. Text

37 a ἔτι γὰρ μικρὸν ὅσον ὅσον
37 b ὁ ἐρχόμενος ἥξει
37 c καὶ οὐ χρονίσει
38 a ὁ δὲ δίκαιός μου ἐκ πίστεως ζήσεται
38 b καὶ ἐὰν ὑποστείληται
38 c οὐκ εὐδοκεῖ ἡ ψυχή μου ἐν αὐτῷ

4.2. Heb. 10:37-38. Textual Witnesses and Variants

The following list of variants is based on the critical editions of the *Novum Testamentum Graece*, including Tischendorf, von Soden, Tregelles, and Nestle-Aland.[84]

γάρ / omit 𝔓[13] 104 vg[ms]
The small textual representation of the reading that omits the conjunction γάρ, and the common use of this preposition to introduce a quotation (1:5, 2:5, 4:4, 7:17, 8:8, 10:16, 10:30) make the inclusion of the preposition the most probable original reading.

μικρόν / μεικρόν 𝔓[13] 𝔓[46] D
The textual variant has no significance with regard to the meaning of the text, and it can be explained as a result of the itacism.[85]

---

[84] Constantinus Tischendorf, *Novum Testamentum Graece*, 8th ed., 3 vols., (Lipsiae: Giesecke & Devrient, 1869-1872); Samuel Prideaux Tregelles, *The Greek New Testament*, 2 vols., (London: Samuel Bagster & Sons, 1857-1879); H. F. von Soden, *Die Schriften des Neuen Testaments in ihrer ältesten erreichbaren Textgestalt hergestellt auf Grund ihrer Textgeschichte*, 3 vols., (Göttingen: Vandenhoeck & Ruprecht, 1913); Klaus Wachtel and Klaus Witte, *Die Neue Testament auf Papyrus. Die Paulinischen Briefe* (ANT 22, ii.2; Berlin / New York: Walter de Gruyter, 1994).

[85] cf. BDF, 13.

ὅσον ὅσον / ὅσον 𝔓⁴⁶* / ὅθεν D*

The quotation from Is. 26:20, μικρὸν ὅσον ὅσον, is considered to belong to the original text. The reading of the single ὅσον in 𝔓⁴⁶* is most probably a case of haplography, which a later corrector rectified by the addition of a second ὅσον above the line. Likewise, the reading ὅθεν in D* could be the combined result of haplography and letter change, which subsequently was modified by the second corrector to the adopted reading.

ὁ ἐρχόμενος 𝔓¹³ 𝔓⁴⁶ / ἐρχόμενος D*

The presence of the article before the participle is well attested and it is most probably the original reading. This text-critical item was discussed also in relation to the Septuagint text. It is most certainly a case where the original readings in both the Greek Habakkuk and the epistle have mutually influenced the transmission of a small group of manuscripts. It is possible that the original copyist of the Codex Claromontanus (D*) tried to correct the manuscript by aligning his copy with the unarthrous reading of the Septuagint text. A later corrector of the Codex D has restored the articular reading. Conversely, the transmission of the LXX manuscripts was influenced by the well-attested reading of the epistle.

καὶ ἐάν 𝔓¹³ / καιν 𝔓⁴⁶

The variants are essentially identical, including the conjunction and the conditional particle. The Hab. 2:3 LXX does not contain the conjunction that is well attested in the Heb. 10:38.

χρονίσει 𝔓¹³ 𝔓⁴⁶ ℵ* D* / χρονιει ℵ² A D² H I K L P Ψ 056 0142 0150 0151

Since both variants are future forms of the verb χρονίζω, this text critical issue has no implications for establishing the meaning of the text.[86] It is important to note that the established reading of the Hab. 2:3 LXX, the aorist subjunctive χρονίσῃ, is not attested in any manuscripts of the epistle.

δίκαιός μου ἐκ πίστεως 𝔓⁴⁶ ℵ H* 33 1739 it^{ar, comp, r} vg cop^{sa, bo} arm Cl Al Thdrt

δίκαιος ἐκ πίστεώς μου D* 1518 1611 it^{d, μ} syr^{p,h} Euseb Faust

δίκαιος ἐκ πίστεως 𝔓¹³ D² Hᶜ I K L P Ψ 056 0142 0150 0151 6 81 104 256 263 365 424 436 459 630 1175 1241 1319 1573 1852 1881 1912 1962 2127 𝔐 it^{b, z} vg^{mss} syr^{pal} cop^{sa, bo} eth geo slav Euseb Chrys Ambr Euthal

Similar to Hab. 2:4, this text critical issue poses difficult challenges in sorting out the original text because of the reciprocal influences between

---

[86] Ellingworth, *Hebrews* 554.

these two pivotal verses. The transmission history of the Pauline version of the Hab. 2:4 quotation, δίκαιος ἐκ πίστεως, proves to be the least troublesome because of its consistency. Indeed, the textual evidence in Gal. 3:11 is uniform because the disputed pronoun, whether 1st or 3rd sg., does not appear in any text. Likewise, with the exception of C*, an uncial of the fifth century which reads δίκαιός μου ἐκ πίστεως, no other manuscript of Rom. 1:17 employs the pronoun. The only other evidence for Rom. 1:17 using a pronoun comes from the writings of the Church Fathers.[87] But this case alone cannot overweigh the evidence that justifies the acceptance of the pronoun-less reading as Pauline. With such overwhelming textual uniformity, it is safe to conclude that in both places Paul quotes Hab. 2:4 purposefully leaving out the pronoun in order to better convey his theological point.[88] The textual variant of C* could be ruled out as a scribal error due to the probable influence from the Heb. 10:38 tradition.

When one considers Heb. 10:37-38 in light of the established Pauline tradition, it is legitimate to expect a significant number of Hebrews manuscripts to contain the pronoun-less version of the quotation. In fact it is remarkable that there was a first century theologian bold enough not to let himself be influenced by the emerging tradition. Manson goes so far as to commend the Author for not succumbing to the pressure of the Pauline tradition when using the Habakkuk quotation.[89] These considerations make the variant δίκαιος ἐκ πίστεως the least probable form of the original text of Heb. 10:37.

Between the two pronominal variants left in contention, a strong case can be made for δίκαιός μου ἐκ πίστεως as the original reading on several counts. Cross influence in the transmission of the manuscripts and the conclusion regarding the original reading of Hab. 2:4 LXX will be presupposed in the following discussion. When the two readings are considered on their own, both external and internal evidence favour the reading δίκαιός μου. First, in terms of textual support, the first variant is vastly superior. Second, since the reading δίκαιός μου is more difficult to explain than πίστεώς μου, the *difficilior lectio potior* is applicable here. Each of the above arguments taken separately is less than conclusive, but together they provide definite support for accepting δίκαιός μου ἐκ πίστεως as the original reading in Heb. 10:38. Increasing certainty about this reading is reflected in the upgrading of the UBS committee's evaluation from {C} in UBS 3rd edition to {B} in the 4th edition.

---

[87] Tischendorf, *Novum Testamentum Graece*.
[88] Koch, "Text" 82 f.; Stanley, *Language* 83.
[89] Manson, "Argument" 135.

ὑποστείληται $\mathfrak{P}^{13}$ $\mathfrak{P}^{46}$ D$^{2, 3}$ / omit D* / ὑποστίλητε D^1
The omission of the verb due to haplography as well as the variant reading of the 2nd plural form of the same verb are to be dismissed as scribal error, since neither fits the context properly.

εὐδοκεῖ / ευδοκιει / ευδοκησει Ψ
The result of this text critical issue does not modify the meaning of the text since all three variants are future forms of the same verb.

ἡ ψυχή μου / μου ἡ ψυχή $\mathfrak{P}^{13}$ $\mathfrak{P}^{46}$ D*$^{, 2}$
Had this critical issue been in a different text, the variant μου ἡ ψυχή would have been dismissed easily as a corruption of the original reading ἡ ψυχή μου. In the present context, the similar form of this reading with the previous δίκαιός μου ἐκ πίστεως, as well as its strong external evidence make the reading more puzzling. It is important to note that no Hebrew text or version other than the LXX mentioned above read the personal pronoun in this way. The internal evidence is in favour of ἡ ψυχή μου since the Author never used the pronominal adjective to precede the noun it qualifies. The only possible example of such an anomaly would be the case discussed above, δίκαιός μου ἐκ πίστεως, where the pronominal adjective qualified the noun πίστεως and not δίκαιος. Even with such a strong external representation, the variant μου ἡ ψυχή is dropped in favour of the variant ἡ ψυχή μου, which is more consistent with the internal evidence.

5. Conclusion

The above investigation concurs with the text of Heb. 10:37-38 as proposed by the critical editions and finds no compelling reason to adopt any emendations. This text will be used in the subsequent analysis.

The text of Hab. 2:3-4, as much in its original Hebrew form as in subsequent forms, has occasioned a number of distinct interpretative traditions. Given the importance of this prophetic oracle, it is warranted to assert that these traditions have exerted their influence on the form and meaning of the quotations from this text by the NT authors. In this chapter, one influence of this nature was traced in the Author's use of Hab. 2:3-4. While the text quoted in Heb. 10:37-38 differs from both the Hab. 2:3-4 MT and LXX, the essential textual components of Hab. 2:3-4 LXX are duplicated in the epistle's quotation. At least four distinctly Septuagintal readings were essential for the text for which underlies the Author's argument at this juncture: the pronoun μου, qualifying both the noun ψυχή and the adjective δίκαιος, the lexical choices, especially the employment of the noun πίστις and the verb ὑποστείληται, and the conditional sentence, ἐὰν ὑποστείληται κτλ. All these readings have made their way into the Hebrews' quotation primarily because of the particular form of the Septuagint text. The explanations for the changes introduced by the Author in the Septuagint text will supply the subject matter for Chapter Nine; this current chapter has established a direct influence at the textual level of Hab. 2:3-4 LXX on Heb. 10:37-38, a text which probably would have been significantly different had the Author used a Hebrew text tradition from which to extract the quotation.

Chapter Eight

The Use of Hab. 2:3-4 in Heb. 10:37-38:
Contextual Considerations

1. Habakkuk in Hebrews: Literary and Historical Contexts

The quotation of Hab. 2:3-4 LXX contributes to the major paraenetic section at the end of the Epistle to the Hebrews which commences in Heb. 10:19 and extends to the end of ch. 12. Extensive discussion on the topic of the epistle's structure has not yielded much consensus, but at least seems to have narrowed down the most probable alternatives to either a threefold division or a fivefold division of the epistle, with a degree of variation within each group.[1] The passage 10:32-39 that contains the quotation from Habakkuk has been understood either as the concluding exhortation of the main theological section opened either in 8:1,[2] or 5:11,[3] or as the opening paragraph in a new section launched by it,[4] or as a paraenesis embedded in the epistle's final argument that extends from 10:19 to the end of ch. 12.[5]

For the purpose of this section the precise position of 10:36-39 in the overall structure of the epistle is of secondary importance since the extensive parallels between the book of Habakkuk, as the original literary context of the quotation, and the main theological ideas of its new context, extend throughout the entire final section of the epistle, Heb. 10:19-12:29. In order to delineate the more distinctive features that might have contributed to the use of Hab. 2:3-4, these parallels may be divided into two categories, even though the division itself cannot be pressed too far. The first category is that of intertextual links, which consists of several points of contact between the book of Habakkuk and other OT passages from which quotations in this section of the epistle were selected. Four OT

---

[1] See, *inter alios*, Guthrie, *Structure* 3 ff. and Christian Rose, *Die Wolke der Zeugen. Eine exegetisch-traditiongeschichtliche Untersuchung zu Hebräer 10,32-12,3* (WUNT II 60; Tübingen: Mohr Siebeck, 1994) 6 ff.

[2] Stanley, "Hermeneutic" 36.

[3] Ellingworth, *Hebrews* 5 f.; Lane, *Hebrews* i: viii; Vanhoye, *Structure* 40.

[4] Rose, *Wolke ad loc.*

[5] Attridge, *Hebrews*; Bruce, *Hebrews*; Neeley, "Discourse"; Spicq, *Hébreux*; B.F. Westcott, *The Epistle to the Hebrews: The Greek Text with Notes and Essays* (London / New York: Macmillan, 1903 [1970 ed.]).

passages, Dt. 32-33, Is. 26, Hag. 2 and Pr. 3, will be investigated for the identification of verbal and thematic parallels with the book of Habakkuk.

The second category relates to the *Sitz im Leben* of the addressees and consists of a set of parallels that can be drawn between their particular situation and the plight of the righteous ones in the book of Habakkuk. The contextualisation of a biblical message to a new, yet similar situation was a hermeneutical approach frequently used not only by other NT writers, but also by other contemporary authors.

It ought to be mentioned at the outset that the Author's distinct understanding of the concept of "faith" as the interpretative key to the lives of the OT heroes and implicitly to the scriptural texts to which he alludes in ch. 11, has been most likely influenced by Hab. 2:3-4 LXX. The prevalence of catch-words between Heb. 10:36-39 and Heb. 11, such as "faith", "righteous", "life/live", "inheritance", and "promise", to name a few, provides sufficient proof of that influence.

2. Literary Context: Habakkuk and the Quotations in Heb.10-12

The four OT texts indicated above are the prime target for the investigation of thematic parallels between the OT texts and the book of Habakkuk. It is important to notice that there are a number of parallels between Habakkuk and other OT passages which are used as quotations in the epistle outside the immediate context of Heb. 10:37-38. From the many examples that can be selected, one of the more evident is the verbal parallels between Habakkuk and Ps. 21 [22 MT], from which the quotation in Heb. 2:13 is drawn. The following table lists several of these verbal parallels.

Habakkuk LXX	Ps. 21 LXX
1:2 ἕως τίνος κύριε κεκράξομαι καὶ οὐ μὴ εἰσακούσῃς	v.3 ὁ θεός μου κεκράξομαι ἡμέρας καὶ οὐκ εἰσακούσῃ
1:2 βοήσομαι πρὸς σὲ ἀδικούμενος καὶ οὐ σώσεις	v.2 ἵνα τί ἐγκατέλιπές με μακρὰν ἀπὸ τῆς σωτηρίας
2:4 ὁ δὲ δίκαιος ἐκ πίστεώς μου ζήσεται	v.27 ζήσονται αἱ καρδίαι αὐτῶν εἰς αἰῶνα αἰῶνος
2:4 ὁ δὲ δίκαιος ἐκ πίστεώς μου ζήσεται	v.30 καὶ ἡ ψυχή μου αὐτῷ ζῇ
3:16 ἐπτοήθη ἡ κοιλία μου ... καὶ εἰσῆλθεν τρόμος εἰς τὰ ὀστᾶ μου	v.15 διεσκορπίσθη πάντα τὰ ὀστᾶ μου ἐγενήθη ἡ καρδία μου ὡσεὶ κηρὸς τηκόμενος ἐν μέσῳ τῆς κοιλίας μου

The cry of the prophet in Hab. 1:2 on behalf of the righteous ones in Judah living in distress under the oppression of evil is in unison with the cry of the psalmist who is under attack from his enemies. Both cries, uttered in the dark hour of God's forsaking them, mirror Christ's agony on the cross, the agony of the righteous one *par excellence*, agony that is portrayed in Heb. 5:7-8 in no less dramatic language than the agony of the prophet in Hab. 3:16 or that of the psalmist in Ps. 21:15 [22 MT]. Moreover, the oracle, which rewards the attitude of faith/trust with life (Hab. 2:4), finds its climactic fulfilment in the resurrection of the "faithful one over the whole house of God" (Heb. 2:17, 3:2, 6), who was brought back to life by God (Heb. 13:20).

The fact that the two quotations from Ps. 21 [22 MT] and Hab. 2 are separated by such a large portion of text decreases the likelihood that the common motifs were operative in the selection of these two texts or that the Author intended them to be acknowledged. Nevertheless, given the extensive verbal and thematic overlap that exists between other quotations in the epistle, the possibility that the pattern would be repeated should not be completely ruled out on the basis of coincidence. Stronger evidence can be gathered in the investigation of the four OT texts mentioned above.

2.1. Habakkuk and Isaiah 26

The quotation from Hab. 2:3-4 is introduced by a short quotation probably from Is. 26:20. The grouping of these two texts was made possible not simply because the text in Isaiah conveniently alludes to the shortness of time before the eschatological visitation, but also because both the context of Hab. 2 and that of Is. 26 include references to the day of God's wrath.

Habakkuk LXX	Is. 26:20, 21 LXX
3:2 ἐν ὀργῇ ἐλέους μνησθήσῃ 3:8 μὴ ἐν ποταμοῖς ὠργίσθης κύριε	μικρὸν ὅσον ὅσον ἕως ἄν παρέλθῃ ἡ ὀργὴ κυρίου ἰδοὺ γὰρ κύριος ἀπὸ τοῦ ἁγίου ἐπάγει τὴν ὀργὴν ἐπὶ τοὺς ἐνοικοῦντας ἐπὶ τῆς γῆς

The theme of the eschatological day of God's wrath is in fact a discernible constant in the context of the other major quotations in the epistle, Ps. 109 [110 MT], Ps. 94 [95 MT], and Ps. 2.

Habakkuk LXX	Ps. 109:5 LXX
3:2 ἐν ὀργῇ ἐλέους μνησθήσῃ 3:8 μὴ ἐν ποταμοῖς ὠργίσθης κύριε	κύριος ἐκ δεξιῶν σου συνέθλασεν ἐν ἡμέρᾳ ὀργῆς αὐτοῦ βασιλεῖς

Habakkuk LXX	Ps. 94:11 LXX
3:2 ἐν ὀργῇ ἐλέους μνησθήσῃ 3:8 μὴ ἐν ποταμοῖς ὠργίσθης κύριε	ὡς ὤμοσα ἐν τῇ ὀργῇ μου εἰ εἰσελεύσονται εἰς τὴν κατάπαυσίν μου

Habakkuk LXX	Ps. 2:12 LXX
3:2 ἐν ὀργῇ ἐλέους μνησθήσῃ 3:8 μὴ ἐν ποταμοῖς ὠργίσθης κύριε	μήποτε ὀργισθῇ κύριος καὶ ἀπολεῖσθε ἐξ ὁδοῦ δικαίας ὅταν ἐκκαυθῇ ἐν τάχει ὁ θυμὸς αὐτοῦ

This evidence confirms the conclusion drawn earlier regarding the importance of the motif of the day of God's wrath, which is a common denominator of the main OT passages employed.[6] The presence of the wrath motif was probably responsible for the concatenation of these two texts in Heb. 10:37-38.

2.2. Habakkuk and Deuteronomy 32, 33

The stern warning in Heb. 10:19-31 concludes with the quotation from Dt. 32, an OT passage from which the Author has already quoted in Heb. 1:6. Immediately following the quotation from Dt. 32, a short paragraph (10:32-34) describes the readers' situation, while another paragraph of exhortation (10:35-39) concludes with the quotation from Hab. 2:3-4. While Deuteronomy and Habakkuk belong to two different corpora of the Jewish Scriptures, there are several common themes and distinct similarity of language between the two books, especially between Hab. ch. 3 and Dt. chs. 32-33. The motif of God's visitation of his people is the most pronounced.

---

[6] The theme is present in the three most frequently quoted or alluded to pslams in the Epistle, Ps. 2, Ps. 94 [95 MT], and Ps. 109 [110 MT]; see *supra* (ch. 3, 3.1).

Hab. 3:3 LXX	Deut. 33:2 LXX
ὁ θεὸς ἐκ Θαιμαν ἥξει καὶ ὁ ἅγιος ἐξ ὄρους κατασκίου δασέος διάψαλμα ἐκάλυψεν οὐρανοὺς ἡ ἀρετὴ αὐτοῦ καὶ αἰνέσεως αὐτοῦ πλήρης ἡ γῆ	καὶ εἶπεν κύριος ἐκ Σινα ἥκει καὶ ἐπέφανεν ἐκ Σηιρ ἡμῖν καὶ κατέσπευσεν ἐξ ὄρους Φαραν σὺν μυριάσιν Καδης ἐκ δεξιῶν αὐτοῦ ἄγγελοι μετ' αὐτοῦ

The Göttingen text of Hab. 3:3 does not adopt the reading ἐξ ὄρους Φαραν even though it is the reading of the uncials W, B, S, and A, and other less important witnesses.[7] With such a substantial textual representation it is probable that the longer reading was part of the Author's *Vorlage*, in which case the two texts are identical in specifying the geographical direction from which God was to come. With this reading the two texts were more suitable to be joined together.

The two texts were associated for reasons other than just this spatial reference. Thackeray discusses the use of the Habakkuk canticle, Ez. 1, Ps. 29, and Ps. 68, as the *Haphtarot* for the Feast of Pentecost. He contends that "the common theme which runs through ... is a theophany in thunder-storm, a triumphal march or ride of the deity across desert, sea or heavens amid a general convulsion of nature" to which he adds, "with these passages should be linked one other ... the blessing of Moses in Deut 33".[8] The thematic and verbal parallels between Dt. 32, 33 and Habakkuk might have contributed both to the use of these two texts and to the development of specific themes, such as that of the final judgement in the paraenesis of ch. 10.[9]

2.3. Habakkuk and Proverbs 3

The quotation from Proverbs and the consequences of the divergences between the Greek and Hebrew texts have been discussed earlier. Attention is drawn here to the divergences between the two texts in Hab. 1:12, where וְצוּר לְהוֹכִיחַ יְסַדְתּוֹ is translated as καὶ ἔπλασέν με τοῦ ἐλέγχειν παιδείαν αὐτοῦ. Of the three noticeable differences, the most important for this section is the translation of יְסַדְתּוֹ as παιδείαν αὐτοῦ,[10] probably generated by the reading of the root יסד, "to establish", as יסר,

---

[7] Ziegler, *Duodecim Prophetae* 268.

[8] H. St. John Thackeray, *The Septuagint and Jewish Worship. A Study in Origins, The Schweich Lectures 1920* (London: Milford, 1921) 47.

[9] See also the argument put forward by Horbury in favour of the messianic link between the Song of Moses and Hab. 2:3-4 (*Messianism* 81).

[10] For the other two differences see the discussion in Chapter Nine.

"to chastise, discipline". The resulting Greek text contains a more specific and emphatic reference to the correction and discipline of God's people.

Hab. 1:12b LXX	Prov. 3:11-12 LXX
κύριε εἰς κρίμα τέταχας αὐτόν καὶ ἔπλασέν με τοῦ ἐλέγχειν παιδείαν αὐτοῦ	υἱέ μὴ ὀλιγώρει παιδείας κυρίου μηδὲ ἐκλύου ὑπ' αὐτοῦ ἐλεγχόμενος ὃν γὰρ ἀγαπᾷ κύριος παιδεύει μαστιγοῖ δὲ πάντα υἱὸν ὃν παραδέχεται

The word παιδεία is the key term for the paraenesis in Heb. 12:4-11 and the occurrence of παιδεία in Hab. 1:12, deems it plausible to envisage that the theme of chastisement might have served as a link between the two texts. It should also be noted that a significant number of manuscripts preserve an intriguing variant reading in Hab. 3:5, εἰς παιδείαν for ἐν πεδίλοις,[11] a reading which continues the emphasis in Hab. 1:12 LXX on the disciplinary role of the theophany.

2.4. Habakkuk and Haggai

Reference to an eschatological climax in the final warning passage brings to a close the main theological discourse of the epistle and offers another example of the common motifs between the OT passages used by the Author.

Habakkuk LXX	Haggai LXX
3:6 ἔστη καὶ ἐσαλεύθη ἡ γῆ ἐπέβλεψεν καὶ διετάκη ἔθνη διεθρύβη τὰ ὄρη βίᾳ ἐτάκησαν βουνοὶ αἰώνιοι	2:6 διότι τάδε λέγει κύριος παντοκράτωρ ἔτι ἅπαξ ἐγὼ σείσω τὸν οὐρανὸν καὶ τὴν γῆν καὶ τὴν θάλασσαν καὶ τὴν ξηράν
3:6 ἔστη καὶ ἐσαλεύθη ἡ γῆ ἐπέβλεψεν καὶ διετάκη ἔθνη διεθρύβη τὰ ὄρη βίᾳ ἐτάκησαν βουνοὶ αἰώνιοι	2:20 καὶ ἐγένετο λόγος κυρίου ἐκ δευτέρου πρὸς Αγγαιον τὸν προφήτην τετράδι καὶ εἰκάδι τοῦ μηνὸς λέγων

---

[11] *L⁰* (711ᵐᵍ) 49ᵐᵍ 613 *C'* 68 239 106 Th Tht Thph. See also Robert Sinker, *The Psalm of Habakkuk* (Cambridge: Deighton, Bell and Co., 1890) 47.

3:17 διότι συκῆ οὐ καρποφορήσει καὶ οὐκ ἔσται γενήματα ἐν ταῖς ἀμπέλοις ψεύσεται ἔργον ἐλαίας καὶ τὰ πεδία οὐ ποιήσει βρῶσιν ἐξέλιπον ἀπὸ βρώσεως πρόβατα καὶ οὐχ ὑπάρχουσιν βόες ἐπὶ φάτναις

2:19 εἰ ἔτι ἐπιγνωσθήσεται ἐπὶ τῆς ἅλω καὶ εἰ ἔτι ἡ ἄμπελος καὶ ἡ συκῆ καὶ ἡ ῥόα καὶ τὰ ξύλα τῆς ἐλαίας τὰ οὐ φέροντα καρπόν ἀπὸ τῆς ἡμέρας ταύτης εὐλογήσω

The theme of eschatological "shaking" is the common ground between the quotation from Haggai, its exposition and the book of Habakkuk. The eschatological manifestation described in Hab. 3 is portrayed in similar terms to those of the Haggai passage, which might have facilitated the association of the two texts. Furthermore, in anticipation of that day, both prophets refer to a year devoid of crops and livestock, a serious test for a faith that resolutely rejoices in eschatological salvation (Hab. 3), or that waits for the return of God's favour toward his people (Hag. 2).

3. Historical Context: Habakkuk and Addressees in Hebrews

Another facet that must be considered in trying to elucidate the possible reasons behind the Author's use of the Habakkuk quotation is the multiple points of contact between the prophetic book and the situation of the addressees. Since the quotation is immediately preceded by a brief description of the persecution experienced by the Christian community, it is natural to search for some clues that would explain, at least in part, the reason for the use of the Habakkuk quotation at this point.[12]

There is no consensus as to the exact identity of the community of faith to which the Author addresses these warnings. A detailed profile of the community is not possible nor is it necessary for the purpose of this section; it will suffice to highlight a few characteristics inferred from pertinent passages. The epistle's first mention of these believers implies that they were hearers and receivers of the Gospel, as a result of the kerygmatic activity of the apostolic generation (2:1-4). The faith that had been established among them for some time had failed to produce in some of them the maturity expected by the Author (5:11-14). That is not to say that the fruit of their conversion, as summarised in 6:1-6, was completely lacking. On the contrary, it seems that the majority of them had quite a strong Christian walk and faith-work (6:11-12). The persecution that they

---

[12] A valuable analysis along the same lines on the use of Hab. 2:4 in Paul's argument in the opening chapters of Romans has been drawn by Rikki E. Watts, "'For I Am Not Ashamed of the Gospel': Romans 1:16-17 and Habakkuk 2:4", in *Romans and the People of God*, eds. S. Sonderlund and N. T. Wright (Grand Rapids: Eerdmans, 1999) 3-25.

had to endure (10:32-34) as a result of their new allegiance to Christ, a persecution that might become even more severe (12:3-4), is singled out as a character-forming experience. The challenges they faced, both the anticipation of continued or intensified persecution on the one hand, and, on the other, the danger of stagnation or even relapse in their faith, are dealt with by the Author with an abundance of warning passages.

The righteous ones in Habakkuk serve as examples for the Christian community addressed in Hebrews. The prophetic book originated in a period of Judah's history described by the prophet in Hab. 1:2-4 by a series of epithets that give the impression of a society in social, political, economic and religious chaos. In addition to this grim situation, the prospect of Chaldean invasion was looming large on the horizon (1:5). In the midst of this context, the prophet laments God's absence or indifference (1:2 f.) and injustice (1:13). The prophet's complaints are answered by God with a message of permanent truth and viability, "the just shall live by faith", which forms the theological centre of the book. The book of Habakkuk concludes with a prayer that climaxes with one of the most memorable expressions of saving faith in the Scriptures. In the midst of uncertainties about the future and the prospect of complete desolation, the prophet resolves to cling to the Lord as his only source of salvation and joy.

The example of the prophet's trust in the face of imminent adversity is a sterling example of faith to the end, one that the Author most certainly wanted to use to inspire his readers to a similar determination to remain steadfast in their faith.

In depicting the situation of the addressees, the Author makes use of terms reminiscent of Habakkuk's situation. First, their possessions, τὰ ὑπάρχοντα (Heb. 10:34), which were confiscated, is cognate with one of the verbs in Habakkuk that describe the total devastation of crop and flock, καὶ οὐχ ὑπάρχουσιν κτλ (Hab. 3:17). Second, the attitude of joy with which the Christians faced the wave of persecution, μετὰ χαρᾶς προσεδέξασθε (Heb. 10:34), echoes the joy expressed by the prophet in his determination to trust, ἐγὼ δὲ ἐν τῷ κυρίῳ ἀγαλλιάσομαι χαρήσομαι ἐπὶ τῷ θεῷ τῷ σωτῆρί μου (Hab. 3:18). Although not immediately recognisable, the theme of rejoicing is not absent from the epistle. It is one of the thematic overlaps between the book of Habakkuk and other Psalms that supply quotations for the epistle.[13] Even more, it is used by the

---

[13] The theme emerges in Ps. 2:11, ἀγαλλιᾶσθε αὐτῷ ἐν τρόμῳ, Ps. 39:17 [40 MT], ἀγαλλιάσαιντο καὶ εὐφρανθείησαν ἐπὶ σοὶ πάντες οἱ ζητοῦντές σε κύριε, Ps. 44:8 [45 MT], διὰ τοῦτο ἔχρισέν σε ὁ θεὸς ὁ θεός σου ἔλαιον ἀγαλλιάσεως παρὰ τοὺς μετόχους σου, and Ps. 94:1 [95 MT] δεῦτε ἀγαλλιασώμεθα τῷ κυρίῳ ἀλαλάξωμεν τῷ θεῷ τῷ σωτῆρι ἡμῶν.

Author to sum up the example of the Saviour, the true model for the believer, who has courageously suffered shame and death for the joy set before him, ὃς ἀντὶ τῆς προκειμένης αὐτῷ χαρᾶς ὑπέμεινεν σταυρόν (Heb. 12:2).

4. Conclusion

This chapter has examined two sets of parallels, one being between the book of Habakkuk as the literary context of Hab. 2:3-4 LXX and the contexts of the other quotations from the last paraenetic section of the epistle, and the other being between the book of Habakkuk and the *Sitz im Leben* of the epistle's addressees. In both cases several thematic links partially explain the reasons behind the Author's use of the quotation from Hab. 2:3-4 LXX. In the previous section an argument was formulated to sustain the contention that thematic parallels between the contexts of the passages quoted by the Author reveal a network of texts, which undergirded the development of his argument. That conclusion is reinforced by the analysis of the context of Hab. 2:3-4 and Heb. 10. The importance of the LXX Hab. will be analysed further in the following chapter. The study of this test case has provided further evidence to reinforce the conclusion reached in ch. 4. The context of Hab. 2:3-4 demonstrates a thematic overlap with the contexts of the other quotations employed in this section of the epistle. It is true that the thematic overlap is not unique to the Greek texts, but is supported by the Hebrew text as well, however, it cannot be denied that in several cases the Septuagint reading supports more directly the thematic associations.

Chapter Nine

The Use of Hab. 2:3-4 in Heb. 10:37-38:
Theological Considerations

1. Introduction

The analysis of the test case continues with an investigation of the theological influence of LXX on the Author of Hebrews in the area of eschatology and Messianism as result of the use of Hab. 2:3-4 in Heb. 10:37-38. As mentioned earlier, the quotation from Habakkuk is one of the very few cases in which the LXX text has undergone considerable change at the hand of the Author.[1] The investigation seeks to establish the reasons for these changes and discusses their legitimacy in light of the larger context of the LXX Hab. It will be argued that the changes reflect the overall message of LXX Hab., which, just as the quotation text itself, has theological nuances distinguishable from its Hebrew text counterpart. The use of Hab. 2:3-4 LXX, a text with a distinct eschatological and messianic message, furnishes the specific Septuagintal contribution to the epistle's theological themes.

The objective of this chapter is to compare the Hebrew and Greek texts of Habakkuk, to identify the major differences between the two textual traditions and to determine if these differences shed light on the distinct theological contribution of the LXX. Methodologically, the necessary data was gathered in a study comprising several stages, beginning with a thorough analysis of the translation technique of the LXX Hab., which

---

[1] Among the other quotations in Hebrews that display some measure of authorial interference one should mention several other instances, such as the quotation from Ps. 94 [95 MT] in Heb. 3 (especially the division of the text between vv. 9 and 10, καὶ εἶδον τὰ ἔργα μου τεσσεράκοντα ἔτη· διὸ προσώχθισα τῇ γενεᾷ ταύτῃ, by which the forty years, τεσσεράκοντα ἔτη, are associated with the Israelites seeing God's works, καὶ εἶδον τὰ ἔργα μου, and not with God's anger toward them, προσώχθισα τῇ γενεᾷ ταύτῃ, as is the case in the LXX Psalm); and the quotation from Ps. 39 [40 MT] in Heb. 10:5-8 (especially the construal of the infinitive phrase τοῦ ποιῆσαι τὸ θέλημά σου with the first part of the verse, ἰδοὺ ἥκω, and not with the second, τοῦ ποιῆσαι τὸ θέλημά σου ὁ θεός μου ἐβουλήθην, as in the LXX). Noteworthy are also the quotation summaries, such as Jer. 38:31-34 [31:31-34 MT], quoted in full in Heb. 8:8-12 and summarized in Heb. 10:16-17, and Ps. 39:7-9 [40:7-9 MT], quoted in full in Heb. 10:5-7 and summarized in Heb. 10:8, 9.

cannot be presented here.[2] The comparative analysis of the two textual traditions reveals that the LXX Hab. is a very literal translation, as in fact is the entire corpus of the LXX Minor Prophets.[3] The information collected in the study of the translator's technique facilitated the evaluation of the differences between the texts of Habakkuk in the Masoretic and Septuagint traditions. These preliminary stages prepared the data for the sketching of a profile of the theological differences between the two textual traditions, and consequently for the assessment of the differences between Hab. 2:3-4 LXX and Hab. 2:3-4 MT in the light of the overall message of LXX Hab.

A study of this nature inevitably builds on several assumptions that can only be acknowledged here without any attempt to justify them. First, the text of the LXX used throughout this study is that of Ziegler's volume on the Minor Prophets in the Göttingen edition.[4] The history of the Greek and Hebrew texts is far too complex, and the textual evidence is far too thin to allow a reconstruction of the Greek text with complete certainty. In the absence of such knowledge, the eclectic text suggested by Ziegler based on

---

[2] Gheorghita, R. "An analysis of the Translation Technique of the Septuagint of AMBAKOYM". Unpublished paper presented to Professor W. Horbury, May 1997. The study of the translation technique and its value continues to be highly disputed among Septuagintalists. The main objective of the analysis of translation technique is to uncover patterns that guided the translation, Anneli Aejmelaeus, "Translation Technique and the Intention of the Translator", in *On the Trail of Septuagint Translators. Collected Essays*, ed. Anneli Aejmelaeus (Kampen: Kok Pharos, 1993) 65-77; S. Olofsson, *The LXX Version. A Guide to the Translation Technique of the Septuagint* (ConBOT; Stockholm: Almqvist, 1990); Emanuel Tov, "The Nature and Study of the Translation Technique of the LXX in the Past and Present", in *VI Congress for the IOSCS - Jerusalem 1986*, ed. C. E. Cox (Atlanta: Scholars Press, 1987) 337-59; Chaim Rabin, "The Translation Process and the Character of the Septuagint", *Textus* 6 (1968) 1-26. But while there are scholars arguing for the priority and indispensability of the study of translation technique for Septuagintal studies, others, especially due to the limited knowledge available on the history of the texts, disclaim it as a pursuit that is, at best, too narrow and, at worst, circular; cf. Schaper, *Eschatology*.

[3] Barry A. Jones, *The Formation of the Book of the Twelve. A Study in Text and Canon* (SBL-DS 149; Atlanta: Scholars Press, 1995) 83. As mentioned earlier, two important studies on the subject have been produced since this dissertation was submitted. First, there is the publication of the first volume on the Minor Prophets corpus (Harl, *Les Douze Prophètes*) in *La Bible d'Alexandrie*. The second work, which has already been alluded to, is a long overdue study of the Old Greek book of Habakkuk exploring the theology and the world view of Habakkuk as represented by the Old Greek text form (Cleaver-Bartholomew, "Analysis". Most conclusions reached in the present study are confirmed by the two subsequent studies.

[4] Ziegler, *Duodecim Prophetae*.

the best available textual witnesses is the most satisfactory compromise.[5] Second, the Hebrew text used for comparing and assessing the LXX Hab. is represented by the Masoretic text, supplemented, when necessary by information from other Hebrew textual traditions, the Habakkuk Pesher from Qumran, and the fragments from the Murabba'ât text of the Scroll of the Minor Prophets.

2. Habakkuk and Septuagint Minor Prophets

A steady stream of research on the Minor Prophets has produced evidence that the collection is not a random grouping of previously separate books, but rather the outcome of an intentional effort to collect, redact and complete a unified canonical writing.[6] Various links between different books in the collection are not unlike internal links found within the individual books of the Major Prophets.[7] While not all scholars agree with this perspective,[8] and even among those who do, not all would agree with the rather neat dogmatic arrangement of the books suggested by House,[9] the level of intertextuality among the books, i.e., quotations, allusions, catch-words, themes, motifs, and various framing devices buttress the

---

[5] The results of this investigation are presented on the basis of the Göttingen text, without special mention of the variant readings attested in other Greek manuscripts, Ziegler, *Duodecim Prophetae*. The majority of the translation techniques' statistics vary insignificantly when these variants are taken into account.

[6] R. J. Coggins, "The Minor Prophets - One Book or Twelve?", in *Crossing the Boundaries. Essays in Biblical Interpretation in Honour of Michael D. Goulder*, eds. S. E. Porter, P. Joyce, and D. E. Orton (BIS 8; Leiden: E. J. Brill, 1994) 57-68; Russell Fuller, "The Form and Formation of the Book of the Twelve: The Evidence from the Judean Desert," in *Forming Prophetic Literature*, eds. J. W. Watts and P. R. House (JSOT-SS 235; Sheffield: Sheffield Academic Press, 1996) 86-101; P. R. House, *The Unity of the Twelve* (JSOT-SS 97; Sheffield: Sheffield Academic Press, 1990); Jones, *Formation*; James D. Nogalski, *Literary Precursors to the Book of the Twelve* (BZAW 217; Berlin: Walter de Gruyter, 1993); *idem*, *Redactional Processes in the Book of the Twelve* (BZAW 218; Berlin: Walter de Gruyter, 1993); J. W. Watts and P. R. House, *Forming Prophetic Literature: Essays on Isaiah and The Twelve in Honor of John D. W. Watts* (JSOT-SS 235; Sheffield: Sheffield Academic Press, 1996); Ehud Ben Zvi, "Twelve Prophetic Books or 'The Twelve': A Few Preliminary Considerations", in *Forming Prophetic Literature*, eds. J. W. Watts and P. R. House (JSOT-SS 235; Sheffield: Sheffield Academic Press, 1996) 125-56.

[7] Coggins, "Minor Prophets".

[8] Zvi, "Twelve" 125 f.

[9] The books are divided thematically, Hosea, Joel, Amos, Obadiah, Jonah, Micah – Sin: Covenant and Cosmos; Nahum, Habakkuk, Zephaniah – Punishment: Covenant and Cosmos; Haggai, Zechariah, Malachi – Restoration: Covenant and Cosmic (House, *Unity*).

tradition that the Minor Prophets were intended to be understood and read as one unit.[10]

A similar set of questions about the origin, development, unity and translation is raised in the discussion of the LXX Minor Prophets, one of the main textual witnesses for reconstructing the history of the Hebrew text. Interest in the LXX Minor Prophets, however, is not limited to the reconstruction of the Hebrew *Vorlage*; recent research increasingly focuses on understanding the corpus as a collection of prophetic books in its own right.[11] Considering the LXX Minor Prophets as a unified collection legitimises the quest for various linguistic and theological particularities that contribute not only to the theology of each individual book but also to the collection as a whole. This particular aspect of the LXX Minor Prophets, while not as vigorously pursued as with other parts of the Septuagint, has been investigated in several studies either on individual books or across the entire corpus, and has proven to be a fruitful enterprise.[12]

As far as the translator issue is concerned, the ongoing dialogue between the proponents of multiple translators[13] and those advocating one translator[14] continues, although in the absence of further textual evidence, the hypothesis of a single translator seems to be gaining momentum, as

---

[10] James D. Nogalski, "Intertextuality in the Twelve", in *Forming Prophetic Literature*, eds. J. W. Watts and P. R. House, (JSOT-SS 235; Sheffield: Sheffield Academic Press, 1996) 102-24. The tripartite division of the Jewish Scriptures, mentioned in the Greek Prologue to the *Ecclesiasticus*, ὁ νόμος καὶ αἱ προφητεῖαι καὶ τὰ λοιπὰ τῶν βιβλίων (v. 25), supplies the earliest evidence to support this view.

[11] Jones, *Formation*.

[12] J. de Waard, "Translation Techniques Used by the Greek Translators of Amos", *Biblica* 59 (1978) 339-50; Jones, *Formation*; Jan Joosten, "Exegesis in the Septuagint Version of Hosea", in *Intertextuality in Ugarit and Israel*, ed. J. C. de Moor (Leiden: E. J. Brill, 1998) 62-85; L. Perkins, "The Septuagint of Jonah: Aspects of Literary Analysis Applied to Biblical Translation", *Bulletin of the International Organization for Septuagint and Cognate Studies* 20 (1987) 43-53; Philip E. Satterthwaite, "The Translator as Imperialist: And Other Aspects of the Septuagint of the Book of the Twelve" (paper presented at the Old Testament Seminar, Cambridge, 1997).

[13] C. R. Jr. Harrison, "The Unity of the Minor Prophets in the LXX: A Reexamination of the Question", *Bulletin of the International Organization for Septuagint and Cognate Studies* 21 (1988) 55-72. See also Jones, *Formation* 87 ff.

[14] Jones, *Formation*; Takamitsu Muraoka, "In Defense of the Unity of the LXX Minor Prophets", *Annual of the Japanese Biblical Institute* (1989) 25-36; and Joseph Ziegler, "Die Einheit der Septuaginta zum Zwölfprophetenbuch", in *Beelage zum Vorlesungsverzeichnis de Staatl. Akademie zu Braunsberg* (Göttingen: Vandenhock & Ruprecht, 1934-1935) 1-16. For a recent contribution on this topic, see Cleaver-Bartholomew, "Analysis" 69-74.

more scholars agree with Jones that "the theory of a single translator to be the most acceptable hypothesis".[15]

3. Habakkuk in Masoretic and Septuagint Traditions

The differences between the two texts can be displayed and analysed in various ways. The present study focuses on the main divergences of morphological, syntactical and lexical nature, while keeping a parallel interest in the way in which the verbs were translated. As the commentary on each passage develops it will become evident that while the divergences have a limited effect on the meaning of the verse in which they occur, their cumulative effect on the overall message of the book, as well as on several theological perspectives is more substantial. A thorough presentation of all the differences would require more space than the present section allows and therefore only the most important will be highlighted in a paragraph by paragraph analysis of the Hebrew and Greek texts of the book of Habakkuk.[16]

At the outset a brief word about the reasons for these changes is in order. The explanation of the divergences between the Hebrew and the Greek texts is one of the most difficult aspects in any comparative study of this nature. This is due essentially to the fragmentary knowledge we have about the history of the texts. In the absence of data it is practically impossible to set objective standards to explain the differences between texts representative of the two textual traditions. The transmission history of the text as well as the translation process itself could be responsible for the divergences encountered in comparing the texts and one can only venture an informed guess as to which of the two bears responsibility for the differences in any given case.

Most of the divergences in the LXX Hab. can be traced to the relationship between the Hebrew MT and the LXX *Vorlage* and can be explained either as the result of the *Vorlage* containing readings close but not identical to the one preserved in the MT, or alternatively, as the result of an erroneous reading by the translator. Intentional divergences which may have been motivated by certain theological affinities of the translator,

---

[15] Jones, *Formation* 89.

[16] A similar approach, including the information from 1QpHab and Naḥal Ḥever, but with primarily text-critical interest is taken by Dominique Barthélemy, "Un archétype commun au pré-M, au S et à 1QpHab?", in *Philologia Sacra. Altes und Neues Testament*, ed. Roger Gryson, (Freiburg: Verlag Herder, 1993) 150-76. A detailed investigation of these aspects is to be found in the works of Cleaver-Bartholomew, "Analysis", and Harl, *Les Douze Prophètes*.

although not as numerous in as literal a translation as the LXX Hab., cannot be completely ruled out. While in most cases the explanations suggested above offer a reasonable solution, the important fact is that, once the translation process has been completed, the target text inevitably conveys a different meaning than the original. This aspect serves as the primary focus for the present study; not the divergences between the textual traditions in themselves, but the implications that these divergences have for the meaning of LXX Hab.[17]

The book of the prophet Habakkuk is perhaps one of the least difficult books to analyse structurally, as indicated by the consensus on the divisions of the book in the major commentaries.[18] There is no complete agreement on all the structural details, as pointed out by Sweeney,[19] but the overall structure of the book seems to be straightforward. The book consists primarily of two distinct sections, the prophet's oracle, τὸ λῆμμα ὃ εἶδεν Αμβακουμ ὁ προφήτης in chs. 1, 2 and the prophet's prayer, προσευχὴ Αμβακουμ τοῦ προφήτου, in ch. 3. While the genres of the two sections are distinct, and the two parts have been preserved separately in at least one ancient tradition, the Qumran Pesher on Habakkuk, most commentators

---

[17] The subject of differences between the Hebrew and Greek texts and their explanations is frequently addressed Aejmelaeus, "Intention"; idem, "What Can We Know about the Hebrew Vorlage of the Septuagint?", in On the Trail of Septuagint Translators. Collected Essays, ed. Anneli Aejmelaeus (Kampen: Kok Pharos, 1993) 77-115; Elias Bickerman, "The Septuagint as a Translation", in Studies in Jewish and Christian History, ed. Elias Bickerman (AGAJU 9/1; Leiden: E. J. Brill, 1976) 167-200; S. P. Brock, "Translating the Old Testament", in It Is Written: Scripture Citing Scripture, eds. D. A. Carson and H. G. M. Williamson (Cambridge, UK: Cambridge University Press, 1988) 87-98; M. H. Goshen-Gottstein, "Theory and Practice of Textual Criticism. The Text-critical Use of the Septuagint", Textus 3 (1963) 130-58; Lester L. Grabbe, "The Translation Technique of the Greek Minor Versions: Translations or Revisions?", in Septuagint, Scrolls and Cognate Writings, eds. George J. Brooke and Barnabas Lindars (Atlanta: Scholars Press, 1992) 505-56, Olofsson, Guide; Rabin, "Process"; Tov, "Translators"; idem, "Nature"; idem, The Text-Critical Use of the Septuagint in Biblical Research, Revised and enlarged, 2nd ed., (JBS 8; Jerusalem: Simor, 1997); Wevers, "Significance".

[18] The book of Habakkuk is served very well by both recent and older commentaries, such as Andersen, Habakkuk; William H. Brownlee, "The Composition of Habakkuk [with reference to 1QpHab]", in Hommages a André Dupont-Sommer, ed. N. Avigad (Paris: Librairie Adrien Maisonneuve, 1971) 255-75; Brownlee, Text; F. F. Bruce, "Habakkuk", in The Minor Prophets. An Exegetical and Expository Commentary. Obadiah, Jonah, Micah, Nahum, and Habakkuk, ed. Thomas E. McComiskey (Grand Rapids: Baker, 1993); Elliger, Buch; Haak, Habakkuk; Horgan, Pesharim; Humbert, Problemes; Rudolph, Habakuk; Smith, Micah - Maleachi; Marvin A. Sweeney, "The Book of Habakkuk", American Schools of Oriental Research Newsletter 39, no. 6 (1988); Ward, Habakkuk.

[19] Sweeney, "Structure" 63.

admit that the thematic unity between the first and the second sections is a strong argument in favour of the book's compositional unity.

The following analysis divides the Book of the Prophet Habakkuk into five sections: 1:1-4, the first complaint; 1:5-11, the first oracle; 1:12-17, the second complaint; 2:1-20, the second oracle and the five vow oracles; and 3:1-19, the prayer of Habakkuk.

3.1. Textual Divergences between MT and LXX Traditions

3.1.1. Hab. 1:1-4

The subscription in 1:1 is followed by a poignant lament addressed to God by the prophet, decrying the deplorable situation in Judah and God's baffling silence and lack of intervention in light of rampant social evil. Even though the translation of the first paragraph is characterised by a high degree of literalness, there are several significant divergences between the two texts.

In verse 1:2, noteworthy is the rare lexical equivalent for the noun חָמָס, which is translated by the passive participle of the verb ἀδικεῖν, and not by an equivalent noun, the more frequent choice in the Septuagint. Both here and in Gen. 16:5 the passive verbal rendering conveys more directly the idea of wrong or evil done against someone, in 1:2 either against the prophet, or, more generally, against the righteous ones (cf. Dt. 28:29, 33).

The following verse contains some of the most notable divergences in the opening paragraph.

Hab. 1:3 MT	Hab. 1:3 LXX
לָמָּה תַרְאֵנִי אָוֶן	ἵνα τί μοι ἔδειξας κόπους
וְעָמָל תַּבִּיט	καὶ πόνους ἐπιβλέπειν
וְשֹׁד וְחָמָס	ταλαιπωρίαν καὶ ἀσέβειαν
לְנֶגְדִּי	ἐξ ἐναντίας μου
וַיְהִי רִיב	γέγονεν κρίσις
וּמָדוֹן יִשָּׂא:	καὶ ὁ κριτὴς λαμβάνει

The 2nd ms. hiphil imperfect תַּבִּיט with God as the implied subject, is translated by the present infinitive ἐπιβλέπειν. The translation reflects either a different *Vorlage*, which had the infinitive הַבִּיט, as in 1:13,[20] or it could be a theologically motivated choice intended to soften the direct

---

[20] Armand Kaminka, "Studien zur Septuaginta an der Hand der zwölf kleinen Prophetenbücher," *Monatschrift für Geschichte und Wissenschaft des Judentums* 72 (1928) 253.

accusation levelled against God, the reading of the Hebrew text וְעָמָל תַּבִּיט. The syntax of the two texts also differs. The verb נָבַט closes the chiastic arrangement תִּרְאֶנִי אָוֶן וְעָמָל תַּבִּיט, whereas in the Greek text the verb ἐπιβλέπειν continues the thought of the verse by adding two direct complements, ταλαιπωρίαν and ἀσέβειαν. The result of this reading is that the implied subject of ἐπιβλέπειν is no longer God, as in the Hebrew text, but the prophet. Furthermore, the structure of the remaining part of the verse is changed. The prepositional phrase לְנֶגְדִּי, which closes the preceding sentence, has as its Greek counterpart ἐξ ἐναντίας μου, which opens the last sentence of v. 4. The translation of this last sentence of v. 3 is quite unclear due to the equivalence ὁ κριτής for מָדוֹן, unique in the LXX, possibly as the result of reading מָדוֹן as a derivative of דִּין.

Mention should be made of the fairly inconsistent translation of the verbs in this paragraph. The actions of YHWH consistently depicted by the Hebrew text in the imperfect, (תַּבִּיט, תִּרְאֶנִי, תּוֹשִׁיעַ, תִּשְׁמָע) are translated by an aorist subjunctive (εἰσακούσῃς), a future indicative (σώσεις), an aorist indicative (ἔδειξας) and a present infinitive (ἐπιβλέπειν). The prophet's action, depicted in the lament by a perfect (שִׁוַּעְתִּי) and an imperfect (אֶזְעַק) are translated as a future perfect (κεκράξομαι) and a future indicative (βοήσομαι). The circumstances that triggered the complaint are depicted in a series of imperfect verbs (יֵצֵא, תָּפוּג, יִשָּׂא, וַיְהִי) and participles (מְעַקֵּל, מַכְתִּיר), and are translated by a mixture of tenses, three perfect indicatives, three present indicatives and one participle. Although not consistent in its verbal equivalents, the Greek translation renders closely the Hebrew text, and the choices here are similar to the ones reflected in the rest of the book. The only difference in the Greek text seems to be a more logical and chronological sequence of events, in view of the repeated use of the indicative verbs.

3.1.2. Hab. 1:5-11

The first response to the prophet's complaint reveals a God who, contrary to the prophet's perception, is actively engaged in dealing with the problems outlined in the lament. God's intention is to act in a way that will defy belief and astonish everybody. He unveils his plan of judging his people by means of a pagan invasion of the ferocious Chaldeans. Different nuances and emphases mark several junctures where the two texts differ.

Hab. 1:5a, b MT	Hab. 1:5a, b LXX
רְאוּ בַגּוֹיִם וְהַבִּיטוּ וְהִתַּמְּהוּ תְּמָהוּ	ἴδετε οἱ καταφρονηταί καὶ ἐπιβλέψατε καὶ θαυμάσατε θαυμάσια καὶ ἀφανίσθητε

Since there are no variant readings for καταφρονηταί, the *Vorlage* most probably contained the reading בּוֹגְדִים instead of בַּגּוֹיִם, the root בגד being exclusively rendered in the LXX Hab. by the Greek equivalents καταφρονεῖν, καταφρονήτης (cf. 1:13 and 2:5).[21] The Hebrew text, in which God summons his people to survey the current political and military landscape, is rendered by the Greek tradition as an emphatic accusation brought against the people.[22]

Furthermore, the verb ἀφανίσθητε, "perish, be destroyed", without a correspondent in the Hebrew text, indicates both a heightened level of God's anger towards his people and a stern judgement of their sin. The Greek rendering is a verdict that anticipates the development of the judgement theme in the book, culminating in verse 2:4.

Hab. 1:5c-6 MT	Hab. 1:5c-6 LXX
כִּי־פֹעַל פֹּעֵל	διότι ἔργον ἐγὼ ἐργάζομαι
בִּימֵיכֶם	ἐν ταῖς ἡμέραις ὑμῶν
לֹא תַאֲמִינוּ כִּי יְסֻפָּר:	ὃ οὐ μὴ πιστεύσητε ἐάν τις ἐκδιηγῆται
כִּי־הִנְנִי מֵקִים	διότι ἰδοὺ ἐγὼ ἐξεγείρω ἐφ' ὑμᾶς
אֶת־הַכַּשְׂדִּים	τοὺς Χαλδαίους τοὺς μαχητάς
הַגּוֹי הַמַּר	τὸ ἔθνος τὸ πικρόν

God's plan of judgement reveals two pairs of noteworthy differences between the Hebrew and the Greek texts of Hab. 1:5c-6. First, in 1:5c-d, the Hebrew participle פֹּעֵל is translated by the Greek verb ἐργάζομαι in a personal mood, and second, the emphatic 1st sg. personal pronoun ἐγώ is added. A similar translation equivalent is used in 1:6 where the participle מֵקִים is rendered by a personal verbal form, ἐξεγείρω. As result of these translation equivalencies the Greek text portrays more emphatically than the Hebrew text that God is the one who has planned and is directly involved in carrying out the punishment on the people.[23] A further clarifying nuance is added by ἐφ' ὑμᾶς, which does not have a correspondent in the Hebrew text,[24] and can be read as a further indictment of the people.

---

[21] A similar choice is found in other passages of the LXX Minor Prophets, Hos. 6:7 and Zeph. 3:4 (Kaminka, "Studien" 55).

[22] This distinct Septuagintal reading is supported also by the quotation from Hab. 1:5 in Acts 13:41; see Harl, *Les Douze Prophètes*.

[23] Sweeney, "Structure" 64.

[24] The two critical editions of the Septuagint of Habakkuk differ at this point; Ziegler (*Duodecim Prophetae*) omits the prepositional phrase, whereas Rahlfs (*Septuaginta*) includes it.

The rest of the paragraph concentrates on a description of God's instrument of judgement, the Chaldeans. The qualifying noun in 1:6b τοὺς μαχητάς, the first in a long string of epithets that describe the Chaldeans' bellicose intentions, has no correspondent in the Hebrew text. The purpose of the invading Chaldeans is συντέλεια, "destruction", which depicted by the Greek text due to the translator reading of the Hebrew pronoun כֻּלֹּה as the noun כָּלָה, an identical consonantal text. The same equivalent is supplied in 1:15.[25] The noun חָמָס, used six times in the book (1:2, 3, 9, 2:8, and twice in 2:17), is translated only here by the Greek equivalent ἀσεβεῖς, yielding a further divergence between the texts. The Hebrew text implies that the Chaldeans come either for the purpose of, or with the end result of "doing violence", a situation reminiscent of the initial complaint of the prophet (1:2). The Greek text describes the coming of the Chaldeans as directed "upon" or "against" the ungodly ones, the very people of God (cf. 1:3), developing even further the condemning emphasis of 1:5 and 1:6.

One of the most difficult renderings in this paragraph comes at the end of v. 11 where the Hebrew phrase זוּ כֹחוֹ לֵאלֹהוֹ, descriptive of the Chaldeans, is translated as αὕτη ἡ ἰσχὺς τῷ θεῷ μου. The major difference between the Hebrew and Greek texts is in the area of the pronominal elements. First, the Greek text does not supply the equivalent of the pronominal suffix for כֹחוֹ. Second, the 3rd ms. sg. Hebrew pronominal suffix is translated as 1st sg. genitive pronoun μου. Even so, the meaning of the verse remains essentially unchanged. The most difficult task is to ascertain the antecedent and referent of the pronoun μου. It could be a collective self-description of the Chaldeans, as suggested by Brenton's translation, who supplies the participle "saying" to improve the flow of the text.[26] Alternatively, it could be an utterance of the prophet, who is just about to address God in the next verse as ὁ θεὸς ὁ ἅγιός μου. In the latter case, the phrase opens the next paragraph in the Greek text, whereas the Hebrew counterpart closes the previous paragraph in the Hebrew text.[27]

The translator's choice of verb tenses and moods in this paragraph reveals two notable aspects. First, as already mentioned, the two Hebrew participles in 1:5, 6 rendered as present indicative verbs, emphasise God's

---

[25] The Naḥal Ḥever 16:36 has the reading [π]άντα εἰς ἀδικίαν ἥξει, indicating a *Vorlage* identical to the Masoretic text (Tov, *Naḥal Ḥever* 51).

[26] Brenton translates "Then shall he change his spirit, and he shall pass through, and make an atonement, *saying*, This strength *belongs* to my god"; L. C. L. Brenton, *The Septuagint with Apocrypha: Greek and English* (Peabody: Hendrickson, 1992).

[27] For further instances in which the division of the Greek and Hebrews texts differ, see Harl, *Les Douze Prophètes* 239.

role in the judgement of his people. Second, the description of the Chaldeans, by far the dominant element in the paragraph, although invariably depicted by imperfect verbs, either simple, or with *waw* conversive or conjunctive, is predominantly accomplished by the use of future indicative verbs, which accentuate the imminence of their arrival. Several other differences between the two texts, although noteworthy, do not directly contribute to the focus of this study.[28]

3.1.3. Hab. 1:12-17

God's answer to the prophetic complaint elicits a mixed reaction from the prophet, a word of praise immediately followed by a second complaint directed at the theodicy of God's means of punishment. Several aspects where the two texts differ deserve attention.

Hab. 1:12 MT	Hab. 1:12 LXX
הֲלוֹא אַתָּה מִקֶּדֶם יְהוָה	οὐχὶ σὺ ἀπ' ἀρχῆς κύριε
אֱלֹהַי קְדֹשִׁי	ὁ θεὸς ὁ ἅγιός μου
לֹא נָמוּת	καὶ οὐ μὴ ἀποθάνωμεν
יְהוָה לְמִשְׁפָּט שַׂמְתּוֹ	κύριε εἰς κρίμα τέταχας αὐτόν
וְצוּר לְהוֹכִיחַ	καὶ ἔπλασέν με τοῦ ἐλέγχειν
יְסַדְתּוֹ:	παιδείαν αὐτοῦ

Noteworthy is the emphatic οὐ μὴ ἀποθάνωμεν, one of the relatively infrequent usages of the subjunctive in the LXX Hab., a translation that offers no help in solving the *tiqqune soferim* in this verse. The noun וְצוּר is rendered by the aorist ἔπλασεν, a rare case of a noun being translated by a verb in a personal mood. Most probably the *Vorlage* had a reading that the translator associated with the root יצ״ר.[29] The most striking difference in the Greek text, however, is in the supplied 1st sg.

---

[28] Among them, in 1:7, the Greek word ἐπιφανής might suggest that the translators read וְנוֹרָא as a cognate of ראה, "to see" not of יר״א, "to fear"(LEH), a possible stylistic addition of ἐξ αὐτοῦ. Verse 1:8 is a rare case of a morphological shift in the target text, though the comparative adjective ὀξύτεροι confers a suitable semantic equivalent for the qal perfect חָדַד. In the same verse is one of several examples of reading the *Vorlage* with a different vocalisation. The consonantal text ערב has been transmitted by the Masoretic tradition as עֶרֶב, whereas the Greek translator read it as a reference to the Arabian steppe. The Naḥal Ḥever 16:33 has the partial reading ρας which points to a reconstructed reading ἐσπέρ]ρας, identical to the Masoretic text (Tov, *Naḥal Ḥever* 51).

[29] In the Hebrew Bible, the noun צוּר is frequently used as a metaphor for God, making it unnecessary to suspect that the translator was reluctant on theological grounds to translate *ad litteram*, cf. Olofsson, *Theological Exegesis*.

personal pronoun which does not have a correspondent in the Hebrew text, and thus radically alters the meaning of the verse. Although the Chaldeans have been appointed to bring judgement on the people, it is the prophet who has been ordained by God to deliver the message of judgement to the people, and as God's mouth-piece, he brings perspective to the events intended to bring about παιδείαν. The infinitival phrase τοῦ ἐλέγχειν παιδείαν αὐτοῦ suggests a *Vorlage* reading that might have contained a derivative of the root יסר, instead of the homeomorph יסד.

The correct translation in 1:13 of בּוֹגְדִים as καταφρονοῦντας supplies an important link with 1:5, with the implication that both the people of God and the Chaldeans are under the same incrimination.

Hab. 1:13c MT	Hab. 1:13c LXX
לָמָּה תַבִּיט בּוֹגְדִים תַּחֲרִישׁ בְּבַלַּע רָשָׁע צַדִּיק מִמֶּנּוּ׃	ἵνα τί ἐπιβλέπεις ἐπὶ καταφρονοῦντας παρασιωπήσῃ ἐν τῷ καταπίνειν ἀσεβῆ τὸν δίκαιον

The translation of the Hebrew text omits the prepositional pronoun מִמֶּנּוּ in 1:13d, which is absent from all Greek variants. One implication of this omission is the possibility that the Greek text operates with an absolute scale for evaluating ungodliness and righteousness, ἀσεβής and δίκαιος, as opposed to a relative scale as implied by the comparative force of מִמֶּנּוּ in the Hebrew text.

The density of the verbs in this passage reveals that the Chaldeans continue to be the focus in the dialogue between God and the prophet. As in previous verses, the Chaldeans' actions are depicted by future indicative verbs with the exception of 1:15, where the three aorist indicative verbs (ἀνέσπασεν, εἵλκυσεν, συνήγαγεν) describe the Chaldeans' past military strategy and not the impending conquest of Judah. The two Hebrew perfect verbs in 1:13 describing God's intention (שַׂמְתּוֹ, יְסַדְתּוֹ) are translated by a perfect verb (τέταχας) and by a noun (παιδείαν), whereas the string of three imperfect verbs, encapsulating the principle reason for the complaint (תוּכָל, תַבִּיט, תַּחֲרִישׁ), are translated as future or present indicatives (δυνήσῃ, ἐπιβλέπεις, παρασιωπήσῃς).

The description of the Chaldeans ends in 1:17, a verse that marks another slight divergence between the two texts. The Greek translation does not take into account the ה - interrogative at the beginning of v. 17. Thus, the impending Chaldean destruction is presented not as a rhetorical question, as in the Hebrew text, but as a *fait accompli*.[30] Several other differences between the two texts do not contribute significantly to the overall message of the LXX Hab.[31]

3.1.4. Hab. 2:1-4

Following the second complaint, the stage is set for the prophet to receive God's answer. This is delivered via a divine oracle that is in essence a promise of life for the righteous and a prediction of destruction for the unrighteous.

Hab. 2:2-4 MT	Hab. 2:2-4 LXX
וַיַּעֲנֵנִי יְהוָה וַיֹּאמֶר	καὶ ἀπεκρίθη πρός με κύριος καὶ εἶπεν
כְּתֹוב חָזֹון	γράψον ὅρασιν
וּבָאֵר עַל־הַלֻּחֹות	καὶ σαφῶς ἐπὶ πυξίον
לְמַעַן יָרוּץ קֹורֵא בֹו:	ὅπως διώκῃ ὁ ἀναγινώσκων αὐτά
כִּי עֹוד חָזֹון לַמֹּועֵד	διότι ἔτι ὅρασις εἰς καιρὸν
וְיָפֵחַ לַקֵּץ	καὶ ἀνατελεῖ εἰς πέρας
וְלֹא יְכַזֵּב	καὶ οὐκ εἰς κενόν
אִם־יִתְמַהְמָהּ חַכֵּה־לֹו	ἐὰν ὑστερήσῃ ὑπόμεινον αὐτόν
כִּי־בֹא יָבֹא	ὅτι ἐρχόμενος ἥξει
לֹא יְאַחֵר:	καὶ οὐ μὴ χρονίσῃ
הִנֵּה עֻפְּלָה	ἐὰν ὑποστείληται
לֹא־יָשְׁרָה נַפְשֹׁו בֹּו	οὐκ εὐδοκεῖ ἡ ψυχή μου ἐν αὐτῷ
וְצַדִּיק בֶּאֱמוּנָתֹו יִחְיֶה:	ὁ δὲ δίκαιος ἐκ πίστεώς μου ζήσεται

At this juncture a general remark about the translation technique employed by the translator of Habakkuk is in order. In the translation process preference seems to have been given to an almost literal word for word translation of the Hebrew text, rather than to a translation that would ensure that the target text mirrors semantically the source text. While in most cases in the LXX Hab. this procedure did not yield significant differences, in this paragraph it did. Since this passage will be analysed in a later section, mention is made here of only two examples. In 2:2 the singular πυξίον translates the plural הַלֻּחֹות, and in the following line, the

---

[30] The Naḥal Ḥever 17:17 text, εἰ διὰ τοῦτο ἐκκενώσει μάχαιραν κτλ, renders more faithfully the rhetoric of the Hebrew text, (Tov, *Naḥal Ḥever* 53).

[31] Several times the number for nouns in the target language does not correspond to the one in the source language. There is also the peculiar translation of כָּלֹה as συντέλειαν, mentioned above, and the addition of ἡ καρδία in 1:15 without support in the Hebrew text. Some lexical choices also are difficult to explain.

number and the gender of the Greek pronoun does not agree with the Greek antecedent, πυξίον, but with the Hebrew one, הַלְּחוֹת. In the following verse, 2:3, the translator supplies the masculine singular pronoun αὐτόν in accordance with the Hebrew text, not perhaps realising that the Greek context would have required the feminine pronoun αὐτήν.

There are several other important differences in this group of verses. First, various lexical choices deserve attention. In 2:3, the verb ἀνατελεῖ translates the Hebrew וְיָפֵחַ, the only occurrence of this equivalence in the LXX. It is possible that the *Vorlage* might have contained ויפרח.[32] A unique LXX equivalent is given also for the verb יְכַזֵּב, translated by the prepositional εἰς κενόν. The Hebrew interjection הִנֵּה in 2:4 is translated by the conditional ἐάν, a rare but legitimate equivalent (cf. KB, BDB), which, however, significantly modifies the meaning of the verse.[33] In the same verse, two further lexical equivalencies must be noted, unique in the LXX, the verb ὑποστέλλειν translating the notoriously difficult lexeme עֻפְּלָה[34] and the verb εὐδοκεῖν which renders the verb יָשַׁר.[35]

The most significant differences between the two texts are the pronominal elements in 2:4. The 1st sg. pronoun translates the 3rd sg. suffix for נַפְשׁוֹ, resulting in a substantial change in the noun's referent. In the Hebrew text the referent is the "one who draws back", whereas in the Greek text the referent is God.[36] A similar change of meaning, due to the graphically similar ו and י, is repeated later in the verse when the Hebrew suffixed noun בֶּאֱמוּנָתוֹ is rendered as ἐκ πίστεώς μου.[37]

The verbs in this paragraph show a continuation of an earlier pattern in translating the narrative material in which all the imperfect Hebrew verbs, both the simple and the conjunctive or conversive *waw* are translated by future indicatives. The depiction of God's answer in Hab. 2:1-2 is less consistent and alternates between aorist and future indicatives. Judging on the use of the indicative mood, the Greek translator has portrayed the

---

[32] Brownlee (*Pesher* 41) adopts this alternative; it is also considered by Andersen, *Habakkuk* 206. Naḥal Ḥever 17:26 uses the future middle of ἐμφαίνω (Tov, *Naḥal Ḥever* 53).

[33] Naḥal Ḥever 17:29 translates ἰδοὺ κτλ (Tov, *Naḥal Ḥever* 53).

[34] The Pesher Habakkuk has the *scriptio plena* עופלה, confirming the MT reading against most of the Versions that might have been based on the root עלף; cf. Brownlee, *Text ad loc.*

[35] Naḥal Ḥever 17:29 uses the feminine adjective εὐθεῖα (Tov, *Naḥal Ḥever* 53).

[36] The Pesher Habakkuk is helpful only indirectly in assessing the person of the pronominal suffix. The word itself is no longer extant, and even if it were its usefulness would be debatable because of the notoriously difficult to distinguish forms of י and ו throughout the manuscript. The form אמנתם used in the commentary indicates that the 3 sing. was the pronominal suffix in the biblical text.

[37] Naḥal Ḥever 17:30 has the reading ἐν πίστει αὐτοῦ (Tov, *Naḥal Ḥever* 53).

events in 2:1-2 in three distinct and successive stages, God's answer anticipated by the prophet, given to the prophet, and transmitted by the prophet. The string of Hebrew imperfect verbs describing the vision is translated by a variety of tenses and moods.

3.1.5. Hab. 2:5-20

Following the revelation of the divine oracle, the prophet delivers further oracles of doom targeting both evil and evildoers. What at first seems to be vow oracles clearly addressed to the Chaldeans, gradually expands to include evildoers among the people of God, culminating in the condemnation of the most serious of all sins, the sin of idolatry. Various differences exist between the two texts, most of them lexical in nature, but they seem to make relatively little contribution to the overall message of the oracles.

In 2:5 the equivalence καταφρονητής for בּוֹגֵד continues the motif begun in Hab. 1:5 LXX, an equivalence which has implications for the identity of the targeted audience. In this passage frequent discordance appears between the person and number of the pronominal elements in the source and target texts. This is a result of the translator seeking to maintain a more uniform rendering by not oscillating between the plural and collective singular,[38] and by opting for indirect speech instead of direct speech in the Hebrew text.[39] The translator chooses a plural form when the Hebrew text employs a collective singular, thus facilitating a clearer reading of the text.[40] Some of these lexical equivalents are difficult to explain,[41] and in only a few cases would a different *Vorlage* reading, or a different reading of the *Vorlage* explain the choice. Three of the more certain examples are first, in 2:14, where כַּמַּיִם יְכַסּוּ עַל־יָם is translated as ὡς ὕδωρ κατακαλύψει αὐτούς, probably as a result of the *Vorlage* reading עֲלֵיהֶם, second, in 2:18, 19, where φαντασίαν and φαντασία translate וּמוֹרֶה and יוֹרֶה, indicating that the translator read a derivative of ראה not of ירה (GELSMP), and third, in 2:19, where the phrase τῷ λίθῳ ὑψώθητι is used for לְאֶבֶן דּוּמָם, with a *Vorlage* reading derivative of the verb רום instead of דּוּמָם.[42]

The translation of the Hebrew verbs in these verses follows a similar pattern observed in the earlier part of the book, where a variety of

---

[38] Cf. 2:6 λήμψονται for יִשְׂאוּ, and ἐροῦσιν for וְיֹאמַר.

[39] Cf. 2:7 δάκνοντες αὐτόν translating יִקּוֹמוּ נֹשְׁכֶיךָ.

[40] Cf. 2:8 δι'αἵματα ἀνθρώπων for מִדְּמֵי אָדָם, and 2:9 ἐκ χειρὸς κακῶν for מִכַּף־רָע.

[41] Some of the many examples that can be adduced include 2:10, in which קְצוֹת־עַמִּים is translated as συνεπέρανας λαούς, 2:11 where וְכָפִיס is translated as κάνθαρος, or 2:15 in which מְסַפֵּחַ חֲמָתְךָ is rendered ἀνατροπῇ θολερᾷ.

[42] Naḥal Ḥever 18:36 has the reading τῷ λίθῳ σιωπῶν, which is closer to the Hebrew text (Tov, *Naḥal Ḥever* 55).

translation options exist for the Hebrew perfect and imperfect conjugations. One aspect is noteworthy. In each of the five segments of this section corresponding to the five vow oracles, two groups of people are primarily addressed, the one(s) accused and the one(s) oppressed. The dynamic of the passage revolves around a discernible pattern, which includes reference to a specific or general evil done by the oppressors against the oppressed and the announcement of imminent punishment for the evildoers. The translator chose aorist indicative verbs to translate the verbs referring to the evil deeds and future indicative verbs to translate the verbs announcing the impending retribution for such acts.

3.1.6. Hab. 3:1-2

Following the preamble to the second section in 3:1, the prophet's prayer responds to the oracle of salvation and condemnation in ch. 2.

Hab. 3:2 MT	Hab. 3:2 LXX
יְהוָה שָׁמַעְתִּי שִׁמְעֲךָ יָרֵאתִי יְהוָה פָּעָלְךָ	κύριε εἰσακήκοα τὴν ἀκοήν σου καὶ ἐφοβήθην κατενόησα τὰ ἔργα σου καὶ ἐξέστην
בְּקֶרֶב שָׁנִים חַיֵּיהוּ בְּקֶרֶב שָׁנִים תּוֹדִיעַ	ἐν μέσῳ δύο ζῴων γνωσθήσῃ ἐν τῷ ἐγγίζειν τὰ ἔτη ἐπιγνωσθήσῃ ἐν τῷ παρεῖναι τὸν καιρὸν ἀναδειχθήσῃ ἐν τῷ ταραχθῆναι τὴν ψυχήν μου
בְּרֹגֶז רַחֵם תִּזְכּוֹר׃	ἐν ὀργῇ ἐλέους μνησθήσῃ

The Greek text presents several significant additions. First, the verbs κατανοέω and ἐξίστημι in 3:2b have no correspondent in the Masoretic text. With these additions and the absence of God's name, the Greek text has a slightly changed syntax, which provides a more balanced symmetrical parallelism, εἰσακήκοα ... καὶ ἐφοβήθην and κατενόησα ... καὶ ἐξέστην. Moreover, the Greek text returns to a theme opened in 1:5 with God's announcement of his works, τὰ ἔργα, and the resulting astonishment, θαυμάσατε θαυμάσια. In 3:2 the prophet witnesses God's ἔργα and stands in amazement, ἐξίστημι.

The second addition, ἐν τῷ παρεῖναι ... τὴν ψυχήν μου, has no correspondent in the Masoretic text. The explicit mention of the καιρός of God's self-revelation, ἀναδειχθήσῃ, is a distinct contribution of the Greek text. The evident parallelism of the form and content of these lines has prompted many scholars to explain the additions as resulting from the conflation of separate translations.[43] Copeland, on the other hand, draws attention to the overall structure of the verse suggesting that "the doublets are not incorporated in a haphazard manner, but are carefully crafted into an expanded translation that aims as a symmetry and parallelism of its own".[44] This view is confirmed by the high degree of similarity of these two verses in the otherwise significantly different textual traditions preserved for the Greek text of Hab. 3, the Septuagint version and the Barberini version.[45]

In the first segment of the verse where the Greek translation can be compared with the Hebrew text, the translation of line 3:2c raises several further issues. First, the phrase בְּקֶרֶב שָׁנִים, used twice, is translated first as ἐν μέσῳ δύο ζῴων and then as ἐν τῷ ἐγγίζειν τὰ ἔτη. It is difficult to assess whether the *Vorlage* contained the same expression, translated differently on stylistic grounds, or whether the translation reflects a close parallelism. Second, the verb γνωσθήσῃ has no correspondent in the Hebrew text, but was probably added to create a complete parallelism. Alternatively, it might be the result of a possible *Vorlage* reading חַיֵּיהוּ. Thirdly and most significantly the translation of שָׁנִים חַיֵּיהוּ as δύο ζῴων draws attention to the possibility of two distinct interpretative frameworks behind the respective texts.[46] The Greek translation might be the result of a *Vorlage* reading שְׁנֵי חיים instead of שָׁנִים חייהו (LEH). As a result the translation identifies the place of God's self-disclosure as the Ark of the Covenant, in contrast to the Hebrew text, in which God's self-disclosure is in the work of renewal and manifestation of power and majesty.[47]

3.1.7. Hab. 3:3-7, 8-15

The prophet's prayer sets the stage for the theophany described in both the Hebrew and Greek texts with similar language and imagery. At the outset one should mention that chapter three presents the most numerous cases of lexical divergence between the Hebrew and Greek texts, including the Barberini tradition. The majority of the deviant readings can be explained as results of the translation process, even though one cannot precisely

---

[43] Maurice Carrez, "Ambakoum Septante", *Revue d'histoire et de philosophie religieuses* 72, no. Ap-Je (1992) 138.

[44] Paul E. Copeland, "The Midst of the Years", in *Text as Pretext: Essays in Honour of Robert Davidson*, ed. R. P. Carroll (JSOT-SS 138; Sheffield: Sheffield Academic Press, 1992) 100.

[45] Copeland, "Midst" 99. The present study does not engage in discussing the complex issues revolving around the Barberini text; both Harl and Cleaver-Bartholomew devote significant space to this matter; Harl, *Les Douze Prophètes* 245 ff., Cleaver-Bartholomew, "Analysis" 333 ff.

[46] Copeland, "Midst" 101.

[47] Copeland, "Midst" 101.

identify the specific cause, as the following examples illustrate. In 3:4, a series of differences, the reading of the adverb שָׁם as the qal perfect of שִׂים, the reading of חֶבְיוֹן as a derivative of אָהב[48] and the possible double translation of the עֻזֹּה, contribute to the semantic departure of the Greek text, "and he set a mighty love of his strength", which conveys almost the opposite meaning of the Hebrew text "and there was / is the concealment of his power". Next, vv. 5-7 contain three readings in which the Greek text departs from the Hebrew. In 3:5, the noun דֶּבֶר, "plague", as part of the phrase conveying a frequently employed image in the OT, was read with the vocalisation דָּבָר, "word, message". The idea communicated by the Greek text is that of a theophany proceeded by a (prophetic) word, a sequence that mirrors the order of events in the book of Habakkuk itself (cf. 2:1-4 and 3:2 ff.). The complementary image of the aftermath of the visitation, the sweeping רֶשֶׁף behind the theophany, is preserved differently in several Greek traditions. None of the better-attested options, ἐν πεδίλοις οἱ πόδες αὐτοῦ, or εἰς πεδία κατὰ πόδας, resemble the Hebrew text. Lastly, the image of a shaking mountain in the Greek text replaces the measuring of the earth in the Hebrew text, due to either a different reading in the *Vorlage*, a derivative of the מוּר, "to set in motion, to shake", or alternatively, an error in reading the manuscript.

Similar differences permeate the translation of the remainder of these verses. The most important as far as the focus of this study is concerned is in 3:9, one of the notoriously difficult verses of the hymn. The Hebrew phrase שְׁבֻעוֹת מַטּוֹת אֹמֶר has been understood in various ways, depending on the way שְׁבֻעוֹת is construed, either as a form of "seven", or as a derivative of שָׁבַע, "to swear" or שָׂבַע, "to be sated".[49] The Greek text translates שְׁבֻעוֹת as τὰ σκῆπτρα,[50] and reads the noun אֹמֶר as a verbal form, λέγει. Furthermore, the most substantial difference is the addition of κύριος in the Greek text, attested in all Septuagint variants, including the Barberini tradition.[51] The Greek text portrays the dialogue of Hab. 3:8 ff. as a conversation between two κύριοι, i.e., μὴ ἐν ποταμοῖς ὠργίσθης κύριε (3:8) and ἐντείνων ἐντενεῖς[52] τὸ τόξον σου ἐπὶ τὰ σκῆπτρα λέγει κύριος (3:9), with marked implications for the overall meaning of the LXX Hab.

The unmistakable focus of these two paragraphs is God. The vision that was first introduced in 2:1-4 and which announced the imminent arrival of

---

[48] Kaminka, "Studien" 250.

[49] Haak, *Habakkuk* 94.

[50] Naḥal Ḥever reads ῥάβδους.

[51] Although the Naḥal Ḥever text is partially missing, it is most probable that the noun κύριος was not part of the text, since the space is insufficient to reconstruct the phrase λέγει κύριος.

[52] ἐντείνω for the root עור found only here in the LXX. Naḥal Ḥever 19:24-25 uses the verb ἐξεγείρω in an identical construction (Tov, *Naḥal Ḥever* 57).

judgement has now taken place. No earlier passage in the MT Hab. is characterised by such frequent shifts between perfect and imperfect verbs. The Greek translator opted for a similar alternation of aorist and future indicatives in the description of God's coming. Although the Greek verbs could be read separately referring either to events that have taken place (the aorist verbs) or to those that are about to take place (the future verbs), it is preferable to read the verbs within the framework of verse 3:16,[53] and to construe the aorists as future verbs, thus enhancing the certainty of the prophetic vision's fulfilment.

3.1.8. Hab. 3:16-19

The soliloquy, which concludes the prophetic book, is one of the most powerful affirmations of trust in the Scriptures. Utmost fear and trembling, the prophet's first reaction to the impending events, is replaced by a vigorous trust in the Lord in spite of the circumstances, a perfect example of what the divine oracle in Hab. 2:4b has already stated.

The divergences between the two texts in this last paragraph contribute to the overall message of the LXX Hab. First, it should be mentioned that throughout 3:16 the dramatic effect of the vision of the theophany is similarly depicted in both texts. The Greek text opens with a mistranslation, in which, due to a possible confusion of consonants, the verb שָׁמַעְתִּי is translated as ἐφυλαξάμην, the translation equivalent of the root שָׁמַר. With this change, the Greek text suggests the closing of the scene opened in 2:1, in which the prophet sets himself ἐπὶ τῆς φυλακῆς μου, waiting for God's answer. Another different nuance of the Greek text of the same verse is introduced by the translation equivalent προσευχῆς for צָלְלוּ, not a correct equivalent, but, as in several other places throughout the book, probably the result of an Aramaic influence through the root צלה, "to pray".[54] The Greek phrase ἀπὸ φωνῆς προσευχῆς is indicative of the intimate relationship between the vision of the theophany and the prophetic prayer. The last line of 3:16, due to another possible case of confusion between the consonants ר and ד, yields the Greek text εἰς λαὸν παροικίας μου, "the people of my sojourning/exile",[55] different from the Hebrew text לְעַם יְגוּדֶנּוּ, "the people who attack us". The lexical

---

[53] See *infra* (3.1.8).

[54] Kaminka, "Studien" 265.

[55] The Greek text departs from the meaning of the Hebrew text, "I will rest in the day of affliction, from going up to the people of my sojourning". If one presupposes a different consonantal Hebrew text reading יגורנו instead of the present text's יְגוּדֶנּוּ, the Greek equivalence would be explained. The ambiguity of the Hebrew text with regard to the executors and receivers of the punishment is perpetuated in the Greek text as well. Both readings are equally possible, i.e., the prophet waits for the destruction to come upon his people, or upon the invaders.

equivalent παροικία μου in the Greek text seems to preserve the ambiguity of the Hebrew text, which refers to the affliction which will come to either God's people or to the conquerors of God's people.

Two divergences are notable in the closing verse 3:19. First, the translation of כָּאַיָּלוֹת as συντέλειαν, which can be explained if the Hebrew word was read as a derivative of the root כלה, confers an eschatological nuance to the Greek text, "strengthen my feet forever, to the end". It can also be perceived as play on words reminiscent of earlier occurrences in 1:9, 15, where συντέλεια was associated with the destruction to be incurred by the Chaldeans. Second, the translation of the musical term לַמְנַצֵּחַ as τοῦ νικῆσαι, an infinitive of purpose, again a possible Aramaic influence from נְצַח, "to conquer" (DT), expresses a renewed assurance of the prophet's victory.

The translation of the verbs in the last paragraph can be divided into two groups; the first depicts the prophet's immediate response to the vision, while the second illustrates his resolve to continue to trust, when humanly speaking it will be impossible. The mixture of perfect and imperfect Hebrew verbs is divided more sequentially in the Greek translation, where the aorist indicative verbs are reserved for the prophet's immediate reaction, and the future indicative ones describe his resolve to trust and rejoice in what ultimately is God's visitation of his people.

On the basis of the above analysis of the Greek and Hebrew texts of the book of Habakkuk several conclusions can be drawn. First, and by far the most important is the overall similarity between these two traditions in which the book of Habakkuk has been preserved. This is to be expected from a translation whose exegetical texture positions it, in Goshen Gottstein's description, "as midways between the *Peshat* character of the Peshitta and the *Derash* features of the Targum".[56] This most probably is due to the intention of the translator who throughout the corpus of the Minor Prophets has succeeded in delivering a highly literal translation. The major themes of the book of Habakkuk are preserved by both texts and, arguably there are more aspects in which the two traditions are identical than in which they differ.

This fact, however, must be taken into consideration with the second conclusion, that there are also significant differences between the two texts, as the above section has shown. While the present study does not intend to advance any proposals for a systematic explanation of these differences, it has insisted throughout that the distinct renderings in the Greek Habakkuk are a potential influence on any careful reader or on the reconstruction of its theology. Careful study of the LXX Hab. will yield

---

[56] Goshen-Gottstein, "Theory" 130.

certain theological nuances different than those resulting from a similar approach with the MT Hab.

3.2. *Thematic Divergences between MT and LXX Traditions*

The overall meaning of the book being the sum of its constitutive elements, the influence of different Septuagintal readings on the overall message of the book cannot be neglected. This section presents a synopsis of the most notable nuances of the LXX Hab., which is built around four selected characters or themes in the book, the person of God, the prophet, the people of God and the circumstances depicted in the book.

3.2.1. *God*

The book of Habakkuk contains one of the most detailed descriptions of a theophany in the entire Scriptures, and the author's interest in describing various aspects of God's character marks the person of God as one of the theological highlights of the book. While the translation's high degree of literalness insures that the portraits of God based on the two textual traditions are similar, the LXX Hab. adds several nuances not present in the Hebrew text.

A first example is the image of God in the two complaints raised by the prophet in 1:2-4 and 1:11-17. The Greek text of the first complaint has a less direct and less critical attitude towards God. This is not to say that the complaints, which are so central to the message of the book, are not faithfully translated, yet it seems that due to either the deliberate intention of the translator, or a slightly different *Vorlage*, the reader of the LXX Hab. presents a less incriminating picture of God. A second distinct nuance occurs in the depiction of God's role in punishing his people, the ἀσεβεῖς belonging to his people. The God portrayed by the Greek text emerges as a deity engaged in a more direct, personal, and emphatic way (ἐγὼ ἐργάζομαι, ἐγὼ ἐξεγείρω, ἐγὼ ἔπλασέν, (cf. 1:5, 6, 12) in the planning and execution of the judgement. Another facet of God's portrait is likewise evident in the Greek text in which God's faithfulness (ἐκ πίστεώς μου) to provide sanctuary for the righteous as well as his delight in them (by implication, εὐδοκεῖ ἡ ψυχή μου) are uniquely accentuated in the Greek text (2:3-4). Lastly, while the image of the coming God is just as dramatic and awesome in the Hebrew text as in the Greek, the latter text provides a more vivid anticipation of the imminent visitation of God through both the choice of verb tenses throughout the translation and elements of intratextuality. More importantly still, the dialogue between divine persons depicted in 3:8, 9 supplies an interpretative framework with far-reaching implications for the LXX Hab. as a whole.

3.2.2. The Prophet

The prophet's mission and role in God's plan concerning his people is the first major difference between the two textual traditions. The conspicuous textual divergence in 1:12 results in a Greek text which confers on the prophet not only the role of spokesman, but also that of interpreter of the events, the one who points to the significance of the punishment for the παιδεία of the people. The second major nuance surfaces in the prophet's resolve to rejoice in the midst of the coming trials and to trust in the Lord for his salvation. The Greek text rewards this resolution with a promise for a final victory, one that is not found in the Hebrew text.

3.2.3. God's People

The reader of the LXX Hab. finds the people of God under stronger condemnation than in the parallel Hebrew text. Several divergences in the translation result in God's people being characterised as οἱ καταγρονηταί, as are the Chaldeans, and being under a condemnation, ἀφανίσθητε, which is not found in the Hebrew text. Thus the distinction between God's people and the Chaldeans is less sharp in the Greek text. Similar inferences can be drawn from the Greek text's use of an absolute scale of righteousness as opposed to the Hebrew's relative one. The major difference appears in the solution for escaping the judgement. The δίκαιος shall live, thus state both texts, but while he does so on account of his faith according to the Hebrew text, the Greek text grants it on the basis of God's faithfulness.

3.2.4. The Circumstances

The Greek text presents the circumstances framing the events in Habakkuk in similar terms as the Hebrew text, yet, given the differences between the two verbal systems one can depict a more organised sequence of events and a predominantly future perspective which add to the sense of imminence of both the Chaldeans' arrival and the theophany. Several other translation equivalencies seem to confer a heightened eschatological perspective on the theophany and its aftermath, such as the land being filled with the glory of the Lord, predicted in 2:14, πλησθήσεται ἡ γῆ, and fulfilled in 3:3, καὶ αἰνέσεως αὐτοῦ πλήρης ἡ γῆ, and the lexical equivalents εἰς καιρόν (2:3), εἰς πέρας (2:3), εἰς συντέλειαν (3:19) and τοῦ νικῆσαι (3:19).

This synoptic analysis of the major differences between the Habakkuk Hebrew and Greek texts supplies the theological parameters for a more detailed study of the central portion of the book, Hab. 2:1-4 LXX.

3.3. Hab. 2:1-4 LXX

The prophetic oracle in Hab. 2:3-4 has been the focus of numerous studies, both as a text in itself, and as one of the most significant scriptural quotations in the New Testament.[57] The present section undertakes to analyse the theological contribution of Hab. 2:2-4 LXX, in light of the entire LXX Hab. as its primary literary and theological context. Initial interest is directed both towards the differences between the MT and LXX of Hab. 2:2-4, as well as towards the way in which differences throughout the book inform the understanding of the Greek text of the oracle.

As an earlier chapter has shown, the quotation from Habakkuk has suffered significant modifications at the hands of the Author. The present inquiry seeks to determine the various ways in which this pivotal passage can be interpreted in its Greek textual tradition, with the purpose of gaining a better understanding of the semantic options that stood before the Author when he made use of the text.

The text critical issues and the changes made by the Author as well as other issues related to the context of Hebrews have already been presented in earlier chapters. Attention is given now only to the differences between the two texts and the way in which overall literary and theological contexts inform the reading and understanding of the central passage in the book of Habakkuk. Here again are the two textual traditions of Hab. 2:2-4.

Hab. 2:2-4 MT	Hab. 2:2-4 LXX
וַיַּעֲנֵנִי יְהוָה וַיֹּאמֶר	καὶ ἀπεκρίθη πρός με κύριος καὶ εἶπεν
כְּתוֹב חָזוֹן	γράψον ὅρασιν
וּבָאֵר עַל־הַלֻּחוֹת	καὶ σαφῶς ἐπὶ πυξίον
לְמַעַן יָרוּץ קוֹרֵא בוֹ:	ὅπως διώκῃ ὁ ἀναγινώσκων αὐτά
כִּי עוֹד חָזוֹן לַמּוֹעֵד	διότι ἔτι ὅρασις εἰς καιρὸν

---

[57] F. F. Bruce, "'To the Hebrews' or 'To the Essenes'?", *New Testament Studies* 9 (1963) 217-32; David S. Dockery, "The Use of Hab 2:4 in Rom 1:17: Some Hermeneutical and Theological Considerations", *Wesleyan Theological Journal* 22, no. Fall (1987) 24-36; Fitzmyer, "Habakkuk"; Koch, "Text"; Lee, "Understanding"; Manson, "Argument"; R. M. Moody, "The Habakkuk Quotation in Romans 1:17", *Expository Times* 92, no. Ap (1981) 204-08; James A. Sanders, "Habakkuk in Qumran, Paul and the New Testament", in *Paul and the Scriptures of Israel*, eds. Craig A. Evans and James A. Sanders (JSNT-SS 83; Sheffield: Sheffield Academic Press, 1993) 98-118; Dwight M. Smith, "O de dikaios ek pisteos zesetai (Rom 1:17)", in *Studies in the History and the Text of the New Testament; In Honor of Kenneth Willis Clark*, eds. B. L. Daniels and M. J. Suggs (Salt Lake City: University of Utah Press, 1967) 13-25; Strobel, *Untersuchungen*; Watts, "Romans"; Walter D. Zorn, "The Messianic Use of Habakkuk 2:4a in Romans", *Stone-Campbell Journal* 1, no. 2 (1998) 213-30.

וְיָפֵחַ לַקֵּץ	καὶ ἀνατελεῖ εἰς πέρας
וְלֹא יְכַזֵּב	καὶ οὐκ εἰς κενόν
אִם־יִתְמַהְמָהּ חַכֵּה־לוֹ	ἐὰν ὑστερήσῃ ὑπόμεινον αὐτόν
כִּי־בֹא יָבֹא	ὅτι ἐρχόμενος ἥξει
לֹא יְאַחֵר:	καὶ οὐ μὴ χρονίσῃ
הִנֵּה עֻפְּלָה	ἐὰν ὑποστείληται
לֹא־יָשְׁרָה נַפְשׁוֹ בּוֹ	οὐκ εὐδοκεῖ ἡ ψυχή μου ἐν αὐτῷ
וְצַדִּיק בֶּאֱמוּנָתוֹ יִחְיֶה:	ὁ δὲ δίκαιος ἐκ πίστεώς μου ζήσεται

The paragraph records God's answer to the second and, in the LXX Hab., the more serious complaint, τὸν ἔλεγχόν μου (2:1), levelled against God. The essence of the complaint is theodicy: a prophet who cannot understand how an eternal, just and holy God could allow or, worse yet, use the godless, ἀσεβῆς, to devour, καταπίνειν, in divine judgement the righteous, τὸν δίκαιον (1:14). Starting with 2:2 the book records God's answer to the prophet's complaint (καὶ ἀπεκρίθη πρός με κύριος), an answer in which many important themes of the book surface. While the textual boundaries of the answer are not entirely clear in either tradition, the present study considers the passage 2:2-4 to be the core of the divine oracle.[58]

3.3.1.   Hab. 2:2b

γράψον ὅρασιν
καὶ σαφῶς ἐπὶ πυξίον
ὅπως διώκῃ ὁ ἀναγινώσκων αὐτά

The first theme in God's answer is the ὅρασις, the prophetic vision which Habakkuk is required to record γράψον, on a tablet ἐπὶ πυξίον. Before giving more information about this prophetic vision, God explains the reason for the specific instructions just given, i.e., that the one who reads the recorded ὅρασις would move with speed, διώκῃ (GELSMP). At this juncture the flow of the Greek text is interrupted by the first grammatical anomaly that constitutes the first significant divergence between the two textual traditions. The plural neuter pronoun αὐτά lacks a referent because there is no explicit or implicit noun in the previous context with which it grammatically agrees. The translation choice that generated this ambiguity of antecedent is explicable on account of the translation technique employed in rendering the pronominal elements in the LXX Hab. As previously noted, the primary concern of the translator is to supply a correct equivalent to the Hebrew word and not to insure that the resultant Greek word fits within the context of the target text. In 2:2 the situation is further complicated by the fact that the Greek text αὐτά is not an

---

[58] So do Carrez, "Ambakoum" and Harl, Les Douze Prophètes 27; Cleaver-Bartholomew extends the unit to include v. 5 as well ("Analysis" 328).

appropriate equivalent for the corresponding pronominal element בֹ in the Hebrew text. Even so, clearly the plural antecedent for the translator was "tablets", הַלֻּחוֹת, rendered by the singular πυξίον in the Greek text.

3.3.2. Hab. 2:3a

διότι ἔτι ὅρασις εἰς καιρὸν
καὶ ἀνατελεῖ εἰς πέρας
καὶ οὐκ εἰς κενόν

At this point full information about the vision (ὅρασις) is given. The prophetic vision, i.e., its fulfilment, is for an appointed time (εἰς καιρόν), it is going to appear and become evident in the end (εἰς πέρας), and is not in vain (οὐκ εἰς κενόν). The reader of the Hab. 2:3 LXX finds clues in the overall LXX Hab., which help to elucidate the meaning of these characteristics. First, the καιρός is explicitly associated with the theophany in 3:2, ἐν τῷ παρεῖναι τὸν καιρόν. The appointed time for the vision is none other than the time of God's self-disclosure, the time when God will be made known. Secondly, the synonymous πέρας and συντέλεια remind the reader both of the destruction to be incurred by the Chaldeans, as well as the final victory promised to and anticipated by the prophet in 3:19, καὶ τάξει τοὺς πόδας μου εἰς συντέλειαν.

3.3.3. Hab. 2:3b

ἐὰν ὑστερήσῃ
ὑπόμεινον αὐτόν
ὅτι ἐρχόμενος ἥξει
καὶ οὐ μὴ χρονίσῃ

With the assurances regarding both the coming of the vision and the things that it will accomplish, one would expect the two following conditional sentences, ἐὰν ὑστερήσῃ κτλ and ἐὰν ὑποστείληται κτλ, to clarify any potential concerns on the part of the prophet about the vision. And this would indeed be the case if not for the pronouns and their antecedents in the Greek text, which generate a second grammatical anomaly with consequences for the overall meaning of the passage.

The apodosis of the first conditional sentence ὑπόμεινον αὐτόν follows closely the Hebrew text, and this is the root of the problem. The translator shows again primary interest in correctly rendering the Hebrew equivalent, to the detriment of being faithful to the semantic flow of the Greek text. The masculine pronoun αὐτόν, a correct rendering of the Hebrew לוֹ, no longer agrees with the noun ὅρασις, as would be required by the text if it were a semantic equivalent of the original. For the Greek text to have maintained the same meaning as the source text, the translator should have supplied the feminine pronoun αὐτήν. As it stands, however, the only masculine antecedent for αὐτόν is the masculine noun καιρός.[59] The departure of the Greek text from the meaning of the Hebrew text is further accentuated by the next phrase ἐρχόμενος ἥξει, which as a masculine entity cannot have as antecedent the feminine ὅρασις, as the source text requires. For a Greek text to have conveyed the idea of the coming vision, (ὅρασις), the translator should have supplied a construction involving the feminine participle ἐρχόμενη ἥξει. With the present reading, however, the Greek text points to the noun καιρός as the most likely grammatical antecedent for ἐρχόμενος ἥξει, which is a significant divergence from the source text.[60] Yet, an alternative reading which also tries to make sense of the masculine construction deserves attention, since one cannot rule out *a priori* the possibility that the phrase ἐρχόμενος ἥξει points not backward but forward. Indeed, in this case the referent of ἐρχόμενος ἥξει in the Greek text is clarified not by the previous lines, (whether vision or time) but by the larger literary context of the book as a whole. It has already been argued that the ἥξει motif, while referring to the imminent arrival of the Chaldeans (1:9), ultimately describes God's coming in the theophany (3:2 ff.), especially v. 3, ὁ θεὸς ἐκ Θαιμαν ἥξει. The essence of Hab. 2:3 LXX is the coming of God. His coming, though initially covert in the form of the Chaldean invasion, will certainly manifest itself in an overt form during the apocalyptic judgement announced by the prophet.

If one takes this stand, then in Hab. 2:3 both αὐτόν and ἐρχόμενος have as referent either a God-chosen representative or, more likely, God himself.[61] The fact that God is also the One who announces the coming, however, seems to be a serious hurdle for this interpretation. How can God, in speaking with the prophet, refer to h imself by using both 1st and 3rd person pronouns? Indeed, this would be an insurmountable problem if not for the overall message of the Greek Habakkuk, especially when one considers the important addition in the Greek text of Hab. 3:9, λέγει κύριος, a text in which the Greek version clearly depicts a dialogue between two κύριοι. This dialogue between two divine beings both confirms and clarifies the interpretative framework for understanding 2:3, and explains how κύριος addresses the prophet in the 1st sg. (cf. 2:4) and yet, using the 3rd sg., foretells the coming of κύριος.

---

[59] The inner logic of the text excludes either πέρας or κενόν as antecedents, even though both neuter nouns would qualify as grammatically appropriate antecedents of αὐτόν, read as a neuter Accusative.

[60] The loss of the proper antecedent in the Greek Old Testament was most likely spotted by Aquila, who uses the masculine noun ὁραματισμός instead of the feminine noun ὅρασις in 2:2, thus supplying a complete equivalency between the source and target texts.

[61] See Andersen, *Habakkuk* 208 and Koester, *Hebrews* 462.

Another aspect that deserves attention is the infinitive absolute in the collocation בֹא יָבֹא, the idiomatic expression that conveys the meaning "it will surely come". This idiom is used only here in the MT Hab., and is translated by a finite verb plus the participle of a semantic, albeit not lexical, cognate verb, ἐρχόμενος ἥξει. This choice is entirely justified in a literal translation, since this formula or an alternative one, a finite verb with the dative of the cognate noun, was the customary way of translating the idiom.[62]

For a reader accustomed with both languages it can be assumed that the idiom's meaning was transferred to the Greek text without any impediment, even though the Greek expression, taken at its own semantic value, does not convey that particular meaning. In other LXX passages the translators rendered such expressions by their dynamic equivalent, through use of adverbs, particles or paraphrases.[63] For the reader of the Greek text unaccustomed with either the Hebrew text or with the translation equivalent of the idiom, the resulting text of Hab. 2:3-4 no longer conveys the idea of certainty. To state it differently, a reader of the Greek text would not have understood consequentially this expression as a reference to the certainty of the vision's coming. The reader would probably have understood the expression as depicting the identity of the coming one and not so much as a reference to the certainty of the event. At best he would have noticed an awkward Greek phrase in need of some clarification from the overall context, a context which itself had to be adjusted in order to make sense.[64]

---

[62] H. St. John Thackeray, *A Grammar of the OT in Greek according to the Septuagint* (Cambridge: Cambridge University Press, 1909).

[63] Thackeray, *Grammar*.

[64] It is interesting that both Brenton and Carrez translate Hab 2:3 LXX by rendering the text according to the Hebrew idiom and not strictly to the Greek expression.

"For the vision is yet for a time, and it shall shoot forth at the end, and not in vain; though he should tarry, wait for him; for *he will surely come*, and will not tarry. If he should draw back, my soul has no pleasure in him: but the just shall live by my faith" (Brenton, *Septuagint ad loc.*)

"Car il y encore une vision pour le moment fixé, Et elle se lèvera pour la fin, et pas pour rien; S'il tarde, attends-le, parce qu'il viendra sûrement et ne s'attardera pas. S'il se retire, mon âme ne se complaît pas en lui, Le juste par ma fidélité vivra" (Carrez, "Ambakoum" 130).

The rendering is doubtful, since it reads the meaning of the Hebrew idiom into the Greek construction, a meaning that the Greek text no longer possesses. The reading of ἐρχόμενος ἥξει proposed above is confirmed by more recent studies:

"If he might be delayed wait for him because the one who is coming will come and he will certainly not be delayed" (Cleaver-Bartholomew, "Analysis" 165)

"[I]f he tarries, wait for him, because he will come, he will not delay" (Lee, "Understanding" 89);

3.3.4. Hab. 2:4

ἐὰν ὑποστείληται
οὐκ εὐδοκεῖ ἡ ψυχή μου ἐν αὐτῷ
ὁ δὲ δίκαιος ἐκ πίστεώς μου ζήσεται

The second conditional phrase must be understood in light of the immediate context. The protasis, ἐὰν ὑποστείληται, speaks of the one who shrinks back or withdraws (ὑποστείληται). This person is the referent of the αὐτῷ in the apodosis, οὐκ εὐδοκεῖ ἡ ψυχή μου ἐν αὐτῷ, the one with whom God is displeased. There are two possible alternatives with regard to the identity of this person. First, the αὐτῷ could be the same person identified as the referent in the protasis of the first conditional sentence, the one who ὑστερήσῃ, for whom the prophet must wait, i.e., God, as argued above. While grammatically this solution is perfectly possible, the logic of the text goes against identifying the one who ὑποστείληται in 2:3 with the one who ὑστερήσῃ in 2:4. The two cannot logically be the same since the one who ὑστερήσῃ, as argued before, is the κύριος himself, the one who is certainly coming and will not delay. It is inconceivable to imply that the one who ὑποστείληται is ὁ κύριος.[65] This logical impediment demands that the identity of the one who ὑποστείληται be found in the subsequent and not preceding line. In other words, a reader would have had to figure out the identity of the referent in the phrase ἐὰν ὑποστείληται κτλ somewhere else and not in the previous conditional statement.

The following line that supplies the essence of the oracle, ὁ δὲ δίκαιος ἐκ πίστεώς μου ζήσεται, is a suitable passage that can inform the reading of the antecedent text, ἐὰν ὑποστείληται οὐκ εὐδοκεῖ ἡ ψυχή μου ἐν αὐτῷ. The two lines ἐὰν ὑποστείληται κτλ and ὁ δὲ δίκαιος κτλ are set in antithetic parallelism, implying that the one who ὑποστείληται is the opposite of ὁ δίκαιος. For the logical coherence of the text the one who ὑποστείληται must be different from the one who ὑστερήσῃ. The one who withdraws (ὑποστείληται) stands in contrast to ὁ δίκαιος, and generically can be identified as an ἀσεβής, if one is to employ the contrasting pair δίκαιος - ἀσεβής used elsewhere in Habakkuk (cf. 1:4, 13).

The two incongruent pronouns, the 1st sg. replacing the 3rd sg., contribute an emphasis on God's role, which is different from the Hebrew text. First, God condemns the one who ὑποστείληται and, by implication,

---

"S'il est en retard, attends-le, car en venant il sera là, et assurément ne tardera pas" (Harl, *Les Douze Prophètes* 272).

The idea of "certainty" in Cleaver-Bartholomew and Harl is conveyed by the phrase οὐ μὴ χρονίσῃ, the two negative adverbs in construction with the aorist subjunctive, and not by the Greek idiom ἐρχόμενος ἥξει.

[65] Manson, "Argument" 130 f.

extends his acceptance to those who do not. His delight is satisfied by the righteous and annulled by the apostate. Second, God makes his covenant faithfulness the only guarantee that the righteous will be sustained. This emphasis on God's activity and involvement in the life of his people concords with the overall tendency of the Greek text to highlight this aspect more frequently than the MT.[66]

The understanding of the Hab. 2:2-4 LXX presented above is the result of reading the text in light of the whole of the LXX Hab. and letting the overall message of the book inform this central paragraph. As often happens with translations that are painstakingly literal, the target text, while having a high degree of conformity to the original, runs the risk of developing internal inconsistencies. These are inevitable when conformity to the source text disregards semantic consequences for the target text. The LXX Hab. has several of these inconsistencies which can be solved either by giving priority to the logic of the text, thus creating grammatical inconsistencies in the process, or alternatively, giving priority to the grammatical features, to the detriment of the text's logic. There is no conceivable reading of Hab. 2:2-4 LXX that can avoid these problems. For a reader of the LXX Hab. unable to consult the Hebrew text, the inconsistencies inherent in the text, either grammatical or logical, must be settled on their own, within the textual parameters of the narrow and extended contexts. The reading proposed by the present study seeks to adopt a middle ground that ensures both grammatical and logical coherence, sacrificing to some extent the smooth flow of the text. This reading, however, could indeed be congruent with the way in which the LXX Hab. was read by the Author, an author who followed the indications from both the immediate and extended contexts in order to elucidate the message of the prophetic oracle.

The eschatological and messianic overtones have been repeatedly emphasised in biblical scholarship.[67] The text is unambiguously set within an eschatological framework established by the use of particular translation equivalencies, εἰς καιρόν, εἰς πέρας, οὐκ εἰς κενόν (2:3). Alongside predominant future verbs, as well as several imported additions of eschatological themes in ch. 3, the terminology of Hab. 2:1-4 enhances the eschatological orientation of the LXX Hab. A similar conclusion can be drawn about the messianic overtones of the passage, primarily the motif of the coming one, ἐρχόμενος ἥξει, whose arrival is not only heralded (2:2 ff.) but also imminently awaited (3:2 ff.), as well as the dialog between the

---

[66] See *supra* (3.1.2).

[67] Strobel's study is to this day the most comprehensive analysis of Hab. 2:3-4 and the traditions it generated, Strobel, *Untersuchungen*; see also Lee ("Understanding"), who, unfortunately, does not interact with Strobel's study.

two κύριοι in ch. 3. Ziegler's contention, "Die Hab-Stelle trägt in der LXX sicherlich messianishen Charackter",[68] has been repeatedly confirmed.[69] Just as important, the significant intertextual links between Habakkuk and other prophetic writings[70] confirm the strong eschatological and messianic orientation of Hab. 2, regardless of its textual tradition.[71]

It would be fair to conclude that these theological motifs, while not completely absent from the MT, are heightened in the LXX. Was this the result of a deliberate messianic, eschatologically-minded translator? To answer this question with certainty is rather difficult. Several commentators subscribe to the evaluation of Manson, who claims that "the LXX interpretation of Hab. ii. 3b-4 is through and through Messianic".[72] The suggestion put forward in the present study is that, as far as the LXX Hab. 2:1-4 is concerned, it can be safely stated that the messianic nuances are inherent in the Greek text without having to assume that they are the result of the translator's deliberate intention.[73] Rather, the text as it stands was the outcome of a translation work in which the "dragoman" type of translator, to use Rabin's phrase,[74] while reasonably accurate and literal, has probably overlooked the significant changes that can creep into the text when little or no attention is given to the dynamic equivalent of the translation. With or without the translator's intention, the LXX Hab. is latently charged with messianic and eschatological overtones that have been noticed and developed further by the NT authors, especially the Author to the Hebrews.

4. The Use of Hab. 2:3-4 in Heb. 10:37-38

The form and content of the Hab. 2:3-4 LXX stand behind the use of this text in three major writings in the New Testament, with the most

---

[68] Joseph Ziegler, *Untersuchungen zur Septuaginta des Buches Isaias*, vol. 12 / 3, *Alttestamentliche Abhandlungen* (Münster: Verlag der Aschendorffschen Verlagsbuchhandlung, 1934) 112.

[69] Horbury, *Messianism*; Manson, "Argument", Strobel, *Untersuchungen*.

[70] *Inter alia*, Dan. 9, Is. 13, Is. 51, and Num. 24:7 LXX.

[71] Horbury, *Messianism*; Strobel, *Untersuchungen*.

[72] Manson, "Argument" 134.

[73] Hays reaches a similar conclusion; he contends, "whether the LXX translators intended it or not, they produced a translation which is readily susceptible to messianic interpretation"; Richard B. Hays, *The Faith of Jesus Christ. An Investigation of the Narrative Substructure of Galatians 3:1-4:11* (SBL-DS 56 Chico, CA: Scholars Press, 1983) 152.

[74] Rabin, "Process" 24.

extensive treatment in the Epistle to the Hebrews.[75] The Author's consistency in the use of the OT provides a natural test case for determining whether or not his use of Hab. 2:3-4 LXX resembles the proposals set out above. The majority of the epistle's quotations conform to known Greek manuscripts, and most of the other modifications in the quoted text can be explained either as evidence of a text tradition that has not survived or merely as stylistic changes that do not alter the meaning of the text. As mentioned earlier, the quotation from Hab. 2:3-4 in Heb. 10:37-38 stands out from the other quotations because of the substantial modifications it has undergone at the hands of the Author. The line of inquiry adopted here seeks to determine if any of the modifications in the quoted text of LXX Hab. can be explained as an outcome of the Author's reading the Greek text of Hab. 2:2-4 as a text in its own right, whose meaning was determined by its larger literary and theological contexts of LXX Habakkuk. The underlying questions that this section seeks to answer relate both to the causes that determined the Author to alter this particular quotation, as well as to his purpose in doing so. If positive evidence can be gathered to substantiate the argument that the LXX text had a determinant contribution to both the necessity of modification and to the particular way in which it was modified, the case for a distinct theological impact of LXX Hab. on the epistle will be strengthened.

For a better display of these changes the two texts are set in parallel columns. The quotation from Isaiah 26:20, which precedes the Habakkuk quotation, is not considered at this juncture.

Hab. 2:3-4 LXX	Heb. 10: 37-38 NTG
διότι ἔτι ὅρασις εἰς καιρὸν καὶ ἀνατελεῖ εἰς πέρας καὶ οὐκ εἰς κενόν ἐὰν ὑστερήσῃ ὑπόμεινον αὐτόν ὅτι ἐρχόμενος ἥξει καὶ οὐ μὴ χρονίσῃ	ἔτι γὰρ μικρὸν ὅσον ὅσον ὁ ἐρχόμενος ἥξει καὶ οὐ χρονίσει ὁ δὲ δίκαιός μου ἐκ πίστεως ζήσεται
ἐὰν ὑποστείληται οὐκ εὐδοκεῖ ἡ ψυχή μου ἐν αὐτῷ ὁ δὲ δίκαιος ἐκ πίστεώς μου ζήσεται	καὶ ἐὰν ὑποστείληται οὐκ εὐδοκεῖ ἡ ψυχή μου ἐν αὐτῷ

---

[75] Sanders, "Habakkuk" 98 ff.

The text of the Greek Hab. 2:3-4 underwent three types of modifications in its use in Hebrews. First, the text develops a new overall structure as different parts of the text shift position. This is the case of the transfer of the possessive pronoun μου from qualifying πίστεως to qualifying δίκαιος, and the repositioning of the clause ὁ δὲ δίκαιός μου ἐκ πίστεως ζήσεται to precede ἐὰν ὑποστείληται κτλ. Since δίκαιός μου is most probably the original reading in Heb. 10:37, and because there is no textual evidence in either the Hebrew or Greek manuscripts for this particular rearrangement of the clauses it is quite certain that both modifications have originated with the Author.[76]

A second category of changes consists of additions to or deletions from the quoted text. The addition of the conjunction καί is required by the rearrangement of the text. It may or may not be considered part of the quoted text, since this conjunction is normally employed by the Author in linking separate texts in previous *catenae* (cf. 1:10, 10:17). The insertion of the masculine nominative article ὁ before the participle ἐρχόμενος is a more significant example of this type of modification.

The third type of changes is the modification in the morphology of certain words, such as the future indicative replacing the aorist subjunctive of Hab. 2:4 LXX. This change in turn requires the dropping of the second negative adverb from the Hab. 2:3 text. All these textual modifications probably originated in the pen of the Author.

Whatever the literary nature of these modifications might be, it should be underlined that behind them lies a theological intention which led to the alteration of the quotation text. The modifications of Hab. 2:3-4 LXX have important theological consequences for the message of the epistle, especially its Christology and eschatology. The following remarks only note the more important observations among the myriad made by many on this topic.[77]   First, the article appended to ἐρχόμενος transforms the messianic potential of the Habakkuk text into a clear messianic reference to the climactic eschatological event of Christ's *Parousia*. Second, the change of the pronoun's position shifts the emphasis from God's

---

[76] Ellingworth, "Old Testament"; Manson, "Argument"; McCullough, "Hebrews"; Schröger, *Verfasser*; Thomas, "Septuagint".

[77] Besides the commentaries on the epistle, some of the more important studies on this topic include Ellingworth, "Old Testament"; Fitzmyer, "Habakkuk"; Erich Grässer, "Das Schriftargument in Hebr 10,37f", in *Ekklesiologie des Neuen Testaments. Für Karl Kertelge*, eds. R. Kampling and T. Söding (Freiburg / Basel / Wien: Herder, 1996) 431-39; Koch, "Text"; Manson, "Argument"; McCullough, "Quotations"; Rose, *Wolke*; Schröger, *Verfasser*; W. Th. In der Smitten, "Habakuk 2,4 als prophetische Definition des Gerechten", in *Bausteine biblisher Theologie. Festgabe für G. Johannes Botterweck zum 60. Geburtstag*, ed. H. -J. Fabry (Bohn: Peter Hanstein Verlag, 1977) 289-300; Thomas, "Septuagint".

faithfulness to the faith of the Christian believer, faith which now stands as the believer's sole responsibility in light of the status acquired as God's righteous one. The inversion of the sentences resolves the ambiguity of the Greek text of Hab. 2:3-4 a solution that not only maintains the contrast between ὁ δίκαιος and the one who ὑποστείληται, but also prevents any reading that would understand ὁ ἐρχόμενος to be the subject of ἐὰν ὑποστείληται.

The changes made by the Author to the Hab. 2:3-4 LXX text concur with the reading of the Greek texts advocated earlier in this chapter. The text of Hab. 2:1-4 LXX, as a tradition of interpretation in its own right, significantly different from the tradition preserved in the Masoretic text, is a text marred by several syntactical and logical inconsistencies. Any subsequent use of the text would have had to address or solve these inner difficulties in order to convey a coherent message, something that the Author himself did.

This study contends that there are several legitimate ways of reading Hab. 2:3-4 LXX in a coherent manner, alternatives that were quite probably pondered by the Author as well. Two of these possible readings are notable. First, one could opt for a reading which essentially understands the referent of the key kernels in the passage, ἀνατελεῖ, ἐὰν ὑστερήσῃ, αὐτόν, ἐρχόμενος, χρονίσῃ, ἐὰν ὑποστείληται, and αὐτῷ, to be consistent throughout. While this reading is characterised by an overall consistency and close similarity to the Hebrew text tradition, upon closer scrutiny it fails to recommend itself as a legitimate reading of the text, mainly because the Greek text displays a significant degree of semantic and logical incongruence, which impedes drawing a coherent sense from the text. One can only say that this reading probably was the sense of the target text intended by the translators, as they sought to reproduce faithfully the Hebrew *Vorlage*. Nonetheless, several reasons, some having to do with the translation technique of the translator, and some with the content of the source manuscript in use, and even with the particular theological outlook, led to the resulting text that resembles the source text in broad strokes, but varies significantly in its details. It might not be too far-fetched to suggest that this reading supplies a meaning for the Hab. 2:3-4 LXX which would not be perceived by a reader of the Greek text unable to consult the Hebrew text.

A second line of interpretation of the Greek text abandons the interest in maintaining consistency of the referents for the pronouns and verbs. Several variations of this interpretation are noteworthy. First of all, there are those who preserve the consistency within 2:2-3, with regard to vision. With the conditional sentence in 2:4a, ἐὰν ὑποστείληται κτλ, the grammatical subject changes from "vision" to a masculine entity, the "coming one". Fitzmyer adopts this position when he translates:

> [2:3] For (there is) still a vision for the set-time, and it will appear for the end, and not for naught; if it tarries, wait for it, because it will surely come and will not delay. [2:4] If one draws back, my soul has no delight in him, but the righteous one because of my fidelity shall find life.[78]

A slightly different approach within the same group keeps consistency with regard to "the vision" only for 2:2-3a, but from the first conditional statement, ἐὰν ὑστερήσῃ κτλ, introduces a masculine subject which dominates the rest of the passage. Noteworthy, the masculine subject of both conditional statements is the same, both grammatically and referentially. Lee adopts this meaning:

> [2:3] For the vision is yet for the point of time, and hastens to the end and not in vain; if he tarries, wait for him, because he will come, he will not delay. [2:4] If he may shrink back, my soul shall not please in him. But the righteous shall live by my faithfulness.[79]

This is also the option taken by Cleaver-Bartholomew, with the significant difference that the referents of the two conditional statements, while grammatically identical, i.e., masculine singular, are clearly different.

> [2:2] And the Lord answered me and said, "Write a vision indeed clearly on a stone in order that the one reading them may pursue it. [2:3] For yet an appearance is on time and he will rise up in the end and not in vain. If he might be delayed, wait for him because the one who is coming will come and he will certainly not be delayed. [2:4] If one might draw back, my soul will not be pleased with him, but the righteous will live by my faith.[80]

The reading proposed by this study is similar to the latter in that it provides a logically and grammatically consistent referent throughout the text, "the vision" limited to 2:2, and a masculine entity as the subject for the two conditional statements, but with different referents. In this reading, the identity of the "anonymous 'he'"[81], while determined in part through grammatical means by tracing the antecedents within the text, is predominantly clarified on considerations of the text's inner logic and theology. As argued previously, the identity of the grammatical subjects in the conditional sentences are determined both by the logic of the text itself, as well as by the broader literary and theological contexts of LXX

---

[78] Fitzmyer, "Habakkuk" 450.
[79] Lee, "Understanding" 89.
[80] Cleaver-Bartholomew, "Analysis" 165.
[81] Manson, "Argument" 133.

Habakkuk. This solution does not solve all the problems of Hab. 2:2-4 LXX, but does offer a plausible explanation for the changes in the text introduced by the Author.[82] First of all, the addition of the article before the participle ὁ ἐρχόμενος is justified on grounds of the LXX's referent for ἐρχόμενος, who according to the LXX Hab., is the Lord, ὁ κύριος (3:8), or God, ὁ θεός (3:2). The purpose for his coming according to LXX Hab. is the salvation of his elect, τοῦ σῶσαι τοὺς χριστούς σου (3:13), a phrase that indicates a possible reason behind the epistle's change from ὁ δὲ δίκαιος to ὁ δὲ δίκαιός μου. In anticipation of the coming of the one who is announced as ὁ ἐρχόμενος and the possibility of his delay, the righteous one in Hebrews must avoid becoming like the ὁ ἀσεβής in Habakkuk, the one who is in danger of drawing back, ἐὰν ὑποστείληται; a perspective which justifies the reshaping of the Habakkuk text by the Author. On the contrary, the righteous one in Hebrews is to imitate the example of the faith and trust of the righteous one in Habakkuk, the one who will find life, typified for the reader of LXX Habakkuk by the prophet (3:17 f.).

One comment about the identity of ὁ δίκαιος, "the righteous one", in Hebrews is in order. There has been a notable tradition of interpretation, especially in Pauline studies, which identifies ὁ δίκαιος with ὁ ἐρχόμενος, thus arguing for a thoroughly messianic reading of Hab. 2:4. According to this interpretation Paul applied the Habakkuk oracle ὁ δίκαιος ἐκ πίστεως ζήσεται to the Messiah himself.[83] While this line of thought might fit within Pauline theology, at least as far as the modified Hab. 2:4 LXX quotation seems to indicate, it was probably never considered by the Author of Hebrews, primarily because of his dependence on the Septuagint text of the oracle. As was argued throughout this chapter, the inconsistencies of the Hab. 2:2-4 LXX, as well as its inner logic, require that the referents of the two participles, ὁ ἐρχόμενος and ὁ δίκαιος, belong to separate groups. That the Author himself wrestled with the meaning of the oracle is very probable; indeed, the alteration of the text stands as an almost certain proof of this fact. Moreover, the specific alteration of the oracle, by which he associates the first participle ὁ ἐρχόμενος with the eschatological coming of the Son, and the second participle ὁ δίκαιος with

---

[82] In the opinion of this writer the most difficult change to explain is the repositioning of the possessive 1st sing. pronoun from its position in LXX, determining "faith", ἐκ πίστεώς μου, to its new location in Hebrews, ὁ δὲ δίκαιός μου, determining the "righteous". As mentioned earlier, Jerome's attempt to read it even in its new relative position as determining "faith", to conform to the LXX textual version, has not found wide support.

[83] This interpretation found an able advocate in A.T. Hanson, primarily in his studies *Paul's Understanding of Jesus* (Hull: University of Hull, 1963) and *Studies in Paul's Technique and Theology* (London: SPCK, 1974). It has been further articulated and defended by Hays, *Faith* 151 ff.

the faithful (as opposed to the apostate), is a further indication that he has never considered identifying ὁ δίκαιος with the Messiah.

These changes are just as indicative of the sense with which the Author read and understood the LXX Hab., as of his method of applying the text to the new situation. They are not only a legitimate rearrangement of the text intended to untangle the meaning of Hab. 2:2-4 LXX, they are also congruent with and supported by the overall message of the LXX Hab.

5. Conclusion

The two traditions analysed in this study, the Septuagint text of Habakkuk and its use in the Epistle to the Hebrews, highlight the distinct way in which the Greek Old Testament influenced the formation of the Author's argument. Hebrews 10:37-38 is a text that explores the meaning of an important prophetic oracle. It is a text with a distinct form and message which can be traced to the Greek textual tradition, and which is unlikely to have had this particular shape and content if the Author had not depended upon Hab. 2:3-4 LXX. The changes that the Hebrew text underwent through translation created an important OT passage with the potential of expressing a crucial messianic idea within an eschatological framework. This potential was developed by the theological acumen of a Christian theologian in the first century. His conclusions are not just the result of reading the Scriptures in the light of God's final, eschatological word of revelation in his Son. They are also the result of reading and reflecting on a particular scriptural tradition, the Greek Scriptures that informed and shaped his message.

Chapter Ten

Summary and Conclusions. Further Investigation

1. Summary and Conclusions

The main objective of this study has been to explore the various ways in which the use of the Septuagint by the Author to the Hebrews has left distinctive marks on the epistle. The study of several verses from the epistle in Part One and the more extensive exploration of one particularly suitable quotation in Part Two, have established that numerous results of the Author's engagement with the OT can be traced to his use of the Septuagint. While this conclusion is in keeping with current scholarly research, the cases surveyed in this thesis were specifically chosen in order to go a step further and explore and assess the possibility of an influence of a more specific nature, a distinct and exclusive Septuagintal influence. This study has maintained that because the Author depended solely on the Septuagint, and since the Septuagint differs in several respects from the Hebrew Scriptures, it is therefore not unreasonable to expect that this distinct and exclusive Septuagintal influence may be located and assessed by means of critical analysis. The investigation targeted and explored primarily those OT texts that present either textual or contextual divergences between the Septuagint and the Hebrew Scriptures, and these in turn were analysed in order to determine their influence on the ideas and the argument of the epistle.

Each chapter focused on one particular aspect: the text and the context of OT quotations, the OT allusions in the epistle, the Septuagintal lexical stock used by the Author, and two theological themes important to the argument of the epistle. The cases investigated have provided evidence that theological nuances of the Septuagint, either absent or less visible in the corresponding Hebrew text, have not only made their way into the epistle but have also influenced the argument of the epistle. These five different, though interrelated, areas in which the Author depended on the Septuagint have left a definite mark on the argument of the epistle. As regards the text and context of the quotations, it was concluded that the Septuagint couldn't be regarded merely as a neutral supplier of the actual wording of the quotations. Important divergences between the Septuagint text and known Hebrew textual traditions reverberate throughout the argument of the epistle. When the particular nuances of the Septuagintal text, as distinct from those of the Hebrew text, are exploited by the Author in the exposition of the quotation, Septuagintal influence must be acknowledged as an important and distinct part of the complex system of factors that contributed to the shaping of the Author's thought as reflected in the epistle.

A similar conclusion is drawn from the Author's use of OT allusions. Although the majority of the epistle's allusions are drawn from texts in which the Hebrew text and its Greek translation are semantically equivalent, some allusions are traceable to biblical texts with notable divergences between the two textual traditions. The Author's dependence on the Greek translation in these cases supports, albeit less unequivocally than in the case of the quotations, the argument for a distinct Septuagintal influence on the epistle.

Likewise, the dependence of the epistle on the lexical riches of the Septuagint, extensive as it is, goes beyond the mere employment of the lexical units. The Septuagintal influence is most distinct in those cases in which the Septuagintal meaning differs from the meaning of the Hebrew word. The Author displays a tendency to explore the Septuagintal meaning of a word and he often imports into the epistle not only the word, but also its distinctive Septuagintal connotation. This too can be considered a case of direct and distinct influence of the Septuagint on the epistle. Finally, two theological themes that are arguably more defined in the Septuagint than in the Hebrew textual traditions have marked the theological contours the epistle's development of those themes.

These conclusions are further confirmed by the more detailed investigation of the test case comprising of the quotation from Hab. 2:3-4 LXX, which is characterised by the most extensive editorial reshaping of any of the quotations in the epistle. While the text of the quotation itself differs from both the Greek and the Hebrew textual traditions, the Septuagintal influence on the way in which Hab. 2:3-4 is used in the epistle is detectable in several places. With regards to the text of the quotation, the essential kernels of the Greek text of Hab. 2:3-4 are preserved in the Heb. 10:37-38 text. The Septuagintal contexts of all the quotations employed in Heb. 10:19-12:29, the immediate literary context of Heb. 10:37-38, display an extensive thematic and verbal overlap. This can reasonably be held responsible, at least in part, for the selection and grouping of the quotations in the final paraenetic section of the epistle. Lastly, it was argued that the very changes introduced by the Author in the quotation's text from Hab. 2:3-4 LXX are not only congruent with the overall theological message of the LXX Hab., but they are also demanded by the particular form and content of the prophetic oracle in its

Septuagintal textual tradition. All these three aspects, the text, context, and theology of the LXX Hab., are directly responsible for the form and content of the Author's use of Hab. 2:3-4.

The Septuagintal influence on all these aspects varies extensively, not only in their degree of impact on the epistle's text and argument, but also in the degree of certitude with which that impact can be documented. Cumulative evidence indicates that all the major ways in which the Author used the OT show the distinct marks of Septuagintal usage. The Author's reliance on the Greek Jewish Scriptures has produced an epistle whose argument at several junctures can be explained exclusively by the use of this particular textual tradition, the Septuagint. Recourse to a Hebrew text tradition would have most probably resulted in an epistle quite different from the one that we now possess.

2. Further Research - Between Necessity and Sufficiency

The following concluding remarks consider the implications of this study and suggest further venues of investigation. The research objectives for the present study were set within the limits of a qualitative investigation of the use of the Greek Scriptures in the Epistle to the Hebrews in order to assess its specific contribution to the content and theology of a first century Christian document, a test case for investigating the role that the Septuagint had for the developing theological thought and canonical writings of early Christianity. The Epistle to the Hebrews was selected from the NT corpus because it recommends itself as most appropriate choice for such an investigation. It is a document penned by a very able author and theologian of an Early Christian community, who used the Greek Scriptures for a multifaceted exploration of the person and work of Jesus, the Christ. Several comments are in order.

First, it must be emphatically upheld that a fair assessment of the role of the LXX in the epistle has to accommodate the instances in which no particular Septuagintal influence can be detected whatsoever. In each category detailed above, examples could be given of instances where no distinct Septuagintal influence was exerted. The vast majority of the quotation material in the epistle consists of scriptural texts in which the Septuagint is a precise reproduction of the Hebrew text. Moreover, the very fact that at times even the Septuagint text of the quotations suffers modifications that diverge from the core meaning of the Greek textual tradition should be taken into consideration in an overall assessment of the Author's dependence on the Septuagint. This is just as true in the case of the Author's lexical stock that frequently shows no particular dependence on the Septuagintal background of a word, phrase or concept.

Second, the concepts of necessity and sufficiency provide a convenient framework within which to assess the Author's dependency on the Septuagint. As mentioned repeatedly, the majority of the studies on the use of the OT in Hebrews highlight the role and importance of the Septuagint. This is most clearly seen in the area of quotations in which the Septuagint provides the actual text for the quotations. While this is true, it seems that most of these studies stop short of acknowledging the possibility of a distinct and unique Septuagintal influence on the epistle. Frequently a divergent reading from the Septuagint is evaluated merely as having been a textual tradition convenient for the Author, but its contribution is not deemed to be distinct and unique. This study suggests that such a conclusion is an insufficient reading of the evidence. Not only did the Septuagint assist the Author in his argument, but also there are several aspects of the epistle that can be explained only as a result of the Author's dependence on the Septuagint, which essentially amounts to an admission of an exclusive influence exerted by the Septuagint.

The boundaries of necessity and sufficiency, then, help to describe more accurately the relationship between the Septuagint and the use of the OT by the Author. The use of the Septuagint is the sufficient cause for the multifarious ways in which the Jewish Scriptures have marked the epistle. Stated differently, the Septuagint as the sufficient explanation maintains that the epistle's use of the OT in quotations, allusions, lexical stock and theology has its form and content *because* the Author based his epistle on the text of and as a result of interaction with the Septuagint. Most scholars acknowledge this point and it is seldom contested. In the language of modal logic the use of the OT in Hebrews is what it is *if* the Septuagint is assumed to be the Author's Scriptures.

At the other end of the spectrum, the issue of necessity elicits a more vigorous debate on whether or not the Septuagint can be considered as the necessary cause for the particular form and content of the Author's use of the OT. Must one conclude that the Septuagint is the only textual tradition that could have generated this particular treatment of the OT? In other words, can it be argued that the epistle's use of the OT has its form and content *exclusively because* the Author's Scriptures were the Septuagint? Is the use of the OT in Hebrews what it is *only if* the use of the Septuagint is assumed? These two extreme positions express in different categories the essence of the questions with which this study commenced; whether or not the Author could have forged the same theological argument had he used a Hebrew text instead of a Greek text.

The evidence for the Septuagint as necessity for the Epistle of Hebrews to be what it is has been outlined in the pages of this work. Since this estimate is primarily qualitative and not quantitative the selective approach pursued here has served well the intended purpose. The text of several quotations, as well as the context, particular allusions, elements of the lexical stock and theological nuances of the Septuagint, can all be considered evidence that at least in several of the cases analysed, the Author's dependence on the Septuagint generated certain points in the epistle whose arguments can be supported only by the Septuagint. Since the Greek text differs from its corresponding Hebrew text in these cases, it can be legitimately concluded that the Septuagint is the necessary component that accounts for the argument of the Author. It is only through the lens of the Septuagint, as the textual tradition on which the Author relied, that much of the epistle could be explained.

Yet, with all this evidence in place, a possible case against considering the Septuagint as a necessary cause behind the text and theology of Hebrews can be built upon the following considerations. First, it is methodologically impossible to prove whether or not the Author could have forged the same argument while working from a Hebrew text. It would be difficult to devise a methodology that could analyse the virtual world of an author's engagement with a text other than the one used. Essentially, the conclusion resulting from such an analysis would run the risk of being highly subjective and speculative.

Second, it is important to acknowledge that the complex history of textual transmission recommends against categorical conclusions. The Masoretic text is considered to be the most reliable Hebrew textual tradition for the tracing of the original biblical texts, yet the evidence from the Judean Desert, while confirming the solidity of the text on which the Masoretic tradition developed, also points to the existence of other slightly divergent Hebrew textual traditions contemporary to the Author. Thus, when considering the question of how a Hebrew text would have influenced the argument of the epistle, one must leave open the possibility that the Author might have used other Hebrew text forms, which would have been less divergent from the Septuagint textual tradition on which the Author based his argument. Based on current textual evidence for both the Hebrew and the Greek texts, one cannot rule out *a priori* the possibility of the existence of a Hebrew text that would be the identical correspondent of the Septuagintal readings, which this study has labelled as distinct or divergent.

Third, the exegetical and hermeneutical procedures of the Author could serve also as a strong caution for granting the Septuagint the status of textual tradition without which the Epistle would have necessarily been different. Much like his contemporaries, the Author displays a remarkable level of creativity, ingenuity and theological boldness. To restrict the boundaries of what a creative writer such as the Author would have been able to argue by expounding from a Hebrew text would be too presumptuous.

The three aspects outlined above seem to be, in the opinion of this writer, a significant argument against accepting too hastily the role of the Septuagint as the necessary condition for the Epistle to the Hebrews, and by extension, to the New Testament. In order to put forward a convincing argument in this respect a qualitative investigation is insufficient; for a definitive answer one needs to undertake a much more comprehensive approach, which would supply a quantitative assessment of that influence as well. Such a thorough examination would have to go beyond the boundaries of the present study in at least two directions. First, it would need to explore further the texts analysed here within the entire spectrum of interpretative traditions in Second Temple Judaism and early Christianity. If one can delineate through such a broad investigation a tradition of interpretation that is anchored uniquely in the Septuagint, i.e., the Greek textual traditions, and yet does not appear in any other interpretative traditions based on the Hebrew text, the Septuagint would indeed have to be reckoned as a distinct, determinant and unique factor that shaped the thought of the Author. Second, the same type of investigation has to be stretched to include not only representative cases, but also the entire epistle. Only an exhaustive investigation of this magnitude, tracing the divergences reflected in the entire epistle between traditions of interpretation generated by the Hebrew and Greek texts, could offer the proper basis on which a final evaluation could be made. Such a trajectory would be the natural development of this study. The limited investigation adopted here situates its author between the positions of sufficiency and necessity. Yes, the Epistle to the Hebrews is what it is *because* the Author used the Septuagint. It would be extremely difficult to confidently conclude that the Author's use of the OT is what it is *exclusively because* the Author used the Septuagint. What this study hopes to have achieved is a presentation in greater detail of the implications of the author's use of and reliance upon the Septuagint for the epistle. The distinct influence of the Septuagint is distinguishable in all the major ways in which the Author made use of the OT.

This consideration leads to a final aspect that ought to be stressed with regard to the role of the Septuagint in shaping the argument of the epistle, especially since it is an aspect that has received only secondary emphasis in scholarship. Scholars often point to the dynamics operative in the shaping of early Christian theology. Lindars and Marshall discuss the dual status of the Scriptures that paradoxically fulfil both the role of servant and master in the formation process of NT theology.[1] One of these roles is also referred to by Ellingworth who has coined the concept of "anacritical reader" as a description of the process of the creative reading of the OT, which was stimulated by the Christ-event.[2] According to him, it seems realistic to envisage the Author engaged in an intense and purposeful searching of the Scriptures, much as the Christians in Beroea from whose experience the term is derived, as he sought to gather and verify scriptural support for the Christian kerygma.[3]

Although the concept of "anacritical reader" offers a valuable contribution to the discussion of the use of the OT in the NT, this study proposes to complement that understanding with the term "epideictic writing" for the Scriptures, and in the Author's case, for the Septuagint. The term derives from the verb ἐπιδείκνυμι, "to show to be true" (*GEL*), which aptly describes the role of the Scriptures in proving that Jesus was the Christ (Acts 18:28).[4] The Scriptures were not only read in light of the Christ-event, but the Christ-event was read in light of the Scriptures.[5] Although the Scriptures were clearly interpreted through the lens of the Chris-event, they also supplied the informative and theologically formative perspective from which the Christ-event had to be interpreted. While this holds true for all NT authors and for their Scriptures, regardless of the form involved, in the Author's case, it was the Greek version of the Scriptures that provided this framework. Those particular nuances that belong to the Septuagint, as opposed to the Hebrew Scriptures, have influenced and shaped the *theolegomena* of the Author. The Septuagint supplied not only an authoritative confirmation of the new message, but also a suitable framework in which the new message could be delivered, thus admirably fulfilling its role as Scripture for the Author to the Hebrews.

---

[1] Lindars, *Apologetic* 59 ff. and Marshall, "Assessment" 18 f.

[2] Ellingworth, "Old Testament" 5.

[3] Acts 17:11, οἵτινες ἐδέξαντο τὸν λόγον μετὰ πάσης προθυμίας καθ᾽ ἡμέραν ἀνακρίνοντες τὰς γραφὰς εἰ ἔχοι ταῦτα οὕτως.

[4] Acts 18:28, εὐτόνως γὰρ τοῖς Ἰουδαίοις διακατηλέγχετο δημοσίᾳ ἐπιδεικνὺς διὰ τῶν γραφῶν εἶναι τὸν χριστὸν Ἰησοῦν. The term "epideictic" is not being used here with its technical meaning proposed by Aune, who characterized in rhetoric categories the Epistle to the Hebrews as "epideictic"; David E. Aune, *The New Testament in Its Literary Environment* (Philadelphia: Westminster Press, 1987) 212.

[5] Clements, "Use" 36. See also the concept of theocentric hermeneutic advocated by Sanders, whereby Luke uses the Scriptures in order to understand Jesus, the early church, and its role; Craig A. Evans and James A. Sanders, "Gospel and Midrash: An Introduction to Luke and Scripture", in *Luke and Scripture,* eds. Craig A. Evans and James A. Sanders (Minneapolis: Fortress Press, 1993) 1-13.

Bibliography

Reference Works and Sources

Aland, K., M. Black, C. M. Martini, B. M. Metzger, and A. Wikgren, eds. *Novum Testamentum Graece*. Stuttgart: Deutsche Bibelgesellschaft, 27th ed., 1993.

Aland, K., M. Black, C. M. Martini, B. M. Metzger, and A. Wikgren, eds. *The Greek New Testament*. New York: United Bible Societies, 3rd rev. ed., 1975.

Archer, Gleason L., and G. C. Chirichigno, eds. *Old Testament Quotations in the New Testament: A Complete Survey*. Chicago: Moody Press, 1983.

Bachmann, H., and W. A. Slaby, eds. *Computer Concordance to the Novum Testamentum Graece of Nestle-Aland, 26th edition, and to the Greek New Testament, 3rd Edition*. Berlin / New York: Walter de Gruyter, 2nd ed., 1985.

Balz, Horst, and Gerhard Schneider, eds. *Exegetical Dictionary of the New Testament*. 3 vols. Edinburgh: T. & T. Clark, 1990-1993.

Barthélemy, Dominique. *Critique textuelle de l'Ancien Testament*. 3 vols. Orbis biblicus et orientalis 50.3. Fribourg / Göttingen: Editions Universitaires Fribourg Suisse / Vandenhoeck & Ruprecht, 1992.

Bauer, Walter. *A Greek – English Lexicon of the New Testament and Other Early Christian Literature*. Translated and revised by W. F. Arndt, F. W. Gingrich and F. W. Danker. Chicago: University of Chicago Press, 1979.

Benoit, P., J. T. Milik, and R. De VauxTov, eds. *Les Grottes de Murabbaʿât*. Discoveries in the Judaean Desert II. Oxford: Clarendon Press, 1960.

Biblia Sacra iuxta latinam Vulgatam versionem. Liber Duodecim Prophetarum. Rome: Libreria Editrice Vaticana, 1987.

Blass, F., and A. Debrunner. *A Greek Grammar of the New Testament and Other Early Christian Literature*. Translated and revised by R. W. Funk. Chicago: University of Chicago, 1960.

Botterweck, G. J., and H. Ringgren, eds. *Theological Dictionary of the Old Testament*. Translated by J. T. Willis. Vol. 1-. Grand Rapids: Eerdmans, 1974-.

Bratcher, Robert G., and William D. Reyburn. *A Handbook on Psalms*. Helps for Translators. New York: UBS, 1991.

Braude, William G. *The Midrash on Psalms*. 2 vols. Yale Iudaica 13. New Haven: Yale University Press, 1959.

Brock, S. P., C. T. Fritsch, and S. Jellicoe, eds. *A Classified Bibliography of the Septuagint*. Arbeiten zur Literatur und Geschichte des hellenistischen Judentums 6. Leiden: E. J. Brill, 1973.

Brooke, A.E., N. McLean, and Henry St. J. Thackeray, eds. *The Old Testament in Greek*. Cambridge: Cambridge University Press, 1906-1940.

Brown, F., S. R. Driver, and C. A. Briggs. *The New Brown – Driver – Briggs – Gesenius Hebrew and English Lexicon*. Peabody: Hendrickson, 1979.

Burrows, Millar. *The Dead Sea Scrolls of St. Mark's Monastery. The Isaiah Manuscript and the Habakkuk Commentary*. 2 vols. New Haven: American Schools of Oriental Research, 1950.

Cathcart, Kevin J., and Robert P. Gordon. *The Targum of the Minor Prophets.* The Aramaic Bible 14. Edinburgh: T. & T. Clark, 1989.

Charlesworth, James H., ed. *The Old Testament Pseudepigrapha.* 2 vols. New York / London: Doubleday, 1983, 1985.

Chilton, B. D. *The Isaiah Targum.* The Aramaic Bible 11. Edinburgh: T. & T. Clark, 1987.

Clines, David J. A., ed. *The Dictionary of Classical Hebrew.* Vols. 1-4; Sheffield: Sheffield Academic Press, 1993-.

Cremer, H. *Biblico – Theological Lexicon of New Testament Greek.* Edinburgh: T. & T. Clark, 3rd English ed., 1883.

Danby, H. *The Mishnah.* Oxford: Oxford University Press, 1933.

Dogniez, C., and M. Harl. *Le Deutéronome.* La Bible d'Alexandrie 5. Paris: Éditions du Cerf, 1992.

Dogniez, Cécile. *Bibliography of the Septuagint (1970-1993).* Supplements to Vetus Testamentum 60. Leiden: E. J. Brill, 1993.

Dorival, Gilles. *Les Nombres.* La Bible d'Alexandrie 4. Paris: Éditions du Cerf, 1995.

Elliger, K., and W. Rudolph, eds. *Biblia Hebraica Stuttgartensia.* Stuttgart: Deutsche Bibelgesellschaft, 1967-1977.

Evans, Craig A. *Life of Jesus Research. An Annotated Bibliography.* Leiden / New York / Köln: E. J. Brill, 1996.

Field, Fridericus. *Origenis Hexaplorum cum supersunt.* 2 vols. Oxford: Clarendon Press, 1875.

Grossfeld, B. *The Targum Onqelos to Leviticus and The Targum Onqelos to Numbers.* The Aramaic Bible 8. Edinburgh: T. & T. Clark, 1988.

Grossfeld, Bernard. *The Targum Onqelos to Genesis.* The Aramaic Bible 6. Edinburgh: T. & T. Clark, 1988.

Harl, M. *Les Douze Prophètes.* La Bible d'Alexandrie 8a. Paris: Éditions du Cerf, 1999.

———. *La Genèse.* La Bible d'Alexandrie 1. Paris: Éditions du Cerf, 1986.

Harlé, P., and D. Pralon. *Le Lévitique.* La Bible d'Alexandrie 3. Paris: Éditions du Cerf, 1988.

Holmes, R., and J. Parsons, eds. *Vetus Testamentum graecum cum variis lectionibus.* Oxford: Clarendon, 1798-1827.

Hübner, Hans. *Vetus Testamentum in Novo. Corpus Paulinus.* 3 vols. Vol. 2. Göttingen: Vandenhoeck & Ruprecht, 1997.

Josephus, Flavius. *The Jewish War.* Translated by H. St. J. Thackeray. 2 vols. Loeb Classical Library. London / Cambridge: William Heinemann / Harvard University Press, 1927-1928.

Josephus, Flavius. *Jewish Antiquities.* Translated by H. St. J. Thackeray (vol. 1); by H. St. J. Thackeray and Ralph Marcus (vol. 2); by Ralph Marcus (vols. 3-4); by Ralph Marcus and Allen Wikgren (vol. 5); by Louis Feldman (vols. 6-7). 7 vols. Loeb Classical Library. London / Cambridge: William Heinemann / Harvard University Press, 1930-1965.

Kautzsch, E., and A. E. Cowley, eds. *Gesenius' Hebrew Grammar.* Oxford: Clarendon, 2nd English ed., 1988.

Kennicott, B. *Vetus Testamentum hebraicum, cum variis lectionibus.* 2 vols. Oxford: Clarendon Press, 1776-1780.

Kittel, G., and G. Friedrich, eds. *Theological Dictionary of the New Testament.* 10 vols. Grand Rapids: Eerdmans, 1964-1976.

Kittel, R., and P. Kahle, eds. *Biblia Hebraica*. Stuttgart: Württembergische Bibelanstalt, 3rd, [5th] ed., 1949.

Jastrow, Marcus. *A Dictionary of the Targumim, the Talmud Babli and Yerushalmi, and the Midrashic Literature*. 2 vols. New York: Pardes Publishing House, 1950.

Koehler, Ludwig, and Walter Baumgartner. *The Hebrew and Aramaic Lexicon of the Old Testament*. Translated and edited under the supervision of M. E. J. Richardson. Revised by Walter Baumgartner and Johann Jakobb Stamm. 4 vols. Leiden / New York / Köln: E. J. Brill, 1994-1999.

Lamsa, George M. *Holy Bible from the Ancient Eastern Text. George M. Lansa's Translation from the Aramaic of the Peshitta*. San Francisco: Harper Collins, 1985.

Le Boulluec A., and P. Sandevoir. *L'Exode*. La Bible d'Alexandrie 2. Paris: Éditions du Cerf, 1989.

Louw, Johannes P., and Eugene A. Nida, eds. *Greek – English Lexicon of the New Testament. Based on Semantic Domains*. 2 vols. New York: United Bible Societies, 2nd ed., 1988, 1989.

Lust, J., E. Eynikel, and K. Hauspie. *A Greek – English Lexicon of the Septuagint*. Part 1: α-ι, Part 2: κ-ω. 2 vols. Stuttgart: Deutsche Bibelgesellschaft, 1992, 1996.

Maher, Michael. *Targum Pseudo-Jonathan: Genesis*. The Aramaic Bible 1b. Edinburgh: T. & T. Clark, 1992.

Martinez, Florentino Garcia. *The Dead Sea Scrolls Translated. The Qumran Texts in English*. Leiden: E. J. Brill, 1994.

McNamara, M., and E. G. Clarke. *The Targum Neofiti 1: Numbers; and Pseudo-Jonathan: Numbers*. The Aramaic Bible 4. Edinburgh: T. & T. Clark, 1995.

McNamara, Martin. *Targum Neofiti 1: Genesis*. The Aramaic Bible 1a. Edinburgh: T. & T. Clark, 1992.

Metzger, Bruce M. *Textual Commentary on the Greek New Testament*. London: United Bible Society, 1971.

Midrash Rabbah on Genesis and Exodus. Jerusalem.

Midrash Rabbah on Leviticus, Numbers, Deuteronomy, Ruth, Esther, Song of Songs, Ecclesiastes, Lamentations. Jerusalem.

Levertoff, Paul P. *Midrash Sifre on Numbers*. London / New York: Macmillan, 1926.

Moulton, J. H. *A Grammar of New Testament Greek*. 4 vols. *Prolegomena*. Vol. 1. Edinburgh: T. & T. Clark, 1908.

Muraoka, Takamitsu. *A Greek – English Lexicon of the Septuagint. Twelve Prophets*. Louvain: Peters, 1993.

Patrologia Latina Database. Chadwyck-Healey Inc, 1991.

Philo, Judaeus. Translated by F. H. Colson (vols. 6-10); with G. H. Whitacker (vols. 1-5). 10 vols. Loeb Classical Library. London / Cambridge: William Heinemann / Harvard University Press, 1929-1962.

Rahlfs, Alfred. *Septuaginta. Vetus Testamentum Graecum. Auctoritate Societatis Litterarum Gottingensis editum. Psalmi cum Odis*. Vol. X. Göttingen: Vandenhoeck & Ruprecht, 1931.

Rhalfs, Alfred. *Septuaginta*. Stuttgart: Deutsche Bibelstiftung, 1979.

Rossi, Johannis Bern De. *Variae Lectiones Veteris Testamenti*. 5 vols. Parmae: Ex Regio Typographeo, 1786.

von Soden, H. F. *Die Schriften des Neuen Testaments in ihrer ältesten erreichbaren Textgestalt hergestellt auf Grund ihrer Textgeschichte*. 4 vols. Göttingen: Vandenhoeck & Ruprecht, 1911, 1913.

Soncino Classics Collection. Institute for Computers in Jewish Life & Davka Corporation, 1991-1996.

Tanakh: A New Translation of the Holy Scriptures according to the Traditional Hebrew Text. Philadelphia: Jewish Publication Society, 1985

Thackeray, H. St. John. *A Grammar of the OT in Greek according to the Septuagint.* Cambridge: Cambridge University Press, 1909.

Thesaurus Linguae Graecae. v. 6.01 Chadwyck-Healey: Silver Mountain Software, 1997.

Tischendorf, Constantinus. *Novum Testamentum Graece.* 3 vols. Lipsiae: Giesecke & Devrient, 8th ed., 1869-1872.

The Tosefta. Translated by Jacob Neusner. New York: KTAV Publishing House, 1979.

Tov, Emanuel. *The Greek Minor Prophets Scroll from Naḥal Ḥever (8Ḥev XIIgr).* Discoveries in the Judaean Desert VIII. Oxford: Clarendon Press, 1990.

Tregelles, Samuel Prideaux. *The Greek New Testament.* 2 vols. London: Samuel Bagster & Sons, 1857-1879.

Turner, Nigel. *A Grammar of New Testament Greek.* 4 vols. *Style.* Vol. 4. Edinburgh: T. & T. Clark, 1976.

Ulrich, Eugen, F. M. Cross, S. W. Crawford, J. A. Duncan, P. W. Skehan, E. Tov, and J. Trebolle Barrera, eds. *Qumran Cave 4. Deuteronomy, Joshua, Judges, Kings.* Discoveries in the Judaean Desert XIV. Oxford: Clarendon Press, 1995.

Ulrich, Eugen, F. M. Cross, R. Fuller, J. Sanderson, P. W. Skehan, and E. Tov, eds. *Qumran Cave 4. The Prophets.* Discoveries in the Judaean Desert XV. Oxford: Clarendon Press, 1997.

VanGemeren, Willem A., ed. *The New International Dictionary of Old Testament Theology and Exegesis.* 5 vols. Carlisle: Paternoster Press, 1996.

Wachtel, Klaus and Klaus Witte, *Die Neue Testament auf Papyrus. Die Paulinischen Briefe.* Arbeiten zur neutestamentlichen Textforschung 22, ii.2. Berlin / New York: Walter de Gruyter, 1994.

Waltke, Bruce K., and Michael P. O' Connor. *An Introduction to Biblical Hebrew Syntax.* Winona Lake: Eisenbrauns, 1990.

Wevers, John William. *Septuaginta. Vetus Testamentum Graecum. Auctoritate Societatis Litterarum Gottingensis editum. Genesis.* Vol. I. Göttingen: Vandenhoeck & Ruprecht, 1974.

Wevers, John William. *Septuaginta. Vetus Testamentum Graecum. Auctoritate Societatis Litterarum Gottingensis editum. Deuteronomium.* Vol. III/2. Göttingen: Vandenhoeck & Ruprecht, 1977.

Wevers, John William. *Septuaginta. Vetus Testamentum Graecum. Auctoritate Societatis Litterarum Gottingensis editum. Numeri.* Vol. III/1. Göttingen: Vandenhoeck & Ruprecht, 1982.

Wevers, John William. *Septuaginta. Vetus Testamentum Graecum. Auctoritate Societatis Litterarum Gottingensis editum. Leviticus.* Vol. II/2. Göttingen: Vandenhoeck & Ruprecht, 1986.

Wevers, John William. *Septuaginta. Vetus Testamentum Graecum. Auctoritate Societatis Litterarum Gottingensis editum. Exodus.* Vol. II/1. Göttingen: Vandenhoeck & Ruprecht, 1991.

Ziegler, Joseph. *Septuaginta. Vetus Testamentum Graecum. Auctoritate Societatis Litterarum Gottingensis editum. Isaiah.* Vol. XIV. Göttingen: Vandenhoeck & Ruprecht, 1939.

Ziegler, Joseph. Septuaginta. Vetus Testamentum Graecum. Auctoritate Societatis Litterarum Gottingensis editum. Duodecim Prophetae. Vol. XIII. Göttingen: Vandenhoeck & Ruprecht, 1943.

Commentaries on Hebrews and on Habakkuk

Andersen, Francis I. *Habakkuk.* Anchor Bible. Garden City: Doubleday, 2001.

Attridge, Harold W. *The Epistle to the Hebrews.* Hermeneia. Philadelphia: Fortress Press, 1989.

Braun, Herbert. *An die Hebräer.* Handbuch zum Neuen Testament 14. Tübingen: J. C. B. Mohr (Paul Siebeck), 1984.

Bruce, Frederick Fyvie. *Commentary on the Epistle to the Hebrews.* New International Commentary on the New Testament. Grand Rapids: Eerdmans, rev. ed., 1990.

――――. "Habakkuk." In *The Minor Prophets. An Exegetical and Expository Commentary. Obadiah, Jonah, Micah, Nahum, and Habakkuk,* edited by Thomas Edward McComiskey. Grand Rapids: Baker, 1993.

Buchanan, George Wesley. *To the Hebrews.* Anchor Bible. Garden City: Doubleday, 1972.

deSilva, David Arthur. *Perseverance in Gratitude. A Socio-Rhetorical Commentary on the Epistle "to the Hebrews".* Grand Rapids: Eerdmans, 2000.

Elliger, Karl. *Das Buch der zwölf kleinen Propheten II: Die Propheten Nahum, Habakuk, Zephanja, Haggai, Sacharia, Maleachi.* Das Alte Testament Deutsch 25. Göttingen: Vandenhoeck & Ruprecht, 1982.

Ellingworth, Paul. *Commentary on Hebrews.* New International Greek Testament Commentary. Grand Rapids: Eerdmans, 1993.

Gordon, Robert P. *Hebrews.* Readings: A New Biblical Commentary. Sheffield: Sheffield Academic Press, 2000.

Grässer, Erich. *An die Hebräer (Hebr 1-6) (Hebr 7,1-10,18) (Hebr 10,19-13,25).* 3 vols., Evangelisch-katholischer Kommentar zum Neuen Testament vii. 1, 2, 3. Zürich / Neukirchen-Vluyn: Benzinger / Neukirchener, 1990, 1993, 1997.

Haak, Robert D. *Habakkuk.* Supplements to Vetus Testamentum 44. Leiden: E. J. Brill, 1992.

Keil, C. F. , and F. Delitzsch. *Biblical Commentary on the Old Testament. The Twelve Minor Prophets.* Vol. 2. Edinburgh: T. & T. Clark, 1871.

Koester, Helmut. *To the Hebrews.* Anchor Bible. Garden City, NY: Doubleday, 2001.

Lane, William L. *Hebrews 1-8, 9-13.* 2 vols., Word Biblical Commentary. Dallas: Word, 1991.

Marti, Karl. *Das Dodekapropheton.* Kurzer Hand-Commentar zum Alten Testament 13. Tübingen: J. C. B. Mohr, 1904.

Moffatt, J. *A Critical and Exegetical Commentary on The Epistle to the Hebrews.* International Critical Commentary. Edinburgh: T. & T. Clark, rep. ed., 1979.

Montefiore, Hugh. *A Commentary on the Epistle to the Hebrews.* Black's New Testament Commentaries. London: Adam & Charles Black, 1964.

Nowack, W. *Die kleinen Propheten.* Handkommentar zum Alten Testament. Göttingen: Vandenhoeck & Ruprecht, 1903.

Roberts, Jimmy Jack McBee. *Nahum, Habakkuk, and Zephaniah.* Old Testament Library. Louisville: Westminster / John Knox Press, 1991.

Rudolph, Wilhelm. *Micha – Nahum – Habakuk – Zephanja.* Kommentar zum Alten Testament 13. Gütersloh: Gerd Mohn, 1975.

Sellin, Ernst. *Das Zwölfprophetenbuch.* Kommentar zum Alten Testament 12. Leipzig: Werner Scholl, 1922.

Smith, J. M. P., William Hayes Ward, and Julius A. Bewer. *A Critical and Exegetical Commentary on Micah, Zephaniah, Nahum, Habakkuk, Obadiah and Joel.* International Critical Commentary. Edinburgh: T. & T. Clark, 1912.

Smith, Ralph L. *Micah – Malachi.* Word Biblical Commentary. Waco: Word, 1984.

Spicq, Ceslas. *L'Épître aux Hébreux.* 2 vols. Paris: Gabalda, 1952-1953.

Weiss, H.-F. *Der Brief an die Hebräer.* Kritisch-exegetischer Kommentar über das Neue Testament 13. Göttingen: Vandenhoeck & Ruprecht, 1991.

Westcott, Brooke Foss. *The Epistle to the Hebrews: The Greek Text with Notes and Essays.* London / New York: Macmillan, rep. ed., 1970.

Secondary Sources

Abegg, Martin G., and Craig A. Evans. "Messianic Passages in the Dead Sea Scrolls." In *Qumran-Messianism. Studies on the Messianic Expectations in the Dead Sea Scrolls*, edited by J. H. Charlesworth, H. Lichtenberger and G. S. Oegema, 191-203. Tübingen: J. C. B. Mohr (Paul Siebeck), 1998.

Aejmalaeus, Anneli. "Septuagintal Translation Techniques – A Solution to the Problem of the Tabernacle Account." In *Septuagint, Scrolls and Cognate Writings*, edited by George J. Brooke and Barnabas Lindars, 381-402. Atlanta: Scholars Press, 1992.

———. "Translation Technique and the Intention of the Translator." In *On the Trail of Septuagint Translators. Collected Essays*, edited by Anneli Aejmelaeus, 65-77. Kampen: Kok Pharos, 1993.

———. "What Can We Know about the Hebrew Vorlage of the Septuagint?" In *On the Trail of Septuagint Translators. Collected Essays*, edited by Anneli Aejmelaeus, 77-115. Kampen: Kok Pharos, 1993.

Ahlborn, E. "Die Septuaginta Vorlage des Hebräerbriefes." Ph. D., University of Göttingen, 1966.

Albl, Martin C. *And Scripture Cannot Be Broken. The Form and Function of the Early Christian Testimonia Collections.* Supplements to Novum Testamentum 46. Leiden / Boston / Köln: E. J. Brill, 1999.

Allen, Leslie C. *Psalms 101-150.* Word Biblical Commentary. Dallas: Word, 1983.

Anderson, H. "The Jewish Antecedents of the Christology in Hebrews." In *The Messiah. Developments in Earliest Judaism and Christianity*, edited by J. H. Charlesworth, 512-35. Minneapolis: Fortress Press, 1992.

Andriessen, Paul. "La teneur judéo-chrétienne de Hé 1:6 et 2:14b-3:2." *Novum Testamentum* 18 (1976): 293-313.

Ashley, Timothy R. *The Book of Numbers.* New International Commentary on the Old Testament. Grand Rapids: Eerdmans, 1993.

Aune, David E. *The New Testament in Its Literary Environment.* Library of Early Christianity. Philadelphia: Westminster Press, 1987.

Backhaus, Knut. *Der neue Bund und das Werden der Kirche. Die Diatheke-Deutung des Hebräerbriefs im Rahmen der frühchristlichen Theologiegeschichte.* Münster: Aschendorff, 1996.

Baer, David A. *When We All Go Home: Translation and Theology in LXX Isaiah 56-66.* Journal for the Study of the Old Testament – Supplement Series 318. Sheffield: Sheffield Academic Press, 2001.

Barr, James. *The Semantics of Biblical Language.* Oxford: Oxford University Press, 1961.

————. "Some Semantic Notes on the Covenant." In *Beiträge zur Alttestamentlichen Theologie: Festschrift für Walther Zimmerli zum 70. Geburtstag*, edited by H. Donner, R. Hanhart and R. Smend, 23-38. Göttingen: Vandenhoeck & Ruprecht, 1977.

Barrett, C. K. "The Eschatology of the Epistle to the Hebrews." In *The Background of the New Testament and Its Eschatology. In Honour of Charles Harold Dodd*, edited by W. D. Davies and D. Daube, 363-94. Cambridge: Cambridge University Press, 1956.

Barth, Markus. "The Old Testament in Hebrews: An Essay in Biblical Hermeneutics." In *Current Issues in New Testament Interpretation*, edited by W. Klassen and G. F. Snyder, 53-78. New York: Harper & Row, 1962.

————. *Les Devanciers d'Aquila*. Supplements to Vetus Testamentum 10. Leiden: E. J. Brill, 1963.

————. "Un archétype commun au pré-M, au S et à 1QpHab?" In *Philologia Sacra. Altes und Neues Testament*, edited by Roger Gryson, 150-76. Freiburg: Verlag Herder, 1993.

Bateman, Herbert W. IV. *Early Jewish Hermeneutics and Hebrews 1:5-13. The Impact of Early Jewish Exegesis on the Interpretation of a Significant New Testament Passage*. American University Studies vii.193. New York: Peter Lang, 1997.

————. "Two First-Century Messianic Uses of the OT: Heb 1:5-13 and 4QFlor 1.1-19." *Journal of the Evangelical Theological Society* 38, no. 1 (1995).

Beckwith, Roger. *The Old Testament Canon of the New Testament Church and Its Background in Early Judaism*. Grand Rapids: Eerdmans, 1985.

Behm, J. "διαθήκη" in *TDNT*, 2:125-34.

Betz, Hans Dieter. *Galatians. A Commentary on Paul's Letter to the Churches in Galatia*. Hermeneia. Philadelphia: Fortress Press, 1979.

Bickerman, Elias. "The Septuagint as a Translation." In *Studies in Jewish and Christian History*, edited by Elias Bickerman, 167-200. Leiden: E. J. Brill, 1976.

Blackstone, Thomas Ladd. "The Hermeneutics of Recontextualization in the Epistle to the Hebrews." Ph. D., Emory University, 1995.

Brawley, Robert L. *Text to Text Pours Forth Speech. Voices of Scripture in Luke – Acts.* Bloomington: Indiana University Press, 1995.

Brewer, David Instone. *Techniques and Assumptions in Jewish Exegesis before 70 CE.* Texte und Studien zum Antiken Judentum 30. Tübingen: J. C. B. Mohr (Paul Siebeck), 1992.

Brock, Sebastian P. "Translating the Old Testament." In *It Is Written: Scripture Citing Scripture*, edited by D. A. Carson and H. G. M. Williamson, 87-98. Cambridge: Cambridge University Press, 1988.

Brownlee, William H. *The Midrash Pesher of Habakkuk*. Society of Biblical Literature – Monograph Series 24. Missoula: Scholars Press, 1979.

Brownlee, William Hugh. "The Composition of Habakkuk [with reference to 1QpHab]." In *Hommages a André Dupont-Sommer*, edited by N. Avigad, 255-75. Paris: Librairie Adrien Maisonneuve, 1971.

————. "The Habakkuk Midrash and the Targum of Jonathan." *Journal of Jewish Studies* 7 (1956): 169-86.

————. *The Text of Habakkuk in the Ancient Commentary from Qumran*. Journal of Biblical Literature – Monograph Series 11. Philadelphia: Society of Biblical Literature, 1959.

Bruce, Frederick Fyvie. "The Earliest Old Testament Interpretation." In *The Witness of Tradition*, edited by M. A. Beek, 36-52. Leiden: E. J. Brill, 1972.

———. "'To the Hebrews' or 'To the Essenes'?" *New Testament Studies* 9 (1963): 217-32.

Buchanan, George Wesley. "The Priestly Teacher of Righteousness." *Revue de Qumran* 6, no. 24 (1969): 553-58.

Buck, Daniel E. "The Rhetorical Arrangement and Function of OT Citations in the Book of Hebrews: Uncovering Their Role in the Paraenetic Discourse of Access." Ph. D., Dallas Theological Seminary, 2002.

Budd, Philip J. *Numbers*. Word Biblical Commentary. Waco: Word, 1984.

Burch, Varcher. *The Epistle to the Hebrews. Its Sources and Message*. London: Williams & Norgate, 1936.

Cadwallader, A. H. "The Correction of the Text of Hebrews towards the LXX." *Novum Testamentum* 34, no. 3 (1992): 257-92.

Caird, George B. "The Exegetical Method of the Epistle to the Hebrews." *Canadian Journal of Theology* 5 (1959): 44-51.

Cambier, J. *Eschatologie ou Hellénisme dans l'épître aux Hébreux*. Analecta Lovaniensia Biblica et Orientalia 2. Bruges / Paris: Descles de Brouwer, 1949.

Carrez, Maurice. "Ambakoum Septante." *Revue d'histoire et de philosophie religieuses* 72, no. Ap-Je (1992): 129-41.

Carson, D. A., and H. G. M. Williamson. *It Is Written: Scripture Citing Scripture. Essays in Honor of Barnabas Lindars, S.S.F.* Cambridge: Cambridge University Press, 1988.

Charlesworth, J. H., H. Lichtenberger, and G. S. Oegema, eds. *Qumran-Messianism. Studies on the Messianic Expectations in the Dead Sea Scrolls*. Tübingen: J. C. B. Mohr (Paul Siebeck), 1998.

Charlesworth, James H. *The Old Testament Pseudepigrapha and the New Testament*. Cambridge: Cambridge University Press, 1985.

———. "From Messianology to Christology: Problems and Prospects." In *The Messiah. Developments in Earliest Judaism and Christianity*, edited by J. H. Charlesworth, 3-35. Minneapolis: Fortress Press, 1992.

———. "Introduction: Messianic Ideas in Early Judaism." In *Qumran-Messianism. Studies on the Messianic Expectations in the Dead Sea Scrolls*, edited by J. H. Charlesworth, H. Lichtenberger and G. S. Oegema, 1-8. Tübingen: J. C. B. Mohr (Paul Siebeck), 1998.

———. "Messianology in the Biblical Pseudepigrapha." In *Qumran-Messianism. Studies on the Messianic Expectations in the Dead Sea Scrolls*, edited by J. H. Charlesworth, H. Lichtenberger and G. S. Oegema, 21-52. Tübingen: J. C. B. Mohr (Paul Siebeck), 1998.

———, ed. *The Messiah. Developments in Earliest Judaism and Christianity*. Minneapolis: Fortress Press, 1992.

Chester, Andrew. "The Parting of the Ways: Eschatology and Messianic Hope." In *Jews and Christians. The Parting of the Ways A.D. 70 to 135*, edited by James D. G. Dunn, 239-315. Tübingen: J. C. B. Mohr (Paul Siebeck), 1992.

Cleaver-Bartholomew, David. "An Analysis of the Old Greek Version of Habakkuk." Ph. D., Claremont Graduate University, 1998.

Clements, Ronald E. "The Use of the Old Testament in Hebrews." *Southwestern Journal of Theology* 28 (1985): 36-45.

Coats, George W. *Moses: Heroic Man, Man of God*. Journal for the Study of the Old Testament – Supplement Series 57. Sheffield: Sheffield Academic Press, 1988.

Coggins, R. J. "The Minor Prophets – One Book or Twelve?" In *Crossing the Boundaries. Essays in Biblical Interpretation in Honour of Michael D. Goulder*, edited by S. E. Porter, P. Joyce and D. E. Orton, 57-68. Leiden: E. J. Brill, 1994.

Collins, John J. *The Sceptre and the Star. The Messiahs of the Dead Sea Scrolls and Other Ancient Literature*. New York: Doubleday, 1995.

Copeland, Paul E. "The Midst of the Years." In *Text as Pretext: Essays in Honour of Robert Davidson*, edited by R. P. Carroll, 91-105. Sheffield: Sheffield Academic Press, 1992.

Cosby, Michael R. *The Rhetorical Composition and Function of Hebrews 11 in Light of Example Lists in Antiquity*. Macon: Mercer University Press, 1988.

Cotterell, Peter, and Max Turner. *Linguistics and Biblical Interpretation*. London: SPCK, 1989.

Craigie, Peter C. *Psalms 1-50*. Word Biblical Commentary. Dallas: Word, 1983.

Cunliffe-Jones, H. "Scripture and Tradition in Orthodox Theology." In *Holy Book and Holy Tradition*, edited by F. F. Bruce and E. G. Rupp, 186-209. Manchester: Manchester University Press, 1968.

D'Angelo, Mary Rose. *Moses in the Letter to the Hebrews*. Society of Biblical Literature – Dissertation Series 42. Missoula: Scholars Press, 1979.

Davis, Ronald Eugene. "The Function of the Old Testament Texts in the Structure of Hebrews: A Rhetorical Analysis." Ph. D., Southern Baptist Theological Seminary, 1994.

Day, John, ed. *King and Messiah in Israel and the Ancient Near East. Proceedings of the Oxford Old Testament Seminar*. Journal for the Study of the Old Testament – Supplement Series 270. Sheffield: Sheffield Academic Press, 1998.

de Waard, J. *A Comparative Study of the Old Testament Text in the Dead Sea Scrolls and in the New Testament*. Studies on the Texts of the Desert of Judah 4. Leiden: E. J. Brill, 1965.

———. "Translation Techniques Used by the Greek Translators of Amos." *Biblica* 59 (1978): 339-50.

Deissmann, Adolf. *Philology of the Greek Bible: Its Present and Future*. London: Hodder and Stoughton, 1908.

deSilva, David A. *Despising Shame. Honor Discourse and Community Maintenance in the Epistle to the Hebrews*. Society of Biblical Literature – Dissertation Series 152. Atlanta: Scholars Press, 1995.

Dockery, David S. "The Use of Hab 2:4 in Rom 1:17: Some Hermeneutical and Theological Considerations." *Wesleyan Theological Journal* 22, no. Fall (1987): 24-36.

Dodd, C. H. *According to the Scriptures: The Sub-structure of New Testament Theology*. New York: Charles Scribner's Sons, 1952.

Driver, G. R. "Linguistic and Textual Problems: Minor Prophets. Part I, II, III." *Journal of Theological Studies* 39 (1938): 154-66, 260-73, 393-405.

Dunn, James D. G. *Christology in the Making*. Philadelphia: Westminster Press, 1980.

Eisenbaum, Pamela M. "Heroes and History in Hebrews 11." In *Early Christian Interpretation of the Scriptures of Israel*, edited by C. A. Evans and J. A. Sanders, 380-96. Sheffield: Sheffield Academic Press, 1997.

Elliger, Karl. *Studien zum Habakuk-kommentar vom Toten Meer*. Beiträge zur historischen Theologie 15. Tübingen: J. C. B. Mohr (Paul Siebeck), 1953.

Ellingworth, Paul. "The Old Testament in Hebrews: Exegesis, Method and Hermeneutics." Ph. D., University of Aberdeen, 1978.

Ellis, E. Earle. "Biblical Interpretation in the New Testament Church." In *Mikra. Text, Translation, Reading and Interpretation of the Hebrew Bible in Ancient Judaism and Early Christianity*, edited by Martin Jan Mulder, 691-727. Minneapolis: Fortress Press, 1990.

———. "The Old Testament Canon in the Early Church." In *Mikra. Text, Translation, Reading and Interpretation of the Hebrew Bible in Ancient Judaism and Early Christianity*, edited by Martin Jan Mulder, 653-90. Minneapolis: Fortress Press, 1990.

Emerton, John A. "Textual and Linguistic Problems of Habakkuk 2:4-5." *Journal of Theological Studies* 28, no. Ap (1977): 1-18.

Enns, Peter. "The Interpretation of Psalm 95 in Hebrews 3.1-4.13." In *Early Christian Interpretation of the Scriptures of Israel*, edited by C. A. Evans and J. A. Sanders, 352-63. Sheffield: Sheffield Academic Press, 1997.

Erickson, Richard J. *James Barr and the Beginnings of Biblical Semantics*. Notre Dame: Foundations Press, 1984.

Evans, Craig A. *Non Canonical Writings and New Testament Interpretation*. Peabody: Hendrikson, 1992.

Evans, Craig A., and Peter W. Flint, eds. *Eschatology, Messianism and the Dead Seas Scrolls*. Grand Rapids: Eerdmans, 1997.

Evans, Craig A., and James A. Sanders. "Gospel and Midrash: An Introduction to Luke and Scripture." In *Luke and Scripture. The Function of Sacred Tradition in Luke – Acts*, edited by Craig A. Evans and James A. Sanders, 1-13. Minneapolis: Fortress Press, 1993.

Fitzmyer, J. A. "Habakkuk 2:3-4 and the New Testament." In *De la Torah au Messie. Melanges Henri Cazelles*, edited by J. Dore, P. Grelot and M. Carrez, 447-57. Paris: Descleé, 1981.

Flint, Peter W., and James C. Vanderkam, eds. *The Dead Sea Scrolls after Fifty Years. A Comprehensive Assessment*. 2 vols. Leiden / Boston / Köln: E. J. Brill, 1998, 1999.

Floyd, Michael H. "Prophecy and Writing in Habakkuk 2,1-5." *Zeitschrift für die alttestamentliche Wissenschaft* 105, no. 3 (1993): 462-81.

Flusser, David. "Messianology and Christology in the Epistle to the Hebrews." In *Judaism and the Origins of Christianity*, edited by David Flusser, 246-89. Jerusalem: Magnes Press, 1988.

———. "'Today if you will listen to His voice': Creative Jewish Exegesis in Hebrews 3-4." In *Creative Biblical Exegesis. Christian and Jewish Hermeneutics Through the Centuries*, edited by B. Uffenheimer and H. G. Reventlow, 55-62. Sheffield: Sheffield Academic Press, 1988.

France, Richard. "The Writer of Hebrews as a Biblical Expositor." *Tyndale Bulletin* 47 (1996): 245-76.

Fuller, Russell. "The Form and Formation of the Book of the Twelve: The Evidence from the Judean Desert." In *Forming Prophetic Literature*, edited by J. W. Watts and P. R. House, 86-101. Sheffield: Sheffield Academic Press, 1996.

Gard, Donald H. "The Concept of the Future Life According to the Greek Translator of the Book of Job." *Journal of Biblical Literature* 73 (1954): 137-43.

Gehman, Henry S. "The Hebraic Character of Septuagint Greek." In *The Language of the Greek New Testament. Classic Essays*, edited by Stanley E. Porter. Sheffield: Sheffield Academic Press, 1991.

Gerhardsson, Birger. *Memory and Manuscript. Oral Tradition and Written Transmission in Rabbinic Judaism and Early Christianity.* Uppsala: Almqvist and Wiksells, 1961.

Glasson, T. F. "'Plurality of Divine Persons' and the Quotations in Hebrews 1.6 ff." *New Testament Studies* 12 (1965-1966): 270-72.

Gleason, Randall C. "The Old Testament Background of Rest in Hebrews 3:7-4:11." *Bibliotheca Sacra* 157, no. Jul-Sep (2000): 281-303.

———. "The Old Testament Background of the Warning in Hebrews 6:4-6." *Bibliotheca Sacra* 155, no. Jan-Mar (1998): 62-91.

Gooding, David W. *The Account of the Tabernacle. Translation and Textual Problems of the Greek Exodus.* Cambridge: Cambridge University Press, 1959.

Gordon, Robert P. "Better Promises: Two Passages in Hebrews against the Background of the Old Testament Cultus." In *Templum Amicitiae. Essays on the Second Temple Presented to Ernst Bammel,* edited by William Horbury, 434-49. Sheffield: Sheffield Academic Press, 1991.

———. "The Targum to the Minor Prophets and the Dead Sea Texts: Textual and Exegetical Notes." *Revue de Qumran* 8, no. 31 (1974): 425-29.

Goshen-Gottstein, M. H. "Theory and Practice of Textual Criticism. The Text-critical Use of the Septuagint." *Textus* 3 (1963): 130-58.

Goulder, Michael D. *The Psalms of the Return. (Book V, Psalms 107-150). Studies in the Psalter.* Journal for the Study of the Old Testament – Supplement Series 258. Sheffield: Sheffield Academic Press, 1998.

Grabbe, Lester L. "The Translation Technique of the Greek Minor Versions: Translations or Revisions?" In *Septuagint, Scrolls and Cognate Writings,* edited by George J. Brooke and Barnabas Lindars, 505-56. Atlanta: Scholars Press, 1992.

Grässer, Erich. "Das Schriftargument in Hebr 10,37 f." In *Ekklesiologie des Neuen Testaments. Für Karl Kertelge,* edited by R. Kampling and T. Söding, 431-39. Freiburg / Basel / Wien: Herder, 1996.

———. "Mose und Jesus. Zur Auslegung von Hebr 3. 1-6." *Zeitschrift für die neutestamentliche Wissenschaft* 75 (1984): 2-23.

Gray, George B. *Numbers.* International Critical Commentary. Edinburgh: T. & T. Clark, 1903.

Greenspoon, Leonard. "The Use and Abuse of the Term 'LXX' and Related Terminology in Recent Scholarship." *Bulletin of the International Organization for Septuagint and Cognate Studies* 20 (1987): 21-29.

Gruenwald, I., S. Shaked, and G. G. Stroumsa, eds. *Messiah and Christos. Studies in the Jewish Origins of Christianity. Presented to David Flusser on the Occasion of His Seventy-Fifth Birthday.* Tübingen: J. C. B. Mohr (Paul Siebeck), 1992.

Guilding, Aileen. *The Fourth Gospel and Jewish Worship.* Oxford: Clarendon Press, 1960.

Guthrie, George H. "The Old Testament in Hebrews." In *The Dictionary of the Later New Testament and Its Developments,* edited by Ralph P. Martin and Peter H. Davids. Downers Grove / Leicester: Inter Varsity Press, 1997.

———. *The Structure of Hebrews: A Text-Linguistic Analysis.* Supplements to Novum Testamentum 73. Leiden: E. J. Brill, 1994.

Hahn, Scott Walker. "Kinship By Covenant: A Biblical Theological Study of Covenant Types and Texts in the Old and New Testaments." Ph. D., Marquette University, 1995.

Hanhart, Robert. "Die Bedeutung der Septuaginta in neutestamentlicher Zeit." *Zeitschrift für Theologie und Kirche* 81, no. 4 (1984): 395-416.

Hanson, Anthony T. *Paul's Understanding of Jesus.* Hull: University of Hull, 1963.
————. "Christ in the Old Testament according to Hebrews." *Studia Evangelica* (1964): 393-407.
————. *Studies in Paul's Technique and Theology.* London: SPCK, 1974.
Harl, Marguerite, Gilles Dorival, and Olivier Munnich. *La Bible grecque des Septante: du judaïsme hellénistique au Christianisme ancien.* Paris: Éditions du Cerf, 1988.
Harris, Murray J. *Jesus as God. The New Testament Use of Theos in Reference to Jesus.* Grand Rapids: Baker, 1992.
Harris, R. *Testimonies.* 2 vols. Cambridge: Cambridge University Press, 1920.
Harrison, C. Robert Jr. "The Unity of the Minor Prophets in the LXX: A Reexamination of the Question." *Bulletin of the International Organization for Septuagint and Cognate Studies* 21 (1988): 55-72.
Hatina, Thomas R. "Intertextuality and Historical Criticism in New Testament Studies: Is There a Relationship?" *Biblical Interpretation* 7, no. 1 (1999): 28-43.
Hay, David M. *Glory at the Right Hand. Psalm 110 in Early Christianity.* New York: Abingdon Press, 1973.
Hays, Richard B. *The Faith of Jesus Christ. An Investigation of the Narrative Substructure of Galatians 3:1-4:11.* Society of Biblical Literature - Dissertation Series 56. Chico: Scholars Press, 1983.
————. *Echoes of Scripture in the Letters of Paul.* New Haven: Yale University Press, 1989.
————. "Echoes of Scripture in the Letter of Paul: Abstract." In *Paul and the Scriptures of Israel,* edited by Craig A. Evans and James A. Sanders, 42-46. Sheffield: Sheffield Academic Press, 1993.
Hegerman, H. "διαθήκη" in *EDNT,* 1:299-301.
Hengel, Martin. *The Septuagint as Christian Scripture. Its Prehistory and the Problem of Its Canon.* Edinburgh: T. & T. Clark, 2002.
————. "'Sit at My Right Hand!'" In *Studies in Early Christology,* edited by Martin Hengel, 119-228. Edinburgh: T. & T. Clark, 1995.
————. *Studies in Early Christology.* Edinburgh: T. & T. Clark, 1995.
Hengel, Martin, and R. Deines. "Die Septuaginta als 'Christliche Schriftensammlung', ihre Vorgeschichte und das Problem ihres Kanons." In *Die Septuaginta: zwischen Judentum und Christentum,* edited by Martin Hengel and Anna Maria Schwemer, 182-284. Tübingen: J. C. B. Mohr (Paul Siebeck), 1994.
Hill, David. *Greek Words and Hebrew Meanings: Studies in the Semantics of Soteriological Terms.* Cambridge: Cambridge University Press, 1967.
Hodgson, Robert. "The Testimony Hypothesis." *Journal of Biblical Literature* 98, no. 3 (1979): 361-78.
Hofius, Otfried. *Katapausis. Die Vorstellung vom endzeitlichen Ruheort im Hebräerbrief.* Wissenschaftliche Untersuchungen zum Neuen Testament 11. Tübingen: J.C. B. Mohr (Paul Siebeck), 1970.
Hoonacker, A. Van. *Les douze petits prophètes.* Paris: J. Gabalda, 1908.
Horbury, William. "The Christian Use and the Jewish Origins of the Wisdom of Solomon." In *Wisdom in Ancient Israel. Essays in Honour of J. A. Emerton,* edited by John Day, Robert P. Gordon and H. G. M. Williamson, 182-96. Cambridge: Cambridge University Press, 1995.
————. "The Cult of Christ and the Cult of the Saints." *New Testament Studies* 44 (1998): 444-69.
————. "Ezekiel Tragicus 106." *Vetus Testamentum* 36, no. 1 (1986): 37-51.
————. *Jewish Messianism and the Cult of Christ.* London: SCM Press, 1998.

————. "Septuagintal and New Testament Conceptions of the Church." In *A Vision for the Church. Studies in Early Christian Ecclesiology in Honour of J. P. M. Sweet*, edited by Markus Bockmuehl and Michael B. Thompson, 1-18. Edinburgh: T. & T. Clark, 1997.

————. "Messianism in the Old Testament Apocrypha and Pseudepigrapha." In *King and Messiah in Israel and the Ancient Near East. Proceedings of the Oxford Old Testament Seminar*, edited by John Day, 402-33. Sheffield: Sheffield Academic Press, 1998.

Horgan, Maurya P. *Pesharim: Qumran Interpretations of Biblical Books.* Catholic Biblical Quarterly Monograph Series 8. Washington, D.C.: Catholic Biblical Association of America, 1979.

House, P. R. *The Unity of the Twelve.* Journal for the Study of the Old Testament – Supplement Series 97. Sheffield: Sheffield Academic Press, 1990.

Howard, George. "Hebrews and the Old Testament Quotations." *Novum Testamentum* 10 (1968): 208-16.

Hughes, Graham. *Hebrews and Hermeneutics: The Epistle to the Hebrews as a New Testament Example of Biblical Interpretation.* Society for New Testament Studies – Monograph Series. Cambridge: Cambridge University Press, 1979.

Hughes, John J. "Hebrews IX 15ff. and Galatians III 15ff. A Study in Covenant Practice and Procedure." *Novum Testamentum* 21, no. 1 (1979): 27-96.

Humbert, Paul. *Problemes du Livre d'Habacuc.* Neuchatel: Université de Neuchatel, 1944.

Hurst, Lincoln D. "The Christology of Hebrews 1 and 2." In *The Glory of Christ in the New Testament. Studies in Christology. In Memory of George Bradford Caird*, edited by L. D. Hurst and N. T. Wright, 151-64. Oxford: Clarendon Press, 1987.

————. *The Epistle to the Hebrews. Its Background of Thought.* Society for New Testament Studies – Monograph Series 65. Cambridge: Cambridge University Press, 1990.

————. "Eschatology and 'Platonism' in the Epistle to the Hebrews." *Society of Biblical Literature Seminar Papers* 23 (1984): 41-74.

Isaacs, Marie E. *Sacred Space. An Approach to the Theology of the Epistle to the Hebrews.* Journal for the Study of the New Testament – Supplement Series 73. Sheffield: Sheffield Academic Press, 1992.

Janzen, Gerald J. "Habakkuk 2:2-4 in the Light of Recent Philological Advances." *Harvard Theological Review* 73, no. Ja-Ap (1980): 53-78.

Jellicoe, Sidney. *The Septuagint and Modern Study.* Oxford: Clarendon, 1968.

Jeremias, Jörg. *Kultprophetie und Gerichtsverkündigung in der späten Königszeit Israels.* Neukirchen-Vluyn: Neukirchener Verlag, 1970.

Jobes, Karen H. "Rhetorical Achievement in the Hebrews 10 'Misquote' of Ps 40." *Biblica* 72 (1991): 387-96.

Jones, Barry Alan. *The Formation of the Book of the Twelve. A Study in Text and Canon.* Society of Biblical Literature – Dissertation Series 149. Atlanta: Scholars Press, 1995.

Joosten, Jan. "Exegesis in the Septuagint Version of Hosea." In *Intertextuality in Ugarit and Israel*, edited by J. C. De Moor, 62-85. Leiden / Boston / Köln: E. J. Brill, 1998.

Juel, Donald H. *Messianic Exegesis.* Philadelphia: Fortress Press, 1988.

Kaminka, Armand. "Studien zur Septuaginta an der Hand der zwölf kleinen Prophetenbücher." *Monatschrift für Geschichte und Wissenschaft des Judentums* 72 (1928): 49-60, 242-73.

Käsemann, Ernst. *The Wandering People of God: An Investigation of the Letter to the Hebrews*. Translated by R. A. Harrisville and I. L. Sandberg. Minneapolis: Augsburg, 1984.

Katz, P. "The Quotations from Dt. in Heb." *Zeitschrift für die neutestamentliche Wissenschaft* 49 (1958): 213-23.

Kennedy, George. *New Testament Interpretation through Rhetorical Criticism*. Chapel Hill: University of North Carolina Press, 1984.

Kistemaker, Simon. *The Psalm Citations in the Epistle to the Hebrews*. Amsterdam: Van Soest, 1961.

Klappert, Bertold. *Die Eschatologie des Hebräerbriefs*. München: Kaiser Verlag, 1969.

Knibb, Michael A. "Eschatology and Messianism in the Dead Sea Scrolls." In *The Dead Sea Scrolls after Fifty Years. A Comprehensive Assessment*, edited by Peter W. Flint and James C. Vanderkam, 379-402. Leiden / Boston / Köln: E. J. Brill, 1998 - 1999.

———. *The Qumran Community*. Cambridge Commentaries on Writings of the Jewish and Christian World 200 BC to AD 200. Vol. 2. Cambridge: Cambridge University Press, 1987.

Koch, Dietrich-Alex. "Der Text von Hab 2:4b in der Septuaginta und im Neuen Testament." *Zeitschrift für die neutestamentliche Wissenschaft und die Kunde der Älteren Kirche* 76, no. 1-2 (1985): 68-85.

———. *Die Schrift als Zeuge des Evangeliums: Untersuchungen zur Verwendung und zum Verständis der Schrift bei Paulus*. Beiträge zur historischen Theologie 69. Tübingen: J. C. B. Mohr (Paul Siebeck), 1986.

Kooij, Arie van der. "Perspectives on the Study of the Septuagint. Who are the Translators?" In *Perspectives in the Study of the Old Testament and Early Judaism. A Symposium in Honour of Adam S. van der Woude on the Occasion of His 70th Birthday*, edited by Florentino Garcia Martinez and Ed Noort, 214-29. Leiden / Boston / Köln: E. J. Brill, 1998.

Kraft, Robert A., and E. Tov, eds. *Computer Tools for Septuagint Studies*. Society of Biblical Literature – Septuagint and Cognate Studies 20. Atlanta: Scholars Press, 1988.

Kraus, Hans-Joachim. *Psalms 1-59, 60-150*. Translated by Hilton C. Oswald. 2 vols. Minneapolis: Augsburg, 1989.

Laansma, Jon. *'I will give you rest': The Rest Motif in the New Testament with Special Reference to Mt 11 and Heb 3-4*. Wissenschaftliche Untersuchungen zum Neuen Testament II 97. Tübingen: J. C. B. Mohr (Paul Siebeck), 1997.

Lee, Bae Gil. "A Developing Messianic Understanding of Habakkuk 2:3-5 in the New Testament in the Context of Early Jewish Writings." Ph. D., Southwestern Baptist Theological Seminary, 1997.

Lee, J. A. L. *A Lexical Study of the Septuagint Version of the Pentateuch*. Society of Biblical Literature – Septuagint and Cognate Studies 14. Chico: Scholars Press, 1983.

Lehne, Susanne. *The New Covenant in Hebrews*. Journal for the Study of the New Testament – Supplement Series 44. Sheffield: Sheffield Academic Press, 1990.

Leschert, Dale F. *Hermeneutical Foundations of Hebrews: A Study in the Validity of the Epistle's Interpretation of Some Core Citations from the Psalms*. Lewiston: Edwin Mellen Press, 1994.

Levine, Baruch A. *Numbers 1-20*. Anchor Bible. New York: Doubleday, 1993.

Lichtenberger, H. "Messianic Expectations and Messianic Figures During the Second Temple Period." In *Qumran-Messianism. Studies on the Messianic Expectations in* the Dead Sea Scrolls, edited by J. H. Charlesworth, H. Lichtenberger and G. S. Oegema, 9-20. Tübingen: J. C. B. Mohr (Paul Siebeck), 1998.

Lincoln, Andrew T. "Sabbath, Rest, and Eschatology in the New Testament (Heb 3:7-4:13)." In *From Sabbath to Lord's Day*, edited by D. Carson, 198-220. Grand Rapids: Zondervan, 1982.

Lindars, Barnabas. *New Testament Apologetic*. Philadelphia: Westminster Press, 1961.

———. "The Rhetorical Structure of Hebrews." *New Testament Studies* 35 (1989): 382-406.

———. *The Theology of the Letter to the Hebrews*. Cambridge: Cambridge University Press, 1991.

Longenecker, Richard N. *Biblical Exegesis in the Apostolic Period*. Grand Rapids: Eerdmans, 1975.

Lust, Jean. "Septuagint and Messianism, with a Special Emphasis on the Pentateuch." In *Theologische Probleme der Septuaginta und der hellenistischen Hermeneutik*, edited by H. G. Reventlow, 26-45. Gütersloh: Chr. Kaiser, 1997.

Lust, Johan. "The Greek Version of Balaam's Third and Fourth Oracles. The ανθρωπος in Num 24:7 and 17. Messianism and Lexicography." In *VIII Congress of the IOSCS*, edited by L. Greenspoon and O. Munnich, 233-57. Atlanta: Scholars Press, 1995.

———. "Messianism and Septuagint." In *Congress Volume Salamanca 1983*, edited by J. Emerton, 174-91. Supplements to Vetus Testamentum 36. Leiden: E. J. Brill, 1985.

———. "Translation Greek and the Lexicography of the Septuagint." *Journal for the Study of the Old Testament* 59 (1993): 109-20.

Luther, J. H. "The Use of the Old Testament by the Author of Hebrews." Ph. D., Bob Jones University, 1977.

MacLeod, David J. "The Literary Structure of the Book of Hebrews." *Bibliotheca Sacra* 146 (1989): 185-97.

MacRae, George W. "Heavenly Temple and Eschatology in the Letter to the Hebrews." *Semeia* 12 (1978): 179-99.

Mai, Hans-Peter. "Bypassing Intertextuality. Hermeneutics, Textual Practice, Hypertext." In *Intertextuality*, edited by Heinrich F. Plett, 30-59. Berlin / New York: Walter de Gruyter, 1991.

Manson, T. W. "The Argument from Prophecy." *Journal of Theological Studies* 46 (1945): 129-36.

Marshall, I. Howard. "An Assessment of Recent Developments." In *It Is Written: Scripture Citing Scripture*, edited by D. A. Carson and H. G. M. Williamson, 1-21. Cambridge: Cambridge University Press, 1988.

McCarthy, Dennis J. "Covenant in the Old Testament: The Present State of Inquiry." *The Catholic Biblical Quarterly* 27, no. 3 (1965): 217-40.

McConville, G. J. "בְּרִית" in *NIDOTTE*, 1: 747-755.

McCullough, J. C. "Hebrews and the Old Testament." Ph. D., Queen's University, 1971.

———. "The Old Testament Quotations in Hebrews." *New Testament Studies* 26 (1980): 363-79.

McGaughey, D. H. "The Hermeneutic Method of the Epistle to the Hebrews." Ph. D., Boston University, 1963.

McKane, William. *Proverbs. A New Approach*. Old Testament Library. London: SCM Press, 1970.

McKnight, Scot. "The Warning Passages of Hebrews: A Formal Analysis and Theological Considerations." *Trinity Journal* 13, no. 1 (1992): 21-59.

McLean, Bradley H. *Citations and Allusions to Jewish Scripture in Early Christian and Jewish Writings through 180 C.E.* Lewiston / Queenston / Lampeter: Edwin Mellen Press, 1992.

Meurer, Siegfried, ed. *The Apocrypha in Ecumenical Perspective.* Translated by Paul Ellingworth. United Bible Society Monograph Series 6. Reading / New York: United Bible Society, 1991.

Milgrom, Jacob. *Numbers Commentary.* JPS Torah Commentary. Philadelphia: Jewish Publication Society, 1989.

Miscall, Peter D. "Isaiah: New Heavens, New Earth, New Book." In *Reading Between Texts. Intertextuality and the Hebrew Bible,* edited by Danna Nolan Fewell, 41-56. Louisville: John Knox Press, 1992.

Mowinckel, S. *He That Cometh.* Translated by G.W. Anderson. Oxford: Blackwell, 1956.

Moyise, Steve. *The Old Testament in the Book of Revelation.* Journal for the Study of the New Testament – Supplement Series 115. Sheffield: Sheffield Academic Press, 1995.

Mulder, Martin Jan. "The Transmission of the Biblical Text." In *Mikra. Text, Translation, Reading and Interpretation of the Hebrew Bible in Ancient Judaism and Early Christianity,* edited by Martin Jan Mulder, 87-137. Minneapolis: Fortress Press, 1990.

Müller, Mogens. *The First Bible of the Church. A Plea for the Septuagint.* Journal for the Study of the Old Testament – Supplement Series 206. Sheffield: Sheffield Academic Press, 1996.

Muraoka, Takamitsu. "In Defense of the Unity of the LXX Minor Prophets." *Annual of the Japanese Biblical Institute* (1989): 25-36.

Murphy, Roland E. "The Personification of Wisdom." In *Wisdom in Ancient Israel. Essays in Honour of J. A. Emerton,* edited by John Day, Robert P. Gordon and H. G. M. Williamson, 222-33. Cambridge: Cambridge University Press, 1995.

Neeley, Linda Lloyd. "A Discourse Analysis of Hebrews." *OPTAT* 3-4 (1987): 1-147.

Nitzan, Bilhah. "Eschatological Motives in Qumran Literature: The Messianic Concept." In *Eschatology in the Bible and in Jewish and Christian Tradition,* edited by H. G. Reventlow, 132-51. Sheffield: Sheffield Academic Press, 1997.

Nogalski, James D. "Intertextuality in the Twelve." In *Forming Prophetic Literature,* edited by J. W. Watts and P. R. House, 102-24. Sheffield: Sheffield Academic Press, 1996.

———. *Literary Precursors to the Book of the Twelve.* Beihefte zur Zeitschrift für die alttestamentliche Wissenschaft 217. Berlin: Walter de Gruyter, 1993.

———. *Redactional Processes in the Book of the Twelve.* Beihefte zur Zeitschrift für die alttestamentliche Wissenschaft 218. Berlin: Walter de Gruyter, 1993.

Oegema, Gerbern S. *The Anointed and His People. Messianic Expectations from the Maccabees to Bar Kochba.* Journal for the Study of Pseudepigrapha – Supplement Series 27. Sheffield: Sheffield Academic Press, 1998.

———. "Messianic Expectations in the Qumran Writings: Theses on Their Development." In *Qumran-Messianism. Studies on the Messianic Expectations in the Dead Sea Scrolls,* edited by J. H. Charlesworth, H. Lichtenberger and G. S. Oegema, 53-82. Tübingen: J. C. B. Mohr (Paul Siebeck), 1998.

Oesterley, W. O. E. "The Old Latin Texts of the Minor Prophets. Part i-iv." *Journal of Theological Studies* 5 (1904): 76, 242-53, 378-86, 570-79.

Olbricht, Thomas H. "Hebrews as Amplification." In *Rhetoric and the New Testament. Essays from the 1992 Heidelberg Conference*, edited by Stanley E. Porter and Thomas H. Olbricht, 375-87. Sheffield: Sheffield Academic Press, 1993.

Olofsson, Staffan. *God is My Rock. A Study of Translation Technique and Theological Exegesis in the Septuagint*. Stockholm: Almqvist, 1990.

―――. *The LXX Version. A Guide to the Translation Technique of the Septuagint*. Coniectanea Biblica – Old Testament Series 30. Stockholm: Almqvist, 1990.

Pardee, Dennis. "YPH 'Witness' in Hebrew and Ugaritic." *Vetus Testamentum* 28, no. 2 (1978): 204-14.

Perkins, L. "The Septuagint of Jonah: Aspects of Literary Analysis Applied to Biblical Translation." *Bulletin of the International Organization for Septuagint and Cognate Studies* 20 (1987): 43-53.

Perrot, Charles. "The Reading of the Bible in the Ancient Synagogue." In *Mikra. Text, Translation, Reading and Interpretation of the Hebrew Bible in Ancient Judaism and Early Christianity*, edited by Martin Jan Mulder, 137-60. Minneapolis: Fortress Press, 1990.

Pietersma, Albert. "Septuagint Research: A Plea to Return to Basic Issues." *Vetus Testamentum* 35, no. 3 (1985): 296-416.

Plett, Heinrich F. "Intertextualities." In *Intertextuality*, edited by Heinrich F. Plett, 3-29. Berlin / New York: Walter de Gruyter, 1991.

Ploeg, J. van der. "L'exégèse de l'Ancien Testament dans l'épître aux Hébreux." *Revue Biblique* 54 (1947): 187-228.

Porter, Stanley E. *Handbook of Classical Rhetoric in the Hellenistic Period (330 B.C. - A.D. 400)*. Leiden / New York / Köln: E. J. Brill, 1997.

―――. "The Use of the Old Testament in the New Testament: A Brief Comment on Method and Terminology." In *Early Christian Interpretation of the Scriptures of Israel*, edited by Craig A. Evans and James A. Sanders. Sheffield: Sheffield Academic Press, 1997.

―――, ed. *The Language of the Greek New Testament. Classic Essays*. Journal for the Study of the New Testament – Supplement Series 60. Sheffield: Sheffield Academic Press, 1991.

―――, ed. *The Rhetorical Interpretation of Scripture. Essays from the 1996 Malibu Conference*. Journal for the Study of the New Testament – Supplement Series 180. Sheffield: Sheffield Academic Press, 1999.

Porter, Stanley E., and Thomas H. Olbricht, eds. *Rhetoric and the New Testament. Essays from the 1992 Heidelberg Conference*. Journal for the Study of the New Testament – Supplement Series 90. Sheffield: Sheffield Academic Press, 1993.

―――, eds. *Rhetoric, Scripture and Theology. Essays from the 1994 Pretoria Conference*. Journal for the Study of the New Testament – Supplement Series 131. Sheffield: Sheffield Academic Press, 1996.

―――, eds. *The Rhetorical Analysis of Scripture. Essays from the 1995 London Conference*. Journal for the Study of the New Testament – Supplement Series 146. Sheffield: Sheffield Academic Press, 1997.

Porter, Stanley E., and Dennis Stamps, eds. *Rhetorical Criticism and the Bible. Essays from the 1998 Florence Conference*. Journal for the Study of the New Testament – Supplement Series 195. Sheffield: Sheffield Academic Press, 2002.

Puech, Émile. "Messianism, Resurrection, and Eschatology at Qumran and in the New Testament." In *The Community of the Renewed Covenant. The Notre Dame Symposium on the Dead Sea Scrolls*, edited by E. Ulrich and J. C. VanderKam, 235-58. Notre Dame: University of Notre Dame Press, 1994.

Quell, J. "διαθήκη" in *TDNT*, 2:106-24.

Rabin, Chaim. "Hebrew and Aramaic in the First Century." In *The Jewish People in the First Century. Historical Geography, Political History, Social, Cultural and Religious Life and Institutions*, edited by S. Safrai and M. Stern, 1007 - 39. Assen: Van Gorcum, 1976.

————. "The Translation Process and the Character of the Septuagint." *Textus* 6 (1968): 1-26.

Rad, Gerhard von. *Wisdom in Israel*. Translated by James D. Martin. London: SCM Press, 1972.

Reid, R. "The Use of the Old Testament in the Epistle to the Hebrews." Th.D., Union Theological Seminary, 1964.

Rendall, R. "The Method of the Writer to the Hebrews in Using Old Testament Quotations." *Evangelical Quarterly* 27 (1955): 214-20.

Rhee, Victor (Sung-Yul). *Faith In Hebrews: Analysis within the Context of Christology, Eschatology, and Ethics*. Studies in Biblical Literature. New York: Peter Lang, 2001.

Riggenback, Eduard. "Der Begriff der ΔIAΘHKH im Hebräerbrief." In *Theologische Studien T. Zahn zum 10 Oktober, 1908 dargebracht*, 289-316. Leipzig, 1908.

Roberts, J. J. M. "The Old Testament's Contribution to Messianic Expectations." In *The Messiah. Developments in Earliest Judaism and Christianity*, edited by J. H. Charlesworth, 39-51. Minneapolis: Fortress Press, 1992.

Rose, Christian. *Die Wolke der Zeugen. Eine exegetisch-traditiongeschichtliche Untersuchung zu Hebräer 10,32-12,3*. Wissenschaftliche Untersuchungen zum Neuen Testament II 60. Tübingen: J. C. B. Mohr (Paul Siebeck), 1994.

Rosner, Brian S. *Paul, Scripture and Ethics. A Study of 1 Corinthinans 5-7*. Arbeiten zur Geschichte des antiken Judentums und des Urchristentums 22. Leiden: E. J. Brill, 1994.

Sailhamer, John. *The Translation Technique of the Greek Septuagint for the Hebrew Verbs and Participles in Psalms 3-41*. Studies in Biblical Greek 2. New York: Peter Lang, 1991.

Sanders, James A. "Habakkuk in Qumran, Paul and the New Testament." In *Paul and the Scriptures of Israel*, edited by Craig A. Evans and James A. Sanders, 98-118. Sheffield: Sheffield Academic Press, 1993.

Satterthwaite, P. E., R. S. Hess, and G. J. Wenham, eds. *The Lord's Anointed. Interpretation of Old Testament Messianic Texts*. Grand Rapids: Baker, 1995.

Satterthwaite, Philip E. "The Translator as Imperialist: And Other Aspects of the Septuagint of the Book of the Twelve." Paper presented at the Old Testament Seminar, Cambridge 1997.

Schaper, Joachim. *Eschatology in the Greek Psalter*. Wissenschaftliche Untersuchungen zum Neuen Testament II 76. Tübingen: J. C. B. Mohr (Paul Siebeck), 1995.

Schiffman, L. H. "Messianic Figures and Ideas in the Qumran Scrolls." In *The Messiah. Developments in Earliest Judaism and Christianity*, edited by J. H. Charlesworth, 116-29. Minneapolis: Fortress Press, 1992.

Schröger, Friedrich. "Das hermeneutische Instrumentarium des Hebräerbriefverfassers." *Theologie und Glaube* 60 (1970): 344-59.

————. *Der Verfasser des Hebräerbriefes als Schriftausleger*. Regensburg: Pustet, 1968.

Scott, Brett R. "Jesus' Superiority over Moses in Hebrews 3:1-6." *Bibliotheca Sacra* 155, no. 2 (1998): 201-10.

Scott, James M. "A New Approach to Habakkuk 2:4-5a." *Vetus Testamentum* 35, no. Jl (1985): 330-40.

Seeligmann, I. L. *The Septuagint Version of Isaiah. A Discussion of Its Problems.* Leiden: E. J. Brill, 1948.

Silva, Moisés. "Bilingualism and the Character of Palestinian Greek." In *The Language of the Greek New Testament. Classic Essays*, edited by Stanley E. Porter, 205-26. Sheffield: Sheffield Academic Press, 1991.

———. "Perfection and Eschatology in Hebrews." *Westminster Theological Journal* 39 (1976): 60-71.

———. "Semantic Borrowing in the New Testament." *New Testament Studies* 22 (1976): 104-10.

Sinker, Robert. *The Psalm of Habakkuk.* Cambridge: Deighton, Bell and Co., 1890.

Smith, Dwight M. "O de dikaios ek pisteos zesetai (Rom 1:17)." In *Studies in the History and the Text of the New Testament; In Honor of Kenneth Willis Clark*, edited by B. L. Daniels and M. J. Suggs, 13-25. Salt Lake City: University of Utah Press, 1967.

Smitten, W. Th. In der. "Habakuk 2,4 als prophetische Definition des Gerechten." In *Bausteine biblisher Theologie. Festgabe für G. Johannes Botterweck zum 60. Geburtstag*, edited by H. -J. Fabry, 289-300. Bohn: Peter Hanstein Verlag, 1977.

Southwell, P. J. M. "Note on Habakkuk 2:4." *Journal of Theological Studies* 19 (1968): 614-17.

Sowers, S. G. *The Hermeneutics of Philo and Hebrews: A Comparison of the Interpretation of the Old Testament in Philo Judaeus and the Epistle to the Hebrews.* Richmond / Zürich: Knox, 1965.

Stanley, Christopher D. *Paul and the Language of Scripture: Citation Technique in the Pauline Epistles and Contemporary Literature.* Society for the New Testament Studies Monograph Series 74. Cambridge: Cambridge University Press, 1992.

Stanley, Steve. "A New Covenant Hermeneutic: The Use of Scripture in Hebrews 8-10." Ph. D., University of Sheffield, 1994.

———. "The Structure of Hebrews from Three Perspectives." *Tyndale Bulletin* 45, no. 2 (1994): 245-73.

Strobel, A. *Untersuchungen zum eschatologischen Verzögerungsproblem auf Grund der spätjüdische-urchristlichen Geschichte von Habakuk 2,2 ff.* Supplements to Novum Testamentum 2. Leiden: E. J. Brill, 1961.

Sundberg, Albert C. *The Old Testament of the Early Church.* New York: Kraus Reprint Co., 1969.

———. "On Testimonies." *Novum Testamentum* 3 (1959): 268-81.

Sweeney, Marvin A. "The Book of Habakkuk." *American Schools of Oriental Research Newsletter* 39, no. 6 (1988).

———. "Structure, Genre, and Intent in the Book of Habakkuk." *Vetus Testamentum* 41, no. 1 (1991): 63-83.

Swete, Henry Barclay. *Introduction to the Old Testament in Greek.* 2nd ed. Cambridge: Cambridge University Press, 1914.

Swetnam, James. "Form and Content in Heb. 1-6." *Biblica* 53 (1972): 368-85.

———. "Form and Content in Heb. 7-13." *Biblica* 55 (1974): 333-48.

———. "The Structure of Hebrews: A Fresh Look. On the Occasion of a New Commentary." *MelTheol* 41, no. 1 (1990): 25-46.

———. "A Suggested Interpretation of Hebrews 9, 15-18." *The Catholic Biblical Quarterly* 27, no. 4 (1965): 373-90.

Synge, F. G. *Hebrews and the Scriptures.* London: SPCK, 1959.

Talmon, S. "The Concepts of *Masiah* and Messianism in Early Judaism." In *The Messiah. Developments in Earliest Judaism and Christianity*, edited by J. H. Charlesworth, 79-115. Minneapolis: Fortress Press, 1992.

Thackeray, H. St. John. *The Septuagint and Jewish Worship. A Study in Origins, The Schweich Lectures. 1920.* London: Milford, 1921.

Thomas, Kenneth J. "The Old Testament Citations in the Epistle to the Hebrews." *New Testament Studies* 11 (1965): 303-25.

———. "The Use of the Septuagint in the Epistle to the Hebrews." Ph. D., University of Manchester, 1959.

Thompson, James W. *The Beginning of Christian Philosophy: The Epistle to the Hebrews.* Catholic Biblical Quarterly Monograph Series 13. Washington, D.C.: The Catholic Biblical Associations of America, 1981.

Thompson, Michael. *Clothed with Christ. The Example and Teaching of Jesus in Romans 12:1-15:13.* Journal for the Study of the New Testament – Supplement Series 59. Sheffield: Sheffield Academic Press, 1991.

Toussaint, Stanley D. "The Eschatology of the Warning Passages in the Book of Hebrews." *Grace Theological Journal* 3, no. 1 (1982): 67-80.

Tov, Emanuel. "Did the Septuagint Translators always Understand Their Hebrew Text?" In *De Septuaginta*, edited by A. Pietersma and C. Cox, 53-70. Missiossauga, Ontario: Benben, 1984.

———. "The Nature and Study of the Translation Technique of the LXX in the Past and Present." In *VI Congress for the IOSCS – Jerusalem 1986*, edited by C. E. Cox, 337-59. Atlanta: Scholars Press, 1987.

———. *Textual Criticism of the Hebrew Bible.* Minneapolis: Fortress Press, 1992.

———. "The History and Significance of a Standard Text of the Hebrew Bible." In *Hebrew Bible / Old Testament. The History of Its Interpretation. From the Beginnings to the Middle Ages (until 1300)*, edited by Magne Saebo, Chris Brekelmans and Menahem Haran, 49-67. Göttingen: Vandenhoeck & Ruprecht, 1996.

———. *The Text-Critical Use of the Septuagint in Biblical Research.* 2nd rev. ed. Jerusalem Biblical Studies 8. Jerusalem: Simor, 1997.

———. "Textual Criticism of the Hebrew Bible 1947-1997." In *Perspectives in the Study of the Old Testament and Early Judaism. A Symposium in Honour of Adam S. van der Woude on the Occasion of His 70th Birthday*, edited by Florentino Garcia Martinez and Ed Noort, 61-81. Leiden / Boston / Köln: E. J. Brill, 1998.

Trebolle Barrera, Julio. *The Jewish Bible and the Christian Bible. An Introduction to the History of the Bible.* Translated by Wilfred G. E. Watson. Leiden / Grand Rapids: E. J. Brill / Eerdmans, 1998.

Turner, Nigel. *Christian Words.* Edinburgh: T & T Clark, 1980.

Überlacker, Walter G. *Der Hebräierbrief als Appell: Untersuchungen zu Exordium, Narratio, und Postscriptum (Hebr 1-2 und 13, 22-25).* Coniectanea Biblica – New Testament Series 21. Stockholm: Almqvist und Wiksell, 1989.

VanderKam, James C. "Messianism in the Scrolls." In *The Community of the Renewed Covenant. The Notre Dame Symposium on the Dead Sea Scrolls*, edited by E. Ulrich and J. C. VanderKam, 211-34. Notre Dame: University of Notre Dame Press, 1994.

Vanhoye, Albert. *La structurelle litéraire de l'épître aux Hébreux.* 2nd ed. Paris: Desclée de Brouwer, 1976.

———. *Structure and Message of the Epistle to the Hebrews.* Subsidia Biblica 12. Rome: Pontificio Institutio Biblico, 1989.

Vermes, Geza. *Scripture and Tradition in Judaism. Haggadic Studies.* Leiden: E. J. Brill, 1961.

Watts, J. W., and P. R. House. *Forming Prophetic Literature: Essays on Isaiah and The Twelve in Honor of John D. W. Watts.* Journal for the Study of the Old Testament – Supplement Series 235. Sheffield: Sheffield Academic Press, 1996.

Watts, Rikki E. "'For I Am Not Ashamed of the Gospel': Romans 1:16-17 and Habakkuk 2:4." In *Romans and the People of God*, edited by S. Sonderlund and N. T. Wright, 3-25. Grand Rapids: Eerdmans, 1999.

Weinfeld, M. "בְּרִית" in *TDOT*, 2:253-78.

Wevers, John W. "The Interpretative Character and Significance of the Septuagint Version." In *Hebrew Bible / Old Testament. The History of Its Interpretation. From the Beginnings to the Middle Ages (until 1300)*, edited by Magne Saebo, Chris Brekelmans and Menahem Haran, 84-108. Göttingen: Vandenhoeck & Ruprecht, 1996.

———. *Notes on the Greek Text of Exodus.* Society of Biblical Literature Septuagint and Cognate Studies 30. Atlanta: Scholars Press, 1990.

———. *Notes on the Greek Text of Genesis.* Society of Biblical Literature Septuagint and Cognate Studies 46. Atlanta: Scholars Press, 1993.

———. *Notes on the Greek Text of Deuteronomy.* Society of Biblical Literature Septuagint and Cognate Studies 39. Atlanta: Scholars Press, 1995.

———. *Notes on the Greek Text of Leviticus.* Society of Biblical Literature Septuagint and Cognate Studies 46. Atlanta: Scholars Press, 1997.

———. *Notes on the Greek Text of Numbers.* Society of Biblical Literature Septuagint and Cognate Studies 46. Atlanta: Scholars Press, 1998.

Williamson, R. *Philo and the Epistle to the Hebrews.* Arbeiten zur Literatur und Geschichte des hellenistischen Judentums 4. Leiden: E. J. Brill, 1970.

Woude, Adam S. van der. "Der Gerechte wird dürch seine Treue leben." In *Studia Biblica et Semitica. Festschrift Th. C. Vriezen*, edited by Adam S. van der Woude and W. C. vanUnnik, 367-75. Wageningen: H. Veenman en Zonen, 1966.

———. "Habakuk 2:4 [Ez 33:12]." *Zeitschrift für die Alttestamentliche Wissenschaft* 82, no. 2 (1970): 281-82.

———. "Pluriformity and Uniformity. Reflections on the Transmission of the Text of the Old Testament." In *Sacred History and Sacred Texts in Early Judaism. A Symposium in Honour of A. S. van der Woude*, edited by J. N. Bremmer and F. Garcia Martinez, 151-69. Kampen: Kok Pharos, 1992.

Wray, Judith Hoch. *Rest as a Theological Metaphor in the Epistle to the Hebrews and the Gospel of Truth. Early Christian Homiletics of Rest.* Society of Biblical Literature – Dissertation Series 166. Atlanta: Scholars Press, 1997.

Wright, J. Edward. "Hebrews 11:37 and the Death of the Prophet Ezekiel." In *The Echoes of Many Texts. Reflections on Jewish and Christian Traditions. Essays in Honor of Lou H. Silberman*, edited by William G. Dever and J. Edward Wright, 147-59. Atlanta: Scholars Press, 1997.

Würthwein, Ernst. *The Text of the Old Testament.* Translated by Erroll F. Rhodes. Grand Rapids: Eerdmans, 1979.

Zemek, George J. "Interpretive Challenges Relating to Habakkuk 2:4b." *Grace Theological Journal* 1, no. 1 (1980): 43-69.

Ziegler, Joseph. "Die Einheit der Septuaginta zum Zwölfprophetenbuch." In *Beelage zum Vorlesungsverzeichnis de Staatl. Akademie zu Braunsberg*, 1-16. Göttingen: Vandenhock & Ruprecht, 1934-1935.

———. *Untersuchungen zur Septuaginta des Buches Isaias.* Alttestamentliche Abhandlungen 12.3. Münster: Aschendorffschen Verlagsbuchhandlung, 1934.

————. *Untersuchungen zur Septuaginta des Buches Isaias.* Alttestamentliche Abhandlungen 12.3. Münster: Aschendorffschen Verlagsbuchhandlung, 1934.

Zorn, Walter D. "The Messianic Use of Habakkuk 2:4a in Romans." Stone-Campbell Journal 1, no. 2 (1998): 213-30.

Zvi, Ehud Ben. "Twelve Prophetic Books or 'The Twelve': A Few Preliminary Considerations." In Forming Prophetic Literature, edited by J. W. Watts and P. R. House, 125-56. Sheffield: Sheffield Academic Press, 1996.

Index of References

Old Testament

Apocrypha

Pseudepigrapha

Qumran

Targumim

Philo

Josephus

Rabbinic Literature

New Testament

Church Fathers

Index of Authors

Index of Subjects

Wissenschaftliche Untersuchungen zum Neuen Testament

Alphabetical Index of the First and Second Series

Brunson, Andrew: Psalm 118 in the Gospel of John. 2003. Volume II/158.

Büchli, Jörg: Der Poimandres – ein paganisiertes Evangelium. 1987. Volume II/27.

Bühner, Jan A.: Der Gesandte und sein Weg im 4. Evangelium. 1977. Volume II/2.

Burchard, Christoph: Untersuchungen zu Joseph und Aseneth. 1965. Volume 8.

– Studien zur Theologie, Sprache und Umwelt des Neuen Testaments. Ed. von D. Sänger. 1998. Volume 107.

Burnett, Richard: Karl Barth's Theological Exegesis. 2001. Volume II/145.

Byron, John: Slavery Metaphors in Early Judaism and Pauline Christianity. 2003. Volume II/162.

Byrskog, Samuel: Story as History – History as Story. 2000. Volume 123.

Cancik, Hubert (Ed.): Markus-Philologie. 1984. Volume 33.

Capes, David B.: Old Testament Yaweh Texts in Paul's Christology. 1992. Volume II/47.

Caragounis, Chrys C.: The Son of Man. 1986. Volume 38.

– see Fridrichsen, Anton.

Carleton Paget, James: The Epistle of Barnabas. 1994. Volume II/64.

Carson, D.A., O'Brien, Peter T. and Mark Seifrid (Ed.): Justification and Variegated Nomism: A Fresh Appraisal of Paul and Second Temple Judaism. Volume 1: The Complexities of Second Temple Judaism. Volume II/140.

Ciampa, Roy E.: The Presence and Function of Scripture in Galatians 1 and 2. 1998. Volume II/102.

Classen, Carl Joachim: Rhetorical Criticsm of the New Testament. 2000. Volume 128.

Colpe, Carsten: Iranier – Aramäer – Hebräer – Hellenen. 2003. Volume 154.

Crump, David: Jesus the Intercessor. 1992. Volume II/49.

Dahl, Nils Alstrup: Studies in Ephesians. 2000. Volume 131.

Deines, Roland: Jüdische Steingefäße und pharisäische Frömmigkeit. 1993. Volume II/52.

– Die Pharisäer. 1997. Volume 101.

Dettwiler, Andreas and Jean Zumstein (Ed.): Kreuzestheologie im Neuen Testament. 2002. Volume 151.

Dickson, John P.: Mission-Commitment in Ancient Judaism and in the Pauline Communities. 2003. Volume II/159.

Dietzfelbinger, Christian: Der Abschied des Kommenden. 1997. Volume 95.

Dobbeler, Axel von: Glaube als Teilhabe. 1987. Volume II/22.

Du Toit, David S.: Theios Anthropos. 1997. Volume II/91

Dunn, James D.G. (Ed.): Jews and Christians. 1992. Volume 66.

– Paul and the Mosaic Law. 1996. Volume 89.

Dunn, James D.G., Hans Klein, Ulrich Luz and Vasile Mihoc (Ed.): Auslegung der Bibel in orthodoxer und westlicher Perspektive. 2000. Volume 130.

Ebertz, Michael N.: Das Charisma des Gekreuzigten. 1987. Volume 45.

Eckstein, Hans-Joachim: Der Begriff Syneidesis bei Paulus. 1983. Volume II/10.

– Verheißung und Gesetz. 1996. Volume 86.

Ego, Beate: Im Himmel wie auf Erden. 1989. Volume II/34

Ego, Beate and Lange, Armin with Pilhofer, Peter (Ed.): Gemeinde ohne Tempel – Community without Temple. 1999. Volume 118.

Eisen, Ute E.: see Paulsen, Henning.

Ellis, E. Earle: Prophecy and Hermeneutic in Early Christianity. 1978. Volume 18.

– The Old Testament in Early Christianity. 1991. Volume 54.

Endo, Masanobu: Creation and Christology. 2002. Volume 149.

Ennulat, Andreas: Die 'Minor Agreements'. 1994. Volume II/62.

Ensor, Peter W.: Jesus and His 'Works'. 1996. Volume II/85.

Eskola, Timo: Messiah and the Throne. 2001. Volume II/142.

– Theodicy and Predestination in Pauline Soteriology. 1998. Volume II/100.

Fatehi, Mehrdad: The Spirit's Relation to the Risen Lord in Paul. 2000. Volume II/128.

Feldmeier, Reinhard: Die Krisis des Gottessohnes. 1987. Volume II/21.

– Die Christen als Fremde. 1992. Volume 64.

Feldmeier, Reinhard and Ulrich Heckel (Ed.): Die Heiden. 1994. Volume 70.

Fletcher-Louis, Crispin H.T.: Luke-Acts: Angels, Christology and Soteriology. 1997. Volume II/94.

Förster, Niclas: Marcus Magus. 1999. Volume 114.

Forbes, Christopher Brian: Prophecy and Inspired Speech in Early Christianity and its Hellenistic Environment. 1995. Volume II/75.

Fornberg, Tord: see Fridrichsen, Anton.

Fossum, Jarl E.: The Name of God and the Angel of the Lord. 1985. Volume 36.

Fotopoulos, John: Food Offered to Idols in Roman Corinth. 2003. Volume II/151.

Frenschkowski, Marco: Offenbarung und Epiphanie. Volume 1 1995. *Volume II/79* – Volume 2 1997. *Volume II/80.*

Frey, Jörg: Eugen Drewermann und die biblische Exegese. 1995. *Volume II/71.*

– Die johanneische Eschatologie. Volume I. 1997. *Volume 96.* – Volume II. 1998. *Volume 110.*

– Volume III. 2000. *Volume 117.*

Freyne, Sean: Galilee and Gospel. 2000. *Volume 125.*

Fridrichsen, Anton: Exegetical Writings. Edited by C.C. Caragounis and T. Fornberg. 1994. *Volume 76.*

Garlington, Don B.: 'The Obedience of Faith'. 1991. *Volume II/38.*

– Faith, Obedience, and Perseverance. 1994. *Volume 79.*

Garnet, Paul: Salvation and Atonement in the Qumran Scrolls. 1977. *Volume II/3.*

Gese, Michael: Das Vermächtnis des Apostels. 1997. *Volume II/99.*

Gheorghita, Radu: The Role of the Septuagint in Hebrews. 2003. *Volume II/160.*

Gräbe, Petrus J.: The Power of God in Paul's Letters. 2000. *Volume II/123.*

Gräßer, Erich: Der Alte Bund im Neuen. 1985. *Volume 35.*

– Forschungen zur Apostelgeschichte. 2001. *Volume 137.*

Green, Joel B.: The Death of Jesus. 1988. *Volume II/33.*

Gundry Volf, Judith M.: Paul and Perseverance. 1990. *Volume II/37.*

Hafemann, Scott J.: Suffering and the Spirit. 1986. *Volume II/19.*

– Paul, Moses, and the History of Israel. 1995. *Volume 81.*

Hahn, Johannes (Ed.): Zerstörungen des Jerusalemer Tempels. 2002. *Volume 147.*

Hannah, Darrel D.: Michael and Christ. 1999. *Volume II/109.*

Hamid-Khani, Saeed: Relevation and Concealment of Christ. 2000. *Volume II/120.*

Hartman, Lars: Text-Centered New Testament Studies. Ed. von D. Hellholm. 1997. *Volume 102.*

Hartog, Paul: Polycarp and the New Testament. 2001. *Volume II/134.*

Heckel, Theo K.: Der Innere Mensch. 1993. *Volume II/53.*

– Vom Evangelium des Markus zum viergestaltigen Evangelium. 1999. *Volume 120.*

Heckel, Ulrich: Kraft in Schwachheit. 1993. *Volume II/56.*

– Der Segen im Neuen Testament. 2002. *Volume 150.*

– see *Feldmeier, Reinhard.*

– see *Hengel, Martin.*

Heiligenthal, Roman: Werke als Zeichen. 1983. *Volume II/9.*

Hellholm, D.: see *Hartman, Lars.*

Hemer, Colin J.: The Book of Acts in the Setting of Hellenistic History. 1989. *Volume 49.*

Hengel, Martin: Judentum und Hellenismus. 1969, ³1988. *Volume 10.*

– Die johanneische Frage. 1993. *Volume 67.*

– Judaica et Hellenistica. Kleine Schriften I. 1996. *Volume 90.*

– Judaica, Hellenistica et Christiana. Kleine Schriften II. 1999. *Volume 109.*

– Paulus und Jakobus. Kleine Schriften III. 2002. *Volume 141.*

Hengel, Martin and *Ulrich Heckel* (Ed.): Paulus und das antike Judentum. 1991. *Volume 58.*

Hengel, Martin and *Hermut Löhr* (Ed.): Schriftauslegung im antiken Judentum und im Urchristentum. 1994. *Volume 73.*

Hengel, Martin and *Anna Maria Schwemer:* Paulus zwischen Damaskus und Antiochien. 1998. *Volume 108.*

– Der messianische Anspruch Jesu und die Anfänge der Christologie. 2001. *Volume 138.*

Hengel, Martin and *Anna Maria Schwemer* (Ed.): Königsherrschaft Gottes und himmlischer Kult. 1991. *Volume 55.*

– Die Septuaginta. 1994. *Volume 72.*

Hengel, Martin; Siegfried Mittmann and *Anna Maria Schwemer* (Ed.): La Cité de Dieu / Die Stadt Gottes. 2000. *Volume 129.*

Herrenbrück, Fritz: Jesus und die Zöllner. 1990. *Volume II/41.*

Herzer, Jens: Paulus oder Petrus? 1998. *Volume 103.*

Hoegen-Rohls, Christina: Der nachösterliche Johannes. 1996. *Volume II/84.*

Hofius, Otfried: Katapausis. 1970. *Volume 11.*

– Der Vorhang vor dem Thron Gottes. 1972. *Volume 14.*

– Der Christushymnus Philipper 2,6-11. 1976, ²1991. *Volume 17.*

– Paulusstudien. 1989, ²1994. *Volume 51.*

– Neutestamentliche Studien. 2000. *Volume 132.*

– Paulusstudien II. 2002. *Volume 143.*

Hofius, Otfried and *Hans-Christian Kammler:* Johannesstudien. 1996. *Volume 88.*

Holtz, Traugott: Geschichte und Theologie des Urchristentums. 1991. *Volume 57.*

Hommel, Hildebrecht: Sebasmata. Volume 1 1983. *Volume 31* – Volume 2 1984. *Volume 32.*

Hvalvik, Reidar: The Struggle for Scripture and Covenant. 1996. *Volume II/82.*

Joubert, Stephan: Paul as Benefactor. 2000. *Volume II/124.*

Jungbauer, Harry: „Ehre Vater und Mutter". 2002. *Volume II/146.*

Kähler, Christoph: Jesu Gleichnisse als Poesie und Therapie. 1995. *Volume 78.*

Kamlah, Ehrhard: Die Form der katalogischen Paränese im Neuen Testament. 1964. *Volume 7.*

Kammler, Hans-Christian: Christologie und Eschatologie. 2000. *Volume 126.*

– see *Hofius, Otfried.*

Kelhoffer, James A.: Miracle and Mission. 1999. *Volume II/112.*

Kieffer, René and *Jan Bergman (Ed.):* La Main de Dieu / Die Hand Gottes. 1997. *Volume 94.*

Kim, Seyoon: The Origin of Paul's Gospel. 1981, ²1984. *Volume II/4.*

– "The 'Son of Man'" as the Son of God. 1983. *Volume 30.*

Klauck, Hans-Josef: Religion und Gesellschaft im frühen Christentum. 2003. *Volume 152.*

Klein, Hans: see *Dunn, James D.G..*

Kleinknecht, Karl Th.: Der leidende Gerechtfertigte. 1984, ²1988. *Volume II/13.*

Klinghardt, Matthias: Gesetz und Volk Gottes. 1988. *Volume II/32.*

Köhler, Wolf-Dietrich: Rezeption des Matthäusevangeliums in der Zeit vor Irenäus. 1987. *Volume II/24.*

Korn, Manfred: Die Geschichte Jesu in veränderter Zeit. 1993. *Volume II/51.*

Koskenniemi, Erkki: Apollonios von Tyana in der neutestamentlichen Exegese. 1994. *Volume II/61.*

Kraus, Thomas J.: Sprache, Stil und historischer Ort des zweiten Petrusbriefes. 2001. *Volume II/136.*

Kraus, Wolfgang: Das Volk Gottes. 1996. *Volume 85.*

– see *Walter, Nikolaus.*

Kreplin, Matthias: Das Selbstverständnis Jesu. 2001. *Volume II/141.*

Kuhn, Karl G.: Achtzehngebet und Vaterunser und der Reim. 1950. *Volume 1.*

Kvalbein, Hans: see *Ådna, Jostein.*

Laansma, Jon: I Will Give You Rest. 1997. *Volume II/98.*

Labahn, Michael: Offenbarung in Zeichen und Wort. 2000. *Volume II/117.*

Lange, Armin: see *Ego, Beate.*

Lampe, Peter: Die stadtrömischen Christen in den ersten beiden Jahrhunderten. 1987, ²1989. *Volume II/18.*

Landmesser, Christof: Wahrheit als Grundbegriff neutestamentlicher Wissenschaft. 1999. *Volume 113.*

– Jüngerberufung und Zuwendung zu Gott. 2000. *Volume 133.*

Lau, Andrew: Manifest in Flesh. 1996. *Volume II/86.*

Lee, Pilchan: The New Jerusalem in the Book of Relevation. 2000. *Volume II/129.*

Lichtenberger, Hermann: see *Avemarie, Friedrich.*

Lieu, Samuel N.C.: Manichaeism in the Later Roman Empire and Medieval China. ²1992. *Volume 63.*

Loader, William R.G.: Jesus' Attitude Towards the Law. 1997. *Volume II/97.*

Löhr, Gebhard: Verherrlichung Gottes durch Philosophie. 1997. *Volume 97.*

Löhr, Hermut: see *Hengel, Martin.*

Löhr, Winrich Alfried: Basilides und seine Schule. 1995. *Volume 83.*

Luomanen, Petri: Entering the Kingdom of Heaven. 1998. *Volume II/101.*

Luz, Ulrich: see *Dunn, James D.G.*

Maier, Gerhard: Mensch und freier Wille. 1971. *Volume 12.*

– Die Johannesoffenbarung und die Kirche. 1981. *Volume 25.*

Markschies, Christoph: Valentinus Gnosticus? 1992. *Volume 65.*

Marshall, Peter: Enmity in Corinth: Social Conventions in Paul's Relations with the Corinthians. 1987. *Volume II/23.*

Mayer, Annemarie: Sprache der Einheit im Epheserbrief und in der Ökumene. 2002. *Volume II/150.*

McDonough, Sean M.: YHWH at Patmos: Rev. 1:4 in its Hellenistic and Early Jewish Setting. 1999. *Volume II/107.*

McGlynn, Moyna: Divine Judgement and Divine Benevolence in the Book of Wisdom. 2001. *Volume II/139.*

Meade, David G.: Pseudonymity and Canon. 1986. *Volume 39.*

Meadors, Edward P.: Jesus the Messianic Herald of Salvation. 1995. *Volume II/72.*

Meißner, Stefan: Die Heimholung des Ketzers. 1996. *Volume II/87.*

Mell, Ulrich: Die „anderen" Winzer. 1994. *Volume 77.*

Mengel, Berthold: Studien zum Philipperbrief. 1982. *Volume II/8.*

Merkel, Helmut: Die Widersprüche zwischen den Evangelien. 1971. *Volume 13.*

Schaper, Joachim: Eschatology in the Greek Psalter. 1995. *Volume II/76.*

Schimanowski, Gottfried: Die himmlische Liturgie in der Apokalypse des Johannes. 2002. *Volume II/154.*

– Weisheit und Messias. 1985. *Volume II/17.*

Schlichting, Günter: Ein jüdisches Leben Jesu. 1982. *Volume 24.*

Schnabel, Eckhard J.: Law and Wisdom from Ben Sira to Paul. 1985. *Volume II/16.*

Schutter, William L.: Hermeneutic and Composition in I Peter. 1989. *Volume II/30.*

Schwartz, Daniel R.: Studies in the Jewish Background of Christianity. 1992. *Volume 60.*

Schwemer, Anna Maria: see *Hengel, Martin*

Scott, James M.: Adoption as Sons of God. 1992. *Volume II/48.*

– Paul and the Nations. 1995. *Volume 84.*

Shum, Shiu-Lun: Paul's Use of Isaiah in Romans. 2002. *Volume II/156.*

Siegert, Folker: Drei hellenistisch-jüdische Predigten. Teil I 1980. *Volume 20* – Teil II 1992. *Volume 61.*

– Nag-Hammadi-Register. 1982. *Volume 26.*

– Argumentation bei Paulus. 1985. *Volume 34.*

– Philon von Alexandrien. 1988. *Volume 46.*

Simon, Marcel: Le christianisme antique et son contexte religieux I/II. 1981. *Volume 23.*

Snodgrass, Klyne: The Parable of the Wicked Tenants. 1983. *Volume 27.*

Söding, Thomas: Das Wort vom Kreuz. 1997. *Volume 93.*

– see *Thüsing, Wilhelm.*

Sommer, Urs: Die Passionsgeschichte des Markusevangeliums. 1993. *Volume II/58.*

Souček, Josef B.: see *Pokorný, Petr.*

Spangenberg, Volker: Herrlichkeit des Neuen Bundes. 1993. *Volume II/55.*

Spanje, T.E. van: Inconsistency in Paul? 1999. *Volume II/110.*

Speyer, Wolfgang: Frühes Christentum im antiken Strahlungsfeld. Volume I: 1989. *Volume 50.*

– Volume II: 1999. *Volume 116.*

Stadelmann, Helge: Ben Sira als Schriftgelehrter. 1980. *Volume II/6.*

Stenschke, Christoph W.: Luke's Portrait of Gentiles Prior to Their Coming to Faith. *Volume II/108.*

Stettler, Christian: Der Kolosserhymnus. 2000. *Volume II/131.*

Stettler, Hanna: Die Christologie der Pastoralbriefe. 1998. *Volume II/105.*

Strobel, August: Die Stunde der Wahrheit. 1980. *Volume 21.*

Stroumsa, Guy G.: Barbarian Philosophy. 1999. *Volume 112.*

Stuckenbruck, Loren T.: Angel Veneration and Christology. 1995. *Volume II/70.*

Stuhlmacher, Peter (Ed.): Das Evangelium und die Evangelien. 1983. *Volume 28.*

– Biblische Theologie und Evangelium. 2002. *Volume 146.*

Sung, Chong-Hyon: Vergebung der Sünden. 1993. *Volume II/57.*

Tajra, Harry W.: The Trial of St. Paul. 1989. *Volume II/35.*

– The Martyrdom of St.Paul. 1994. *Volume II/67.*

Theißen, Gerd: Studien zur Soziologie des Urchristentums. 1979, ³1989. *Volume 19.*

Theobald, Michael: Studien zum Römerbrief. 2001. *Volume 136.*

Theobald, Michael: see *Mußner, Franz.*

Thornton, Claus-Jürgen: Der Zeuge des Zeugen. 1991. *Volume 56.*

Thüsing, Wilhelm: Studien zur neutestamentlichen Theologie. Ed. von Thomas Söding. 1995. *Volume 82.*

Thurén, Lauri: Derhethorizing Paul. 2000. *Volume 124.*

Treloar, Geoffrey R.: Lightfoot the Historian. 1998. *Volume II/103.*

Tsuji, Manabu: Glaube zwischen Vollkommenheit und Verweltlichung. 1997. *Volume II/93*

Twelftree, Graham H.: Jesus the Exorcist. 1993. *Volume II/54.*

Urban, Christina: Das Menschenbild nach dem Johannesevangelium. 2001. *Volume II/137.*

Visotzky, Burton L.: Fathers of the World. 1995. *Volume 80.*

Vollenweider, Samuel: Horizonte neutestamentlicher Christologie. 2002. *Volume 144.*

Vos, Johan S.: Die Kunst der Argumentation bei Paulus. 2002. *Volume 149.*

Wagener, Ulrike: Die Ordnung des „Hauses Gottes". 1994. *Volume II/65.*

Walker, Donald D.: Paul's Offer of Leniency (2 Cor 10:1). 2002. *Volume II/152.*

Walter, Nikolaus: Praeparatio Evangelica. Ed. von Wolfgang Kraus und Florian Wilk. 1997. *Volume 98.*

Wander, Bernd: Gottesfürchtige und Sympathisanten. 1998. *Volume 104.*

Watts, Rikki: Isaiah's New Exodus and Mark. 1997. *Volume II/88.*

Wedderburn, A.J.M.: Baptism and Resurrection. 1987. *Volume 44.*

Wegner, Uwe: Der Hauptmann von Kafarnaum. 1985. *Volume II/14.*

Welck, Christian: Erzählte ‚Zeichen‘. 1994.
Volume II/69.

Wiarda, Timothy: Peter in the Gospels . 2000.
Volume II/127.

Wilk, Florian: see *Walter, Nikolaus.*

Williams, Catrin H.: I am He. 2000.
Volume II/113.

Wilson, Walter T.: Love without Pretense. 1991.
Volume II/46.

Wisdom, Jeffrey: Blessing for the Nations and
the Curse of the Law. 2001. *Volume II/133.*

Wucherpfennig, Ansgar: Heracleon Philologus.
2002. *Volume 142.*

Yeung, Maureen: Faith in Jesus and Paul. 2002.
Volume II/147.

Zimmermann, Alfred E.: Die urchristlichen
Lehrer. 1984, ²1988. *Volume II/12.*

Zimmermann, Johannes: Messianische Texte
aus Qumran. 1998. *Volume II/104.*

Zimmermann, Ruben: Geschlechtermetaphorik
und Gottesverhältnis. 2001. *Volume II/122.*

Zumstein, Jean: see *Dettwiler, Andreas*

For a complete catalogue please write to the publisher
Mohr Siebeck • P.O. Box 2030 • D–72010 Tübingen/Germany
Up-to-date information on the internet at www.mohr.de